KONTUM

Battles and Campaigns

The Battles and Campaigns series examines the military and strategic results of particular combat techniques, strategies, and methods used by soldiers, sailors, and airmen throughout history. Focusing on different nations and branches of the armed services, this series aims to educate readers by detailed analysis of military engagements.

Series editor: Roger Cirillo

An AUSA Book

KONTUM

The Battle to Save South Vietnam

Thomas P. McKenna

The University Press of Kentucky

Scholarly publisher for the Commonwealth,
serving Bellarmine University, Berea College, Centre College of Kentucky,
Eastern Kentucky University, The Filson Historical Society, Georgetown
College, Kentucky Historical Society, Kentucky State University, Morehead
State University, Murray State University, Northern Kentucky University,
Transylvania University, University of Kentucky, University of Louisville,
and Western Kentucky University.
All rights reserved.

Editorial and Sales Offices: The University Press of Kentucky
663 South Limestone Street, Lexington, Kentucky 40508-4008
www.kentuckypress.com

Maps by Dick Gilbreath

15 14 13 12 11   5 4 3 2 1

Library of Congress Cataloging-in-Publication Data

McKenna, Thomas P., 1930–
  Kontum : the battle to save South Vietnam / Thomas P. McKenna.
    p. cm. — (Battles and campaigns)
  Includes bibliographical references and index.
  ISBN 978-0-8131-3398-0 (hardcover : alk. paper)
  ISBN 978-0-8131-3401-7 (ebook)
  1. Kontum, Battle of, Kon Tum, Vietnam, 1972. I. Title.
  DS557.8.K56M35 2011
  959.704'342—dc22   2011012746

This book is printed on acid-free paper meeting the requirements of the
American National Standard for Permanence in Paper for Printed Library
Materials.

Manufactured in the United States of America.

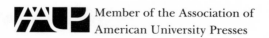 Member of the Association of
American University Presses

To all those who served
during the Vietnam War
in the struggle to preserve
South Vietnam's independence.

Contents

Illustrations follow page 152

Maps

Preface

From September 1971 to June 1972, I was a US Army infantry lieutenant colonel assigned as a military adviser to the Army of South Vietnam. As one of the participants in the Battle of Kontum, I have tried to describe what we endured there and what we accomplished without indulging in too much of what my grandmother called "tooting your own horn."

The North Vietnamese invasion of South Vietnam in the spring of 1972 was a major military campaign involving hundreds of thousands of troops on both sides. The enemy attacked with the latest Soviet and Chinese tanks and artillery, and the South Vietnamese and their American allies were supported by their own tanks and artillery, thousands of helicopters, fixed-wing gunships, and bombers—including B-52s that could drop more than 100 tons of bombs on a single three-plane mission. The battles along the Demilitarized Zone (DMZ) in the North, at Kontum in the Central Highlands, and at An Loc in the South were large battles with massive violence and staggering losses on both sides. The survival of South Vietnam as an independent nation depended on the outcome of these battles. Although more than 30,000 books have been written about the Vietnam War, the history of what the Americans called the Easter Offensive is not as well known as that of the campaigns and battles involving American units and extensively covered by the American media during the years from 1965 to October 1971.

For example, in Stanley Karnow's Pulitzer Prize–winning *Vietnam: A History* the only mention of the Battle of Kontum consists of 26 completely misleading words. He writes, "The Communists showed relative restraint in the Central Highlands, where they besieged the town of Kontum, even though a South Vietnamese division fled rather than fight."[1] We all make mistakes, but it is disappointing to see a careless inaccuracy like this in what presumes to be a definitive history of the Vietnam War. What actually happened was quite different. Nearly three weeks before the attack on Kontum City, part of the 22nd Army of the Republic of Vietnam (ARVN) Infantry Division broke and ran at Tan Canh and Dak To II northwest of Kontum City. In contrast, the 23rd ARVN Infantry Division stood, fought, and held at Kontum. They blocked the North Vietnamese army (NVA) from cutting South Vietnam in half. The North Vietnamese attack on Kontum—with two divisions plus additional independent infantry, artillery, and tank regiments—was not "restrained" from the viewpoint of those of us who fought there. Yet future students of the Vietnam War who read only Karnow's history will have no inkling of what really happened at Kontum in the spring of 1972.

The Battle of Kontum was major drama on a big stage with many players on our side, and we would not have prevailed without all of them. One man who stood out above all others in this struggle was Mr. John Paul Vann. He was a retired US Army lieutenant colonel and a US Department of State Foreign Service officer serving with ambassador rank. His civilian rank was equivalent to a major general. Vann was the senior adviser to the II Corps commander, an ARVN lieutenant general who controlled an area larger than one-fourth of Vietnam. Although I was serving two levels below Mr. Vann, he was the sort of man who might show up any place at any time, so I met him many times. While writing this book, I interviewed Vann's military deputy, a man with whom I had more frequent contact: retired brigadier general George E. Wear. In Korea, when Wear was a major, he had known John Paul Vann, a captain at the time. As a result of this long acquaintance, Wear was the only man in II Corps who called him "John"; to everyone else he was "Mr. Vann."[2]

Almost all of my descriptions of John Paul Vann are confined to his actions leading up to and during the Easter Offensive. Neil Sheehan's Pulitzer Prize–winning book *A Bright Shining Lie: John Paul Vann and America in Vietnam* describes him in full. It is a history of Vann's part in the Vietnam War and a definitive biography with details about his military service, his civilian service in Vietnam, and his death.

In a review of Neil Sheehan's *A Bright Shining Lie,* General Bruce Palmer wrote,

> I found that one of the most heartening and positive aspects was telling the story of our advisers, the unsung heroes of

Vietnam. Virtually all of the movies, TV programs, and flashy novels about Vietnam concern the trials of regular US combat units. Rarely if ever do we hear about the advisers, often alone, or in very small groups, serving in a foreign, war-torn land, doing their job on their own with no US backup support nearby, and knowing that their very survival is not in their hands, but dependent on their South Vietnamese friends. For telling this story in a compelling way, Sheehan deserves our thanks and high praise.[3]

This book is intended to be a thorough description of the Battle of Kontum and the events leading up to it, but with only enough information about what was happening elsewhere in Vietnam to place Kontum in context. Dale Andradé offers an excellent history of the entire Easter Offensive in all of South Vietnam in *Trial by Fire: The 1972 Easter Offensive: America's Last Vietnam Battle* (revised as *America's Last Vietnam Battle: Halting Hanoi's 1972 Easter Offensive*). Decisions made in Washington and Hanoi and at the Paris peace talks soon impacted those of us "on the tip of the spear" in the combat zone, so I have included brief descriptions of these official meetings to provide necessary background information.

A battle is best described in chronological order, but doing so was difficult with respect to the actions leading up to and during the Battle of Kontum. Many contemporaneous accounts and primary sources are undated or not organized by the hour or even by the day. If various sources disagreed on when something happened, I used the most reliable source—when I could determine that. Vietnam is across the international dateline, so the date there is always a day later than in the United States. To deal with this difference, I used the local dates found on letters, logs, and other documents created in Vietnam and the US dates for events taking place in the United States. The Vietnam datelines on American newspaper articles were not always accurate but were seldom off by more than one day. News stories in the military newspaper *Pacific Stars and Stripes* were more accurately dated. Determining the time of day when something happened was especially difficult. Military messages between Saigon and Washington and the messages that Mr. Vann in Pleiku sent to General Creighton W. Abrams in Saigon were in Zulu (Z) or Greenwich Mean time even though the US military in South Vietnam was operating on Hotel (H) time, which was the same as the South Vietnamese time but an hour later than North Vietnam's time. A further complication was that the NVA used North Vietnam's time even in South Vietnam.

Some true war stories would be difficult to believe even if they were told in a work of fiction. However, memories of traumatic events that occurred more than three decades ago are sometimes hazy, so whenever possible I have checked sources against each other, with experts in certain fields, and against the contemporary written accounts. In 1971–1972, while I was in Vietnam, I wrote letters to my parents and my wife, most of which they saved, and exchanged recorded cassette tapes with my wife. We had half-a-dozen tapes in use but almost always recorded over the ones we received, so only two tapes recorded in Vietnam survived. My letters and the two tapes were an invaluable source of information. They reminded me of names and incidents long forgotten and confirmed critical dates and events during the battles in 1972.

An unexpected benefit of my research was reconnecting with men who served with me in Kontum. Many of them shared their own memories, maps, and photos with me. These materials provided significant information and were invaluable primary sources.

To preserve the tenor of the times and military character of conversations or messages, I use the "14 May 1972" date format and the 24-hour time system. The US Armed Forces, most foreign nations, and most airlines use the 24-hour system. It saves adding a colon and AM or PM to every time reference and avoids confusion when neither AM nor PM is inserted. So noon is 1200, 1:45 PM is 1345, and 1:45 AM is 0145. Some accounts add the word *hours* to the time, but it is unnecessary unless other numbers follow the time reference, as in "At 1350 hours 1,200 men attacked." In most cases, I give yards and meters or miles and kilometers as they were used in the original sources. (For anyone unfamiliar with the metric system, a meter is 1,000 millimeters and only 3.37 inches longer than a yard, so considering meters and yards as equal is accurate enough for the lengths involved in this account [or, as we sometimes said in Vietnam, "Close enough for government work"]. A kilometer, 1,000 meters, is 62.5 miles. To convert kilometers to miles, divide by two and then add a fourth of the result. Thus, 100 kilometers divided by two equals 50, and adding a fourth of that, or 12.5, produces a total of 62.5 miles.)

I have included a glossary to define or explain the acronyms, organizations, and military jargon we used. There are now many printed and online sources for complete descriptions of the weapons, aircraft, and vehicles used by both sides during the Vietnam War, so I give only minimal descriptions of them in this account. An exception is the enemy's T-54 medium tank. It played an important part in the Easter Offensive, so it must be described in enough detail to explain why just the sight of one could send ARVN soldiers fleeing in terror. This tank was about 30 feet long, 11 feet wide, and 8 feet high, and it weighed 36 tons. It was powered by a 580-horsepower V-12 engine and could move as fast as 30 miles an hour—with a great deal of loud clanking, grinding, and roaring. The main gun fired a 100-mm shell that could penetrate up to 390 millimeters of armor a kilometer away. There was a 7.62-mm coaxial machine gun beside the main gun, and above the turret a .51-caliber (12.7-mm) machine gun that could be fired by the tank commander. The North Vietnamese had two versions of this tank: the Soviet-designed and produced T-54 and the Chinese-made Type 59 (often called the "T-59"), which was almost an exact copy of the T-54. There were few external features to distinguish them. For example, the T-54 had an infrared searchlight, and the Type 59 did not. However, those distinguishing searchlights could be removed by the crew or shot off in combat. At the division and regimental level, we had no need to distinguish between the two types. The NVA employed both T-54s and Type 59s during their Easter Offensive and probably used both in the Central Highlands. What was most important to those of us being shot at by those tanks was that both of them carried a big 100-mm main gun.[4]

Vietnamese names have the family name (surname) first and the given name last. For example, Colonel Ly Tong Ba's surname is "Ly," and his given name "Ba." However, the Americans in Vietnam used the European and American form for Vietnamese names and knew Ly Tong Ba as "Colonel Ba," so that usage is employed here.

When I could not determine an individual's complete or correct name, I substituted a pseudonym in italics. Except for portions deleted, anything written in the 1970s—including my own letters home—is quoted exactly as written. Spelling, punctuation, grammar, or factual errors are not corrected. Emails, letters, or statements that came to me in the course of writing this book are sometimes corrected for spelling, punctuation, and other small errors. Ellipses are used to indicate where something is omitted from a quotation or transcription. Where conversations—including my own speech—are quoted, what was said is written as accurately as I can remember it. Even if the words are not the original words, the content is accurate.

Military units that were something other than infantry are identified by type, such as "armored cavalry," "artillery," or "sapper." So all units mentioned should be assumed to be infantry unless identified as something else. Except for US Army aviation units, no US Army units of battalion or larger size were involved in fighting during the Easter Offensive. I have added "ARVN" or "NVA" to unit names for clarification when needed. The military units described here are, from largest to smallest: division, regiment, battalion (or squadron for cavalry), company (or troop for cavalry and battery for artillery), and platoon (the artillery did not have platoons).

The Viet Cong (VC), the South Vietnamese Communist insurgents, were almost wiped out during their Tet Offensive in 1968. Those VC losses and the continuing infiltration of NVA soldiers into South Vietnam gradually increased the proportion of northerners in the enemy forces. During the Easter Offensive, it was estimated that the enemy combat and combat support units were approximately 80 percent North Vietnamese and 20 percent VC.[5] There were only a few instances where an independent VC unit could be identified. So in this account, enemy forces identified as "NVA" may have included some VC.

The acronym ARVN was often used to describe the South Vietnamese army we were advising as well as groups of South Vietnamese soldiers or even one individual, as in "The Arvins are moving out" or "An Arvin was killed in the ambush." It was not good grammar, but it was the way we often talked.

Prologue

Kontum: Now and Then

Isn't it strange that a country can be so pastoral, yet so
deadly?
        —Dickey Chappell, war correspondent killed in 1965

If you were to visit Kontum today, you would probably find a peace-
ful, bustling Central Highlands city of around 35,000. Most of
the inhabitants would belong to the various ethnic minorities, the
people the French called "Montagnards." The main agricultural
products would be coffee, tea, cassava, rubber, and lumber. This
pleasant city has a gentle climate. It would be difficult to find any
evidence of—or even to imagine—the major battle that took place
here long ago. During the last two weeks of May in 1972, Kontum
was the scene of a violent struggle between the equivalent of three
divisions of Communist North Vietnamese soldiers, who were
attacking to seize the city, and the one South Vietnamese division
defending it. At least 30,000 refugees were packed into Kontum.
Communist artillery, rockets, and mortars were pounding the city,
and many buildings were burning. The enemy held almost half
of the town, and their troops and tanks were assaulting day and
night to take the remainder of it. It was close, brutal, often toe-to-
toe combat. Helicopter and fixed-wing gunships and aerial bombing both inside and outside Kontum aided the South Vietnamese
troops. During just 25 days, B-52 bombers alone dropped about
60 million pounds of bombs around Kontum.[1] Tactical air fighter-
bombers dropped additional millions of pounds of bombs both
inside and outside the city. Day after day during the battle, aircraft
were being shot down in flames; soldiers on both sides were being

killed and wounded; and the air was filled with the smell of cordite, smoke, and rotting bodies.

In the spring of 1972, 12 Communist North Vietnamese divisions plus many independent units—about 200,000 men in all—supported by an estimated 1,000 tanks and the latest Soviet and Chinese artillery and anti-aircraft guns, invaded South Vietnam in what the Americans called the Easter Offensive. It was the biggest across-the-border invasion and the largest military offensive anywhere in the world since the Communist Chinese attacked across the Yalu River into Korea 22 years earlier in October 1950.[2] Although virtually no US Army ground combat units took part in the Easter Offensive—they were in the process of withdrawing from Vietnam—there were American advisers with the South Vietnamese army, marine, and air force units. Also, US Army aviation units, the US Air Force (USAF), the US Navy, and navy and marine aircraft crews were involved. Many Americans were wounded or killed during this campaign.

No US Army or US Marine ground units returned to Vietnam to respond to the invasion, but the USAF response was swift and massive. From bases in the United States, Korea, and the Philippines, waves of fighters, bombers, tankers, and cargo aircraft flowed to Southeast Asia. Some of those aircraft crews were flying combat missions three days after they received orders to deploy. The US Navy responded by tripling the number of aircraft carriers off the Vietnamese coast from two to six, with almost 500 aircraft, plus 20 cruisers and destroyers. It was the largest collection of naval power assembled since World War II.

The Easter Offensive was not like the attack on cities by the indigenous VC guerillas during Tet in 1968. In 1972, we were fighting the NVA, and for the first time in the Central Highlands the enemy had tanks. The Communists were not just testing; they were trying to conquer South Vietnam that spring. They made repeated, all-out attempts to seize the outposts, fire-support bases (FSBs), and cities they wanted. Their goal was to defeat South Vietnam or at least to seize and hold enough key cities to relegate the United States to a weak bargaining position in the Paris peace talks.[3] This offensive was a massive three-pronged invasion. In the North, the enemy attacked into the I Corps area with six divisions of about 8,700 men each. Three Communist divisions attacked II Corps in the Central Highlands, and another three attacked into III Corps north of Saigon, the South Vietnamese capital.[4]

A famous Vietnam War correspondent told me, "The main show was up north, Kontum was just a sideshow." The invasion did start in the North—across the DMZ into I Corps—so the Americans, the South Vietnamese, and the media initially focused their attention on the North. Maybe most of the reporters remained there, but after the NVA attacked in force into two other areas of South Vietnam, all three fronts became equally important. If the Communists' invasion from the North down Highway 1 had seized all the important coastal cities, they might have also seized Saigon. If An Loc in the South had fallen, they might have seized Saigon from that direction. If Kontum and the Central Highlands had fallen, South Vietnam would have been cut in half and defeated by the Communists. For those of us who were there, wherever we were fighting was the most important place in Vietnam.

1

Autumn in the Highlands, 1971

In the final analysis, it is their war. They are the ones who have to win it or lose it. We can help them, we can give them equipment, we can send our men out there as advisers, but they have to win it, the people of Vietnam.

—John F. Kennedy

I went to war in a first-class seat on a chartered, civilian jumbo jet. It was September 1971, and I was an infantry lieutenant colonel going back to Vietnam for my second one-year tour there. The airplane was full of military personnel, and the officers were assigned seats in the first-class section. Sitting next to me was an infantry colonel, an army aviator, who introduced himself as Robert S. Keller. He was going to be the senior adviser to the 23rd ARVN Infantry Division. I was going to be the G-3 (operations) adviser to that same division. Colonel Keller would be my commanding officer.

The 23rd ARVN Infantry Division was under II Corps in Pleiku, so after a couple days of personnel processing and orientations in Saigon I moved on to Pleiku for more processing and some briefings by the II Corps advisers in the large American military compound in Pleiku. Transient officers staying overnight were assigned to individual "hooches" in a row of identical small buildings. As I was walking across a big lawn, returning from dinner one beautiful evening, someone's radio was tuned to the Armed Forces Network (AFN), and Joan Baez was singing "The Night They Drove Old Dixie Down." Just as she sang "See there goes Robert E. Lee,"

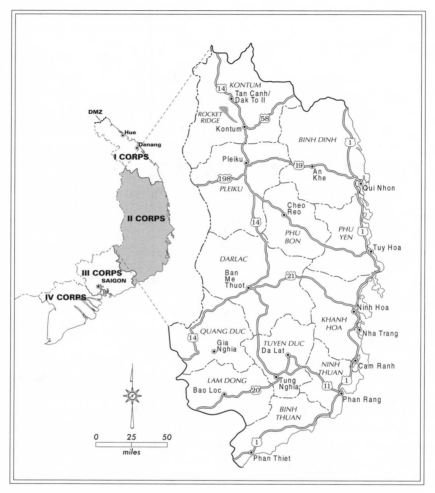

II Corps: major cities, highways, and boundaries of provinces. Small inset map shows the position of II Corps within South Vietnam.

there was the heavy CRUMP! CRUMP! CRUMP! of mortar rounds falling in the compound. A siren wailed, and I ran to the nearest bunker. Welcome back to Vietnam!

During my first tour in Vietnam, I learned that when you live with intermittent incoming artillery or rocket fire, you become somewhat used to it. To me, the US Military Assistance Command, Vietnam (MACV) compound at Pleiku seemed less dangerous than trying to cross a busy street in Saigon. However, Brigadier General George E. Wear, the II Corps deputy senior adviser, saw the reaction of high-ranking visitors to II Corps headquarters:

> The area containing the US Advisory compound [Pleiku Barracks] [and] the II Corps headquarters building with adjoining ARVN living quarters was the prime target for 120-mm rockets. They didn't do much damage unless a direct hit. We were rocketed on an average of about every two weeks or so during the 20 months I was there. Occasionally, a direct hit would produce US or ARVN casualties. We could tell when the first rocket landed whether they were going to be a problem. Alarms were sounded, artillery fired in the general direction of the launch sites, and we went on about our business. If they started landing during dinner, we usually kept on eating.
>
> I realized near the end of my tour up there that not a single [visiting] full colonel or higher ever spent a night [in Pleiku] in all the time I was there. Colonels and generals would show up during the day for some reason or another and then would quickly depart.[1]

By 1971, many of the American and South Vietnamese military and pacification experts thought the war was won. However, the South Vietnamese had reached the limits of what they could do to defend themselves, and our government had reached the limits of what it would give them to do it. The North Vietnamese were unfortunately willing to intensify their struggle for final victory, and massive aid from China and the Soviet Union would give them the means to do it.[2]

As we withdrew from Vietnam, our government's attention was turning toward other places and other problems. Even the Central Intelligence Agency (CIA) was paying less attention to Vietnam. It published a national intelligence estimate on Vietnam in April 1971 and did not publish another one until October 1973, 18 months later.[3] The media were also turning away from Vietnam. War news was disappearing from magazine covers, the front pages of newspapers, and TV news programs.

At the peak of our involvement, there were 543,400 Americans in South Vietnam.[4] We took over the war, and many of the South

Vietnamese military units were relegated to guarding government installations and hunting down local Communist forces while the Americans went into the jungle to seek big battles with the NVA.

The American people and Congress were increasingly opposed to continued involvement in Vietnam, and there was no chance this trend would be reversed.[5] US troop strength there was now less than 100,000 and falling fast. Most of our allies' forces were already withdrawn, and world opinion generally did not support our efforts in Vietnam. Some Western governments were even supporting our enemies. In May 1971, Swedish foreign minister Torsten Nilsson announced that Sweden was expanding its assistance to the VC with an initial donation of $550,000 worth of medical supplies and hospital equipment.[6]

President Richard M. Nixon's claim that he had a plan to get us out of Vietnam was a major factor in his election in 1968. After his inauguration, he revealed the plan as "Vietnamization"—to turn the war over to the South Vietnamese. He started withdrawing American troops while building up the South Vietnamese government and armed forces. The North Vietnamese said the purpose of Vietnamization was to change the color of the corpses.[7]

General William C. Westmoreland, the MACV commander, returned to Washington to become chief of staff of the army in July 1968. He was replaced by his deputy, General Creighton W. Abrams, who was given the responsibility of withdrawing his US ground forces while building up the South Vietnamese forces. When Nixon took office, there were about 850,000 troops in South Vietnam's armed forces. This number was soon increased to more than a million, and the Americans replaced the South Vietnamese's World War II–era weapons with the same weapons used by the US armed forces. More than a million M-16 rifles, 12,000 M-60 machine guns, 40,000 M-79 grenade launchers, and 2,000 artillery pieces and mortars were given to the Vietnamese. They also received new tactical radios; 46,000 vehicles, ships, and boats; and 1,100 helicopters and other aircraft.[8]

The Americans created ARVN in their own image as much as possible. The organizational structure, equipment, ranks, supply system, and personnel system were almost exact copies of those in the US Army. Starting with the smallest element, ARVN had infantry platoons of about 30–40 men and infantry companies of 150–200 men in four platoons and a headquarters element. There were three or four companies in a battalion, and three or four battalions in a regiment. The configuration varied by division, and the 23rd ARVN Division had three companies per battalion and four battalions per regiment.

The ARVN artillery batteries, armor companies, and armored cavalry troops had fewer men than similar infantry units, but they were also organized in battalions—or squadrons for the cavalry. An ARVN infantry division also had an artillery regiment consisting of three artillery battalions with 105-mm howitzers. Each infantry regiment had two 81-mm mortars, and each infantry company had two 60-mm mortars. ARVN was plagued by desertions, so most units had fewer men present for duty than was authorized.

The South Vietnamese also had the Airborne Division and Ranger battalions in Ranger groups. They were moved around the country like chess pieces to block enemy threats or to plug holes in the defenses. In addition, Border Ranger battalions were manning static bases along the border. Most of the troops in Border Ranger battalions were from local ethnic groups, like the Montagnards, but most of their officers were Vietnamese. The Border Rangers did not receive the same training as the regular Ranger battalions, and they were not moved around the country to deal with military emergencies.

Regional Forces (RFs), or "Ruffs," were recruited in each province. The RFs were organized like ARVN units and were under the command of the province chiefs, most of whom were ARVN officers. They could be deployed anywhere in their home province but were seldom sent to other provinces. They were as well armed—including their own artillery—and almost as well trained as the ARVN units. Popular Forces (PFs), or "Puffs," were also recruited in each village. These forces had the same small arms as ARVN or the RF, but they stayed near their homes and guarded local bridges, government buildings, and their own villages.

The Ruff Puffs had more men under arms than all the regular forces combined. Under the upgrading program started by General Abrams, they had a higher priority than ARVN for new equipment, such as M-16s. They were able to defend against the local VC and even launch limited operations against them, but they lacked the logistical support required to spend extended periods of time in the field. They were not able to engage in lengthy battles with the NVA. Although the Ruff Puffs and civilian police guarded much of the government infrastructure, some of ARVN's manpower was also committed to guarding government installations—including its own camps—and to clearing roads of mines and ambushes.

Included in the change of direction under General Abrams was a campaign to retrain the South Vietnamese armed forces. More than 12,000 ARVN officers were sent to the United States for advanced training, and 350 five-man teams of American advisers were sent to train the RFs and PFs on their new weapons.[9] Because the Americans were withdrawing and the South Vietnamese were being strengthened with new weapons and training, General Abrams considered the advisers essential to his effort to turn the war over to the Vietnamese, and he wanted to improve the quality of the officers selected for adviser assignments. In early 1970, Abrams told Secretary of Defense Melvin R. Laird and chairman of the Joint Chiefs of Staff General Earle G. Wheeler that he was "actively shifting talent from U.S. units into the advisory thing. We've got to dig in there and get some blue chips out of the one bag and stick them in the other."[10]

The advisers had varying degrees of rapport with and success in dealing with their Vietnamese counterparts. If the ARVN officer did not speak enough English or the American officer did not speak enough Vietnamese—and few did—then they had to communicate through an interpreter, which further complicated their relationship and ability to get anything accomplished. The basic technique was for the adviser to tell his counterpart what he recommended and tell his American superior the same thing. The other American adviser would then tell his counterpart, who would tell his Vietnamese superior or subordinate. When that system worked well—and that did not always happen—the ARVN counterparts would receive orders from their superiors that paralleled their advisers' recommendations.

The advisers and their counterparts often had a difficult relationship. In addition to the language and cultural differences, the advisers were often younger and sometimes lower in rank than their Vietnamese counterparts. In the early 1960s, the American captains and lieutenants advising ARVN battalions and companies in the field were on their first tour in Vietnam. Few of them were old enough to have experienced combat in Korea, but they were advising men with years of combat experience, sometimes going back to serving with the French against the Viet Minh ten years earlier. In those circumstances, the advisers tended to concentrate on equipment and logistical matters. However, after the mid-1960s, when US involvement surged, the advisers became their counterparts' link to vital US helicopter airlift, artillery and tactical air support, and B-52 strikes. The relationship became much closer then. In December 1968, at the height of the war, 11,000 American advisers were working with the South Vietnamese armed forces.[11] By the time the last US advisers left Vietnam in early 1973, many ARVN officers had worked with as many as 20 to 30 different advisers.[12]

South Vietnam had its own air force, the South Vietnamese Air Force (VNAF). The performance of VNAF's A-1 and A-37 fighter-bomber pilots was excellent, and its AC-47 gunship and C-123 cargo aircraft crews were almost as good. VNAF fighter-bomber pilots were more experienced than the Americans, and after years of bombing in their own country, they knew the territory. However, both the Americans and the South Vietnamese held VNAF helicopter crews in contempt. The only exception was the crews of VNAF helicopter gunships. ARVN had no helicopters of its own; they all belonged to VNAF, and VNAF was a separate service with its own chain of command. VNAF troop-lift helicopter units were seldom responsive to ARVN officers, and their support for ARVN was notoriously poor.

VNAF helicopter pilots sold rides to unauthorized civilians, charged refugees for evacuation flights, and sometimes sold their equipment on the black market. Whenever we were flying in a VNAF helicopter without seat belts or doors and with a VNAF "cowboy" pilot at the controls, I maintained a tight grip on some part of the interior frame and hoped for the best. How well the engines were being maintained was also a worry. If we informed our ARVN counterparts that our helicopter support for a mission was coming from VNAF rather than from a US unit, we could see disappointment and even fear in their eyes. ARVN soldiers could see the stark contrast between VNAF pilots and the US helicopter pilots who risked their lives to resupply and evacuate advisers. VNAF helicopter pilots had a bad reputation for refusing to fly medical evacuation (medevac), troop transport, or resupply missions if they might encounter hostile fire.

VNAF medevac pilots sometimes refused to pick up ARVN casualties in the battle area. Their medevac pilots would even hover four or five feet off the ground, ready for a fast getaway but so high only the walking wounded could get onboard. The advisers were ordered not to call for a "dustoff" (an American helicopter medevac mission) unless there was an American casualty because the USAF advisers with VNAF were trying to force ARVN commanders to put pressure on VNAF to do its job. We complied, but it was hard to tell a counterpart that we could not call for a dustoff to pick up his wounded men and that he would need to use his chain of command to complain about VNAF so they would be forced to do their job.

On paper, the South Vietnamese armed forces looked impressive, but, as with many military organizations, the actual strength present for duty was usually less. The II Corps commander, Lieutenant General Ngo Dzu, visited the 23rd Division one day and invited the division commander, Brigadier General Vo Vanh Canh, Colonel Keller, and me to join him for an informal lunch at a local restaurant. General Dzu told us that a few weeks earlier he and another ARVN general ate lunch in a civilian restaurant. When Dzu had asked their waiter, a young man of military age, why he was not in the army, the waiter told them that he *was* in the army, but that his company commander allowed him to work full-time as a waiter as long as he split his civilian wages with the commander. This practice was not uncommon. These "ghost" soldiers were typical of the graft and corruption that crippled ARVN.

ARVN's American-style organization, training, and equipment were deceptive in some ways because the South Vietnamese armed forces and their government also operated in the traditional Oriental way. The ARVN officers were influenced by ancient mandarin traditions and their experience under the French colonial system. The higher their rank, the greater the likelihood their promotions were based more on political influence than on military merit.[13] Personal alliances, social class, and graft often carried more weight than the abstract ideal of a nation to be built—or saved. After the 1963 coup d'état in which South Vietnamese president Ngo Dinh Diem was overthrown and murdered, his successors were always on their guard. So loyalty to the president rather than to professional competence was often the main criterion for promotion to the higher ranks and subsequent assignments. Too many ARVN officers, especially the higher-ranking ones, seized the opportunity for immediate financial gain from their positions even though doing so undermined continued American support and put their own futures and their country's future at risk. In the late 1960s, to be appointed as province chief of a wealthy province reputedly required a bribe of 10 million piasters, about $50,000. The payoff was sometimes made through the aspiring province chief's wife, who would "lose" that amount to the wife of her husband's patron during a game of mah-jongg.[14]

Both early military background and religion caused some rifts within ARVN. Most of the higher-ranking ARVN officers had received their earlier military training from the French, but the lower-ranking officers and many of the noncommissioned officers (NCOs, such as sergeants) received their training from the Americans, so there were some differences in military culture, standards, and methods between the higher and lower ranks. ARVN was 69 percent Buddhist, but most of the higher-ranking commanders were from the Catholic minority. In 1966, a US military study of the South Vietnamese officer corps revealed that only one field-grade ARVN officer had been wounded in action during the 12 years since the war with the Communists had started in 1954.[15]

The Communist North Vietnamese referred to the war as the "American War" to distinguish it from their earlier "Japanese War," in which they had fought the Japanese, who occupied Indochina during World War II, and the "French War," in which they had fought the French, who had returned to Vietnam after World War II.

The NVA was organized and equipped like the Soviet and Communist Chinese armies, which furnished their advisers and equipment. The North Vietnamese officers tended to be professionals who were commissioned and promoted based on military merit.[16] Most NVA soldiers received 12 weeks of basic training. Specialists were trained for an additional two to nine months, depending on the specialty. During training, a three-man cell was formed, and unless there were casualties or transfers, it remained intact as long as the men were in the army. The cell members supported each other in combat, provided comradeship to prevent homesickness and low morale, and ensured that any wavering or loss of revolutionary zeal by one member would be detected and probably reported by the other two. Three cells composed a nine-man squad.[17]

A full-strength NVA infantry division was made up of three regiments of about 2,500 men each, plus organic artillery; anti-aircraft, engineer, signal, and medical battalions; and a transport company—all totaling around 9,600 men. Some divisions had a regiment rather than a battalion of artillery. The infantry regiments had three infantry battalions of 600 men each.[18] Tank battalions with about 38 tanks each were sometimes attached to the divisions. The number of tanks in an NVA tank unit could vary according to the mission or the tactical situation or availability of tanks.

South Vietnam was made up of four areas for administrative and military purposes. In various contexts, they were called "corps," "military regions," or "regional assistance commands." They were numbered from first (I Corps) at the DMZ on the border with North Vietnam to fourth (IV Corps) in the Mekong Delta. Within each corps area, the corps commander, an ARVN major general or lieutenant general, was in command of all the South Vietnamese troops. A US Army major general or lieutenant general was in command of all US troops in that area and served as the senior adviser to the ARVN corps commander. By late 1971, the American organization within each corps area was designated a "regional assistance command." However, II Corps was different because John Paul Vann, a US Foreign Service officer, was appointed as senior adviser to the Vietnamese II Corps commander and as "director" of the Second Regional Assistance Group (SRAG, the advisers to II Corps) in May 1971. Although Vann was a retired US Army lieutenant colonel, he was now a civilian and could not "command" the US Army troops, so a US Army brigadier general was appointed to serve under Vann as his deputy and to command the US troops in II Corps. A lengthy letter of instructions from General Abrams to Vann described Vann's mission and the responsibilities and relationships involved.[19]

Under both the French colonial administration and the South Vietnamese government, some Vietnamese considered the Central Highlands a place of exile where a civil servant or military officer was sent as punishment or just because he was considered below average in some way. Saigon or the coastal cities were considered more desirable postings. II Corps was a strategically important area, but Lieutenant General Ngo Dzu was in command there even though he was obviously not the best man for the job.[20]

Brigadier General Wear described how Lieutenant General Dzu operated:

General Dzu apparently came from a well-to-do Vietnamese

family. He graduated from the ARVN Military Academy with the first class in about 1958 along with President [Nguyen Van] Thieu. He was in his early forties when I served with him and had attended our Command and General Staff College. Spoke English very well. Had a wife and 10 or 12 kids in Saigon. He was more a politician than soldier and became heavily involved in black-market activities, if not drug running. We got along fine, although I had little admiration for him as a soldier.

General Dzu did not spend much time in Pleiku. He operated mostly out of Nha Trang or, for some reason, his ancestral home, Qui Nhon. The First Field Force, Vietnam headquarters, was in a French Hotel on the beach in Nha Trang. That was where Dzu's main headquarters was. Also, where John Vann spent most of his time. [Vann] had a nice home near the headquarters where his significant other, Julie, lived.

[Dzu's] pattern soon became like this: On Sunday afternoons, he would arrive at the corps headquarters building and stop by my office. He liked our Scotch, so I would invite him over to the barracks, have a couple Scotches with him, invite him for dinner in our mess. He had a fairly nice house in the town of Pleiku. On Monday mornings, he would attend the morning briefing, harangue his staff for an hour or two (I never knew what about), and go up to his office in the headquarters building directly above my office. I would stay around and at about 10:00 he would come down to my office accompanied by his chief of staff, Colonel Bien. He would say: "General Wear, I have many things to do down on the coast and must leave shortly. You take care of things in the Highlands. I tell Colonel Bien to tell the staff that you are in charge." With that he would leave, and we wouldn't see him until the following Sunday afternoon.[21]

Brigadier General Wear knew one reason why Dzu always followed Mr. Vann's advice:

In September 1971, General [Frederick C.] Weyand [Abrams's deputy] informed Vann that the US Criminal Investigation Department was convinced that Dzu was a ringleader in the flow of drugs from Laos and Cambodia to the US troops in Vietnam. Vann accosted Dzu with this information, and Dzu denied the charge. [He] admitted to doing a little contraband smuggling with his brother, a VNAF pilot, but claimed that they were not involved with drugs. Vann believed him and intervened with Abrams and Weyand to save Dzu's hide. That gave Vann a lot of control over Dzu.[22]

The ARVN troops in II Corps included the 22nd and 23rd Infantry Divisions and 11 Ranger battalions in Ranger groups. Other Ranger and airborne battalions from the strategic reserve were sometimes deployed there. II Corps was the largest but least populated of the four corps areas. It included 30,000 square miles—47 percent of South Vietnam's total area—and was about the size of South Carolina. Its eastern boundary was 320 miles of irregular coastline along the South China Sea. About two-thirds of South Vietnam's entire coast was in the 23rd Division's area of operations.[23] On the western side were a 175-mile border with Cambodia and a 65-mile border with Laos. The southern boundary of II Corps was only 56 miles from Saigon. There were three distinct geographic regions in II Corps: the fertile coastal plain along the coast; the Highland Plateau, averaging 3,000 feet high; and the Annamite Mountains, with peaks up to 8,500 feet high in Kontum Province. Most of the population of II Corps lived on the flat, narrow strip of coast along the South China Sea. Highway 1, the French Foreign Legion's "Street Without Joy," connects all the major coastal cities. In peacetime, it is possible to drive on Highway 1 all the way from the Chinese border to Cau Mau at the southern tip of Vietnam. From October through February, when the northeastern monsoon rains fall on the coast, the Annam Cordillera Mountain Range blocks them from falling in the highlands. Then, after a month or so of transition, the southeastern monsoon brings rain to the highlands while the coast remains dry.[24]

There are high, barren plateaus, dense jungle, and tall, jagged mountains in the Central Highlands. One of the best-known cities in the Highlands is Dalat, a mountain resort in a beautiful setting. To drive from Dalat to Ban Me Thuot in the early 1970s, it was necessary to go down to the coast on Highway 11 (now 20), north on Highway 1, and then back up into the Highlands on Highway 21 (now 26), driving over roughly three sides of a square. Pleiku is 203 kilometers north of Ban Me Thuot on the north–south Highway 14, and Kontum is another 47 kilometers farther north. Highway 21 connects Ban Me Thuot to the coast near Nha Trang, and Highway 19 connects Pleiku to the coast at Qui Nhon. However, vehicle travel on any of these mountain roads was dangerous during the war. There could be mines buried in the road; you were always vulnerable to enemy ambushes; and VC or NVA forces were sometimes able to seize a narrow pass and block traffic for weeks or months.

Three million people, about 18 percent of the total national population, lived in II Corps. Half a million people were scattered over the Central Highlands, and half of them were Montagnards.[25] There were few ethnic Vietnamese in the Central Highlands. More than 50 percent of Kontum Province's population was composed of the ethnic minorities such as Bahnar, Jarai, Koho, Manong, Rhade Xo Dang, Ba Na, Gie Trieng, Brau, Gia Rai, Ra Rai, and Ro Mam. The French called them "Montagnards" (Mountain People), and some Vietnamese called them "Moi" (savages.) The Americans called them "Yards," an affectionate rather than a derisive nickname. Most of us considered the Yards good people who made good soldiers. As many as 800,000 Montagnards died during the war.[26]

The headquarters of the 23rd ARVN Division was in Ban Me Thuot. It was a city of 70,000 but looked more like a small town of about 2,000. Trash was strewn in the streets, and mold crept up the trunks of trees and the sides of buildings. Red dust covered the lower several feet of trees and buildings. The streets were dirt, with many Jeep-jarring potholes. Government installations were surrounded by barbed wire, protected by sandbags at critical points, and guarded by soldiers or national policemen. However, it was basically a nice place with beautiful pine trees and a wide variety of flowers. There were giant poinsettia trees and other flora that reminded me of Hawaii. The climate was pleasant and cool during the dry-cold months and downright cold in January and February, when I slept under three blankets. During the hot, wet months, it rained a great deal, but neither the heat nor the humidity were as oppressive as they were in the Mekong Delta, where I spent my first tour in Vietnam.[27]

We saw spectacular sunsets where the mountains met the sky out toward Cambodia, only 30 miles to the west. Double- or triple-canopy jungle with giant trees covered much of the Central Highlands. In some areas, the tangle of tree limbs, leaves, and vines blocked the sunlight, and the jungle floor below them was dark and dank. The logs trucked through Ban Me Thuot were the largest I have ever seen. Flying over the jungle, we could see broad, fast-flowing rivers and high, dramatic waterfalls. Deer and big-game animals roamed the jungles of the Central Highlands. Former US president Theodore Roosevelt may have hunted around Ban Me Thuot in the early twentieth century. Just before dark one evening as some of us were flying back to Ban Me Thuot in a Huey, there were low-hanging clouds, so the pilot, Colonel Keller, was skimming just above the treetops. The doors were open, and I saw an elephant running through the jungle below us. The 23rd Division commander, Brigadier General Vo Vanh Canh, told me he once saw a herd of 30 elephants below his helicopter.

In late 1971, a tiger skin was on sale for $150 in the Ban Me Thuot market. An American major I knew bought a stuffed tiger to take home. His wife may not have been so enthusiastic about that souvenir.[28] A friend who was a US Navy doctor during the Vietnam War told me he operated on a marine who, while sitting in a night ambush position, was bitten by a tiger when he reached out to check on the man next to him. Another friend who served in Special Forces in the Highlands in 1964 told about a puzzling radio report they received from one of their teams at an outlying camp. The team radioed the coded number of friendlies (ARVN troops) killed in action (KIA) and wounded in action (WIA) but added one "EIA." When asked what "EIA" meant, the outpost said one of their Yards had gone outside the perimeter wire at night to go to the toilet and was "eaten in action" by a tiger.

There had been 10,000 Americans in Ban Me Thuot only a few years earlier, and 3,000 were still there in early 1971. Now only 250 of us remained. The advisers to the 23rd Division were in Advisory Team 33. An excellent and popular Vietnamese beer coincidentally had the team's name, a big "33," on the label. Our advisory team had been 180 strong in the spring of 1971 but was now down to 80 and scheduled for reduction to 50 by the end of June 1972. Rumors said the schedule might be accelerated.

The withdrawal of American forces from Vietnam, or "draw-down," started in late 1969. President Nixon gave MACV a total troop-strength ceiling to be reached by the end of each quarter. MACV then met those ceilings by selecting which units would be sent home and when they would depart. It was important to do this in an order that would still provide necessary support for the remaining units, but this support was not being maintained in the First Field Force, Vietnam, which included all the US units in II Corps. Brigadier General Wear describes how the problem was resolved:

> The MACV staff was not letting me help decide which units should leave next. . . . In September or October, I mentioned the problem to Vann and pointed out how we were becoming unable to support some of the remaining units. Vann contacted his mentor, Weyand, with the problem. Weyand told John that Abrams was personally handling that issue and that he would set up a meeting with Abrams for Vann and me. Weyand said that the best time to meet with Abrams was at breakfast with him in his quarters. Accordingly, the date was set, and Vann and I were at Abrams's quarters at a few minutes prior to the seven o'clock breakfast meeting. We were let in by a MSGT [master sergeant] aide and found ourselves in a room with a breakfast table set up for three people. At exactly 0700, Abrams came in, just grunted to us, and invited us to sit down with him. Over breakfast of eggs and bacon, etc., Vann and I outlined our problem and requested that we have a say in the II Corps withdrawal schedule. We covered some specifics of the problem. All during breakfast, Abrams never uttered a word. When breakfast was over, Abrams stood up and said, "I'm not about to buy that pile of shit," and left. As Vann and I exited the building, John said, "Well, George, I guess we didn't do very well in there!" However, a day or two later the MACV G-3, Maj. Gen. John Carley, called me and said, "I don't know what you and Vann discussed with Abrams, but at the morning briefing he directed me to clear all future withdrawals from IFFV [I (First) Field Force, Vietnam] with Wear.[29]

In November 1971, the US senior adviser to one of the provinces down on the coast reported to Brigadier General Wear that the province chief, an ARVN colonel, was using a large portion of his regional forces to guard a US airbase left vacant as part of the US withdrawal. When the adviser asked his counterpart why he was using his troops that way instead of for securing the population, the province commander told him that Lieutenant General Dzu had ordered him to guard the empty base. Wear asked Dzu about it and was told, "General Wear, things are going to get rough up here, and the United States will have to come back and use that airbase." Wear responded, "General, please listen to me carefully. For political reasons, the United States will not send troops, airplanes, etc., back into Vietnam, regardless of how bad the situation is." Wear was not sure Dzu understood his point, but he did rescind the order to guard the empty base.[30]

When the 23rd Division command group traveled by helicopter, Colonel Keller would displace one of the command-and-control (C&C) ship pilots to fly the aircraft himself. I liked to have him at the controls because he was an excellent and experienced pilot. During the previous decade, most US Army pilots had served at least 2 one-year tours flying in Vietnam, and many were veterans of three or four tours. They had done their duty and gone home for good. So most of the American pilots supporting us in 1971–1972 were warrant officers about 20 years old, just out of flight school, and with around 200 hours of total flying time. But they were still far better than VNAF Huey pilots we flew with. Colonel Keller had served in the 10th Mountain Division during World War II, and we respected him very much for that. However, he had no previous experience as an adviser and did not build the necessary relationship with his counterpart. When Colonel Keller flew the helicopter, the copilot occupied the other front seat. This left Keller's own counterpart, the division commander, back in the passenger compartment with me and any other advisers or ARVN staff officers accompanying us that day. Most of the time I was the one who sat beside and talked with the division commander. We pointed out places on the map and on the ground and discussed past, present, and future operations.[31]

The Vietnam War was the first helicopter war. While serving in Vietnam from May 1966 to March 1973, the 1st Aviation Brigade had at least some degree of control over 4,000 rotary-wing and fixed-wing aircraft and 24,000 troops.[32] The workhorse helicopters were the UH-1H utility helicopters, the Hueys. Starting in 1959, Bell Aircraft produced more than 16,000 Hueys.[33] The ones armed with only an M-60 machine gun mounted in the door on each side were "slicks" because they had no weapons mounted on the exterior. Slicks carried troops or served as C&C ships during operations. UH-1H Hueys with 7.62-mm miniguns in the doors and 2.75-inch rockets mounted externally were "gunships" or just "guns." The guns always worked in pairs. Those external weapons on the Hueys caused drag and made the guns slower than the slicks they were escorting. In late 1971, the US aviation units supporting us were turning many of their helicopters over to VNAF and going home. All the Huey gunships were going to VNAF because in US units they were being replaced by the new AH-1G Cobra gunships, armed with a nose turret, which contained a combination 7.62-mm multibarrel minigun and a 40-mm grenade launcher called a "thumper." There was another minigun or a 20-mm cannon in a pod. On the "stub wings," there were up to nineteen (depending on the launcher) 2.75-inch rockets. We called the Cobras "snakes." VNAF never received Cobras.[34]

The troops or supplies we needed to support operations were sometimes carried on CH-47 helicopters flown by US or VNAF pilots. The CH-47 was a big, twin-engine, tandem-rotor helicopter. It could carry a 10,000-pound payload, as opposed to the Huey's 4,600-pound payload. The actual weight carried depended on the altitude, weather, and capability of the individual aircraft. The official name for the CH-47 was "Chinook," but we usually called it a "Hook" because it had a hook in a bomb bay–type opening in the deck. A heavy load, such as a 105-mm howitzer suspended in a sling, could be carried beneath the aircraft. Some of the US CH-47 crews referred to themselves as "Hookers."

The LOH-6 "Cayuse" light observation helicopter, called a "Loach," was used by the air cavalry scouts and carried only the pilot and an observer/gunner with a machine gun. Two snakes always flew cover for the Loach and brought death and destruction on any enemy that fired at their "little bird." In some places, the Loach could fly between the trees while searching along a jungle trail. While doing this, a scout pilot could come face to face with the enemy. A Loach pilot told me he saw an enemy soldier step from behind a tree, wave at him, and then shoot at him. The round came through the Plexiglas bubble and hit his foot pedal. His gunner shot the man who did it.[35]

Operation Jefferson Glenn, the last major ground operation for US ground forces, ended on 8 October 1971 with 2,026 enemy casualties. On 12 November, President Nixon announced that henceforth only the South Vietnamese would take offensive actions and that the US ground forces would play a defensive role only.[36] In October 1971, Vo Van Sung, the Communist delegate general at the Paris peace talks, said the North Vietnamese would launch a new military offensive in 1972.[37]

2

Fighting in Phu Nhon

We don't have 12 years experience in this country. We have one year's experience 12 times.
—Lieutenant Colonel John Paul Vann
at the end of his 1962–1963 tour in Vietnam

A steady stream of NVA soldiers and equipment was flowing toward us down the Ho Chi Minh Trail. Staff Sergeant John L. Plaster was a Special Forces soldier in the Studies and Observations Group (SOG) running secret operations deep into Laos and Cambodia. In early October 1971, he was flying as a Covey rider (an airborne controller) with a forward air controller (FAC), Captain Glenn J. Wright, whose call sign was "Covey 593." They were over Highway 110 E in Laos where that part of the Ho Chi Minh Trail ended at the triborder area—the place where the borders of Vietnam, Cambodia, and Laos meet. It was the NVA's main route into the Central Highlands of South Vietnam. As Plaster and Wright flew over the highway, Plaster noticed long, parallel lines of bushes on either side of the road. They circled back for a closer look and saw some of the bushes move. They were camouflaged enemy soldiers—many of them. Plaster noted the interval between "bushes" and the length of the two columns and calculated the force at about 2,000 men, probably an entire enemy regiment. He radioed his SOG commander to request a B-52 strike on this target. A B-52 strike was not approved, but they got something even better: priority for all US tactical air strikes in Southeast Asia.

Wave after wave of fighter-bombers arrived about ten minutes apart to bomb the NVA regiment with 500-pound bombs, cluster bombs, and napalm. So many bombers were arriving that they had to split the target area with another Covey FAC and Covey rider from SOG so all the air assets could be used as efficiently as possible. They bombed until dark and then returned at daylight to bomb some more. The more they bombed, the more hidden enemy vehicles, camps, and supply dumps were exposed, and they, too, were bombed. As the enemy tried to reassemble his units dispersed by the earlier bombing, they were plastered again. Wiping out almost an entire NVA regiment with all its equipment and supplies was a major blow against the enemy infiltrating into South Vietnam.[1] There would be many less—maybe thousands less—Communist soldiers available to attack us in the future.

In early November, we started an ARVN offensive named "Operation 23/7" in Phu Nhon, northwest of Ban Me Thuot near the Cambodian border. We used four infantry battalions, including those in the division's 45th Infantry Regiment. The senior adviser to that regiment was Lieutenant Colonel John C. Grant and his deputy was Major *George* Dodge, a tall redhead with a great sense of humor. The 11th and 23rd Ranger Battalions were placed under our operational control, and we were supported by the US "Sidekick" Cobra gunships, the 17th Air Cavalry (A Troop, 7th Squadron), and CH-47 Hooks. We brought along 105-mm howitzers and lifted them into FSBs with the Hooks.

Our division forward command post was set up in a pyramid tent next to an old dirt airstrip high on a windy hill. We erected a small wall tent nearby for the advisers to live in and furnished it with some canvas cots. However, Colonel Keller flew most of the advisers back to Ban Me Thuot every evening, and then we would return with him to Phu Nhon every morning after breakfast. We always left a couple advisers in the Phu Nhon Division Tactical Operations Center (DTOC) to hold the fort overnight.

The typical soil in the Highlands is red, laterite clay, which turns to dust during the dry season. A strong wind we called "the Hawk" howled day and night and covered everything with fine, red dust. Helicopters landing and taking off sent clouds of dust swirling everywhere. It covered our clothes and equipment. It was in our hair and eyes and got down inside our sleeping bags. When I undressed back in Ban Me Thuot after even one day at Phu Nhon, there would be red dust inside my undershorts.[2]

Enemy activity and possibly base camps were reported just

across the border, so we put in air strikes on identified targets and then used helicopters to insert troops to do bomb damage assessments (BDAs), kill or capture any living enemy soldiers, and collect enemy weapons. In mid-November, we used a three-plane B-52 "Arc Light" strike to destroy a reported enemy base camp across the border in Cambodia. After the strike, one of our battalions swept the area and found a large cache of enemy weapons and ammunition. As the ARVN officers and troops searched the surrounding area, they found more and more weapons caches. They were overjoyed about their success, and the commanding general wanted to see what they had captured and to congratulate them. So the lucky battalion cleared a landing zone and established a secure perimeter around it. Colonel Keller flew the command group, including Lieutenant General Dzu, who was visiting the division that day, across the border to see the results. We landed in the strike zone and walked around. It was my first time in Cambodia. The holes left by our 500-pound bombs were impressive. No bodies were visible, but plenty of evidence indicated that this zone was a base camp the enemy had vacated just before our bombs hit.[3]

We walked around the area where the captured booty was being collected in piles about 4 feet high and 15 feet in diameter. There were AK-47s, rocket-propelled grenades (RPGs), a mortar, an antiaircraft gun, thousands of hand grenades, baskets full of Russian plastic explosives, an inflatable raft, and a great deal of ammunition—all made in Russia or China. It was a major coup to capture so many items the enemy could have used to kill us.

VNAF slicks started extracting the loot, and the two generals decided to go. We called for our orbiting helicopter to pick us up. Just as we cleared the trees, enemy mortar rounds started falling on our troops below. The enemy followed up his mortar barrage with a counterattack that got between two ARVN companies and overran the battalion headquarters. The ARVN regimental commander and his adviser barely escaped by running across a shallow river. All the captured weapons and explosives not already extracted were recaptured. What a loss![4]

The captured weapons we extracted were displayed in Phu Nhon and later in Ban Me Thuot, where a high-ranking American civilian from the Department of Defense came to see them. He told me he had come to Vietnam recently with Secretary of Defense Melvin Laird and was left behind as a "spy" to get a better evalua-

tion of the military situation. I asked if American government officials coming to Vietnam for only a week or so could get an accurate
sense of what was going on. He sidestepped the question by saying
there was an amazing difference between the optimism of Americans in Saigon and the more pessimistic view in Pleiku. Those of
us out in the field knew there was a similar gap between Pleiku and
where we were.[5]

One day I was alone in the pyramid tent we used for our forward
CP at Phu Nhon when "Rogues Gallery"—our boss, Mr. John Paul
Vann—called on the radio to inform us he was inbound and would
arrive in ten minutes. I "rogered" the transmission and called for
someone in our adjacent advisers' tent to come mind the store
while I went out to meet our visitor.

When Mr. Vann's helicopter landed, I walked over to meet him,
saluted, and reported to him. He demanded, "Why isn't Colonel
Keller here to meet me?" I told him Colonel Keller was flying his
counterpart over the area where our operation was in progress and
asked if he would like me to brief him. He remained rankled about
not being met by the senior adviser himself but accompanied me
into the pyramid tent, where I briefed him on what we were doing,
why, how, and what results had been achieved so far. He asked some
questions, including why almost all the advisers returned to Ban
Me Thuot every evening. Vann seemed satisfied with my briefing
but was obviously still dissatisfied with his reception party. Shortly
after we finished, Colonel Keller radioed to say he was inbound.
After he landed, Vann and Keller had a private conversation out
on the airstrip. From then on, all the advisers involved in Operation
23/7 lived and slept at Phu Nhon.

Mr. Vann's service in Vietnam had started in 1962 when he was
an army lieutenant colonel and senior adviser to the 7th ARVN
Infantry Division in the Mekong Delta. He was not a large, physically impressive man, but he dominated whatever space he was in.
His usual garb was cowboy boots, slacks, and a short-sleeved sport
shirt—usually white and frequently worn with a necktie. He seldom wore a flak jacket even when bullets were buzzing around and
incoming artillery was throwing shrapnel his way. Although he had
replaced a lieutenant general and his State Department rank was
the civilian equivalent of a major general, he was no longer in the
army and wore no rank insignia. As a result, strangers sometimes
failed to accord him the recognition or deference he deserved—

and demanded. When this happened, he promptly enlightened the offenders about the proper protocol where John Paul Vann was concerned. Someone told me a story about how on one occasion when Vann came aboard a US Navy ship in the South China Sea, he was not given the six side boys, full guard, and band due a person of his rank. Vann was not one to overlook a slight like this, and he complained to his hosts about the lack of ceremony appropriate for his rank.

Vann followed the military maxim "Ride to the sound of the guns!" He was able to identify the time and place where he could best influence the outcome of an important phase of a battle. He seemed to be inexhaustible and had far more energy and drive than most men his age (58 in 1972). He stayed up late and got by on less sleep than most of us need. A busy man on a tight schedule, he probably packed more travel, asking questions, and issuing orders into a day than any other American in Vietnam. John Paul Vann was arrogant, egotistical, and cocky. He could be abrasive, blunt, and opinionated. But he was also a hard-driving, hands-on, competitive commander who got results. His subordinates knew that he was interested in their welfare and that—if necessary—he would risk his own life to save theirs. This was why he was valued by his superiors, respected by his peers, and supported by his subordinates.

Brigadier General Wear, who knew Mr. Vann better than anyone else in Vietnam, described him:

> John Vann's title, since he wasn't military, was director, US Advisory Command, Military Region II. John's State Dept. rank was FSO1 [Foreign Service Officer 1]. The State Dept. also tacked on to his rank "Viet Nam Only." I don't think they wanted a John Vann with that rank serving anywhere else in the world.
>
> John scooted about in an OH-58, which he flew most of the time although he had never taken the pilot training or received his wings. His official pilot was [a] WO [warrant officer] who was a fine pilot and kept John alive when things got rough. John told me that weather had never stopped him. I reminded him that this was different than the Delta. Shortly after arriving, he and the WO got caught in very bad weather and had to land in the jungle and spend the night

there. That chopper didn't have the instruments to fly in rough weather like the Huey.

John lived mostly in Nha Trang. He had a room in Pleiku Barracks adjoining my suite. We had a door cut between them so we could get together and he could use the amenities in my suite. John was a night man, while I am a day person. He wouldn't get up until nine or so but stayed up until one or two in the morning. I was up for the six o'clock intelligence briefing, etc. but liked to go to bed by ten or so. I finally convinced him that midnight bull sessions weren't my thing.

John would do crazy things. He would ride his motorcycle all the way from Nha Trang to Pleiku at night! Arriving around daylight in Pleiku, he would grouse because [some] ARVN unit had stopped him and demanded identification, etc. He would also drop in at a District HQ and order the senior adviser to do something that he had no authority to do. The adviser would call me, and I would talk to John, who would always relent. For some reason, John liked me and never once treated me other than [as] an equal. I was embarrassed when he returned from a trip to Hong Kong [with Julie] and brought me back several presents.

In about mid-November, John showed me an efficiency report he had filled out on me. It was a special report for promotion to Maj. Gen. The report was exceptionally laudatory. Abrams's endorsement was, "Wear should be wearing two stars now."[6]

As the Americans withdrew from Vietnam, they transferred much of their own equipment to the South Vietnamese, who also received some new equipment shipped directly from the United States. By the end of 1971, the Americans had provided ARVN with 1,202 artillery pieces, including 12 of our big 175-mm guns.[7] By early 1972, ARVN had the same M-16 rifles and some of the M-48 medium tanks the American units were using. VNAF had F-5 fighter-bombers and other ground attack and transport aircraft, both propeller driven and jet propelled. The South Vietnamese now had the equipment they needed, but did they have the will? The Asian concern about "saving face" often inhibited commanders from taking risks that might turn out wrong or from making attacks that might produce many casualties. This attitude also contributed to their reluctance to admit and accurately report defeats and problems that higher headquarters needed to know about to access the situation accurately. There was a general lack of aggressiveness in the South Vietnamese commanders, which often manifested itself in overreliance on air support.[8] Using artillery and bombing to knock out bunkers and supporting weapons and to inflict casualties on the enemy before attacking makes sense. However, there comes a time when it is necessary for the infantry to attack to gain or regain an objective or to follow up when the enemy is reeling from attacks by artillery or bombing. ARVN commanders were all too often not aggressive enough to achieve maximum results.

Some ARVN soldiers were psychologically intimidated by the North Vietnamese, whom they believed were better soldiers. The South Vietnamese troops were especially worried when they were near the border, out west in what the Americans referred to as "Indian Territory." In April 1971, Lieutenant General Arthur S. Collins Jr. was the commanding general of the US Army's First Field Force, Vietnam, and the adviser to the ARVN II Corps commander. Collins persuaded the corps commander, Major General Lu Lan, to launch an ARVN operation in the Plei Trap area in northwest Kontum Province. After about a week, all but one battalion was withdrawn. The remaining battalion was ordered to sweep north to end up at Ben Het, a Border Ranger camp near the border with Cambodia and Laos. About the second night of the sweep, the NVA blew bugles and hit the battalion with mortar fire. According to the last report from the two-man advisory team, the ARVN soldiers panicked, threw down their weapons, and ran off toward Ben Het. Only a few members of the battalion reached Ben Het, and the advisers were never heard from again. Experiences like this gave Collins a low opinion of ARVN soldiers in general and of the higher-ranking Vietnamese officers in particular.[9]

Operation 23/7 at Phu Nhon continued into late December with the II Corps commander and staff in charge. Seen from my level, that operation was achieving results, but it was apparently an exception for ARVN operations in the western Highlands near the border. Brigadier General Wear described Lieutenant General Collins's frustration with ARVN's performance:

For the remainder of the time LTG Collins was there, he seemed to expect me to see that the ARVN performed effectively, which they seldom did. He would call me by telephone (usually late at night) two or three times a week and point out how some ARVN unit did not perform very well (as if I didn't know). General Collins understood how poorly the ARVN performed (primarily because of poor leadership) and continually whined about it. I understood that the folks in Saigon (Abrams, etc.) got tired of his continued pessimistic reports.[10]

The last week in November 1971 Mr. Vann and Brigadier General Wear flew to Saigon to attend the MACV Weekly Intelligence Briefing given by Major General William E. Potts, the MACV J-2, the highest MACV intelligence officer. Potts and Wear had attended the Armed Forces Staff College together. According to Wear,

the gist of the briefing was that an estimated 50,000 NVA troops, along with tanks and artillery pieces, were making their way down the Ho Chi Minh Trail and would be in position to attack in the Highlands area by late January or early February. No one but me seemed to be surprised by this information. After the briefing, Abrams discussed the withdrawal of troops program, and no one said anything about how we were going to meet the threat in the Highlands. Before leaving, I went over to Potts and asked him if he was sure that the NVA information was correct, and he assured me that he was sure and that he didn't know what plans were being made to meet it.

On the way back to Pleiku on the plane, I asked John if he heard what I did. John said that those estimates were always overblown and that a large attack in our area would give us an opportunity to destroy lots of them [the enemy]. He also said he had been hearing about enemy tanks for years, but none had ever shown up. He also said that if ARVN troops became surrounded, they would have to fight. John then informed me that the State Department was ordering him to spend two months in the states as part of their program to ensure that their top people did not lose contact with things at home. He had been resisting this visit but could no longer put it off. He had been assured by Weyand that he would be recalled after 30 days to meet the threat in the Highlands. John left in early December and returned about the middle of January.

During the month Vann was gone, Dzu hardly made an appearance in Pleiku. Nobody but me, my G-2 (Colonel Irv Paul), and my G-3 (Colonel Dillon Snell) seemed to be concerned about the coming events. Also, the withdrawal of US forces continued, including the Air Force Recon Squadron based at the Pleiku Air Base. Their O-1 and O-2 flights over the Highlands area had been our eyes on enemy movements, etc.[11]

Although there were continuing intelligence reports about an impending enemy offensive, even the MACV headquarters could only guess at when it might start. Down at our level, the advisers who had rest and recreation (R&R) leave approved for specific dates were allowed to go as scheduled but were required to leave contact information so they could be recalled if needed.

When Major *George* Dodge, deputy senior adviser to the 45th Regiment, showed up in Ban Me Thuot on his way to R&R, I asked, "You were waiting until early next year to go on R&R. How come you're leaving now?" He explained, "We were eating with the Yards, and they served cold, curdled duck's blood soup. It had some veins and entrails in it, but if you squeezed lime juice on every spoonful, it wasn't bad. In fact, I ate three bowls of it. After that, Colonel Grant decided I'd been in the field too long and really needed to go on R&R right away."

Major Dodge's description helped when a similar soup, maybe cold monkey's blood, was served during a meal I ate with some Montagnards. It was served in a small, thick ceramic cup without a handle—the type some Chinese restaurants use for tea. So the portion was thankfully small. There was half a lime on the side, so I squeezed all of it over the soup until a clear layer of lime juice covered the entire surface. Then I drank it all, emptying the cup without stopping, while thinking only "lime juice, lime juice, lime juice" as it slithered down my throat. It was not considered impolite to decline a second serving.

3

A Hundred Tons of Bombs

You always write it's bombing, bombing, bombing. It's not
bombing! It's air support!
                    —USAF colonel David H. E. Opfer

We resisted using tactical air strikes against any targets we could
hit with our artillery. However, the ARVN artillery had some lim-
itations. During the briefings that the high-ranking US officers
visiting II Corps received, some of them complained about the
ARVN artillery's performance. These officers were invariably the
ones who had served one or more previous tours in Vietnam with
US units that had had an unlimited supply of 105-mm rounds for
training and firing. In contrast to that unrestricted flow of ammunition, by 1972 the ARVN artillery was limited to 20 rounds per
tube (gun) per day,[1] which severely restricted live-fire training and
even fire support in combat.

The maximum range of the artillery pieces available was also
important. All NVA artillery was designed by the Soviet Union and
manufactured by either the Soviets or China. The Soviet D74 122-
mm field gun had a range of 23,900 meters, and the Soviet M-46
130-mm gun could hurl a shell 27,500 meters. All ARVN artillery
came from the United States. The US M101 105-mm howitzer was
the mainstay. It was fast to load and fire, and a six-tube battery
manned by experienced crews could hit an enemy target with 60
rounds in one minute. It had a barrel life of about 20,000 rounds.
However, it had a range of only 11,270 meters. That was nearly
eight miles but not far enough to duel with the NVA.

The US M114 155-mm howitzer fired a shell almost three times as powerful as the 105 but threw it only slightly farther: 14,600 meters. The US 8-inch gun was the most accurate US artillery piece and had a maximum range of 16,800 meters. The 175-mm "Long Tom" could throw a 174-pound projectile 32,000 meters, but the powder charge necessary to do this wore out the barrel after only 400 rounds. Also, the 175 was notoriously inaccurate at extreme ranges. ARVN did not have many 175s, and the ones it did have were not part of the 23rd Division's artillery and were never assigned to support us. When it came to long-range artillery duels, the NVA had us outgunned. So tactical air or B-52 strikes were usually required to knock out the enemy's long-range guns.[2]

Other air support came from USAF fixed-wing AC-130 gunships with the radio call sign "Spectre." These gunships were C-130 troop and cargo carriers modified into a flying, side-firing weapons platform. Their armament included two 20-mm Vulcan automatic guns, a 40-mm Bofors automatic gun, and a 105-mm gun capable of firing all types of 105-mm shells to hit targets as far as 12,000 meters away. All those guns could be fired at ground targets while circling thousands of feet above them. Extensive electronic target acquisition and tracking equipment enhanced the AC-130s' capabilities. The ammunition fired by miniguns included tracer rounds, which burned red, so they—and the troops on the ground—could see where their fire was hitting. Spectre gunships could carry tens of thousands of pounds of ammunition for their guns. They were able to spend hours on station, circling above the battlefield, dropping flares at night, and becoming familiar with the battlefield and the friendly voices from the ground. This time on station gave Spectre crews an airman's knowledge of the battlefield that only an FAC could equal and that a fighter-bomber pilot in a "fast mover" jet could not acquire.

The USAF also flew old, twin-tail-boom C-119 "Flying Boxcars" as gunships with the call sign "Shadow." They were converted to AC-119G side-firing weapons platforms with four 7.62-mm miniguns and a load of up to 50,000 rounds of ammo for them. They specialized in mowing down enemy troops attacking US or ARVN bases. The AC-119G Shadow crews carried calling cards saying, "When uninvited guests drop in . . . call for 'THE SHADOW,'" and, following the theme of an old radio show, "Who knows what evil lurks below the jungle canopy? THE SHADOW KNOWS!" Other C-119s were converted into AC-119Ks. Their call sign was "Stinger," and they specialized in hunting down and destroying enemy trucks on the Ho Chi Minh Trail. In addition to four 7.62-mm miniguns, they carried two 20-mm multibarreled Gattling cannons and 4,500 rounds of ammunition for them.

VNAF's fixed-wing gunships were modified World War II C-47 "Gooney Birds" converted into AC-47 "Spooky" gunships with three 7.62-mm six-barreled miniguns mounted in the door, which was on the left. Each minigun could fire up to 6,000 rounds per minute. The AC-47s were older than some of the "Spooky Squadron" pilots who flew them. In late 1972, the USAF started turning its AC-119s over to VNAF.[3]

Tactical air strikes were most effective against bunkers, artillery pieces, and armored vehicles. However, a fighter-bomber has to make multiple passes over the target and has to locate it again before each successive pass, so the helicopter gunships and the fixed-wing gunships were usually the most accurate and responsive close air support we had against groups of enemy soldiers. Enemy troops in the open were their ideal target. They could maintain eyeball contact with the target while they orbited overhead during offensive or defensive operations and could maintain constant communication with the advisers or commanders on the ground. They could quickly pounce on a machine gun emplacement or even a single enemy soldier if we could identify the target for them.[4]

Troops in close contact with the enemy preferred their fighter-bomber air support "low and slow" for accuracy, and VNAF's propeller-driven Skyraiders flew lower and slower than the jets. VNAF A-1 Skyraider pilots were also generally the most accurate because they were more experienced than the American fighter-bomber pilots. The US fighter-bombers providing our tactical air support could come from USAF bases or from US Navy or US Marine planes flown off aircraft carriers in the South China Sea. The USAF aircraft flown included the F-4 Phantom and the F-105. The navy and marines flew the Chance Vaught A-7 Corsair II and also the F-4.[5] The fighter-bombers could carry napalm, rockets, or anti-personnel cluster bomb units (CBUs) or bombs weighing 250, 500, 750, or even 1,000 pounds. Some mixing of that ordnance was possible, depending on the aircraft type, but the FACs usually had to work with what the aircraft came with. If many missions were flown against the same target—for example, a large bunker complex—the FAC could request specific ordnance on the follow-up missions.

The USAF initially required FACs to be experienced jet fighter pilots so they would better understand the capabilities of the fighter-bombers they were working with. However, as the war progressed, this requirement had to be relaxed to find enough pilots to fill all the FAC positions. Some pilots became FACs right after flight school and only two months in a FAC training course.[6] The US Army advisers were an important link between the ARVN forces on the ground and the USAF FACs in the air. Without those advisers, the USAF could not strike so close to ARVN troops, and the strikes could not be adjusted to achieve maximum results.

Using the USAF's B-52 Stratofortresses—long-range strategic bombers—in a tactical air support role was one of the most important innovations of the Vietnam War. General William C. Westmoreland realized the B-52's tactical bombing potential, so on 14 May 1965 he sent a memorandum on the subject to his superior, Admiral Ulysses S. Grant Sharp, who was commander-in-chief Pacific. Westmoreland described a 15 April 1965 operation during which 443 tactical air sorties dropped more than 900 tons of bombs in a 12-square-kilometer area. The results were "magnificent" but still limited because the bombs hit scattered targets over many hours. He pointed out that if the same bombs had been evenly distributed, the results would have been better. There would also be a big advantage in dropping all the bombs at once, plus the surprise and shock gained through bombing from 30,000 feet, where the B-52s probably would not be seen or heard by the enemy on the ground. The Strategic Air Command (SAC) did not like the idea of diverting so many of its strategic nuclear bombers to tactical bombing missions in a regional conflict. However, with Westmoreland, Sharp, and Secretary of Defense Robert McNamara all in favor of it, on 18 June 1965 the first B-52 tactical strike hit a suspected VC base north of Saigon. The first B-52 tactical strike in support of US ground forces was in November 1965. The B-52 missions in South Vietnam were code-named "Arc Light."[7]

When Arc Lights were first flown, requests for them had to be approved by the commander-in-chief Pacific and the Joint Chiefs of Staff. Even later, despite their demonstrated effectiveness in South Vietnam, their use was controlled so tightly that White House approval was sometimes required. President Lyndon Johnson's tight, personal control of which targets could be bombed produced protests that we could not have an effective bombing campaign when the president of the United States had to personally approve even a tactical air strike on a "monkey bridge," one of the small, hand-made footbridges found in the jungle. Although this description was almost certainly an exaggeration, it was sometimes cited as an example of how we were fighting with one hand tied behind our back.[8]

The B-52 Stratofortress is affectionately known as the "Buff" (Big Ugly Fat Fellow). It was designed in 1948 and first flew in 1954. This aircraft was developed as a strategic bomber to penetrate the enemy's airspace at 500 miles an hour while flying at altitudes as low as 200 feet or as high as 50,000 feet. The B-52 has a 185-foot wingspan and carries more than 45,000 gallons of fuel internally— enough to provide an average combat range of 8,800 miles. It can carry up to 70,000 pounds of bombs.[9] The undersides of the SAC's B-52s were a nuclear-blast-reflective white, but that light color made them easier for North Vietnamese anti-aircraft crews to see against the blue sky in the daytime and against the black sky at night, so in Southeast Asia the B-52s' undersides were painted black to make them more difficult for enemy gunners to locate.[10]

The B-52Ds were given a "Big Belly" upgrade, and starting in March 1966 Arc Light missions were flown by B-52s carrying a total of 108 bombs per aircraft. Eighty-four 500- or 750-pound bombs were carried internally, and 24 more could be slung under the wings on external racks. On most missions, the B-52s carried a mix of 500- and 750-pound bombs.[11] If each bomber carried 70,000 pounds of bombs, then the three-plane formation could drop 210,000 pounds of bombs—more than 100 tons of high explosives— on the target. The aircraft crews were not always told what their target would be on Arc Light missions.

Arc Lights were planned to kill or destroy everything within a rectangular "box" one kilometer wide and three kilometers long by saturating it with 500- and 750-pound bombs. The bombs were usually dropped from at least 30,000 feet by three planes flying in echelon. The boxes could be reduced to one-by-two or even one-by-one kilometer to concentrate the bombs, in which case the bombers flew in trail rather than in echelon. The smaller the box, the greater the destruction within it. The bombers never flew a pattern over or toward friendly troops because an early or late bomb release might result in friendly casualties.[12]

After SAC was ordered to fly Arc Light missions, it developed a system to bomb accurately from around 30,000 feet and even through cloud cover when the B-52s could not see the target. This also meant they could hit a target hidden under the jungle canopy. The ability to hit a target they could not see gave the B-52s an important all-weather capability fighter-bombers lacked. The USAF achieved this accuracy by modifying the Combat Sky Spot system they already had. A network of six or more ground radar sites was set up in South Vietnam. An air force crew in a van or building used their ground-based radar/computer unit to track the incoming B-52s, guide them to the target, and tell them when to release their bombs. Arc Light bomb runs in II Corps were controlled by a USAF radar site with the call sign "Bongo" located on a hill in Pleiku.

The system was so accurate that enemy troops massed for an attack could be hit without hitting friendly troops who were less than a kilometer away. That minimum safe distance could be reduced to only 300 meters if the friendly troops were protected by bunkers or foxholes.[13] However, although 300 meters might be safe in theory, BDAs indicated the overpressure from so many big explosions so close could cause broken ear drums; bleeding eyes, ears, and noses; disorientation; and other injuries you would not want to inflict on friendly troops.[14]

To provide an adequate margin of safety, Arc Lights were normally not placed closer than three kilometers from friendly troops, but in cases of emergency they could be brought in closer. Captain Christopher E. Scudder was air operations adviser at II Corps. When one of the FSBs was under siege, he brought the bombs in almost to their defensive wire, maybe as close as 100 meters from the friendly troops. Shortly after the bombs fell, the ARVN defenders were forced to abandon this base. However, they held out long enough to force the attackers to form a lucrative target, and the Arc Light gave them a chance to withdraw without being overrun in the process.[15] Bringing the bombs in that close to friendly troops was done only when those troops were in extreme danger of being overrun.

The B-52s could bomb from 29,000 to 38,000 feet, but most of the Arc Light missions were flown at 32,000 to 34,000 feet. Before takeoff, the navigator was given the time to be at the initial point, and he was responsible to get them there on time. Even when flying the six-hour trip from Guam, the B-52 crews rarely missed the scheduled time on the target by more than three minutes. Using their own sources and information from the incoming aircraft, the USAF radar sites entered the temperature, the wind speed, the aircraft's altitude and speed, and the bomb load's characteristics into their computer. The navigator punched a code into his transmitter-receiver, and the ground radar team sent him a heading, altitude, and airspeed for his bomb run. As the aircraft neared the target, a countdown came from the ground, " . . . five, four, three, two, one," and on "Hack!" the navigator hit the switch to release the bombs. The navigator had an eight-power periscope looking down, so he could see the bombs fall to impact. However, on most missions the Arc Light bombers dropped their bombs into the clouds and could not see them impact. There were no known friendly casualties from Arc Lights.

Americans who flew over a target area just after an Arc Light hit usually saw any enemy soldiers who were still alive wandering around in a daze with blood running out of their noses and ears. The helicopter crews often put them out of their misery. ARVN troops were sometimes sent in to collect prisoners of war (POWs) and equipment. On one such foray into an Arc Light target area, ARVN troops captured an NVA nurse and a pedal-operated Singer sewing machine.[16] The intelligence-collection effort was focused on identifying new targets for more Arc Lights rather than doing BDAs after targets were hit. However, some BDAs were done by accident rather than by design. John Paul Vann's pilot, Chief Warrant Officer (CWO) Robert Richards, described an impromptu BDA he and Vann performed. They were flying near where an Arc Light had just hit, so they flew low over the target box even before the dust had settled. In addition to the dead, numerous NVA soldiers were wandering around in a daze. Vann was not one to pass up a chance like that. He grabbed the CAR-15 he always carried in the helicopter and fired at the enemy soldiers until his ammo was gone.[17]

A semiannual Arc Light Operations Security Briefing at MACV revealed some weaknesses in safeguarding the information on when B-52s would be taking off from U Tapao in Thailand, from which half the B-52 missions were flown. The USAF called the tower over an insecure phone line to give the bomber takeoff times up to 12 hours in advance. The takeoff times were then posted in the tower, where Thai operators regularly worked. Adding two hours, plus or minus only ten minutes, to the takeoff time would predict fairly accurately when the bombs would be falling in Vietnam. The bus schedule for transporting the bomber crews was phoned to the motor pool, where the dispatcher was a Thai. The NVA were very interested in knowing the time on target because if they knew some of their units had been detected and were probably targeted, they could move them to a new location before the bombs fell. There were also reports that Soviet Navy signal intelligence trawlers were positioned off Guam to report when B-52 flights departed from Anderson Air Force Base (AFB).[18]

The B-52s were John Paul Vann's major weapon in this fight, and he was willing to break the Arc Light rules whenever he thought he could get away with it. He bragged to Captain Jack R. Finch, the Team 33 G-3 air adviser, about "stealing" Arc Light missions from Lieutenant General James F. Hollingsworth, the III Corps senior adviser, by diverting them in flight within a four-hour window during which changes could be made. This diversion gave II Corps additional Arc Lights at the expense of III Corps, which had planned and requested them and was counting on them as already allocated to III Corps. These diversions could also be risky. Shackling the coordinates of the divert both accurately and quickly put pressure on Vann's staff. If an aircraft or ARVN unit did not get the warning in time, they could be caught in the target box.

Sometimes we could see the B-52s flying high above us on their way to and from missions. When an Arc Light hit, the earth shook. Even many kilometers from the impact area, we could hear and feel the long drum roll of heavy explosions. They rippled along the ground, one after another for three kilometers. The target area disappeared in billowing smoke filled with fire and shrapnel. At night, the rumble of the explosions and flashes of fire reminded me of the thunder and heat lightning of summer evening storms along the horizon when I was a boy living out on the Great Plains in Norfolk, Nebraska.

Referring to the use of B-52 strategic bombers in a tactical bombing role, an air force officer commented tongue in cheek, "Frankly, that's no longer an Air Force weapon. We fly the airplanes, but the army puts in the target request; they handle the clearing, etc. The only thing we do is hand out the aircraft strike warning to our own aircraft, so they won't have bombs dumped on them."[19]

4

The Looming Threat

In order to fulfill the goals of Chairman Ho Chi Minh, all
young men must fight. . . . A costly battle is ahead. Much
sacrifice and heartache will precede our victory. . . . The
armed forces must be increased. All youths, regardless of
past deferments, must serve. . . . Victory is in sight.
                        —North Vietnamese general Vo Nguyen Giap,
                                                    December 1971

The heavily armed NVA was moving into position to attack us.

During 1971, the Soviets sent 350 ships loaded with war material—a million tons of it—to North Vietnam.[1] By 1972, they had
replaced all the equipment previously lost by the NVA and VC. The
NVA now had more tanks and heavy artillery than ever before.[2] An
ARVN lieutenant general described the warning signs, the NVA's
plans, and the dire consequences if the enemy's coming offensive
succeeded:

> Starting in the fall of 1971, intelligence reports began to
> stream into II Corps Headquarters revealing the enemy's
> preparations for a major offensive campaign in the Central
> Highlands during the approaching dry season. Prisoner and
> returnee sources further disclosed that large enemy forces
> were moving into northern Kontum Province from base areas
> in Laos and Cambodia and [that] their effort would concen-
> trate on uprooting border camps and fire bases in northwest-
> ern Kontum, and eventually, "liberating" such urban centers
> as Pleiku and Kontum. In conjunction with this effort, the
> reports indicated, other enemy forces in the coastal lowlands

were to increase activities aimed at destroying ARVN forces, particularly in northern Binh Dinh Province, where enemy domination had long been established. If these concerted efforts succeeded and joined forces, South Vietnam would run the risk of being sheared along Route QL-19 [Highway 19] into two isolated halves.[3]

Captured enemy documents, defectors, and other intelligence sources confirmed that the Communist B-3 Front would act as a corps headquarters to control all the units participating in the attack on II Corps. NVA lieutenant general Hoang Minh Thao would be in command. The B-3 Front's subordinate units were identified as the 2nd and 320th NVA Infantry Divisions plus the entire 203rd Tank Regiment[4] from Hanoi High Command and other independent infantry and artillery units. VC main and local-force units supplemented the NVA units. All those nondivisional units assigned to the B-3 Front equaled another division, so the equivalent of three enemy divisions would be attacking into the Central Highlands in II Corps. A captured document revealed that both 122-mm and 130-mm Soviet field guns with ranges up to 27,500 meters were being infiltrated into the triborder area. This attack would be the enemy's first use of either armor or artillery in the Central Highlands. The main thrust of the offensive would be attacks on Tan Canh and Dak To II and the FSBs on Rocket Ridge, the American name for a large hill mass running northwest from Kontum that the enemy used to fire rockets at Kontum. Next the NVA would attack the main population centers of Kontum City and Pleiku City. In Binh Dinh Province on the Coastal Lowlands, the NT-3 "Gold Star" NVA Division, augmented by VC units, would lead the attack.[5]

The 2nd NVA Infantry Division had entered South Vietnam in 1967. They had fought the Americans in Kontum and Darlac provinces and thereafter had remained in the Highlands. They were experienced soldiers who knew the territory. The 320th NVA Infantry Division was formed in 1951 and had participated in the French defeat at Dien Bien Phu. The 320th's organic units were the 48th, 52nd, and 64th Infantry Regiments and the 54th Artillery Regiment. The total strength of the division and its special battalions was 10,400 men. However, information that the 2nd NVA Artillery Regiment and the 7th NVA Engineer Regiment were now supporting the 320th indicated that an unusually big attack was coming. The 7th NVA Engineer Regiment was building a road four meters wide to be used by tanks moving to attack Kontum. It was to be completed by the end of March. Enemy sources said the attack would begin the first week in April and the objectives would be ARVN outposts along Highway 14 northwest of Kontum City and then the city itself.[6]

At a Weekly Intelligence Estimate Update on 20 November 1971, Major General William E. Potts, the MACV intelligence chief, said that by the end of the year about 16,000 enemy soldiers would have infiltrated into South Vietnam to join the Communist B-3 Front—about four times as many infiltrators as in the previous year.[7] Forewarned of a major enemy attack, in late 1971 General Abrams requested through the commander-in-chief Pacific, Admiral John S. McCain, advance authority to retaliate in specific ways not then authorized by higher headquarters. He asked for authority to launch air attacks on the enemy's MiG fighters on the ground at bases in North Vietnam, their active ground-control intercept radars, and occupied surface-to-air missile (SAM) sites within range of the DMZ. Washington responded that those actions were pending approval.[8]

Under pressure to hold down American casualties, in late 1971 Mr. Vann told his advisers, "To achieve a reasonable balance between advisory credibility and combat risk for advisers, I desire that U.S. advisers limit their activities in combat to a level commensurate with their counterparts."[9] In other words, as an adviser I should follow my counterpart's example and not take any more risks than he does. A good and sensible policy, but we advisers would sometimes find it impractical to comply.

Speaking at a MACV Special Intelligence Update conference in Saigon on 28 December 1971, Brigadier General George E. Wear said:

> I wish I could be a lot more optimistic than I really am about the ARVN in II Corps. And I think this time last year I was. They can just about handle the local forces within the boundary. Our experience has been, as you well know, that when the NVA well-trained units come across the border, the ARVN just hasn't stood up against them. They have just been able to keep the lid on to fill the gaps as the U.S. [units]

have moved out, helped by the fact that the VC and NVA south of our northern three provinces have apparently just not been getting the supplies to be able to do very much. Our war is now almost completely limited to Kontum, Pleiku, and Binh Dinh.

The two divisions [the ARVN 22nd and 23rd Infantry Divisions] I don't think have really improved in the 17 months I've watched them. Their strength runs about the same, 71 to 76 percent assigned to authorized. His battalions he puts in the field are a little over 300, 320 or something like that. The leadership problem you know, which is the same. The airborne brigades were our real fighting force last year in both those battles. . . . The division commanders commit the corps ranger group, those three battalions, *all* the time to spare their own battalions. . . . But of course, when you look at what the enemy's got, and what the ARVN's got, we shouldn't have any trouble up there.

General Dzu spent the whole Christmas holidays up there, visiting around with the troops. And he's making it very clear that there isn't anybody to help. And maybe that could have been one of the problems. We, as advisers, whenever one of their infantry elements was attacked, we brought in gunships and air and so forth. I have noticed that when a unit really got into it, and didn't have a choice, they fought pretty well.[10]

One evening in Ban Me Thuot, some of the off-duty officers gathered in our small Officers Club for some serious drinking. After extended discussion, they decided the Team 33 motto should be "We Go Now." One of them, the Catholic chaplain, translated it into Latin as "Nunc Imos" and had it painted on the Team 33 sign at the compound gate. At another time in another place, that motto would hold special significance for some of those advisers.[11]

5

The Year of the Rat

Americans do not like long, inconclusive wars—and this is
going to be a long, inconclusive war. Thus we are sure to win
in the end.
                    —North Vietnamese prime minister Phan Van Dong

New Year's Day! It was now 1972, the Year of the Rat in the Asian
calendar.

Around 140,000 American troops still remained in Vietnam,
but only 20,000 of them were in combat units.[1] In January, President Nixon announced the withdrawal of 70,000 more Americans to reduce total strength to no more than 69,000 by 1 May.[2]
Those cuts were soon translated into actions down at our level.
The US military telephone switchboards closed on 3 January, and
all circuits were transferred to ARVN. From now on, all military
telephones, lines, and switchboards would be operated and maintained by ARVN. This change was unwelcome for the remaining
Americans. To ensure there was some backup for communications
between the US elements, a single sideband radio net was set up.
The radios used were civilian shortwave radios. Based on plans to
phase out the Regimental Combat Assistant Teams (RCATs), our
G-4 adviser, Major Richard C. Gudat, started transferring the regimental adviser buildings back to ARVN.

The strength of the South Vietnamese armed forces was now:[3]

120 infantry battalions in 11 infantry divisions
58 artillery battalions
19 armored battalions

Engineer, signal, and other supporting arms and services

A national reserve consisting of a marine division, an airborne division, and 21 Ranger battalions

37 Border Ranger defense battalions in bases along the border

Territorial forces consisting of 1,679 RF companies and 8,356 PF platoons for a total of 550,000 soldiers stationed in their home provinces.

116,000 officers in the National Police

An air force with more than 1,000 aircraft

A navy with 1,680 craft of various types

More than 4 million men in the People's Self-Defense Forces, a part-time hamlet militia

However, ARVN was losing the equivalent of a division a year through desertions (approximately 5,000–6,000). This rate of desertion meant that more and more men had to be drafted. The deserters and even the dead were sometimes maintained on the rolls so their commanders could continue to draw and steal their pay. The strength an ARVN infantry battalion actually had in the field was sometimes barely half of its authorized strength.

Many optimists expected this year to be one of continued progress in South Vietnam. A South Vietnamese presidential election was held in October 1971 without disruption by the VC, which was still trying to recover from its disastrous losses during the Tet Offensive in 1968. VC influence in the rural areas was now the lowest in many years. ARVN troops were receiving a continuing flow of American equipment, and they were operating in the enemy's base areas.[4] However, something ominous was present for the pessimists to point to: the continuing buildup of NVA forces compared to the continuing withdrawal of American forces. If the enemy attacked before the South Vietnamese were completely ready to defend themselves—and the available intelligence indicated an attack was imminent—1972 could end in disaster. The North Vietnamese Political Bureau resolved that 1972 would be the year of "decisive victory." It defined victory as forcing the United States "to end the war by negotiating from a position of defeat."[5]

The North Vietnamese were sending nearly their entire army south. On 10 January 1972, MACV headquarters estimated 39,000 enemy troops had already infiltrated into South Vietnam since the start of the new year, compared to 27,400 during the same period in 1971. Many of them would arrive in the B-3 Front's area during January and February. Equally important, the NVA was now bringing in big T-54 main battle tanks, which were much more threatening than the lighter P-76 tanks the NVA had previously used on a limited basis in the South. It also increased its artillery strength and deployed at least 52 anti-aircraft artillery battalions in Laos. Some of these battalions were equipped with 100-mm guns, an extremely potent anti-aircraft weapon.[6]

During late 1971 and early 1972, reconnaissance missions detected large numbers of NVA supplies, troops, and tanks coming down the Ho Chi Minh Trail, moving toward Kontum Province. This was the first time tanks were found coming so far down the trail.[7] In early January, the commander of the USAF reconnaissance squadron called Brigadier General Wear and asked him to take a flight with him to see some new developments. Wear described what he saw: "As we low-leveled over the area just north of Ben Het, it was very obvious that heavy vehicles had crossed the river. The brush was torn down along the banks, the tall elephant grass was matted down, etc. A few days later O-1 pilots from that squadron reported seeing camouflaged tanks in the area just east of where we saw the crossing. I flew over the area a few days after that in my Huey, did not see tanks, [but] started to receive heavy ground fire. I stayed out of that area after that. [No more] tank sightings were reported until [tanks] rolled into Tan Canh."[8]

On 25 January 1972, a pair of Cobra pilots from the 361st Aerial Weapons Company, the Pink Panthers, attacked two enemy tanks in the Plei Trap Valley in Kontum Province just east of the Communists' Base Area 609 on the border. It was the first time enemy tanks were sighted that far into Kontum Province. The pilots saw four other tanks under trees, and another Cobra team reported six sets of tank tracks. These discoveries indicated that at least one NVA tank company was in the area. There were more tank sightings on 30 January and others on subsequent days. However, because none of those tank sightings was confirmed by ARVN ground reconnaissance, most of the II Corps advisers—including John Paul Vann—refused to believe there were enemy tanks in II Corps.[9] In the early 1970s, the US Army did not have a good field manual on enemy armor, its vulnerability, and how to destroy it.[10]

During the first 20 days of January 1968—before the Tet attacks—

enemy infiltration had been 26,000. On 20 January 1972, MACV intelligence estimated that enemy infiltration for the month was already 50,000. General Abrams thought President Nixon should know this, and Ambassador Ellsworth Bunker volunteered to send the information flagged so the president would see it.[11]

John Paul Vann commented at a 22 January 1972 Commanders Weekly Intelligence Evaluation Update, "I have one observation. It's beautiful what the enemy is planning to do, because it appears in II Corps that he's going to make the same basic tactical error that he made in Tet '68, and that is fragment his forces in so many different directions that he will not put a real weight of effort on any one attack. And that loans [sic] itself very well to the way our forces are already deployed. We are making some adjustments of the forces in line with the most likely scenario so as to require a minimum of movement once the attack starts."[12]

US reconnaissance also detected a massive NVA buildup just north of the DMZ, but we did not launch preemptive strikes against those lucrative targets because of a November 1968 agreement with the North that required the United States to halt bombing north of the DMZ in exchange for the Communists' pledge that they would participate in meaningful negations in Paris and would not violate the DMZ or shell South Vietnamese cities.[13] Although we did not bomb north of the DMZ, when General Abrams requested more Arc Lights in January, the number of Arc Light sorties authorized per month across South Vietnam was increased from 1,000 to 1,200.[14]

Toward the end of January, Colonel Keller offered me the opportunity to exchange assignments with Lieutenant Colonel Ralph A. Matthews, the senior adviser to the 44th Infantry Regiment. This exchange struck me as a good chance to gain some different experience, so I jumped at it. However, Lieutenant Colonel Mathews was not exactly enthusiastic about the swap. He apparently worked out a transfer to a different assignment because I was actually replaced by Lieutenant Colonel James W. "Bill" Bricker. The time between my old and new assignments seemed like a good opportunity to take much-needed R&R. Everyone serving in Vietnam was allowed to go on 2 one-week R&Rs, which were not deducted from our annual leave allowance. I chose to go to Bangkok, Thailand, and departed Ban Me Thuot on 28 January.

Colonel Ly Tong Ba took command of the 23rd Infantry Division in February 1972. Ba had spent a year in the United States training at the Armor Center at Fort Knox, Kentucky, and had returned to Vietnam in 1959. Unlike many of the higher-ranking ARVN officers, he had a reputation for being honest rather than corrupt. His wife came from one of the richest families in Bac Lieu Province. Her family had once owned around 4,000 hectares (almost 10,000 acres) of rice fields.[15] Ba was also related to the wife of General Cao Van Vien, the chairman of the South Vietnamese Joint Chiefs of Staff. Vien claimed he never favored Colonel Ba because he was a relative.[16] There was also a "family" relationship between Colonel Ba and John Paul Vann. Ba's mother and the mother of Vann's fiancée, Julie, were sisters.[17] Colonel Ba's selection to command the division would prove to be a wise and fortunate choice.

Master Sergeant Lowell W. Stevens was a Special Forces soldier who spent a total of six and a half years in Vietnam. He also served in MACV SOG, running operations across the border into Laos and Cambodia. Stevens had nothing but respect for the NVA because they were disciplined soldiers. He killed them when he had to, but he respected them as good fighters. In early 1972, Stevens spent most of his time as a "Covey rider," flying out of Kontum airfield in an OV-10 with the Covey FACs. He first found new roads extending through the jungle to the southeast from the border with Laos while flying with a Covey FAC in February 1972. The NVA were using bulldozers and other heavy equipment to build roads at night. In the past, they had concealed their new roads with vines and limbs before daylight, but now they were brazenly leaving them uncovered and plainly visible from the air. One road was extended 600 meters just overnight. The enemy tanks and other vehicles would be able to use these roads to move into position for attacks against Dak To II, Tan Canh, and the ARVN bases farther south. By early May, there was a new road clearly headed toward Polei Kleng, a Border Ranger camp 22 kilometers west–northwest of Kontum. Master Sergeant Stevens reported all this road building to the Kontum Province senior adviser, Colonel Stephen W. Bachinski, and used his map to show him where it was located. However, Bachinski scoffed at Stevens's eyewitness reports of NVA road building in the jungle and made no mention of it in his monthly reports to MACV.[18]

I arrived back in Ban Me Thuot from R&R on 4 February, picked up my mail, and packed my few possessions, and the next day a Huey flew me down to the extreme south of the II Corps area to become senior adviser to the 44th Infantry Regiment. The regiment's headquarters was in Song Mao, Binh Thuan Province, just inland from Highway 1 and between Phan Rang and Phan Thiet.

My new counterpart was Lieutenant Colonel Tran Quang Tien. He was a capable, extremely thin, middle-aged officer. He had assumed command in the fall of 1971, so he was also fairly new to the regiment. He spoke passable English and had learned French while serving in the army under the French. I spoke some French, so we could communicate in two languages without an interpreter. Colonel Tien and I established a good working relationship that lasted throughout my tour in Vietnam.

An ARVN infantry regiment had an authorized strength of 3,650 men.[19] Many of the 44th Regiment's soldiers were Nungs, an ethnic minority in Vietnam, considered by many ARVN and American officers to be the best and most loyal soldiers.[20] The 44th Regiment was reputed to be one of the best in ARVN. After a battle in the fall of 1971, a US Army brigadier general suggested that the 44th be recommended for the US Valorous Unit Award (equal to an individual Silver Star), but Lieutenant Colonel Matthews, the regimental senior adviser at the time, did not want to push it, and Colonel Keller thought the battle was won by the US air cavalry, so the recommendation died for lack of support.[21]

Only a few years earlier, there had been 65 to 70 Americans in an RCAT assigned to advise an ARVN regiment. There had been advisers with each battalion and company and with each of the principal regimental staff officers. Now only two of us were with each regiment: a lieutenant colonel senior adviser and a major or captain as deputy senior adviser. In many ways, we were more liaison officers between the regimental commander and the American supply system and air support than we were advisers on how to fight the war. Our first big cohort of advisers had come to Vietnam in 1962, so it was time for this change.

My deputy was Major Tony *Swachek,* and the temporary third member of my team was Captain *Jack A. Martin.* My ARVN interpreter was Sergeant *Hao,* a good interpreter and a good, reliable soldier. There were eight Americans in Song Mao when I arrived, but the drawdown would soon leave only three or four of us. Small MACV teams like mine did not have an American medic with them. Every American soldier carried the standard wound packet in a pouch on his pistol belt, but other than that advisers were sent into the jungle with only some Band-Aids and a tube of Bacitracin as our medical kit. What we did have was "dustoff," the helicopter medevac system. We had confidence that if we were wounded, we would be extracted by helicopter and whisked away to excellent medical care. Not only the pilots whose job was medevac but also any American helicopter pilot available would risk his own life to save a fellow American on the ground.

After about a week in Song Mao, Lieutenant Colonel Tien informed me that the regiment was moving to An Khe to replace a unit that had allowed sappers (combat engineers) to get into the ammo dump and blow it up. An Khe was a town on Highway 19, the winding, mountain road between Pleiku and Qui Nhon on the coast. A couple days later we moved out in a vehicle convoy to make the two-day, 500-kilometer drive to An Khe. We drove north along the coast on Highway 1 and then up into the Highlands on Highway 19.

When we arrived in An Khe, the results of the sapper attack were still visible in the form of destroyed defensive bunkers and blasted areas where the enemy sappers' explosive charges had set off the ARVN ammunition dump. Colonel Tien went to work rebuilding the defenses and deploying his troops to secure the area.

The NVA's sappers were more like an elite force than suicide bombers. They were essentially assault engineers who were good, basic infantrymen with additional training and experience to qualify them as demolition experts. One US unit's published "Lessons Learned" described how the enemy sappers operated:

Sapper attacks have been preceded by detailed, [clandestine] reconnaissance to include identifying anti-intrusion devices and determining the extent of protective wire. This task may take place three to seven days prior to the attack and is followed by attack rehearsals. The night of the sapper attack the enemy will neutralize obstacles by tying down trip flares, mines, etc, and will approach to within a few hundred meters of the position. Then they will slowly work their way through the wire using the least likely avenues of approach along low ground. Sapper attacks usually take place between 2400 and 0200 hours. They may be preceded by mortar fire to get US personnel to move inside bunkers. Once launched, the sapper attack will be rapidly executed with one or two squads heading for specifically predetermined targets such as ammo storage, POL [petroleum, oil, and lubricants] storage, artillery positions, and CPs. Half of the sappers will be armed with 7 to 14 CHICOM [Chinese Communist] grenades and 20 kilograms of TNT. The remaining sappers will have AK-47s.[22]

The US 1st Cavalry Division (Airmobile) had been stationed at An Khe since 1965, when it had first arrived in Vietnam, until most of its units left Vietnam. The US Army engineers built a large base and a 6,200-foot paved runway for the "Cav" just north of the town of An Khe. When the US Army departed and turned the base over to the Vietnamese, everything not secured by ARVN for its own official use was quickly taken for personal use. Except for the concrete floors, every part of every American-built building was gone by the time we arrived there in February 1972.

While the 1st Cavalry Division was based outside An Khe, a local Vietnamese entrepreneur opened an establishment in the town named the "The Million Fingers Massage Parlor, Laundry, and Tank Wash." The American division commander was concerned about the massage parlor's potential impact on his troops' health and morals and threatened to close it down. The owner quickly responded to these new market conditions by changing his sign to "No More Whorehouse, Only Laundry."[23]

I decided my RCAT would live with some other Americans in an 1871 two-story French colonial mansion at the south end of the runway. There were 13 rooms and four fireplaces. It must have been a grand place a hundred years ago, but it had been occupied by the Japanese army from 1941 to 1945, by the French from 1945 to 1954, by the Vietnamese from 1954 to 1965, and by the Americans since then. The 1st Cavalry Division used the building for various purposes. They built an airfield control tower on the roof and painted the entire exterior of the building light green. From then on, it was known as the Green House. Fortunately, it was inside our regiment's security cordon. The Green House had sleeping rooms with steel army cots, running water, and even intermittent electricity. There was also a wet bar and a refrigerator to keep our beer cold. We were living in the lap of luxury compared to most of the other advisers out in the field with ARVN combat units. Another boost to our morale came when an AFN FM radio station resumed broad-casting from Pleiku.

In early February 1972, MACV intelligence estimated Communist troop infiltration down the Ho Chi Minh Trail was 65,700 since the beginning of the year, with 26,200 of them going to the B-3 Front in II Corps. They were headed our way. Over the past four years, MACV's end-of-the-year reevaluation of infiltration estimates confirmed that those estimates were never off by more than one percent.[24]

Brigadier General Wear had recommended a series of strong blocking positions on the avenues of approach to Kontum. Each position would be formidable enough to force the NVA to assemble a significant force to assault it, which would create a "target-rich" environment for Arc Lights and tactical air strikes. When the ARVN defenders were finally forced to withdraw from each successive blocking position, they could fall back to the next one, and the process would start over again. Repeatedly going through this process would wear down the NVA forces before they could attack Kontum. However, Mr. Vann did not follow this recommendation and instead set up a strong forward defense with ARVN forces concentrated in the Tan Canh/Dak To II area.

Brigadier General Wear remained concerned about the deployment of ARVN forces in the Highlands:

> Gen. Abrams came up to Pleiku in about February 1972 for a briefing on the situation. . . . When that was over, Vann said to Abrams, "Gen. Wear has a different proposal for the units at Tan Canh." Abrams's answer, with just the three of us (including Dzu) there: "Tell Gen. Wear to have faith." I still don't know exactly what he meant.
>
> As the three of us came on downstairs, I asked Abrams if I could talk to him in my office. After the two of us were in my office, I said something like the following: "Sir, I know what I am supposed to say. That our plan is great, etc. But I can tell you from my seventeen months experience up here, and visiting the troops in the Dak To area almost every day, that their morale is terrible, that Dzu has no confidence in the success of it, and that he is cowardly and doesn't have the stomach for a fight. I am sure the entire force up there will collapse when the first major attack comes. Sir, we are facing

a disaster unless we pull the majority of the forces deployed around the Dak To/Tan Canh area out and place them in blocking positions along the highway to Kontum." Abrams sat there a minute, and then said, "Thank you," and left.[25]

With a major enemy attack expected during Tet, the three-day celebration of the lunar New Year starting on 15 February, the 2nd Airborne Brigade, part of the South Vietnamese strategic reserve, was sent to strengthen the defenses in Kontum Province in February. Their headquarters was set up near Vo Dinh, a small town about 16 kilometers north of Kontum City on Highway 14, and their units occupied FSBs on the southern end of Rocket Ridge.[26] Lieutenant General Dzu then defined the command structure. The 22nd ARVN Division commander was placed in command of the Dak To area, which would include Tan Canh and the Border Ranger camps at Ben Het, Dak Mot, Dak Pek, and Dak Seang as well as the troops on FSBs 5 and 6. Colonel Nguyen Ba Thinh, the Kontum Province chief, was responsible for Kontum City, and Colonel Tuong (full name not known), the II Corps deputy for operations, was given command in Pleiku.[27]

In addition to the increase in B-52 sorties from 1,000 to 1,200 a month, General Abrams received authority to surge to 1,500 sorties at his discretion. The Communist uprising and offensive in 1968 had started during Tet, so many observers believed the offensive we were expecting would also begin then. To disrupt any such plans, the Americans struck first with a massive air assault. At 0500 on 12 February, a 48-hour maximum air effort began against the B-3 Front. During that period, virtually all available tactical air, gunship, and B-52 strikes were deployed to disrupt the NVA's attack preparations.[28] During the first three weeks of February, more than 80 B-52 missions were flown in the Tan Canh area alone. The Arc Light and tactical air strikes near the western border disrupted the NVA's movement of its logistics units into forward attack positions and bought valuable time for the defenders to prepare.[29]

Highway 19 is a steep, winding, two-lane asphalt road between Pleiku in the Highlands and Qui Nhon on the coast, 90 road miles away. It makes many sharp turns and goes through narrow passes with high mountains on either side. Some areas are heavily forested on both sides. In the 1960s, the US Army had cleared away the jungle and the tall elephant grass where enemy ambushes could hide near the road. However, in this struggle between man and jungle, by 1972 the jungle was winning. My "pucker factor" always redlined while driving through the narrow passes, especially the place where 1,200 Frenchmen were killed or wounded when Groupe Mobile 100 was ambushed in 1954. We put sandbags under our Jeep's seats and covered the floor with more sandbags to dampen the blast (we hoped) if we drove over a mine. Nevertheless, driving down Highway 19 was risky.

Mr. Vann and Brigadier General Wear held periodic meetings for the advisers in Qui Nhon down on the coast. On 4 March, I drove my Jeep down Highway 19 to one of those meetings and came into the city on a straight two-lane road with French plane trees on either side. I saw motorbikes leaning against or chained to some of the trees and then a sudden burst of flame about 100 yards ahead. From a distance, it looked like a motorbike gas tank fire, but it turned out to be a Buddhist monk who had doused himself with gasoline and then lit a match. Self-immolation was an act the bonzes (Buddhist monks) used to protest against persecution by the Saigon government.

Lieutenant Colonel Tien, my counterpart, impressed me as an energetic, demanding officer who was willing to take the war to the enemy. He planned a battalion-size operation out of An Khe for 7 March. VNAF helicopters were requested and approved to lift the troops to a position near their objective. However, on the morning of the operation VNAF claimed that its helicopters were unavailable—not an unusual occurrence. Many ARVN commanders would have cancelled or at least rescheduled the operation. However, Tien ordered his troops to walk into the area of operations.[30]

For years, VNAF's undependable and inadequate helicopter support for ARVN had often been augmented or replaced by US Army helicopter units. Now the US Army aviation units were disbanding, but VNAF—despite the hundreds of helicopters being transferred to it—was not assuming greater responsibility. A bad, basic mistake had been made years earlier when South Vietnam's troop-lift and gunship helicopters were placed in VNAF with USAF advisers rather than in ARVN with US Army advisers who were experienced in using helicopters to support ground troops.

As the number of NVA troops in the Highlands increased, and as they drew closer to the ARVN defenders, more enemy soldiers either were captured or deserted the Communist army rather than die in the coming battles. Nguyen Trong Huy was an NVA Hoi

Chanh who rallied to ARVN troops 19 kilometers north of Kontum on 14 March. When interrogated, a Hoi Chanh—a North Vietnamese who had deserted his own army—was more likely to be cooperative and truthful than a POW. Huy claimed to be a master sergeant, a squad leader of the 4th Squad, 2nd Platoon, C-25th Transportation Company, 64th Regiment, 320th NVA Infantry Division. The 64th NVA Regiment, designated the "Tay Ninh Group," was commanded by Colonel Khuat Duy Tien, and the 320th Division commander was Colonel Kim Tuan. The division commander and his staff departed North Vietnam in October 1971 to "prepare the battlefield in the Highlands." The 64th NVA Regiment departed the North on 8 November 1971 and arrived at Base Area 609 on the border between Cambodia and Kontum Province shortly afterward. Huy told the ARVN interrogators that the 64th Regiment had three infantry battalions (the K-7, K-8, and K-9) of 300 men each and eight specialized companies for reconnaissance, antiaircraft, 75-mm recoilless rifle, 82-mm mortar, engineer, signal, medical, and transportation. The K-7 Battalion was hit by an air strike on 12 March and suffered heavy casualties. The next day the battalion lost another 65 men in a fight with ARVN troops. Sergeant Huy had heard that the next campaign would be "violent and great" and would involve the 64th Regiment and the D-19 Sapper Battalion supported by tanks in an attack against Kontum City.[31]

Starting in mid-March, more frequent encounters with battalion-size NVA units occurred. The enemy was showing a new willingness to engage in battle. A Hoi Chanh and several POWs were taken during a fight near Rocket Ridge. They revealed that the 320th NVA Infantry Division would join the B-3 Front in a major offensive from April to September. They also confirmed that there were many tanks in the base areas and that those tank units would participate in the coming attacks.[32]

On 24 March, the ARVN 23rd Ranger Battalion was inserted into a rugged, mountainous area 30 kilometers north of Kontum to do a BDA after an Arc Light strike. The battalion became heavily engaged with an enemy force and then was quickly surrounded. The Rangers held out for four days of repeated ground attacks and attacks by fire, and they suffered more than 100 casualties. The 11th Ranger Battalion was able to link up with them, but much artillery support and many tactical air strikes and B-52 strikes were required before the Rangers could break out and withdraw from the battlefield.[33] Another engagement started when the 95th Border Ranger Battalion from Ben Het was operating north of its camp and tangled with the 141st NVA Regiment of the 2nd NVA Division.

At the end of March, elements of the 47th ARVN Regiment and the 2nd ARVN Airborne Brigade were in heavy fighting along Rocket Ridge. Then, during the first week in April the 48th and 52nd NVA Regiments of the 320th NVA Division made human-wave assaults against the ARVN bases on Rocket Ridge. In all those engagements, the attacking NVA forces suffered heavy casualties during the fighting and from Arc Lights as well as US and VNAF tactical air strikes. A prisoner taken on Rocket Ridge said the pounding they received during their attacks rendered four or five NVA battalions combat ineffective. However, he also said replacements were streaming in from the North.[34]

On 23 March, the US delegation announced that the Paris peace talks would be suspended until the Communists agreed in advance on the issues to be discussed and then would enter into serious discussions about them.[35]

In the last week of March 1972, POWs said the 2nd NVA Infantry Division was also operating in the area. Its subordinate units included the 1st and 141st NVA Infantry Regiments, the D10 Sapper Battalion, the 14th NVA Artillery Battalion, and the 12th NVA Anti-Aircraft Artillery Battalion. Two battalions of the independent 28th NVA Infantry Regiment and two battalions of the 40th NVA Artillery Regiment were soon identified as operating east of Highway 14 north of Kontum City. All these newly identified enemy units meant that the equivalent of three rather than two divisions would be attacking Kontum.[36]

While the NVA was assembling for a major attack, the US Army was disassembling units that would play a major part in the coming battle. The 17th Aviation Group was closing four of its bases, reducing its aviation companies from 27 to 9, and inactivating four of its five aviation battalions.[37] By early April, the 361st Aerial Weapons Company, the Pink Panthers, was the only Cobra gunship company still operational in II Corps, and it was scheduled to stand down on 7 April. John Paul Vann knew this company would be an essential asset in the coming battle, and he did not want to lose it. He convinced MACV to keep the 361st around through the coming battle. He also requested additional antitank assets.

6

The North Vietnamese Invasion

> One thing Hanoi cannot do in the remaining months of this dry season: it cannot launch a nationwide military offensive on anything approaching the scale of Tet 1968.
> —CIA intelligence estimate, January 1972

When the Communists would be able to launch their invasion depended in part on the weather. Enemy activity in the Highlands usually peaked from February to April because that was a period of good, dry weather not seriously affected by either monsoon cycle. The monsoon rains started in May, and they would make moving supplies down the Ho Chi Minh Trail and maneuvering in the jungle much more difficult.

At the Communist Party's Nineteenth Plenum in Hanoi late in 1970, there was discussion about whether to give priority to invading the South or to rebuilding the North. A year later the arguments for invasion were the strongest. The Vietnamization program in the South appeared to be succeeding, and more of the population was progressively being brought under government control. The ARVN was growing stronger and was acquiring more modern arms from the Americans. Both of those developments were reasons to attack sooner rather than later. Despite the ARVN's increased size and modern weapons, however, when it launched Operation Lam Son 719 into Laos in early 1971—without its US advisers or US air support—its performance against the NVA was poor. That result encouraged a sense of military superiority on the part of the North Vietnamese and some sense of military inferiority on the part of the South

Vietnamese. The US Armed Forces were being withdrawn, and US public opinion was unlikely to allow Nixon to send any American ground units back to Vietnam. Moreover, the American presidential campaign would start with the New Hampshire primaries in the spring of 1972, and the Communists hoped a victory for them in the spring would mean a defeat for Nixon in the fall.[1] The principal proponents of invasion in 1972 were General Vo Nguyen Giap and First Secretary Le Duan of the Communist Party. Giap hoped the Easter Offensive would lead to final victory over the South and perhaps even trap the tens of thousands of Americans still there.[2] The Communists decided they should attack in early 1972.

When the enemy had launched attacks all over South Vietnam during Tet in 1968, they had assumed that the people would rise up to support them and that the Communists could seize and control enough of the cities and population to force the South Vietnamese government to accept a coalition government including Communists, who could then take over the Saigon government. However, the vast majority of the populace had not supported the Communists, the VC had been driven back with heavy losses, and—after having revealed themselves—most of the VC leaders had been killed and their infrastructure destroyed. There was no prospect of launching a similar uprising anytime in the near future. So the Communists' only alternative for total victory within the next few years was to use their army to launch a conventional invasion into South Vietnam. Another negative factor for them was that Nixon was improving relations with both China and Russia, which may have caused the North Vietnamese to worry that Nixon might convince their two biggest arms suppliers to stop supporting them.

Time magazine summed up why the North Vietnamese might attack in the spring of 1972 rather than wait for all the Americans to leave:

> A more important question is why the Communists would want to attack in 1972, instead of waiting a year for U.S. withdrawal to run its course. An offensive timed to the President's Peking visit would clearly be a signal from Hanoi that it will not tolerate any possible deal on Viet Nam cooked up by the U.S. and China. Beyond that, some Pentagon officials are convinced that the Communists want the psychological benefit of a "visible victory." According to this theory, Hanoi and the Viet Cong have decided not to settle for a uni-

lateral American withdrawal, which the world might inter-
pret as simply a political decision made by the White House.
Instead, the Communists want a tangible triumph, à la Dien
Bien Phu, which they can hold up as their own.[3]

If the North Vietnamese succeeded in taking over South Vietnam in 1972, it would be a humiliating defeat for the United States.
Our remaining troops would be forced to flee under enemy pressure rather than being gradually withdrawn in an orderly manner.
Many of us there would probably be killed or captured. Defeat by
the Communists would mean prison camps or death for many of
the 17 million South Vietnamese. A North Vietnamese military victory over the United States could have far-reaching effects around
the world and especially in Southeast Asia, which might be desta-
bilized. Communist prestige would soar and ours decline in Korea,
the Philippines, and Indonesia. Even Japan might loosen its ties to
the United States and be receptive to Communist overtures.

Their leaders told the NVA soldiers who invaded South Vietnam
that they must achieve victories, seize territory, and control large
populations to maximize their country's position at the bargaining
table. Then President Nixon would be forced to accept conditions
favorable to North Vietnam.[4] President Nixon revealed how much
he—and America—had riding on the outcome of the Communist
invasion when he said at a press conference, "The South Vietnamese lines may bend [but] not break. If this proves to be the case,
it will be the final proof that Vietnamization has succeeded."[5] Of
course, the opposite was also true. If the South Vietnamese lines did
break, then Nixon's critics could claim Vietnamization had failed.

Before launching an invasion of the South, the North Vietnamese needed to raise tens of thousands of men to fill their 15 divisions and to provide replacements for combat losses. To accomplish
this goal, they lowered the draft age from 17 to 16 and raised the
upper age from 30 to 35. They also lowered the physical standards
and drafted previously exempt classes of young men, including
skilled workers, technicians, university students, and even those
who showed promise of becoming future government and Communist Party leaders. Perhaps most significantly, they now drafted the
sixth and seventh sons of families who had already sent five sons to
war. Draft teams were sent into the countryside to find the necessary men, and POWs captured later in the South said those teams

stripped entire districts of all men between ages 14 and 45. A Hanoi government newspaper exhorted, "The Fatherland is calling, the front lines are waiting." NVA personnel strength was increased overall from about 390,000 in 1968 to 430,000 by the end of 1971.[6]

Speculation about exactly when the attack would come naturally focused on the Tet holidays starting on 15 February, but there were also reasons to argue for the week of 21–28 February, when President Nixon planned to visit China, or as late as the US presidential elections in the fall. In the end, it was none of these significant dates: the attack occurred when the NVA decided they were ready to attack. They launched their offensive on 30 March. The Americans called the North Vietnamese invasion in the spring of 1972 the "Easter Offensive" because it started at the beginning of the Easter holidays. However, the North Vietnamese called it the "Nguyen Hue Offensive," named for a legendary Vietnamese national hero who had led his army hundreds of miles through the jungle and mountains from central Vietnam to the outskirts of Hanoi, where he surprised and defeated the invading Chinese in the spring of 1789. He later became Emperor Quang Trung.[7]

Unlike the Communist attacks during Tet 1968, an uprising in which the lightly armed VC led the charge, for the Easter Offensive of early 1972 the North Vietnamese had 15 combat divisions, including 2 VC divisions manned mainly by North Vietnamese. They would leave only one division in North Vietnam to defend the North and to serve as a reserve. The other 14 divisions would be committed outside the country. Two were already in Laos and Cambodia, and the other 12 divisions totaling 150,000 men were available to attack South Vietnam.[8] This would be the largest military offensive and across-the-border invasion anywhere in the world since the fall of 1950, when the Communist Chinese Peoples Liberation Army attacked across the Yalu River into South Korea.[9]

This was General Vo Nguyen Giap's offensive. The battle at Khe Sanh and the failed Tet Offensive in 1968 had cost him about 100,000 casualties, but by 1972 he was ready to try again for a knockout blow. This time he had a different approach. Giap rebuilt the NVA into a Soviet-style force capable of launching a conventional attack with the newest tanks, artillery, and anti-aircraft weapons from Russia and China. During the Battle of the Bulge in December 1944, the German Wehrmacht's 19 divisions and 950 tanks had sent the Americans reeling backward with heavy losses. Giap's force was almost as formidable. He attacked with 14 divisions plus many independent units and an estimated 1,000 tanks.[10]

General Giap possessed the most technically advanced, mobile, anti-aircraft defenses ever deployed with a field army in combat up until this offensive. One of his most deadly weapons was the Soviet-made "Strella," code-named the "SA-7 Grail" by the North Atlantic Treaty Organization. This handheld, heat-seeking SAM could destroy aircraft flying at altitudes up to 10,000 feet. A two-man team, loader and gunner, could shoulder-fire it and bring down an aircraft all by themselves. The first reported kill was on 2 May when a Strella destroyed a US Army helicopter flying a rescue mission in I Corps. An AC-130 was destroyed about the same date. Despite the missile's subsonic speed, the Strella destroyed at least one jet fighter-bomber. For a heavier punch, the NVA had large Russian-made SAMs, which could bring down B-52s. They also had .51-caliber machine guns; 23-mm, 37-mm, 57-mm, 85-mm, and 100-mm anti-aircraft guns—some with tracking radar for fire control; ZSU 23-4 (four-barreled) 23-mm and twin-barreled 37-mm automatic guns; plus some ZSU-24s that fired anti-aircraft rockets. A few of these anti-aircraft weapons were mounted on self-propelled armored chassis. One of the most lethal was the S-60 57-mm gun with a maximum effective altitude (range) of 28,000 feet. When mounted on a T-55 tank chassis, it was designated the ZSU-57-2. The NVA used a network of aircraft spotters who reported incoming aircraft so the gun crews could be alerted and ready to fire when US or VNAF aircraft came within range. The Americans responded by attacking the enemy anti-aircraft gun emplacements with B-52 strikes.[11]

Some significant enemy weapons would be used in South Vietnam for the first time during the Easter Offensive. Lighter PT-76 amphibious tanks had previously been employed in the South, but now many hundreds of Russian T-54 and Chinese Type-59 medium tanks accompanied the Communist troops. The NVA's new 130-mm artillery piece could shoot farther than any enemy gun previously used in South Vietnam. Another unpleasant surprise was the AT-3 Sagger wire-guided missile, which could destroy ARVN tanks, bunkers, and other structures from a distance with deadly accuracy.[12]

An NVA record says it deployed the following forces to the Central Highlands battlefield: two infantry divisions (minus), four separate infantry regiments, four battalions of sappers, two regiments of artillery with 76 guns, one tank battalion, six anti-aircraft battalions with 72 guns, and two regiments of engineers.[13] This claim that only one NVA tank battalion was deployed in the Central Highlands may be true because only one, the 297th, was positively identified by ARVN and US sources. However, one separate company of PT-76 amphibious tanks was also positively identified in the Highlands.

At the height of the US involvement in 1969, there were 550,000 US troops on the ground in South Vietnam plus significant US air and naval forces outside the country. When the North Vietnamese invaded South Vietnam on 30 March, about 95,000 US military personnel were still in Vietnam, but only 6,000 of them were combat troops. Seven US Army divisions and two US Marine divisions had already departed. The only US combat units remaining in Vietnam were the 3rd Brigade (Separate) of the 1st Cavalry Division (Airmobile) and two battalions of the 196th Light Infantry Brigade. They were scheduled to depart within the next few months.[14] The 1st Squadron, 1st Cavalry Regiment, was the last American armored unit in Vietnam, and it left in April 1972.[15] Two-thirds of the air and naval forces were gone. Only a few USAF fighter squadrons remained to support the remaining American units and their South Vietnamese allies.[16]

Except for a few small units providing security for other American units, no US Army infantry units participated in active combat during the Easter Offensive.[17] The small size of our fighting force and the political pressure to avoid more American casualties meant the South Vietnamese would have to bear the brunt of all ground combat.[18] This would be the first time they would defend their country against a major enemy offensive without significant American help on the ground. Other than the advisers, virtually the entire US contribution would come from the air. B-52 and tactical air strikes, fixed-wing gunships, the tactical airlift of the C-130s, helicopter gunships, and air cavalry reconnaissance would play important roles in the battle.

When the invasion started, the South Vietnamese forces were deployed throughout the country, and even part of the general reserve—the marine and airborne divisions—was already committed in the I and II Corps areas.[19] The CIA in Saigon estimated the total enemy strength in South Vietnam was 180,000 to 190,000, including the VC. The South Vietnamese had 1.2 million men under arms in their armed forces, but only 421,263 of them were in ARVN. The hundreds of thousands in the RFs and PFs were not as well trained and unlikely to be committed outside their own provinces or even outside their own villages.

Nhan Dan, an authoritative Hanoi newspaper, proclaimed in late March that a return to full-scale warfare using large units was necessary to defeat the Nguyen Van Thieu government and its US allies. MACV intelligence predicted an impending, large-scale attack, yet when the offensive started on Thursday, 30 March, both General Abrams and Ambassador Ellsworth Bunker were outside of Vietnam. Abrams was spending an extended Easter weekend with his wife in Thailand, and Bunker was visiting his wife, who was ambassador to Nepal. Back in Washington, Secretary of Defense Melvin Laird was about to depart for a golfing vacation in Puerto Rico. The entire US defense and foreign-affairs establishments had to scramble to cope with the crisis, which the North cited as proof that the invasion caught the Americans by surprise.[20]

However, the Easter Offensive and even its timing did not come as a complete surprise to the South Vietnamese and their American advisers. In fact, as the Communist buildup progressed, MACV intelligence predicted the offensive would start on 1 April. They were off by only two days. However, it was surprising when the initial attack came across the DMZ rather than from farther south into II or III Corps. The DMZ route had the advantage of quick access to the coastal Highway 1 and was convenient to the NVA's POL pipeline. This was a major consideration now that the NVA was using the tanks, armored personnel carriers (APCs), and trucks of a conventional army.[21]

The Easter Offensive began at 0200 on 30 March when a massive artillery bombardment pounded the South Vietnamese forces in northern I Corps. Then more than 200 T-54 tanks and 40,000 enemy soldiers in six NVA divisions and two independent regiments attacked into the DMZ from the north across the Ben Hai River and from Laos in the west. The ARVN 3rd Infantry Division and the two marine brigades defending the border were hit hard.[22] In the first 24 hours of the attack, more than 5,000 artillery and rocket rounds struck the 12 major ARVN bases along the DMZ. Almost all of the ARVN forward artillery batteries were wiped out.[23]

The 3rd ARVN Division troops on the DMZ were trained and experienced in counterguerilla warfare but were not trained to stand up against an enemy equipped with tanks and heavy artillery. The division's own lack of aggressiveness worked against it. After the invasion started, if the division had patrolled out beyond its own lines to learn where the enemy was and what he was doing, it could have learned when the NVA troops were resting, resupplying, and regrouping, and the ARVN troops could have done the same. With no idea about when the enemy would attack again, all of the defenders had to remain on full alert all the time. That wore them down, so they were already exhausted when the enemy finally did attack.[24]

Brigadier General Vu Van Giai, the 3rd ARVN Infantry Division commander, was one of the best ARVN generals, but his division was probably the worst ARVN division. It had been created only six months earlier by taking one regiment from the 1st Division and forming two new regiments from the castoffs other units sent when ordered to provide troops. Brigadier General Giai was not given authority over the ARVN tank units and the marine brigade operating in his area of responsibility. This lack of unity of command was a fatal flaw in the defense of I Corps.[25] The I Corps commander, Lieutenant General Hoang Xuan Lam, ordered the 3rd ARVN Division to counterattack, but the counterattack failed, the ARVN casualties were high, and a great deal of equipment was lost.[26] When Brigadier General Giai sensed he was losing control of the situation and asked Lieutenant General Lam for advice and assistance, he was offered the solution of shooting any insubordinate commanders on the spot.[27] When the defenses along the DMZ collapsed, the marine brigade made a tactical withdrawal into the mountainous jungle, but the 3rd ARVN Division's withdrawal disintegrated into a rout as it was pushed back by fast-charging enemy tanks and successive waves of NVA infantry. As the division fell apart, the American advisers were extracted by helicopter, which further deepened the defenders' sense of impending doom.

On 31 March, an Airborne Division CP and the 3rd Airborne Battalion were airlifted from Tan Son Nhut Air Base in Saigon to Kontum. To accomplish this airlift, all in-country aircraft were flown around the clock to their maximum capability. During this 36-hour effort, eight C-130s transported 425 tons of troops and equipment to the Central Highlands. Their ground time at Tan Son Nhut averaged an hour, and at Kontum each aircraft was unloaded in 15 minutes. Many of the return flights carried refugees. VNAF

C-123s assisted in the effort. In the Highlands, the paratroopers assumed responsibility for the defense of Kontum City and the southern part of Kontum Province.[28]

In the first ten days of the offensive, the NVA captured eighty-one 105-mm howitzers, thirty-two 155-mm howitzers, and four 175-mm guns. These weapons were then turned against the South Vietnamese. Most of those lost artillery pieces were in isolated FSBs, to which they had been brought by helicopter and from which they could be extracted only by helicopter. When the time came to evacuate the heavy artillery pieces, enemy anti-aircraft fire made it impossible to lift them out by helicopter.[29]

The Americans were stunned to learn that almost an entire ARVN regiment surrendered to the enemy at Camp Carroll just south of the DMZ. On 2 April, after the 56th ARVN Infantry Regiment of the 3rd Division had been shelled and attacked for three days, Lieutenant Colonel Pham Van Dinh, its commander, betrayed his country. He ran up a white flag and surrendered his men—about 1,800 of them—and five artillery batteries to the enemy. The NVA was handed 22 American-made 105-mm, 155-mm, and 175-mm artillery pieces, which were then used against ARVN. Lieutenant Colonel William Camper, Dinh's US Army adviser, described what happened: "Colonel Dinh . . . told us he was going to surrender Camp Carroll. . . . [He] offered me the choice of surrendering. I said I would not surrender, that we would find some other way to get out. He said that we (myself and Major Brown) could hide among his troops when they went out the gate to surrender to the North Vietnamese and once we were outside the perimeter, we could fall down in the grass and crawl away. I dismissed this as ridiculous."[30]

The 3rd Division advisers were fortunately able to divert a big Chinook helicopter to pick up the two 56th Regiment advisers. With a pair of snakes flying cover, the courageous Hook pilot extracted the Americans only minutes before the surrender.[31]

The next day, the traitorous former commander of the 56th Regiment made a propaganda broadcast over Radio Hanoi calling on ARVN soldiers to surrender to the National Liberation Front (NLF, the Communist shadow government in South Vietnam): "Find out how to get in touch with the NLF in order for you to return quickly to the people. Your action will effectively assist in ending the war quickly and also save your life. . . . My personal feeling is that the NLF is going to win the war. The NLF is ready all the time to welcome you back. The NLF is expecting you to return very soon."[32]

From the beginning of US involvement in South Vietnam, American participants had speculated about how hard ARVN would fight when the chips were down. Dinh's craven surrender made us wonder about how steadfast our own counterparts would be if they decided the NVA might win a battle we were fighting—or the war. However, during the entire course of the Vietnam War, the 56th ARVN Infantry Regiment was the only ARVN unit to surrender en masse.[33]

Brigadier General Wear described the months from February to April 1972:

> During the February to April time frame, Vann continued to spend most of his time in Nha Trang. Dzu would spend a day or two in the Corps Headquarters in Pleiku, constantly on the telephone to his commanders or whomever. Everyone seemed to be waiting for the enemy to attack. I visited Tan Canh almost every day. Colonel Kaplan was always very upbeat and seemed to have faith that the troops in the area would put up a good fight. I attended the intelligence briefings each morning at a secure Special Forces or CIA office in Pleiku Barracks. The reports indicated a large buildup of enemy forces in the Dak To area.
>
> I will always remember 4 April 1972. On that day, everything seemed to be falling apart. Among other things, I flew up to the old US Firebase English in Binh Dinh Province, which was being attacked. The US Lt. Col. adviser . . . was trying to hold the place together. When it was overrun a few days later, the [adviser] was wounded but [was] picked up by a very brave helicopter pilot. Visiting him in Pleiku hospital, he was shocked that his ARVN troops had bugged out so quickly. Coming back from that visit on the 4th, I stopped by the Korean unit . . . [in] An Khe Pass. They had just had a popular captain killed and were not in a happy mood. Also, on that day one of my key staff officers, Colonel Snell, completed his year and left for home. When I landed at our pad near the Corps Headquarters, I realized that I was really beat and shouldn't be flying a helicopter. I decided at that

moment, landing at Pleiku on 4 April, to ground myself, and I never flew a chopper after that.[34]

By 4 April 1972, MACV headquarters was claiming 52 enemy tanks destroyed in all corps areas since the NVA offensive had started five days earlier.[35] The South Vietnamese marines west of Dong Ha proved that the T-54 tanks were not invincible by killing 40 of them with M-72 light antitank weapons (LAWs).[36] Individual ARVN soldiers firing M-72s were also taking a toll on the T-54s. They knocked out 33 tanks in nine days. In ARVN armor units equipped with the newly issued M-48 medium tanks, good crews using good tactics, performed well against the T-54s, in part because the M-48's fire-control optics were superior. VNAF's First Air Division, supported by Air Squadron 518, demolished 15 tanks in the first three days of April. Then they demolished 75 tanks of the 203rd NVA Tank Regiment in three days.[37]

The population of Quang Tri fled south on Highway 1 to escape the NVA artillery bombardment, but the NVA followed them down the highway. The enemy artillery observers intentionally adjusted their fire onto the refugee columns. On 9 May, President Thieu denounced this butchery, which killed or wounded 25,000 innocent civilians.[38] Thieu's announcement was probably necessary to recognize the South's loss and to tell the world about this atrocity, but it was bad for the morale of other civilians who were fleeing the enemy invasion and contributed to some of the subsequent scenes of panic.

Giap's next thrust was into III Corps, almost 600 kilometers south of the fighting in I Corps. On 5 April, more than 20,000 NVA troops in three divisions supported by tanks and artillery attacked the district town of Loc Ninh, only 100 kilometers from Saigon. Loc Ninh fell two days later. The invaders rapidly rolled on to assault An Loc, the provincial capital. An Loc was a tougher nut to crack. Even after it was attacked in force on 13 April, the defenses did not crumble. When the NVA's initial attempt to take An Loc was repulsed, it could have spread panic across South Vietnam by bypassing this provincial capital and charging on toward Saigon. Instead, its forces were committed to a prolonged siege of An Loc. Most of the city was destroyed, and the outcome was often in doubt. However, with considerable help from the USAF and VNAF, the defenders held the city, and the enemy was eventually forced to withdraw after suffering staggering losses of men and equipment.[39]

Before the Vietnam War, the US Army had last fought a counterinsurgency war against indigenous guerillas during the Philippine Insurrection from 1899 to 1902. American officers and NCOs who were trained to defeat the Russians in big battles on the plains of central Europe led the army we took to Vietnam. Many of them were veterans of World War II or the Korean War or both, which we considered "conventional" wars. We knew what our bombers, tanks, and artillery could do against an enemy who massed his forces for large-scale attacks. For ten years, we grumbled about fighting a Communist Vietnamese enemy who seldom massed his forces or even stood and fought long enough to make a good target for us. So when the NVA launched the Easter Offensive—a conventional attack with many divisions supported by tanks and artillery—it did present an opportunity of sorts. Major John D. Howard, an adviser in An Loc, said, "This was the war we came to fight."[40]

The North Vietnamese knew they could cut South Vietnam in half along the east–west Highway 19 by seizing and controlling Qui Nhon on the coast and the Highland cities of Pleiku and Kontum. So General Giap, with his attacks in I Corps to the north and in III Corps to the south under way, opened a third front in II Corps. On 9 April, his Gold Star Division attacked to the south in coastal Binh Dinh Province. Then on 12 April, the 320th NVA Division attacked the two ARVN airborne brigades defending Rocket Ridge in the Central Highlands.[41] The North Vietnamese apparently reasoned that making major attacks into three widely separated areas of South Vietnam would confuse the Saigon government as to where the main threat was and where it should send its national reserves. Any one of the NVA's attacks could succeed so spectacularly that South Vietnam would collapse. However, there were fatal flaws in the strategy of launching three separate attacks. The attacks were so widely separated that they were not mutually supporting, and spreading its forces across three attacks did not leave the NVA with adequate reserves to exploit successes and allow any one of the attacks to overwhelm the South Vietnamese defenders. Also, the 600 kilometers between the NVA forces in I Corps and those in III Corps must have been a command and control problem for Giap. Our air superiority prevented him from flying between these areas to exercise any personal control or to confer with his subordinate commanders as the top ARVN and American generals could.

By early April, all 12 of the 23rd ARVN Division's infantry battalions were in the northern part of II Corps. The four battalions of the 44th Regiment were at An Khe, the 45th Regiment was in Pleiku, and the 53rd Regiment was defending Kontum City.[42] Some of the ARVN units in II Corps were already involved in heavy combat. On 1 April, the 22nd Division's 47th Regiment at Dak To II repulsed a sapper attack supported by indirect fire. For the next five days, the regiment fought a tenacious enemy force only 300 meters north of their CP. More than 10,000 rounds of artillery, 70 tactical air sorties, and four Arc Lights were required to repel the attackers.[43]

The North Vietnamese correctly sized up President Nixon when they assumed he would not return American ground forces to Vietnam. However, they badly underestimated his resolve and his willingness to increase US airpower in the region. Nixon's response to the NVA invasion was a terrible, swift sword in the form of renewed and heavier than ever bombing of the North. The USAF response was fast and overwhelming as a vast air armada surged toward Southeast Asia:

> The 45 days following the start of the Easter Offensive saw the Air Force demonstrate global mobility and power on a massive scale. From bases in Korea, the Philippines, and the United States, additional fighters, bombers, gunships, electronic warfare planes, search and rescue units, transports, and tankers moved in a swift, smooth flow to Southeast Asia. In some instances, units were in combat just three days after they received orders to move. The strike forces built up rapidly: Fighters doubled to almost 400, B-52 bomber strength increased to 171, and the number of tankers rose to 168. . . . B-52 sorties in South Vietnam built from 689 in March to 2,223 in May. Fighter sorties of all branches (including the South Vietnamese air force) rose from 4,237 in March to 18,444 in May.[44]

By 31 March 1972, our MACV Advisory Team 33 was down to 26 officers and 14 enlisted men.[45] On 20 April, President Nixon announced a reduction in US troop strength from 69,000 to 49,000 to be reached by 1 July. President Thieu was informed of this latest cut while he was struggling to stop a major invasion by the NVA, now equipped with Soviet and Chinese tanks and artillery.[46] However, the number of Americans involved in the war was actually increasing. "Withdrawing" air force units were moved from Vietnam to Thailand, and some flew bombing missions en route to Takhli Air Base in Thailand. USAF troop strength in Thailand increased from 32,000 to 45,000 during April and May. Fifty more B-52s were moved to U Tapao Air Base in Thailand, and the number of USAF personnel on Guam tripled from 4,000 to 12,000. Naval personnel strength doubled from the beginning of the year to 39,000. So the reduction of 20,000 Americans in Vietnam was more than offset by the increase of 40,500 Americans added to the forces engaged in the conflict but stationed outside Vietnam.[47]

On 3 April, a forward base for the smaller, slower FAC aircraft was established at Pleiku. USAF fighter-bomber missions continued to be flown from bases around Saigon or from Thailand, but a facility set up at Bien Hoa enabled F-4s from Thailand to refuel and rearm for another strike in Vietnam before returning to their base.[48] After so many years of war, some VNAF pilots were credited with more than 3,000 combat missions. The South Vietnamese government found a hero in one 25-year-old A-1 pilot, Captain Tran The Vinh, who knocked out 21 NVA tanks during the Easter Offensive. A photo of him giving the jaunty thumbs-up sign was made into posters, which were widely distributed. He died on 9 April when his Skyraider was finally shot down.[49]

Around 10 April, John Paul Vann knocked on the door of Brigadier General Wear's bedroom suite early in the morning. This was unusual because Vann seldom got up before nine or ten. He was excited about a plan to entice a large group of VC to defect. The go-between would be a double agent named "John" who was in contact with the group somewhere in the mountains south of Ban Me Thuot. The agent told Vann this group would defect only if Vann would personally meet with them and guarantee they would be treated fairly by the US and ARVN forces. Vann removed his ID card and other identification documents from his wallet and put them in the safe he shared with Wear. He said he planned to have his WO pilot fly him and the double agent to a clearing on a mountain.

Brigadier General Wear was dumbfounded and reminded Mr.

Vann that the action in Kontum Province would soon explode and that he was the big boss in the area. He needed to be available to deal with Dzu and all the crises certain to arise. Vann responded with something like, "George, you are beginning to sound like all the other generals I have worked with over here." He went on to say that they badly needed a success story coming out of the Highlands and this could be it.

Wear pointed out that Vann was leaving him as the final authority in the entire corps area. He reluctantly agreed to cover for Vann for 72 hours but warned that if Vann was still absent without leave (AWOL) after three days, then Wear would have to report his absence to General Weyand. Vann agreed to this stipulation and flew away in his OH-58. Wear did not hear from him or the pilot until the morning of the second day, when Vann returned, bleary eyed from lack of sleep and with a two-day growth of beard. He told Wear, "That bastard John lost his nerve." Wear was too busy from then on to ask the pilot what happened, so he never learned more about the incident.[50]

The bizarre disorganization of our on-again, off-again bombing campaign against strategic targets in North Vietnam was an obstacle to be overcome before that campaign could achieve maximum results. Back in November 1968, we had agreed to stop bombing the North if the Communists would stop shelling and attacking cities in the South. They never kept their part of the agreement. So, finally, on 6 April 1972 US fighter-bombers flew deep into the North to strike Communist targets 100 kilometers north of the DMZ. On 15, 16, and 17 April, B-52s bombed North Vietnam for the first time since 1969. Nixon could not be certain how the Russians and Chinese would react to this bombing, but he was certain the North Vietnamese invasion was intended to destroy South Vietnam.[51] On 29 and 30 April, B-52s flew 700 missions over North Vietnam. By 9 May, US bombing of North Vietnam equaled the previous high level of 1967–1968.[52]

When the NVA invasion started, the number of C-130s stationed at Tan Son Nhut was quickly increased to 44, the maximum that could be accommodated there. Without those aircraft and their crews, it might have been impossible to stop and repel the Communist onslaught.[53]

An article in *Air Force* magazine later summarized the USAF's contribution to the defense: "Cargo aircraft weaved their way through smoke, flak, and the dangerous Strella missiles to land when they could or drop when they could not. Gunships flew protective sorties around embattled garrisons, laying down a curtain of fire to suppress enemy attacks. Amidst the carnage, FACs flew calmly, calling out targets and monitoring enemy movements. And through it all, the search and rescue units worked to recover downed airmen."[54]

When the Easter Offensive started, the US Navy had two aircraft carriers with a total of 170 aircraft in the Gulf of Tonkin. Six weeks later there were six aircraft carriers with almost 500 aircraft plus 20 cruisers and destroyers off the Vietnamese coast. This naval task force was the largest assembled since World War II.[55] Nixon ordered a blockade of North Vietnam, and the navy mined the approaches and harbors so effectively that no major ship entered or left any of those ports for the remainder of the war.[56]

President Thieu issued an order to hold Kontum, Quang Tri, and An Loc at all costs. He feared that if the North Vietnamese seized and held them, the psychological and political repercussions would lead to the collapse of South Vietnam. The highest-ranking officer in the South Vietnamese armed forces, General Cao Van Vien, considered An Loc the most important because it was so close to the capital. However, he also thought if Kontum were lost, it would be impossible to defend Pleiku, and the enemy would drive to the coast and cut his country in half. South Vietnam would not survive if that happened.[57]

Secretary of State Henry Kissinger described the challenges facing General Abrams:

> For four years General Abrams had performed, with dignity, one of the most thankless jobs ever assigned to an American general. He took over a force of 540,000 men in 1968 but was immediately shackled by mounting restrictions. He was continually given assignments that made no military sense. Starting in the middle of 1969, he was asked to dismantle his command at an ever-accelerating rate while maintaining the security of South Vietnam and putting the South Vietnamese forces into a position from which they could undertake their own defense. He succeeded to a remarkable degree. By the time Hanoi struck in 1972, more of the countryside than ever before was under Saigon's control; most of

the South Vietnamese units had vastly improved. Still, deep down, General Abrams knew that he was engaged in a holding action in a battle for which even a small strategic reserve of American ground forces would almost surely have been decisive. For three years his command had been turned into a withdrawal headquarters. Now he was urged to win the crucial final battle.[58]

7

Attacking in An Khe Pass

Nothing in life is so exhilarating as to be shot at without
result.

—Winston Churchill

Highway 14, the vital main supply route between Pleiku and Kontum, went through the Chu Pao Pass, a place the Americans called "Kontum Pass," north of Pleiku and about ten kilometers south of Kontum. Chu Pao Mountain dominated the pass, and it was a natural fortress full of caves, making it easy to defend and difficult to assault. The Americans called it the "Rock Pile." In early April, the 95B NVA Regiment seized the pass and concentrated its new, heavy anti-aircraft artillery around its positions on the Rock Pile. The anti-aircraft fire at this location was so intense it limited aerial observation and air support in the pass. On 4 April, an ARVN helicopter assault using VNAF helicopters was launched to retake the pass and reopen the road to Kontum. USAF tactical air bombed the landing zone to prepare it for the helicopter assault, but because of poor coordination between ARVN and VNAF the assault was four hours late.[1] The long delay allowed the enemy to regroup and move to meet the assaulting force with enough firepower to defeat it. ARVN attempts to eliminate the Communist roadblock and reopen the road to Kontum would go on for several months. There were many ARVN failures, and any ARVN successes were quickly followed by the NVA's retaking the Rock Pile and again blocking the road.

At An Khe, the North Vietnamese invasion seemed far away from us because most of the action was up north in I Corps, and neither the *Stars and Stripes* nor AFN was saying much about it. On 11 April, the invasion suddenly hit home when the Communists seized An Khe Pass and blocked Highway 19 between Pleiku in the Highlands and Qui Nhon on the coast.

In early April, POWs revealed that the VC K2 Battalion of Gia Lai Province and several VC local-force sapper companies were deployed along Highway 19 with the mission of interdicting it between the Mang Yang and An Khe passes.[2] The NVA forces involved were the 12th Regiment, 3rd Division, supported by the NVA 200th AA Battalion. Early on 11 April, one of the VC sapper units attacked the Republic of Korea (ROK) Capital "Tiger" Infantry Division compound on a hilltop overlooking Highway 19, and other Communist units seized control of the highway.[3] The Koreans were responsible for securing this part of Highway 19. However, the ROK battalion stationed near An Khe Pass was not able to clear it, so the 44th ARVN Regiment was ordered to drive out the Communists.[4]

Captain *Patrick* O'Neil, the adviser to an ARVN armored cavalry unit, and I took Sergeant *Hao* in my Jeep and followed Lieutenant Colonel Tran Quang Tien and his troops down Highway 19 to the east until the 44th Regiment soldiers in front of us ran into enemy fire. The regimental commander began maneuvering his troops and engaged the enemy to push them back. On the American tactical radio net, we heard a report about two Americans and an Englishman—all civilians—being caught in an ambush farther down Highway 19. Both Americans were killed.[5]

Mortar rounds were hitting a Korean outpost on top of a nearby hill, and one would occasionally come close to us. We could see enemy troops milling around down in the valley south of the highway and firing mortars at the outpost on the hilltop. I radioed for air support, and before long my radio came to life with, "This is Covey Five-Zero-Seven. You have a target for me?" I gave Covey 507 the coordinates and description of the target and told him I was in a Jeep just off the south side of the highway. He said, "Covey Five-Zero-Seven. OK. Fast Draw Six, I've got your target. See some trucks down there, too. But I can't find you along the south side of the highway." We both wanted to be certain the bombers diving from thousands of feet above could identify and avoid my Jeep. I unrolled one of the orange panels used to mark the friendly lines and drop zones or to point toward the enemy and radioed the FAC when the panel was laid across our Jeep hood.

Covey 507 said, "Still don't see you. . . . OK! Got you." About five minutes later, the FAC called back to say, "I've got F-4s at 16,000. I'm going to mark the target, and then they'll take care of those mortars for you."

It amazed me how fighter-bomber pilots, flying hundreds of miles an hour, could dive from so high they were out of sight and then hit a pinpoint target with a bomb. They often flew into heavy anti-aircraft fire and then flew through it again and again on multiple passes to drop their bombs and use their machine guns to destroy the target. And they did it all without flying into each other or the FAC or a mountain.

We watched for the fighters, and they soon appeared—one, two, three of them, rolling in to bomb the target one after another. Looking through my big field glasses, I could see the enemy troops and mortars disappear in balls of fire and clouds of smoke. Then each F-4 made several more passes to strafe the target area. The mortar fire stopped.

It would be impossible for me to choose between the crews of the US Army helicopters; the B-52s; the AC-130 gunships; the C-130 cargo aircraft; the fighter-bomber pilots from the USAF, US Marine Corps, and US Navy; or the FACs to say which I most admired and appreciated for the many times they saved those of us on the ground. But the FACs carried the extra burden of having to keep several balls in the air at the same time. The FACs were not only our link to the air support we needed; they were an American voice reassuring us when we felt we were alone and in danger. They had a bird's-eye view of the action and could see both the friendly and enemy forces during an attack. A FAC could call for and adjust artillery fire and bring an overpowering array of aerial firepower to help us.

The 44th Regiment's troops were moving against stiff opposition from an enemy fighting from prepared positions. Nevertheless, with the help of Cobra gunships and air strikes, they were making progress. At the end of the first day, Lieutenant Colonel Tien told me they counted at least 50 enemy bodies—a big victory for our side. During Senate Foreign Relations Committee hearings in mid-April, Secretary of State William P. Rogers stated, "We have no Americans in ground combat today."[6]

The next day, as our troops moved down the highway to the east, clearing out the enemy, we followed at a distance in our Jeep.

Mortar rounds were falling around us again, and Captain O'Neil, Sergeant *Hao,* and I jumped out of the Jeep and dove for cover in a ditch beside the road. We were scrunched down, hugging the ground, when I heard a helicopter approach from our rear. I turned my head and watched while an OH-58 landed on the road, and Mr. Vann got out. He came striding toward us through intermittent mortar fire and occasional rifle shots cracking overhead. He was not wearing a helmet or flak jacket. Common sense told me it was still risky to stand up, but I had to stop cowering in the ditch and report to him. I told O'Neil and *Hao* to stay where they were, stood up, and trotted down the road to report to John Paul Vann.

After I briefed him on the situation, he asked if the ROK commanders had contacted me. I told him we had no contact with them but could use their help. Mr. Vann said he was going to fly down to Qui Nhon to tell the ROK commanders they needed to get into the fight immediately because security for An Khe Pass and this part of Highway 19 was their responsibility. After Vann's helicopter left, the mortar fire died down.

About an hour later, a Huey landed on the road, and two men got out. One of them was a big man, and I recognized the insignia of a Korean full colonel. The other man was the colonel's interpreter, an ARVN sergeant who spoke Vietnamese and Korean. I walked over to meet the colonel, saluted, and introduced myself. He shook my hand in a perfunctory way, and I started to brief him on the situation. He held up his hand, turned, and said something in Korean to his interpreter, who asked me—in broken English—if we had a Vietnamese interpreter. I waved to Sergeant *Hao* to join us. After a brief exchange between the two Vietnamese, I was astonished to learn that the ROK colonel wanted me to speak English to my interpreter, who would then relay in Vietnamese what I said to the other interpreter, who would relay it in Korean to the ROK colonel. He would respond or ask me questions through the same process.

In 1959–1960, I had served a year in Korea and so knew that all the higher-ranking Korean officers could speak excellent English. Many of them were graduates of US Army schools. Out of extreme arrogance, this Korean officer would not speak directly with me because he was a full colonel and I was only a lieutenant colonel. Here we were in the middle of a battle, ROK and ARVN troops were being killed, we could be killed while standing there, and he insisted on playing out a senseless charade. I shook my head in disbelief but decided to go along with his silly game to get the Koreans into the fight. Looking directly at the Korean colonel, I spoke in English and then waited while my words were translated into Vietnamese, then from Vietnamese to Korean, and finally the colonel's comments or questions came back by the same circuitous route. All the while, occasional mortar rounds were landing nearby, and now and then we heard the sharp CRACK of bullets passing by.

The Korean soldiers had a reputation as fierce fighters. Shortly after they arrived in Vietnam, a Korean unit had suffered some casualties when they were fired on from a village, so they had wiped out the village.[7] However, the ROK "Tiger" Division, which had responsibility for securing An Khe Pass, had engaged in virtually no fighting during the previous three years.[8] A US government report said the Koreans were under orders from their government to avoid combat to minimize casualties, so it took a special effort on our part to get them to agree to clear the enemy out of An Khe Pass. This "special effort" was probably Mr. Vann's threatening to cut off their post exchange store privileges.[9]

Later that day the Koreans finally joined the fight. They brought a significant additional weapon—a flame-throwing APC. It was an M-132, a standard M-113 with the .50-caliber machine gun cupola replaced with an M-8 cupola containing a flamethrower. It could shoot a stream of flame up to 200 meters for half a minute.[10] When the Koreans located an NVA position, the M-132 would pull forward to where it had a clear shot at the enemy. Then it would fire a series of short bursts of fire with a WHOOSH, WHOOSH, WHOOSH like a giant blowtorch. We were impressed, and the NVA must have been terrified. Captain O'Neil joked that every time it shot flame, it was proclaiming, "I am the king of the valley!" The Koreans moved slowly down the road, burning and shooting as they cleaned out the NVA. When they finally joined the fight, they fought like "tigers" should.

Overall, the Koreans were valuable allies in Vietnam, where their total casualties were 4,407 KIA and nearly 10,000 WIA. They inflicted many times more casualties on the Communists.[11]

A continuing flow of truck convoys from Qui Nhon was required to resupply Pleiku and the troops beyond it in Kontum as well as the outposts still farther west. With the An Khe Pass closed, no supplies were arriving in Pleiku overland from the coast, and by 16 April John Paul Vann said there was only a three-day supply of some items in Pleiku. C-130s started flying in supplies, including fuel. Some C-130s carried 4,500 gallons of fuel in large bladders. C-141s joined the effort. On the return flight, the cargo planes often carried refugees, many of them military dependents. Vietnamese are smaller than Americans, and because their situation was desperate, the aircraft were packed with far more than the normal number of passengers. One C-141 brought out 394 refugees—four times the normal passenger load. People who saw it arrive at Tan Son Nhut were amazed at the continuing stream of refugees pouring out of this one airplane.[12]

After the Koreans were coerced into doing their duty in the An Khe Pass, they eventually cleared out the NVA. They declared Highway 19 reopened on 26 April, more than two weeks after it was first closed. They then relapsed into inactivity. Several days of road repair were required before trucks could travel from Qui Nhon to Pleiku.[13] The 44th Regiment's area of responsibility was then expanded to include the An Khe Pass.[14] The Koreans claimed they killed 705 NVA soldiers during the fighting and said their own casualties were 51 killed and 115 wounded. However, later reports said 110 Koreans were killed, and 384 wounded. Most of their casualties occurred when they attacked fortified enemy positions on Hill 638, which dominates An Khe Pass.[15]

With the NVA still controlling Highway 14 both north and south of the city, Kontum was cut off and surrounded. Having the main supply route from Pleiku held by the enemy increased the sense of isolation that the defenders of Kontum already felt. However, NVA control of Highway 14 also meant the troops defending Kontum could not escape down this highway, knowledge of which helped to strengthen their resolve to stand and fight. One adviser remarked that the NVA might have made a mistake when they denied ARVN that escape route.[16]

The NVA employed .51-caliber (12.7-mm), 14.5-mm, 23-mm, 37-mm, and 57-mm anti-aircraft weapons in the An Khe Pass, in the Kontum Pass between Pleiku and Kontum, around Rocket Ridge northeast of Kontum, and around their base areas. Accurate .51-caliber fire was reported at altitudes of 2,500 feet above ground level, and 37-mm fire with airbursts was reported at up to 6,000 feet above ground level. Crew-served and individual weapons augmented the anti-aircraft guns. The enemy usually employed two or three weapons firing from different directions. Their targets, the pilots of American and VNAF aircraft, rated the efficiency of the NVA's anti-aircraft fire to be excellent and their accuracy deadly. When US or VNAF aircraft were flying at a low level or inserting troops, the NVA sometimes fired RPGs and even mortars at them.[17]

When Brigadier General Wear returned from a visit to Tan Canh in mid-April, he briefed Mr. Vann on the deteriorating situation there and again advised him to pull some troops from the Tan Canh/Dak To area and use them to create blocking positions. Vann seemed to agree and set up a meeting for Wear, as the senior US Army officer in II Corps, to tell General Frederick C. Weyand, General Abrams's deputy, about his concerns. Wear describes the meeting:

> I took my G-2, Colonel Irv Paul, with me. When we arrived at Weyand's office, he was not alone. Abrams, [with] whom I had previously had this same discussion, was also there. I felt that I was probably being set up by someone—Weyand, Vann, or whoever. Neither Abrams nor Weyand said a word. I told them that I wanted to be sure that we were reading off the same sheet of music and that they saw the picture as I did, or was I missing something? Colonel Paul gave a rundown on the enemy situation as we knew it, and then I reviewed the ARVN deployments. I then pointed out the morale of the ARVN forces, the problems they had the previous year against only small enemy forces, and recommended that we adopt my blocking-position plan in Kontum Province, etc. Neither of them said a word.
>
> When I was finished, Abrams said something like, "We know all that shit, what else do you have?" I . . . asked Col. Paul to step out and then told them that Dzu was cowardly and did not have the stomach for a fight; I also pointed out the weaknesses and poor morale of the ARVN troops in the Highlands. I told them that I was quite sure that the troops in the Dak To/Tan Canh area would not fight, just as they had demonstrated in the Plei Trap and Fire Base 6 battles. I told them that we were facing a catastrophe if we didn't get reinforcements or, at least, redeploy the forces now in that area.

Weyand said something like, "Wear, we are not going to let that happen." Abrams asked me if that was all. When I said yes, he said, "Thank you," and I left. Col. Paul was waiting for me outside the office. It was almost noon, but nobody invited us to lunch, . . . [so we] flew back to Pleiku.[18]

Weeks before the fighting in An Khe Pass, I had applied for my second and last R&R to meet my wife in Hong Kong. The international airfares were so low that my wife could fly roundtrip from Los Angeles to Hong Kong for $368. Much to my surprise, considering the increased action in our area, the R&R was approved, and on 24 April I went to Camp Alpha at Tan Son Nhut to leave on R&R.

8

Our Firebases Fall

The requirement to defend all will probably mean we will lose much.

—Warning that Mr. Vann deleted
from a II Corps message to MACV

Although the advisers were supposed to just advise and in fact had no command authority over the ARVN forces, John Paul Vann, a civilian US State Department Foreign Service officer, exempted himself from that rule and essentially assumed command of all the South Vietnamese forces in II Corps during the Easter Offensive. Lieutenant Colonel Stanislaus J. Fuesel, the II Corps artillery adviser, said, "If I had attempted to do what Vann did, he would have fired me." Indeed, although Vann tried to give the appearance of only advising—or at least working through—Lieutenant General Dzu, it was clear who was really in charge. Some of the ARVN officers on the II Corps staff referred to Dzu as "Mr. Vann's man."[1]

Vann's biographer, journalist Neil Sheehan, explained Vann's approach to defending Kontum City and ultimately the Central Highlands:

John Vann planned to defeat his enemy as he had seen Walton Walker defeat the North Koreans in the Pusan Perimeter. He would not throw away infantry as Westmoreland had done in sending men against fortified positions in the wilderness. The roles had been reversed. To win the war, the Vietnamese Communists had to come to him, and when they advanced out of the mountains, he would break them on his

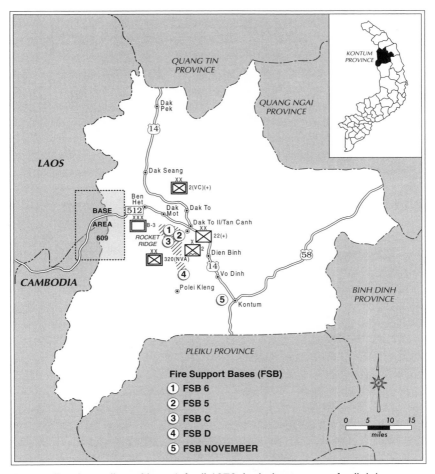

Kontum Province, dispositions 1 April 1972. Includes names of adjoining provinces and countries. Small inset map shows the location of Kontum Province within South Vietnam.

strongpoint. The apparent objective of the NVA offensive in II Corps was Kontum, a garrison and trading center with a population of about 25,000, the capital of the province of the same name and the northernmost town of substance in the Highlands. Kontum was guarded to the north by the regimental base at Tan Canh on a plateau near the district headquarters of Dak To twenty-five miles up the ascending asphalt ribbon of Route 14. Just below Tan Canh and to the west of it, a series of ridgelines ran in a north–south direction, parallel to Route 14 and back down toward Kontum. These were known collectively as Rocket Ridge. . . . The U.S. Army had built a string of fortified artillery positions, called fire support bases or fire bases for short, down Rocket Ridge to shield the road and the northwest approaches to Kontum and had bequeathed these to the ARVN. Before the Vietnamese Communists could attack Kontum, they first had to overrun Tan Canh or crack the firebase line along Rocket Ridge.[2]

The chain of FSBs along Rocket Ridge dominated the valleys and highways on either side of it. Those FSBs and the Border Ranger camps along the border were positioned to control the surrounding area with their own artillery fire and by tactical air strikes.

Almost 50 kilometers north of Kontum City on Highway 14, there was a district town named Dak To. Five kilometers south of it was an airfield named Dak To I. Adjoining Dak To I on the south was a big ARVN base named Tan Canh, and four kilometers west of it was another airfield named Dak To II. Lieutenant General Dzu was worried his forces in the Tan Canh/Dak To area would not be able to withstand an attack by the large enemy force headed his way. He proposed to reinforce his forward defenses by moving the two regiments of the 22nd ARVN Division in Binh Dinh Province on the coast to Kontum Province in the Highlands. Mr. Vann strongly opposed this move because it would leave Binh Dinh Province without any regular ARVN troops and defended by only its own province forces. Vann convinced Dzu to leave the two 22nd Division regiments in Binh Dinh and to free up 22nd Division forces to reinforce Tan Canh and Dak To by extending the 23rd Division's area of responsibility north to include part of Kontum. The II Corps order of battle in the Highlands then included the 22nd Division's controlling its own 42nd and 47th Infantry Regiments and three Border Ranger battalions, plus scout companies, some armored cavalry, and province forces—all supported by 50 tubes of 105- and 155-mm artillery. The Airborne Division controlled six airborne battalions and one Border Ranger battalion and was supported by 16 tubes of 105-mm artillery. The forces in Kontum City were two Ranger battalions and the Kontum Province RF and PF units. The

14th and 19th Cavalry Regiments (actually battalion size) had 50 M-41 light tanks, but the tanks were strung out between Pleiku and Ben Het.[3]

This force seemed formidable, but it was spread over a large area in rugged terrain with a limited road network. Resupply was a problem because the main supply route was the two-lane Highway 14 north from Kontum. Moreover, some of those ARVN units were on isolated FSBs and could be resupplied only by helicopter. Scattering rather than massing the tanks ignored one of the main principles of employing armor. A large force of tanks attacking together can terrify, overwhelm, and defeat the enemy, but the same number of tanks attacking a few at a time can be destroyed a few at a time. Another serious problem was the lack of unity of command. In the Tan Canh/Dak To II area, the commanding general of the 22nd Division commanded his own troops and other forces northeast of Kontum City, including the Border Ranger camps at Ben Het, Dak Mot, Dak Pek, and Dak Seang, plus FSBs 5 and 6. But all the Ruff Puffs belonged to the Kontum Province chief, Colonel Long, who commanded in Kontum City. The II Corps deputy chief of staff for operations was in command in Pleiku. The Airborne Division was ultimately under the control of Saigon and could be withdrawn at any time.[4] As if to emphasize that last point, during 20–24 April the 3rd Airborne Brigade, consisting of the 1st, 2nd, and 3rd Airborne Battalions, was pulled out of II Corps and sent to help defend Hue in I Corps.[5]

At the same time that the NVA invaded I Corps, it increased its pressure on the Border Ranger camps and the FSBs along Rocket Ridge. The 48th and 52nd NVA Infantry Regiments of the 320th NVA Infantry Division were soon in contact with the ARVN units along Rocket Ridge. The friendly forces were pounded with 20-mm and 82-mm mortars, 122-mm rockets, and 105-mm artillery. Analysis of shell fragments positively identified the 105-mm shells as both American and Chinese made.[6]

On 31 March, while attempting to resupply FSB Delta on Rocket Ridge, a "Big Windy" Chinook from the 180th Assault Support Helicopter Company (ASHC) was shot down east of the FSB. The crew managed to get into Delta, but over the next few days all attempts to extract them were unsuccessful. Determined to rescue the crew, a force of five Hueys from the 57th Assault Helicopter Company and six snakes from the 361st Aerial Weapons Company arrived to try again at first light on the morning of 3 April. They were surprised to catch enemy troops in the open launching an assault on the base. It was the 52nd Regiment, 320th NVA Division, making the enemy's first major ground assault in the area. The regiment overran part of the FSB, but the defenders, supported by the helicopters and tactical air strikes, drove it out with heavy losses, including 353 KIA. The Chinook crew was extracted the next day.[7]

Enemy activity around Dak To II was increasing, and by early April MACV had an accurate count of the NVA units in the area. At 0430 on 3 April, the D-10 Sapper Battalion of the 2nd NVA Division attacked the Dak To II airfield with explosive charges and RPGs. The airfield was under continuing attacks by fire through the day, and aircraft reported receiving heavy anti-aircraft fire from north of the airfield. While operating only a kilometer northeast of the airfield, two ARVN M-41 tanks were destroyed by recoilless rifle fire. The ARVN defenders captured three prisoners, who revealed that the 1st and 141st regiments of the 2nd NVA Division were in a staging area on the mountain north of Dak To II and would attack Tan Canh and Dak To II at 0100 on 4 April. They said the NVA 17th Signal, 18th and 19th Transportation, 20th Medical, 12th Anti-Aircraft, and 14th Heavy Weapons Battalions were also in the vicinity. The enemy was clearly ready to launch a major attack against ARVN installations in this area. The airfield at Dak To II was the main terminal from which the FSBs on Rocket Ridge were resupplied. Moreover, enemy control of Tan Canh and Dak To II would threaten FSBs 5 and 6 and open the door to an NVA advance down Highway 14 or through the valley west of Rocket Ridge.[8]

Base Area 609, a large Communist supply depot, was located in the area where the borders of Vietnam, Cambodia, and Laos meet. It was only 15 kilometers west of Dak To II and Highway 14, which runs southeast to Kontum, so the NVA units in western Kontum Province would be supplied from the stockpiles in Base Area 609, and Highway 14 would be their main supply route.[9]

The NVA described its buildup:

The three-border area became alive as if infused with fresh vitality: once again, it was crowded with troops. Many new encampments sprang up; every night, from the strategic corridor, a continuous stream of tanks, artillery prime movers, and trucks poured into the theater.

. . . The High Command reinforced the Highlands with the 2nd Division (under strength), the 320A Division, the 24B Infantry Regiment, the 2 OB Sapper Battalion, and a large number of armed branch, specialized, and technical units. For the first time, the Highlands main-force group had made a big leap forward in both quality and quantity.

Seeing that we were feverishly preparing the battlefield and moving large forces, the enemy predicted that our main strategic offensive and principal direction of attack in the entire South Vietnam was the Highlands. Therefore, since the beginning of 1972 he sent in the 47th Regiment to join the 42nd Regiment in beefing up the defense of the Tan Canh area. At the same time, he stepped up probing activities and sent aircraft to attack our depots and transport lines. On the average, Routes 128, 70, 60, and 50K were attacked by 15 to 29 aircraft sorties daily. Within the space of five days—from 9 to 13 February—alone, thousands of U.S. aircraft of all types carried out bombing strikes in the Highlands.[10]

By early April, only two US air cavalry troops were left in the II Corps area, but they, the FACs, and other pilots reported some tank sightings. However, there were no cases where a second pilot could confirm seeing those same tanks. Neither the ARVN officers nor their advisers at Tan Canh and Dak To II were receiving the US pilots' reports on tank sightings. In early April, some ARVN long-range reconnaissance patrols reported seeing enemy tanks but could not provide accurate descriptions, so their reports were discounted, and it was assumed they actually saw only trucks. At II Corps, most of the senior ARVN officers and their advisers thought there could not be any large concentrations of enemy tanks in the Highlands because none had been both detected and confirmed.[11]

To counter the threat of heat-seeking, ground-to-air missiles being used by the NVA, all Hueys were modified to thrust their engine heat upward rather than to the rear. The Huey door gunners were generally relaxed when flying high, but now, faced with the danger of being blown out of the sky, the door gunners were alert and ready to pop and throw thermite grenades to divert any heat-seeking missiles.[12] The "seeker" on the Strella would home in on the grenade, which was hotter than the helicopter exhaust.

When a scout or C&C helicopter pilot marked a target with smoke, he could usually count on the NVA's opening fire on him. Some "Lessons Learned" published by the 17th Aviation Group described techniques developed to avoid being shot down. Rather than turning quickly to mark the target immediately after it was discovered, the Loaches would mark with smoke during a high-speed run from a different direction, while covered from above by the guns. The Hueys would drop smoke from above small-arms range. The "Lessons Learned" also pointed out that units requesting reconnaissance by the air cavalry tended to think of early morning as the best time to find out if the enemy had moved during the night or would pop up in an unexpected place. However, the slanting rays of the early morning and late afternoon sun made it difficult to see because of shadows and limited light in wooded areas. Also, flying into the rising or setting sun could cause a "whiteout" in which a scout pilot would have limited visibility to his front, and the gunships would have difficulty seeing the scout aircraft. Little or no information was gathered under those conditions.[13]

However, air cavalry scout pilot Captain Jim Stein—call sign "Scalp Hunter Lead"—who was shot down ten times during two tours in Vietnam, said,

> I never heard of or . . . remember having difficulties seeing. . . . Most little birds [OH-6s] had one or two rotor blades painted white, so the lead gunship front seater, who was responsible to watch the little bird at all times, could ID us. We flew with Willie P [white phosphorus] and smoke grenades to identify targets. A Willie P would be attached to the observer's M-60, and if we came under fire, his first move was to pop the Willie P as the pilot would make the call. This was done to get a quick mark on the target, alerting the guns that we were in contact and receiving fire. Also, if the pilot was hit and couldn't make the call, it alerted the guns and C&C of contact and the possibility a little bird was going down. . . . During this period of the battle, we were not flying missions to find the enemy and insert troops. Our mission [in the spring of 1972] was to find the enemy and two days later fly into the area and see which direction they were moving. Most of the time . . . the enemy . . . would see us first and fire at us, but sometimes we lucked out and saw them first.

They gave themselves away more than we found them. We knew they were near, but they could hide.[14]

An air cavalry squadron had a headquarters, a headquarters company, and three lettered troops, A, B, and C. Each cavalry troop consisted of a headquarters, a scout platoon with eight OH-6 light observation helicopters, a gun platoon with eight Cobra gunships, a lift platoon with eight UH-1H Hueys, and an infantry platoon that could be inserted by the lift helicopters. For a typical mission, the troop would employ a C&C ship, three gunships, three scouts, and four lift ships. The minimum force they used on a mission was a C&C ship, two gunships, and two scouts. Most of their aircraft could carry enough fuel for close to two and a half hours of flying time.

In February, the 7th US Squadron of the 17th Air Cavalry Regiment ceased tactical operations to prepare its men and equipment to depart Vietnam. The squadron was scattered at various bases. US units still in Vietnam were experiencing significant racial tensions, drug use among the lower-ranking enlisted men, and alcoholism among the NCOs. So it was even more difficult to cope with those morale and discipline problems in a unit that was not intact, had ceased tactical operations, and was preparing to go home, but the squadron commander managed to hold it all together.

Captain Martin S. Kleiner was the operations officer of C Troop, 7th Squadron. Elements of C Troop were at An Khe, Tuy Hoa, and An Son. The troop was scheduled to depart Vietnam on 6 April, but that plan was suddenly changed when the North Vietnamese launched their invasion on 30 March. On 2 April, the squadron commander was ordered to reconstitute C Troop. He directed Captain Kleiner to take the operating elements forward to Camp Holloway at Pleiku and begin conducting reconnaissance and attack missions in the triborder area. A Troop was already in the United States, but B Troop was still operating out of Camp Holloway. The reconstituted C Troop flew to Camp Holloway, where it was placed under operational control of the II Corps G-3 adviser. It was assigned reconnaissance missions, usually along the border northwest of Pleiku. After returning from a reconnaissance mission, C Troop was debriefed by the II Corps G-2 and G-3 advisers. The old military maxim of "find 'em, fix 'em (hold them in place), and fight 'em" had to be modified to eliminate most of the "fight 'em" part because the air cavalry was now operating in many areas no longer covered by US or even ARVN artillery fire support. Also, to hold down casualties, C Troop was prohibited from employing its own US infantry platoon, which was still with it, and had to rely on Vietnamese troops when it was necessary to put boots on the ground. Even the ARVN infantry platoon was seldom used unless there was a downed aircraft. After one staff briefing, Brigadier General Wear pulled Captain Kleiner aside and told him, "Your mission is to not get another American killed."

Unfortunately, some more Americans assigned to C Troop were killed. When C Troop was reconstituted, it was necessary to reassign some of the pilots. One junior lieutenant, who was one of the least aggressive pilots in the troop, was a qualified OH-6 pilot but had been serving as supply officer and flying Hueys. When Captain Kleiner told him he would be flying as an OH-6 scout pilot, the lieutenant responded he really did not want to be a scout pilot. Kleiner, then 24 years old, explained in a fatherly way that the lieutenant was wearing pilot's wings, was trained as scout pilot, was needed to fly reconnaissance missions, and so was obligated to do so. The lieutenant said he understood. He was soon taking a checkout ride in an OH-6 with the troop's most aggressive pilot flying the Loach. The pilot made a risky third pass over an NVA platoon near Kontum, and they were shot down. It was three days before their bodies could be recovered. C Troop soon lost two more scout aircraft near Pleiku, and three more Americans were killed.

Troop B of the 7th Squadron was working in Kontum Province and providing valuable information on the enemy until 27 April, when it stood down (ceased operations) to prepare for redeployment to the United States.[15] The 7th Squadron of the 17th Air Cavalry Regiment was officially redeployed to the United States that spring. *Stars and Stripes* reported the redeployment as part of the continuing withdrawal of American forces from Vietnam. The unit guidon and a personnel roster with a zero balance were sent home with a lieutenant who was not a pilot, but the personnel and aircraft unofficially remained in Vietnam and their duty extended indefinitely.[16]

Some of the pilots who returned to the United States with A Troop of the 17th Air Cavalry in February were assigned to Fort Bragg, North Carolina, where they were flying old C Model Hueys with the XM 26 ENTAC wire-guided antitank missiles mounted on them. One and a half months after arriving at Fort Bragg, they were redeployed back to Vietnam with their ENTAC firing helicopters to help stem the tide of North Vietnamese tanks attacking into I Corps.[17]

By mid-April 1972, there were increasing clashes between ARVN troops in the Tan Canh/Dak To II area and instances of the enemy probing the South's defenses. The 2nd and 3rd Airborne Brigades on Rocket Ridge were repeatedly attacked by fire, and on 14 April the 11th Airborne Battalion on FSB Charlie, 30 kilometers northwest of Kontum at the northern end of Rocket Ridge, was hit by more than 300 rounds of 105-mm artillery and 75-mm recoilless rifle fire. Then the 48th Regiment, 320th NVA Division, attacked them in force. Tactical air strikes and Cobra gunships inflicted heavy casualties on the attackers, and the paratroopers put up a good fight. However, at 2230 that night the 11th Airborne Battalion was forced to withdraw. Major John J. Duffy, the battalion senior adviser, was the last to leave, and he withdrew under covering fire from the snakes. Duffy estimated that five of the nine NVA antiaircraft guns around the base were destroyed and that a thousand Communist bodies were piled up on the perimeter wire.[18]

The ARVN troops at FSB Delta on Rocket Ridge were overrun and pushed off their base at 1850 on 21 April. The defenders, an airborne company and a company from the 2nd Ranger Group, held out as long as they could but were forced to withdraw when the NVA infantry attacked with three tanks. A marine F-4 controlled by Covey 546 swooped in to hit the enemy with three bombs as they came through the perimeter wire on one side of Delta while the ARVNs withdrew on the opposite side of the base. The fact that tanks participated in the enemy attack was noted in the II Corps adviser's Daily Staff Journal.[19]

We did not know it at the time down at the regimental level, but a new American antitank weapon was coming to Vietnam. It was a *t*ube-launched, *o*ptically tracked, *w*ire-guided missile called TOW and was mounted on both helicopters and Jeeps.

Brigadier General Wear's last visit to Tan Canh and Dak To II was on 21 April. At Tan Canh, he found Colonel Phillip Kaplan and his counterpart, Colonel Le Duc Dat, in the DTOC bunker, busy plotting positions and sending messages. Kaplan briefed Wear on what was going on, and Wear got the locations of the ARVN units so he could plan B-52 strikes as closely as possible. In that period, II Corps was able to get three or four Arc Lights during each 24-hour period. Wear then flew to Dak To II, where he talked to Lieutenant Colonel Robert W. Brownlee, senior adviser to the 47th ARVN Regiment. Wear got the locations of the regiment's battalions, which were generally positioned around the airstrip, for his Arc Light planning. Brownlee pointed to a man slouching in a chair in the corner and said, "That's Colonel Minh, the regimental commander. He's been drunk now for several days."

Brigadier General Wear could feel the gloom in this bunker. As they waited in the doorway for Wear's helicopter to return, Brownlee asked, "General, what do you expect me to do?" Wear was the main advocate for pulling most of the troops in that area back to successive blocking positions, and he was also the most realistic about the probability of a debacle if it was not done. So he wanted in the worst way to take Brownlee and his deputy with him when he left. However, his answer was, "Colonel, just do the best you can to hold this regiment together." His chopper landed, and Wear left. A few days later Dak To II was overrun, and the 47th Regiment quickly dissolved.[20]

By 22 April, MACV was estimating that a total of 127,000 enemy troops had infiltrated into South Vietnam since the beginning of the year.[21] After South Vietnamese units in I Corps disintegrated and fled in disorder, the US personnel in Pleiku conducted defensive drills to practice defending their own compounds. They could feel the threat coming closer and closer.

Brigadier General Wear became so sick he could not remember where he put a B-52 strike. At this point, Vann, a somewhat dramatic man, got down on his knees and begged his old friend to go to Clark AFB, where he could get better medical treatment. Wear reluctantly agreed and left for the Philippines on 22 April. The day after Wear arrived at Clark, Vann's chief of staff, Colonel Joseph J. Pizzi, called to tell him that Tan Canh was under attack. Wear immediately flew back to Vietnam, but General Weyand met him at Tan Son Nhut and told him to return to Clark because his replacement, another brigadier general, was already in II Corps to sign off on B-52 strikes. On his return to Clark AFB, Wear was diagnosed with tropical sprue, an extremely debilitating fungus infection of the stomach.[22] Brigadier General John G. Hill Jr., an army pilot who had graduated from flight school in July 1970, replaced Brigadier General Wear. He served as commanding general of US

Armed Forces and as the deputy senior adviser in II Corps until June 1972.[23]

The North Vietnamese made no attempt to win the hearts and minds of the South Vietnamese civilians. Perhaps the NVA was punishing them because they failed to rise up to support the VC attacks during Tet in 1968. Whatever the reason, the enemy had a callous disregard for the plight of the civilians fleeing from them and intentionally shelled the columns of refugees walking on the roads. Some ARVN soldiers were mixed in with the refugees, but their presence could not justify the wanton killing of so many innocent civilians. The NVA wanted to terrorize the populace and to force them into the defended cities such as Kontum, where they would become a burden for the ARVN defenders. Sanitation conditions in the cities left much to be desired even in peacetime, and with tens of thousands of refugees essentially "camped out" in a city there was a significant danger of disease spreading through them and to the ARVN defenders. Having so many refugees in town also interfered with military operations, and every aircraft bringing in food and medical supplies for refugees meant one less load of food, ammunition, and other supplies for the defending soldiers. In addition, the NVA infiltrated spies and even sappers into the cities with the refugees, which created a serious security problem.

By 23 April, 4 of the 19 FSBs north and west of Kontum were held by the Communists. FSB Charlie fell on 14 April, Delta on 21 April, and FSBs 5 and 6 were evacuated on 23 April by order of the corps commander because they were considered untenable.

The North's official history provides the Communists' version of these events:

> The 2nd Infantry Division (minus) conducted deception operations to attract the enemy's attention to the area north of Dak To. This enabled the 66th Infantry Regiment to complete preparations to attack the headquarters of the puppet 22nd Division and the 42nd Regiment at Tan Canh. Cadre and soldiers of the 66th Regiment secretly built a new road over 100 kilometers long, bringing rice and ammunition all the way up to the assault assembly areas. . . . Front engineering troops built roads to a point only five or six kilometers from enemy positions to ensure that our tanks and artillery

could move forward to carry out the planned attack against the enemy's rear.

On 30 March 1972 . . . Division 320A attacked the 2nd Airborne Brigade's defensive line west of the Po Co [Poko] River, destroying or crippling two enemy battalions and clearing the route of advance to Kontum city. The defensive positions held by the puppet 42nd and 47th Regiments at Dak To and Tan Canh were now isolated.[24]

A draft of the 20 April 1972 "Daily Commanders Evaluation," prepared for Mr. Vann's approval before dispatch to General Abrams at MACV headquarters, described a bad situation:

The ARVN battalion[s] in the Highlands have been in contact almost daily for three weeks, and have suffered severe casualties, and for the most part are maldeployed for a mid intensity war. To properly deploy them would involve giving up district headquarters and population centers. The requirement to defend all will probably mean we will loose [sic] much. Replacements are not coming in to fill losses. Lieutenant General Dzu is reaping the results of sustained poor leadership throughout the chain of command and failure to insist on high standards of performance in training, target acquisition and operations. ARVN failure to insist VNAF perform adequately has led to acceptance of VNAF's substandard performance especially in the vital VR [visual reconnaissance] program and flexibility to respond to many missions.

On the original draft of this message, a handwritten marginal note next to this paragraph says, "Deleted by JP Vann, who wrote, 'We don't need to tell them what they already know.'" The next paragraph sent to General Abrams reported, "A thin line of advisers, FACs, and two air cav troops are holding the corps efforts together. I hope that this U.S. effort will continue to sustain the corps in the forthcoming defensive fight."[25]

9

The Collapse at Tan Canh

It is inconceivable that the South can't hold out against
the North Vietnamese. They are just too good and well-
equipped an army for that—unless the North Vietnamese are
all Prussians and the South Vietnamese are all Italians. . . .
There is always that possibility, of course.
                                    —A Rand Corporation senior analyst

The ARVN 22nd Infantry Division was a large division with four
rather than the usual three regiments and four rather than the
usual three battalions in each regiment. In February 1972, the division commander was Major General Le Ngoc Trien, an officer who
was tired, burned out, and actively lobbying for a new assignment.
His deputy, Colonel Le Duc Dat, who was stationed in Kontum,
wanted to be the division commander and had enough political
influence to get the job despite John Paul Vann's lobbying for
another candidate. Vann had known Dat when he was a province
chief in III Corps and considered him incompetent and corrupt.
Colonel Dat's adviser was Colonel Phillip Kaplan, who became
the commanding officer of MACV Advisory Team 22 and senior
adviser to the ARVN 22nd Division in August 1971. Kaplan had
graduated from Officer Candidate School in 1949 and had served
as a platoon leader in Korea, so he was an experienced combat
leader.[1] After Dat took command, Kaplan established a reasonably
good relationship with him but thought several of the regimental
commanders should be fired.[2]

   While Brigadier General Wear continued to advocate a series of
blocking positions on the enemy's avenue of approach to Kontum,
President Thieu was admonishing his generals not to give up any

more territory. So Vann's strategy was to establish a stronger forward defense to hold the territory northwest of Kontum. He convinced Lieutenant General Dzu that this tactic was necessary, and on 27 January Dzu ordered Colonel Dat to set up a 22nd Division forward CP at Tan Canh. This placed the division headquarters closer to the units it would be controlling during the NVA offensive. Dat's 42nd Regiment was already at Tan Canh, and his 47th Regiment would be moved from Pleiku to Dak To II,[3] about five kilometers west of Tan Canh.

Lieutenant Colonel Robert W. Brownlee Jr., senior adviser to the 47th Regiment, was quoted in *Time* magazine about the NVA's probable intentions in the Highlands: "The enemy's got a new goddamn division and three good regiments across the border in this area, and Tet is coming and Nixon's going to Peking. If I were a Communist political commander I'd say screw the casualties and hit 'em."[4] The 9th Airborne Battalion was also at Dak To II and had one company deployed on a ridge farther north. The Ben Het Border Ranger Camp was five kilometers west of Dak To II. The 40th and 41st Regiments, half of the 22nd Division, would remain on the coast to defend Binh Dinh Province.[5] Binh Dinh was an important province of a million people as well as being the intersection of coastal Highway 1 and Highway 19 that connected Pleiku and the Highlands with the coast.[6]

Elements of the 19th ARVN Cavalry Regiment were sent to Tan Canh to reinforce the 22nd Division's own organic 14th Cavalry Regiment. Although these ARVN tank units were called regiments, they were more equal to a US tank battalion in numbers of men and tanks. Colonel Dat sent this additional armor to Ben Het Border Ranger Camp because he thought any NVA tank attacks would come from that direction. However, the II Corps senior armor officer, Lieutenant Colonel Tuong, argued against this disposition because he thought the tanks should be uncommitted and free to use in counterattacks rather than in fixed positions inside Ben Het.[7]

Colonel Dat was one of those South Vietnamese who believed the northerners made better soldiers. He thought the NVA was superior in just about every way and was probably invincible. This view was ironic because Dat was from the North himself. When Kaplan admonished him about things he failed to do, Dat would sometimes say, "We've been fighting this war a long time." Kaplan's response would be, "That's the trouble!" Dat once sent Mr. Vann a gift, a statue of a Greek warrior with the inscription, "From one warrior to another." Around mid-April, Vann was in the 22nd Division DTOC ticking off for Dat all the basic actions he needed to take, such as "Get out there on the high ground in front of you," "Make contact with the enemy as soon and as far out as possible," and "Bring maximum firepower to bear on him." At one point, Vann said bluntly, "Colonel Dat, you are going to be the first division commander to lose your division because you are going to be overrun!" It was a prophetic statement, but Dat's response was, "Oh, that won't happen." As Vann left Tan Canh, he told Kaplan, "I'll send you a postcard in the POW camp." Kaplan responded, "Not to me, you won't, because I won't be in one." If the 22nd Division were overrun, he intended either to escape or to die trying.[8]

The 22nd ARVN Division compound at Tan Canh was 300 to 400 yards long and about as deep. In addition to the 22nd Division headquarters and three battalions of the 42nd Regiment, some engineers were stationed there, for a total of about 1,200 ARVN troops. Logistics units and other support troops were in a nearby compound, for a total of about 4,000 ARVN soldiers in the immediate area.[9]

Most of the M-41 tanks available to the 22nd Division were at Ben Het on Colonel Dat's order. The 42nd Regiment's CP; its 1st, 2nd, and 4th Battalions; its scout company; and its reconnaissance platoon were at Tan Canh. Most of its 3rd Battalion was eight road miles southeast at Dien Binh on Highway 14, but one company of the 3rd Battalion was on FSB 5, and one of its platoons was on FSB 6.[10] The 42nd ARVN Regiment—the linchpin of Vann's forward defense strategy—ominously had a bad reputation.[11] General Cao Van Vien had seen the 42nd Regiment run from the enemy several times and considered it the worst regiment in his army.[12]

Colonel Dat and his regimental commanders knew the NVA was out there someplace, building up for an attack, and moving toward them. Yet they failed to patrol aggressively or to operate far enough from their bases to learn the size, type, and location of the enemy units. Kaplan, Wear, and Vann pressured Dat to be more aggressive and to locate targets to hit with Arc Lights, but to no avail. The 22nd Division did equip small reconnaissance teams with Starlight night-vision scopes and radios and sent them out to find the NVA, but the teams made no contact. The patrols would only go two to three kilometers beyond their perimeter, not far enough to find the enemy units. Only the 9th Airborne Battalion at Dak To II ventured far enough to make contact with the enemy. It was the first to capture a POW, a 17-year-old from the 320th NVA Infantry Division. When the teenage soldier got out of the helicopter at Tan Canh, he asked, "Is this Saigon?"[13]

In early April, prisoners taken during combat northeast of Dak To said the mission of the 2nd NVA Division and the independent 66th NVA Regiment of the B-3 Front was to take Dak To II and Tan Canh. The 1st and 141st NVA Regiments and the D10 Sapper Battalion, all part of the 2nd NVA Infantry Division, were staging north of Dak To airfield and would lead the assault. The prisoners said that T-54 tanks from a battalion of the 203rd NVA Tank Regiment would join in the attack. The enemy had already reconnoitered the Tan Canh compound four times, and their attack preparations were in the final stages.[14]

In an effort to disrupt the enemy's timetable and to kill as many of the NVA soldiers as possible, more than 100 Arc Lights were used in the 22nd Division's area in the Highlands during a 60-day period ending in early April.[15] Operating outside the perimeters of Tan Canh and Dak To on 19 April, the 1st Battalion of the 42nd Regiment was cut off and surrounded by an estimated two enemy battalions. Not surprisingly, Colonel Dat's relief efforts were ineffective. The isolated troops were not resupplied, so they eventually ran out of ammunition. Two days later only 63 men from the original 360 made it back to their regimental compound.[16]

Mr. Vann's original strategy for a forward defense that would position the 22nd Division forward CP and the 42nd Regiment at Tan Canh and the 47th Regiment at Dak To II was based on his belief that if ARVN troops were surrounded, they would have to stand and fight regardless of the odds against them. If the ARVN troops at Tan Canh could hold out, they would control the approach down Highway 14 to Kontum. However, if the enemy attacked with tanks, that would be a different ball game, and the ARVN troops might not hold out. Despite repeated reports of tank sounds and tank tracks, Vann still did not believe there were any NVA tanks in II Corps. But now, with the enemy attack imminent, he decided to modify his strategy. Perhaps he also decided that Wear's blocking-position strategy was best after all. Whatever his reasons for this change, a major consideration was that John Paul Vann no longer had any confidence in Colonel Le Duc Dat. Referring to Dat, he said, "I'll shoot the little bastard myself if he runs."[17]

Every day during this period, Colonel Phillip Kaplan either saw John Paul Vann in person or talked to him on the radio.[18] Only a day or two before the main enemy attack, Vann and Dzu came to Tan Canh and told Kaplan and Dat, "We ought to start planning and thinking about pulling some forces back toward Kontum. We've got too much up here." They were concerned that the NVA would cut the roads and any ARVN tanks, trucks, and artillery unable to withdraw overland would be lost. The division had twenty-two 105-mm and 155-mm artillery pieces in the area, and more artillery was with the airborne battalion there. Vann and Dzu were now willing to give up the Tan Canh and Dak To area by pulling the division headquarters and the 42nd and 47th Infantry regiments back to Kontum.

Dat and Kaplan understood they were to start planning the withdrawal, but not to execute it until they received orders to do so. Executing a withdrawal when the enemy is already probing and likely to attack at any time is an extremely difficult and dangerous maneuver. Kaplan went over the withdrawal process with Dat. Units would be displaced half a battalion at a time, and strict discipline would be maintained to control the movement. Dat did order ten artillery pieces to be moved south to Binh Dinh on Highway 14, but only four were actually moved. The other crews were too scared to drive through the intermittent artillery and mortar fire on the highway.[19]

Incoming indirect fire on the 22nd Division DTOC at Tan Canh averaged 50 rounds a day from 5 April until midmonth, when it gradually increased to 200–300 rounds a day. It continued to increase until more than 1,000 rounds a day were hitting the DTOC area. On Saturday, 22 April, one battalion of the 42nd Regiment was operating outside the compound when enemy artillery and rockets began falling on Tan Canh at the rate of several rounds a minute. One rocket hit a 105-mm howitzer position, and more than 900 rounds of artillery ammo in the position exploded.[20]

Captain John B. Keller was an adviser in Dak To District about five kilometers north of Tan Canh on Highway 14. At 2330 Saturday night, 22 April, he reported to the II Corps operations center that enemy vehicles were moving to his west–northwest. He requested a Stinger gunship and said the district artillery was firing on the vehicles while they waited for the gunship to arrive. Next to an entry about his report typed into the II Corps adviser's DTOC journal, the note "TRUCKS" was hand printed. This note may indicate that, despite the NVA tanks used in the attack on FSB Delta, the II Corps adviser staff still assumed any enemy vehicle sounds were more likely to be coming from trucks rather than from tanks.[21]

Contacts with large NVA units increased over a two-week period, and by Sunday, 23 April, hostile forces surrounded the entire Tan Canh/Dak To area. The enemy held key terrain overlooking Tan Canh, from which they were able to place observed fire on the ARVN compound. The attacks by fire were not only intensifying, but also becoming much more accurate.

Around 0900 on Sunday, Captain Raymond H. Dobbins, the acting senior adviser to the 42nd ARVN Regiment, was lying in an exposed position on top of a bunker directing US air strikes on targets that his counterpart, the regimental commander, gave him. One battalion of the 42nd, supported by four M-41 tanks, was trying to clear the enemy out of an area near its perimeter. One of the tanks, from the ARVN 1st Squadron, 14th Cavalry, was returning through the main gate at Tan Canh with a wounded crewman when the tank was suddenly destroyed with a FLASH! BANG![22] The ARVNs assumed the tank was hit by an RPG and reported that to Dobbins, who radioed it to Major Jon R. Wise in the 22nd Division DTOC. Wise discussed it with the senior adviser, Colonel Kaplan, and his deputy, Lieutenant Colonel Terrence McClain. The RPG's maximum effective range was about 300 meters, but the nearest enemy was more than 500 meters from the tank, so they doubted an RPG had knocked it out. Kaplan, McClain, and Major George W. Carter, senior adviser to the 14th Armored Cavalry Regiment, left the bunker to see for themselves. As they walked toward the stricken tank, they heard a strange, high-pitched, warbling sound and saw a streak as another missile knocked out another M-41 near the main gate about 150 meters north of them. McClain noticed copper wire trailing from the missile and gathered up 30 to 40 meters of it as he ran toward the second tank. There was a hole about the size of a silver dollar in the armor on the front of the tank, and lying on the ground were the tail assembly and part of the motor from the missile. Two more missiles were quickly fired from high ground in the vicinity of a Buddhist pagoda. The three advisers returned to the DTOC to examine the parts McClain had collected.

The 22nd Division DTOC at Tan Canh was in a large bunker about 100 by 40 by 30 feet and rising 6 to 8 feet above ground level. There were windows between the ground and the roof, which was covered with sandbags and timbers treated with creosote to provide overhead cover. When Colonel Kaplan was inside the bunker, he did what most of us did when we were going to be in a relatively safe place for a while. He removed his helmet and his web gear—heavy with a pistol, ammo, and full canteen—and hung them on a wall peg. The advisers examined the missile tail assembly, which was about three inches in diameter and had two bobbins of wire and two jet nozzles attached to it. This missile was a sophisticated new weapon being employed against them, and they all agreed its use might signal the start of the enemy's main offensive in the Highlands.

At 1031 on Sunday, the 22nd Division DTOC suddenly exploded in fire, smoke, and flying shrapnel as another missile came in through a window. Everyone inside was knocked down, several walls were knocked out, and equipment was strewn around. Twenty ARVN soldiers were dead, and more were seriously wounded. No Americans were killed, but Kaplan had a bleeding shrapnel wound on top of his head, and several of the other advisers were even more seriously injured. Kaplan's interpreter lost part of his ear. The explosion ignited the creosote on the dry timbers, which started burning and filled the bunker with acrid smoke. Kaplan quickly moved to put out the fire. He grabbed a five-gallon container of water they used to make coffee and started to throw it on the flames. Then he realized the fire was already out of control and thought, "This is ridiculous. It's like pissing on a forest fire." He turned around and said, "Get everybody out of here!" An hour later the DTOC bunker collapsed into a smoldering ruin.[23]

Major Julius G. Warmath and Captain David Stewart, the division signal adviser, started working to reestablish vital communications. The advisers had their own much smaller bunker constructed partially above ground, the same as the division DTOC bunker. They used it only for protection from artillery and rocket attacks and for storing rations, LAWs, and other supplies. However, communications equipment was already set up there and functioning, so they moved into it. A few minutes after the Americans left the DTOC bunker, Dat and his staff finally came out of the burning, collapsing bunker. The Vietnamese asked if they could also use the advisers' bunker, and Kaplan agreed. Shortly after noon, they again had a functioning DTOC.[24]

Colonel Kaplan called for a medevac of the seriously wounded Americans and about 40 wounded Vietnamese. Major Warmath assisted Lieutenant Colonel McClain with evacuating all the wounded. They talked the medevac helicopters in through the incoming artillery and rocket fire and helped carry litter patients to the aircraft. Other advisers were busy directing tactical air strikes on enemy targets near the compound. At 1100, John Paul Vann landed through heavy enemy fire to check on the deteriorating situation. He remarked on the absence of any ARVN counter battery fire. Vann directed his pilot to evacuate some of the wounded in his own OH-58, and he, the senior adviser to the corps commander, stayed at the helipad for several hours helping to organize the wounded for loading and even loading some of them himself—all while under heavy artillery and rocket fire. He pointed out that some of the ARVN casualties were being evacuated by American helicopters rather than by VNAF, whose job it was to evacuate ARVN soldiers to ARVN hospitals. Vann's visits usually lasted about 20 minutes, but he may have stayed longer on this particular day to help evacuate the wounded and to determine if Kaplan was really able to carry on as the division adviser. Kaplan's head wound was not deep, but it bled profusely, so he was covered with blood. Before Vann left, he and Kaplan discussed extraction plans in case the advisers needed to be rescued from Tan Canh. There was one US Army infantry company in Pleiku for security at the II Corps headquarters, and it could be used to secure an extraction of the advisers. When Vann left, he took with him several Vietnamese civilians who were employed by the advisers.[25]

This attack was the first time the Soviet AT-3 Sagger antitank missile was used in Vietnam, and on this same day it was used both at Tan Canh in II Corps and against ARVN M48A3 medium tanks in I Corps. Eight Sagger attacks on the M48A3s caused the targeted tanks to explode and burn immediately—something not good for tanker morale. The Soviet AT-3 Sagger was eventually used in all four corps areas. It was a wire-guided, antitank missile 700 millimeters (2.3 feet) long and 120 millimeters (4.72 inches) in diameter. It had a range of 2,500 meters (2,735 yards) and could penetrate 400 millimeters (15.75 inches) of armor—the equivalent of 16 sandbags. However, it did have some vulnerabilities. The wire might break, and the missile could not be fired at night or in heavy vegetation because the gunner had to maintain constant visual contact with both the missile and the target to have constant control of the missile. Because the gunner was exposed while guiding the missile, the ARVN troops were instructed to fire at his suspected location.[26]

The South Vietnamese developed an interesting and apparently effective tactic to defend against the Sagger. An operator controlled the Sagger with a joystick connected to the launcher by a 15-meter control wire. When a puff of smoke from the launcher warned ARVN tanks that a Sagger had been fired, all ARVN tanks other than the targeted vehicle would fire all over the area 15 meters around the plume of smoke emitted at the launcher, with the intent to kill or at least disrupt the operator. The target tank counted to five and then made a sudden move in any direction—an evasive maneuver requiring strong nerves and quick reaction by the targeted tank crew.[27]

At Tan Canh, the Sagger missile explosion in the bunker not only destroyed the DTOC but also had a devastating effect on Colonel Dat and greatly reduced his troops' morale and confidence in their ability to defend Tan Canh. By noon, Saggers had destroyed all five M-41 tanks in the compound and several more bunkers. McClain and Warmath worked constantly through the afternoon to complete the evacuation of all ARVN wounded. The bombardment of Tan Canh continued in the normal pattern until 1900, when a new type of indirect fire was used. The enemy lined up ten RPGs on the high ground near the airstrip. While a heavy artillery barrage held down the ARVN troops, the NVA fired rockets into the ammunition dump. A direct hit started a fire that destroyed hundreds of thousands of rounds of small-arms ammunition, mortar rounds, and M-72s—all munitions the ARVN troops would need to defend Tan Canh. The advisers' billets nearby were severely damaged.

At 2100 Sunday evening, Captain Richard Cassidy, the senior adviser in Dak To District, told the 22nd Division TOC that his counterpart, the district chief, had said tanks were moving through Dak Brung hamlet and toward the Dak To District headquarters. Cassidy requested a Spectre C-130 gunship. His request was approved, and at 2300 a Spectre arrived over Dak Brung and scanned the area with its infrared and television tracking systems. After 15 minutes of searching, the gunship located a column of 18 tanks moving from the east toward Dak To District headquarters. Spectre reported this movement and attacked the tanks with its 105-mm gun.[28] Next, the 9th Airborne Battalion north of Dak To II reported to Colonel Kaplan that it not only heard tanks but also could see their headlights. Kaplan relayed those reports to II Corps and requested a Spectre gunship. When the Spectre arrived, it confirmed 11 tanks and soon spotted 10 more. Despite weeks of reports about tank tracks, there had been no positive confirmation by a US observer who actually saw an NVA tank in the corps area, so John Paul Vann still doubted that there were enemy tanks in the Highlands. When Kaplan reported Spectre's sightings, Vann was skeptical and said, "Well, if there are tanks, congratulations, because these are the first positive tanks that anybody has found in MR II."[29] Kaplan thought that "congratulations" was not exactly the best thing to say to a man with a couple dozen enemy tanks headed his way.

Spectre was firing 105-mm high-explosive (HE) rounds, which normally would not kill a tank. HE rounds were effective against troops, trucks, and bunkers but could not penetrate a tank's armor. A lucky hit from above on a T-54's rear deck, where the engine and fuel were located, might knock out the tank, but the most it could accomplish normally would be to stun and terrify the crew—maybe enough so they would abandon their tank. Spectre reported three tanks knocked out near Dak Brung, and the local Ruff Puffs found a T-54 abandoned but apparently undamaged. Some NVA sappers came down the road, scared off the Ruff Puffs, and reclaimed the tank, which they drove away.[30]

Around midnight, the NVA tank column turned south toward Tan Canh. Colonel Kaplan pushed the ARVN artillery commander to fire on the tanks before they could reach his defensive line, and a battery of four 105s fired one volley toward the tanks. Spectre reported that one round hit a POL truck and another landed within five feet of a tank. Kaplan congratulated the artillery commander, but before the ARVN artillerymen could fire again, Communist counter battery fire drove them into their bunkers. There was no more ARVN artillery fire against the oncoming tanks.

The FSBs on Rocket Ridge were on hilltops and located close enough to be mutually supporting with artillery fire. But Tan Canh was on a small hill in a relatively flat area and not within support-ing artillery range of the nearest FSBs or Border Ranger camps. Tan Canh and Dak To II were within 105-mm artillery range of each other. However, Dak To II was under extremely heavy attacks by fire at the same time Tan Canh was being attacked, so it did not fire in support of Tan Canh that morning.

The enemy armored column crossed two bridges over unfordable streams to reach Tan Canh. Both bridges should have been rigged for demolition, and ARVN engineers should have been standing by to destroy them if necessary. This action required reliable communications back to the DTOC so the engineers could receive an order to blow the bridges. However, the bridges were not prepared for demolition and were defended by only a platoon of local forces with no antitank weapons. As might be expected, the lightly armed Ruff Puff defenders fled when confronted by NVA tanks. This lack of coordination between the regular forces and the territorial forces as well as ARVN's failure to seize this opportunity to block the NVA advance allowed the enemy tanks to continue rolling toward Tan Canh. On the outskirts of Tan Canh Village, some of the tanks stopped, and others drove back toward Dak To. Spectre requested permission to fire on the tanks in Tan Canh Village, but it was denied because there were ARVN dependents in the village.[31] With enemy tanks closing in, Colonel Kaplan checked with his advisers to be certain they understood the escape and evasion plan.

The NVA was still probing and bombarding FSBs 5, 6, and Yankee; Dak To District headquarters; and Dak To II. However, it was employing a tactic the North Vietnamese called "striking at the head of the snake." In this case, the head of the snake was the 22nd ARVN Division CP at Tan Canh, and destroying it was most likely the NVA attack's main objective. On Sunday night, Dat said to Kaplan, "We will be overrun tomorrow. Maybe six o'clock." He had already lost the battle psychologically.[32]

Kaplan now realized that without new leadership, the troops at Tan Canh would most likely not hold against a big attack. Colonel Dat was physically unharmed but mentally incapacitated. He would not respond to Kaplan's recommendations or take any command action. Sunday evening Kaplan and Vann made plans to replace Colonel Dat. Radio contact between Tan Canh and Pleiku required relays and was intermittent at best. Also, Kaplan had difficulty discussing such a delicate matter on the radio without ARVN officers overhearing him. Removing Dat without a replacement already in Tan Canh might give the impression that Dat was being extracted to save him from capture or death, and just a rumor of that might start a panic. Lieutenant General Dzu finally agreed to send up Colonel Tuong from corps headquarters "to be in charge while Dat was called to Pleiku to discuss the planned withdrawal of his forces." After that personnel exchange took place, the change of command would be announced. This plan fell apart when Tuong declined the honor of commanding the 22nd Division.[33]

A long, sleepless night was ahead for Kaplan. Three successive Spectre gunships worked the area until dawn. Although their 105-mm guns were able to slow or temporarily stop the T-54s, they were unable to knock them out because they had only HE rounds rather than high-explosive antitank (HEAT) ammunition, which could penetrate a tank's armor plating. After this NVA tank attack, the AC-130s supporting us in II Corps started carrying HEAT rounds. The 22nd Division's troops had a 106-mm recoilless rifle with armor-piercing ammunition covering the road the enemy tanks were using, but it never fired a shot. Hundreds of LAWs had previously been distributed throughout the division, and the ARVN soldiers were trained to use them. Captain Dobbins persuaded his counterpart, Lieutenant Colonel Thong, to break down one company of his regiment into small hunter-killer teams and send them out to destroy the oncoming enemy tanks. That effort was rewarded when the hunter-killer teams reported they knocked out two T-54s west of the town.[34]

At 0326 on Monday, Spectre reported that ten of the enemy tanks were moving to the high ground north of the compound near the airstrip. The remaining armor was proceeding south of Tan Canh Village and then west toward the ARVN compound. This Spectre returned to Pleiku to refuel and rearm and was replaced by another Spectre gunship armed only with two 20-mm and two 40-mm cannons, neither of which could stop, let alone destroy, a T-54.[35]

The news that a column of tanks was headed toward Tan Canh created a flurry of activity there. The 42nd Regiment commander, Lieutenant Colonel Thong, sent his deputy to an abandoned water tower on the perimeter to direct air strikes on the tanks. The deputy's adviser, 24-year-old Captain Kenneth J. Yonan, grabbed a radio and went with his counterpart so he could communicate with US aircraft and the other advisers. However, when the enemy tanks reached Tan Canh, they unknowingly occupied positions that prevented the two observers in the water tower from leaving. Yonan was able to direct some of Spectre's fire on enemy troops, but he and his counterpart were trapped in the tower, and his radio eventually went silent.

The attack started at dawn when a long line of tanks attacking abreast charged out of the morning mist with guns blazing, engines roaring, headlights on. The tanks and an infantry assault force hit the southern perimeter. The enemy infantry were from the 1st Regiment, 2nd NVA Division, and the tanks were from the 297th NVA Tank Battalion.[36] Unlike some enemy attacks in other places, this tank and infantry assault was well coordinated. The ten tanks that Spectre had reported moving to the high ground north of the Tan Canh compound were now firing their main guns into the compound in support of an infantry attack on the northern perimeter, which the 42nd Regiment's reconnaissance company was defending. The regiment repulsed the first battalion-size attack but was eventually overwhelmed by successive waves of yelling Communist soldiers.[37]

Both friendly and enemy accounts claim someone popped tear gas during the battle. The NVA version is that "the enemy used toxic chemical dispensers to fire asphyxiating and tear gases in a bid to stop our advance. Well prepared in advance, combatants poured water from their canteens onto the towels and gauze masks they carried and used them to cover their mouths and noses, then continued to fight."[38]

A year earlier Tan Canh had been attacked by infantry and sappers who penetrated the minefield, where around 100 of them had been killed inside the wire. The ARVN soldiers had held fast on this occasion, and Kaplan thought they should be able to hold fast now. However, this time was different because the NVA attacked with tanks, and the big T-54s had a devastating effect on the ARVN defenders. Kaplan observed, "The tanks just froze our leadership." Almost all of the eight South Vietnamese tanks had been knocked out before the NVA tanks attacked, and the crews of the remaining ARVN tanks abandoned their light M-41 tanks and ran when they saw the big T-54s coming.[39] The intense bombardment, the attacking waves of Communist infantry, and above all the tanks were too much for the ARVN support troops. About a thousand of them fled in terror.

Captain James T. Vaughan was on duty in the II Corps Tactical Operations Center in Pleiku the night of 23–24 April when Tan Canh fell. Listening on the radio, the two captains on duty followed the action as the defenses unraveled at 22nd Division headquarters. Reports of large-caliber artillery rounds, including 130-mm, falling on the defenders were followed by reports of tanks attacking with their lights on. As the situation grew worse, more and higher-ranking Americans joined the two duty officers to listen to radio exchanges between FACs, helicopters, and the advisers at Tan Canh. It was chaos. Vaughan thought, "The night seemed like it would just never end."[40]

At first light on Monday, around 0600, there was a direct hit on the new DTOC in the advisers' bunker. Colonel Kaplan went to the exit and saw that some sandbags had dropped into the doorway. He started to throw them out of the way and then thought, "We're doing absolutely nothing in this bunker. We can't see anything. We don't know what's going on. The reports we get, I don't know if they're accurate or any good. This is no place to be if you have to fight."[41] Colonel Dat was just sitting, staring, and not exercising any leadership. He would not implement any of Kaplan's recommendations. At this point, Kaplan realized he was no longer an effective adviser to an ARVN division commander but just the squad leader of nine Americans. He assembled the advisers, said, "Let's go, guys," and led them out of the bunker.[42] Kaplan reflected later, "It's better to die on your feet shooting than to suffocate or burn to death in a bunker."[43]

Colonel Kaplan had lost everything but the clothes on his back in the DTOC bunker fire but had managed to come up with a flak vest and an M-16. Incoming artillery rounds and rockets were now falling at the rate of about four a minute and the entire defensive perimeter was under assault by enemy infantry and tanks. Kaplan sent a message, "Get ahold of John Vann and tell him that I want him up here."[44] Vann understood what that meant and was soon in the air, inbound in his OH-58 with CWO Robert Richards flying and Captain Dolph A. Todd following them in another OH-58. They decided the advisers at Tan Canh should move west to a road between the adviser buildings and the minefield around the compound, where they could be picked up by the helicopters.[45]

The advisers reached the road, and about 20 minutes later Dat and some of his officers came out of the bunker and stood around it, only 30 yards from the Americans. One of the advisers yelled at them to get down because they would attract the enemy's attention. They went back into the bunker, and Kaplan never saw Dat again. One report said Dat was last seen walking across the airstrip at Tan Canh when the enemy shot at him and he fell. The NVA claimed that both Dat and Kaplan died on the battlefield.[46]

The first T-54 tank Kaplan saw in Vietnam suddenly broke through the defenses and came roaring down the road toward them. The advisers crouched behind some buildings to hide from the tank. Lieutenant Johnny M. Jones had an M-72 LAW, and Kaplan asked, "Jones, do you know how to use that thing?" Jones responded "You betcha!" So Kaplan told him, "Well, my friend, get yourself a tank. We'll cover you." Jones knew the best place to hit a tank is in the rear where it has the least armor and where the engine is located. As soon as the tank passed, he stepped out, aimed at the engine, and pulled the trigger. The LAW misfired, and the tank disappeared around a corner. Another T-54 came down the same road, so the advisers hid again. As soon as the second tank passed, Lieutenant Colonel McClain tried to kill it with another M-72, but it also misfired, and the second tank disappeared around the corner.[47]

NVA tanks were already inside the compound at Tan Canh, the rescue helicopters were inbound, and the advisers needed to move fast. The road they had originally selected was no longer a safe place for the extraction. They decided part of an old road in the minefield appeared to be the next best place, so they crossed the road to the edge of the minefield. Their next hurdle was to get through the minefield without being blown up. One of the advisers, Staff Sergeant Walter H. Ward, saw the route some ARVN soldiers had taken through the minefield, so the other advisers lined up behind him, and he led them safely to their pickup point. Some of the ARVN soldiers took other routes and were blown to pieces when they stepped on mines. The nine advisers found whatever cover they could and used their radio to talk in the two OH-58s. Three advisers, about the maximum load, got into each helicopter. Kaplan, McClain, and Stewart, the communications officer, remained behind with a radio. As the two small helicopters took off, some panicked ARVN soldiers grabbed on to the skids and dangled below while the OH-58s struggled to gain altitude and escape the increasingly heavy enemy fire.[48]

With ARVN soldiers dangling below the rescue helicopters and three advisers still in extreme danger while they waited to be rescued from Tan Canh, Vann decided the OH-58s should land at Dak To II rather than risk the long trip back to Pleiku. The six advisers and the hanging Vietnamese were dropped at Dak To II. As Vann's helicopter took off again, it was severely damaged by enemy fire and barely made it back to Pleiku. Captain Todd returned to Tan Canh in the other OH-58, extracted Kaplan, McClain, and Stewart, and flew them to Pleiku.

As soon as Kaplan was in the air, he used the OH-58's radio to contact an inbound Huey, the C&C ship he normally received around 0800 every morning. This day it was Gladiator 715 from the 57th Assault Helicopter Company. Kaplan diverted it to pick up the six advisers left at Dak To II. Gladiator 715 picked up the advisers and took off from Dak To II but was quickly shot down in flames and crashed on a sandbar in the Dak Poko River. An explosion was heard, and smoke from the fire could be seen from Dak To II. Because of the many people who saw it go down and the nature of the crash, it was assumed there were no survivors. However, without any immediate way to confirm this assumption, the crew and passengers were reported MIA.[49]

Colonel Kaplan, Lieutenant Colonel McClain, and Captain Stewart arrived in Pleiku at 0830 that morning. At the II Corps TOC, Vann and several of the other senior leaders debriefed Kaplan. Captain Vaughan later described the senior adviser to the 22nd Division: "He was pretty muddy and tired, as I recall. However, he had his head up and acted the part of the leader. I was always very impressed with Colonel Kaplan—thought he was a real soldier."[50] Lieutenant General Dzu asked Kaplan, "Where's Colonel Dat? Why didn't he come out with you?" Dzu said they should not have had so much of their force outside Tan Canh, but Kaplan thought the opposite. Contradicting his own point about concentrating their forces in Tan Canh, Dzu then asked why they had not moved more elements to the south. Kaplan had the impression the corps commander was looking for a scapegoat.[51]

During a telephone conversation with Mr. Vann, Charles Mohr, the *New York Times* Saigon bureau chief, obtained Vann's own description of how he extracted some of his advisers under enemy fire. The day Tan Canh was overrun Vann made eight trips into the area to extract American advisers who were escaping and evading (E&E) the enemy. His helicopter was hit by ground fire on all of his first four trips. On his second trip, the chopper was shot up so badly it was unflyable, and a replacement was sent to pick up the stranded passengers and crew. On his third trip, Vann's OH-58 was hit going in and going out. The OH-58 was built to carry four passengers, but most of that day it was carrying five inside and another three hanging outside on the skids. As he landed at Dak To II to extract the advisers, his helicopter took more hits but was still flyable. However, as the Americans were climbing aboard, 15 to 20 panicked ARVN soldiers tried to get into—or at least hang on to—the helicopter. The pilot had his hands full trying to take off, so Vann, sitting in the left-hand seat, literally had to beat off the ARVNs with his rifle butt. As the chopper lifted off, the heavy exterior weight on the right side tipped it until the rotor blades hit the ground. The chopper flipped over twice and broke into five pieces. All passengers, including Vann, were injured to some degree. Those in the backseat were hurt the worst. The ARVNs who caused the crash then fled on foot, leaving Vann and another injured American to use their rifles to fight off two squads of attacking NVA. Ground fire was so intense that Cobras had to be called in to suppress it before a slick (Huey) could land to extract them. The slick got in and took all the Americans out, but it received nine hits in the process.[52]

The two 42nd Regiment advisers at Tan Canh, Captain Dobbins and Captain Yonan, were in the meantime separated from the division advisers and from each other. Captain Dobbins managed to E&E to a prearranged point, where he was picked up later. Captain Yonan sent his last radio transmission from the water tower where he was directing air support. Aerial searches for missing advisers failed to find him, and he was reported as MIA. In a press conference in Pleiku on 24 April, the day Tan Canh fell, John Paul Vann said he thought four enemy tank battalions were involved in the attack and that "we were expecting armor to be employed for the last two months."[53]

Although NVA often wildly exaggerated its own accomplishments, the following enemy account of the attack on Tan Canh is generally accurate:

Amid thick smoke, the 66th Regiment and the 37th Battalion moved close to the fences of the enemy base. From its secret staging position at the Lower Po Co underwater bridge, the

7th Tank Company went into attack. Our nine T-54 tanks roared down Route 14 like fierce tigers, zipped past the district capital of Dak To, and dashed toward Base 42 (Tan Canh).

At 0510 on 24 April, three color flares shot up in the sky, tracing dimly lit curves in the morning mist. From various directions, our troops charged simultaneously. When the man in front fell, the one behind him took his place: in this manner, the 7th Battalion went into attack to seize a bridgehead. Our tanks violently fired on both flanks of the counterattacking enemy, creating favorable conditions for ground troops to charge toward the interior of the base. One after another, enemy bunkers were collapsed by our tank fire, B-40 [RPG] rockets, and infantry handheld explosives. Several gun nests that put up resistance were crushed by our tank tracks. 7th Battalion commander Pham Van Vuong—with a style of command marked by close contact with his men—was very active and courageous. Always present at the fiercest fighting to resourcefully and promptly resolve all difficult situations, he led his battalion and the tanks in quickly making a deep thrust into the enemy's command center. Pham Van Vuong was later honored by the party and the government with the title of Hero of the People's Armed Forces.[54]

The NVA's official history provides another Communist version:

On 24 April the 66th Infantry Regiment, with tank and artillery support and in coordination with 1st Regiment, 2nd Division, attacked the Dak To–Tan Canh defensive line, inflicting heavy casualties on the enemy's 22nd Division (minus), 4th Tank Regiment, and two enemy artillery battalions. One enemy troop element that broke and ran was caught in a loose net established by the 28th Infantry Regiment and captured en masse. Colonel Le Duc Dat, commander of the puppet 22nd Division, died on the battlefield, and Deputy Division Commander Colonel Vi Van Binh and the entire headquarters staff of the 22nd Division were captured.

An area of northern Kontum with a population of more than 25,000 people was liberated. For the first time in the history of the Central Highlands, our forces had destroyed an enemy divisional base camp located behind a fortified line of defenses.[55]

After dark Tuesday night, 25 April, reports of enemy tanks continued to flow into the II Corps headquarters—three tanks here, five there, nine more in another place. A few were spotted west of Dak To II and others 28 kilometers south near Polei Kleng. The enemy was clearly on the move all night. Some of the NVA tanks and trucks were brazenly driving with their headlights on. Spectre and Stinger gunships and tactical air strikes were called in, and they destroyed dozens of NVA tanks, trucks, and guns. Spectre alone hit 30 to 50 trucks.[56]

10

A Debacle at Dak To

Under the command of Platoon Leader Nguyen Nhan Trien, tank number 377 plunged into a group of enemy [ARVN] tanks and destroyed them one after another. [His] combat team set a record knocking out five tanks in one battle in the Highlands theater.
—*History of the Central Highlands People's Armed Forces in the Anti-U.S. War of Resistance for National Salvation*

The ARVN base at Dak To II was five kilometers due west of Tan Canh. There was a small airstrip on slightly higher ground to the north and a steep mountain north of the airfield. The 22nd ARVN Division's 47th Regiment defended this base. Lieutenant Colonel Robert W. Brownlee Jr. was the regimental senior adviser. His deputy was Captain Charles H. Carden. The regimental CP, most of the regiment's 1st Battalion, and part of the 9th Airborne Battalion were at Dak To II. C Company of the regiment's 1st Battalion was well to the south, and the remainder of the airborne battalion was to the north–northeast. The 47th Regiment's 2nd Battalion was north–northwest of Dak To II. Nine kilometers to the west–southwest of Dak To II was FSB 6, manned by the 1st Company of the 72nd Ranger Battalion and one platoon from the 1st Company, 3rd Battalion, 42nd Regiment, the regiment whose headquarters and other battalions were at Tanh Canh. Seven kilometers almost due south of Dak To II was FSB 5, manned by the remainder of the 72nd Ranger Battalion and one company of the 3rd Battalion, 42nd Regiment. The remainder of the 3rd Battalion was 13 road kilometers away at Dien Binh on Highway 14.

As at Tan Canh, this hodgepodge of intermixed units at widely

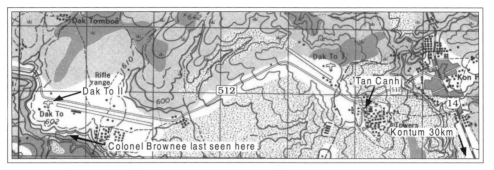

The battles at Tan Canh and Dak To II.

separated locations violated the principle of unity of command, and the many small outlying positions were more vulnerable than fewer, larger troop concentrations would be. However, there may have been other considerations for this configuration. For example, after spending years at the same base, the troops there would know the territory, and something would be lost by moving them to consolidate units. The airborne battalion could be withdrawn at any time, so it was better to spread the paratroops among the various locations. Also, the airborne troops were more likely than the other ARVN soldiers to aggressively patrol out from their bases, and by doing so they might stiffen the other defenders' spines. Nevertheless, the best that can be said for such a complex disposition of troops is that it might confuse the NVA intelligence officers trying to determine where the various ARVN units were located.[1]

Toward the end of March, there were several unsuccessful sapper attacks against Dak To II. In early April, the NVA established a position north of the airstrip with about 200 men, recoilless rifles, and .51-caliber anti-aircraft guns—all dug in. They scored 11 hits on a VNAF chopper carrying Colonel Kaplan, Colonel Dat, and some of the Vietnamese staff. One .51-caliber round blew the door gunner's head to pieces. The NVA was issuing a challenge with this move, but the 22nd Division's response was ineffectual. For five days, the 47th Regiment tried to drive out the NVA troops in this position by using three battalions of infantry, tanks, and 10,000 rounds of artillery fire. All that harassment finally wore down the NVA, so they packed up and left. The 47th should have wiped out that much smaller enemy force in a day. Kaplan considered the regimental commander, Colonel Minh, totally inept at using his available firepower and called this encounter, "the worst example of leadership I have ever seen anyplace." Both Dat and Kaplan thought Colonel Minh incompetent, and they finally managed to get him relieved a few days before the main NVA attack.[2]

A POW from the 400th NVA Sapper Regiment, who was captured on 6 April, said two of his regiment's battalions, K3 and K37, were operating in the Tan Canh/Dak To area. He also revealed that four or five of the 320th NVA Infantry Division's battalions had suffered so many losses from ground combat and Arc Lights that they were combat ineffective. He added, however, that a steady stream of replacements was arriving in the Communist B-3 Front, so those units would soon be back to full strength and combat ready.[3]

The Airborne Division was part of the South Vietnamese government's strategic reserve. Perceiving a greater need somewhere else, the Joint General Staff shifted the Airborne Division's light command post and one airborne brigade of three battalions out of II Corps on 20 April. To compensate for this troop loss, the 6th Ranger Group would be transferred from Hue to II Corps. The 23rd ARVN Division assigned its own 53rd Regiment to assume responsibility for the paratroopers' former area of operations.[4]

Our concerns about our own troops' will to fight were increased by the reports about how ARVN was responding elsewhere. A 22 April *Pacific Stars and Stripes* article headlined "Scared S. Viets Refused to Fight at Hoai An—Adviser" quoted an extracted, wounded adviser who said the Communists were able to capture the district capital because both ARVN and the local militiamen refused to fight the NVA and abandoned the town without a fight. The militia forces guarding the town "neatly stacked arms, changed into civilian clothes and joined the local population." ARVN soldiers refused to leave the safety of their bunkers in their camps. Speaking from his hospital bed, the adviser said, "They were good at hunting down the Viet Cong but were scared of the North Vietnamese."[5]

The enemy attacks on Tan Canh and Dak To II were planned as a one-two punch—two successive phases of one big attack—on Monday, 24 April. While attacking Tan Canh, the NVA continued to soften up Dak To II with heavy artillery and rocket bombardments. As soon as its assault on Tan Canh overwhelmed the ARVN defenders and sent them reeling south, the NVA turned to Dak To II. The attacks by fire increased as the enemy probed the base's defenses.

It was the 2nd NVA Division supported by attached units that attacked Tan Canh and then Dak To II. However, there is some discrepancy among the NVA, ARVN, and US accounts as to which NVA units participated in each attack. The units attacking Tan Canh were probably the 66th NVA Infantry Regiment, the 37th NVA Sapper Battalion, artillery from the 40th and 675th NVA Artillery Regiments, and the 7th Tank Company of the 297th NVA Tank Battalion. The units attacking Dak To II were probably the 1st Regiment, 2nd NVA Division, reinforced with the 10th Sapper Battalion. They were supported by four tanks diverted from Tan Canh, which were probably from the 7th NVA Tank Company.[6]

In preparation for their attack on Dak To II, the Communists built a road 200 kilometers long over a high mountain and through dense forests to bring ammunition and supplies to their staging area. At night, they carried logs from two or three kilometers away to bury them close to the ARVN perimeter barbed wire, where they would be available for building underground shelters when the fighting broke out.[7] If the 22nd Division troops had aggressively patrolled well beyond their own lines, they could have detected those preparations.

Captain Carden, the deputy senior adviser, saw two T-54s move onto the airfield. One positioned itself at the west end to cover the road from Ben Het, the Border Ranger Camp where Colonel Dat had foolishly sent most of his armor. The other T-54 stopped in the center of the airstrip, turned its 100-mm gun on the 47th Regiment's CP bunkers, and systematically destroyed all of them one by one. The defenders' last two operating M-41 light tanks managed to move to a position on the flank of the T-54 and 800 meters away. They boldly fired three rounds each at the T-54, but the M-41s' 76-mm guns were no match for the T-54's heavy armor. The NVA tank quickly recovered, spun its turret around, and used its 100-mm main gun to destroy one M-41 with a first-round hit and the other M-41 with a second-round hit.[8] Cobra gunship pilot Pete Peterson spotted an enemy tank on the runway at Dak To and fired one of his 2.75-inch rockets at it. He hit the tank, but the tank ignored it. Peterson tried again with a second rocket. Still no results. The type of rockets his Cobra was armed with could not knock out a T-54.[9] It was lucky that the TOW helicopters were on the way.

About this time, a relief column of 12 M-41 light tanks from the 2nd Armored Brigade and a platoon of infantry left Ben Het to counterattack the enemy at Dak To II. They crossed the bridge at Dak Mot and were barely one kilometer along the five-kilometer drive to Dak To II when they were ambushed. A large NVA force was waiting for them on the adjacent high ground. The enemy scattered the ARVN infantry and used recoilless rifles, RPGs, and possibly Sagger missiles to destroy 9 of the 12 ARVN tanks. The 3 surviving M-41s scurried back to Ben Het. Even if the M-41s had reached Dak To II, all 12 of them probably would have been destroyed by the two T-54s lying in wait on the airfield.[10] This push was the last ARVN attempt to counterattack during the battles for Tan Canh and Dak To II.

Things were falling apart fast at Dak To II. After dealing with the evacuation of the advisers from Tan Canh, Lieutenant Colonel Brownlee and Captain Carden had reported the crash of the Huey carrying six of them and then turned their attention to their own situation. Brownlee and Carden tried to locate their counterparts, but the regimental TOC was deserted, and none of 47th Regiment's officers could be found. Those officers apparently decided the battle was already lost and deserted their troops. Without officers to control them, the troops abandoned their posts and fled Dak To II en masse. Brownlee and Carden no longer had counterparts to advise, and the compound was rapidly being overrun. It was time for them to leave. They burned some documents, grabbed their radio and a few supplies, and went out over the defensive perimeter to the southeast.[11]

Moving cautiously through small arms and mortar fire, the two American advisers managed to reach the Dak Poko River. There was a footbridge, but the river around it was already clogged with wounded and dead ARVN soldiers who had been mowed down by the NVA as they tried to cross the bridge. Brownlee and Carden moved about 700 meters west along the north bank of the river until they reached a spot where they could cross. It was a wide river, approximately 50 meters across, but they made it to the south side— where they found the bank was about 20 meters high. Captain Carden climbed to the top and looked back at Colonel Brownlee, who motioned to him to continue going south. Brownlee was ill, had a cold, and needed to catch his breath. Carden went about 100 meters beyond the river to get out of a mortar barrage and found Sergeant Cao Ky Chi, their interpreter. They called out to Colonel Brownlee and started to go back to search for him but were driven out of the area by intense small-arms fire. Carden and Chi evaded some NVA soldiers and made their way to FSB 5, where they were extracted with the troops manning that base. When Carden last saw him, Brownlee had his helmet and web equipment, a compass, a .45-caliber pistol, an M-16, and a Claymore mine bag full of M-16 clips. Carden thought Brownlee had a good chance of surviving if he made it to the top of the riverbank. For the next few days, an air cavalry troop and several advisers, including Mr. Vann, flew over the entire area looking for Brownlee and Captain Kenneth J. Yonan, who had been last seen in the water tower at Tan Canh. They were never found.[12]

I knew Lieutenant Colonel Brownlee because we both had attended the adviser meetings in Qui Nhon. He was 42—almost exactly a year older than I—and a large man. At An Khe, we heard how the two 47th Regiment advisers at Dak To II escaped over the defensive perimeter at the south side of the compound as enemy tanks smashed into the north side. Knowing Brownlee and knowing what had happened to him could happen to any regimental adviser made his loss more personal to me. We decided to get into better shape in case we had to make a similar escape and evasion. We did not want to need a rest stop if enemy soldiers were in hot pursuit. Every evening before dinner we did some calisthenics and then ran from the Green House to the end of the 6,200-foot runway built by the US Army engineers for the 1st Cavalry Division and back to the Green House. The main purpose of that two-and-a-third-mile run was to help us survive if we ever needed to E&E, as Brownlee and Carden did—but we also worked up a good appetite for dinner.

An NVA history described the attack on Dak To II:

> Our artillery shifted its bombardment to the Dak To 2 Base. At 0800, when it had become obvious that Base 42 [Tan Canh] could be annihilated, the Front's Command advocated a quick and bold attack on the Dak To 2 Base.
>
> The 1st Regiment (2nd NVA Division), reinforced with the 10th (Sapper) Battalion, carrying out the task of interdicting the enemy between Dak To and Tan Canh, was ordered to strike directly at the den of the (ARVN) 47th Regiment at the Dak To 2 Base. Four T-54 tanks and one self-propelled 57-mm AA gun were also ordered to leave Base 42 [Tan Canh] to join the fight. Under the command of Platoon

Leader Nguyen Nhan Trien, tank number 377 plunged into a group of enemy tanks and destroyed them one after another. Nguyen Nhan Trien's combat team set a record knocking out five tanks in one battle in the Highlands theater. Enemy resistance was swiftly crushed. Our troops were in complete control of the Dak To 2 Base.[13]

By 25 April, ARVN equipment losses already reported in II Corps included twenty-three 105-mm howitzers, seven 155-mm howitzers, and ten M-41 tanks. On the morning of 25 April, the NVA was preparing to tow away three American-made 105-mm howitzers abandoned by ARVN at Dak To II when a flight of F-4s used laser-guided 2,000-pound bombs to destroy them.[14]

The US Army's artillery crews have a strong tradition of never abandoning or surrendering their guns in working order. If they cannot take their guns with them, they destroy them and all remaining ammunition. The US advisers tried to instill this ethic in the ARVN artillery officers, many of whom were sent to the US Army's Artillery School at Fort Sill, Oklahoma, where they should have learned it firsthand. Yet in numerous instances ARVN allowed the NVA to capture 105-mm and 155-mm artillery pieces in good working order and with large stocks of ammunition. The NVA formed new artillery units to use the captured American artillery pieces to fire the captured American artillery rounds at us.[15]

The remnants of the 22nd Division fled Tan Canh and Dak To II in terror. A few ARVN stragglers reached Vo Dinh on Highway 14. The 300 to 400 soldiers of the 47th Regiment who reached Ben Het were airlifted from there to Kontum City.[16] In addition to the fleeing ARVN soldiers trying to evade combat or capture, a growing stream of civilian refugees was moving south down Highway 14 toward Kontum City. A FAC covering the area northeast of Kontum reported, "There were three busloads of refugees coming down the road. The North Vietnamese opened up on them with RPGs—blowing hell out of those buses. People began flying all over."[17]

When Tan Canh was overrun, one of the ARVN soldiers manning a radio monitoring station escaped by taking a dead NVA soldier's uniform and wearing it over his own ARVN uniform. As he worked his way back toward Kontum, he saw enemy tanks on Highway 14 run over the bodies of civilians killed by the enemy artillery.

When he got close to friendly lines, he removed the NVA uniform and made contact with an ARVN unit.[18]

After being involved in heavy combat in the Hue area, the 6th Ranger Group was transferred to II Corps to replace the Airborne Division troops who were pulled out on orders from Saigon. The Rangers initially went to FSB Bravo north of Vo Dinh on Highway 14. Their senior adviser, Major James Givens, and his deputy, Captain William H. J. Vannie, followed the action on their radio as Tan Canh and Dak To II were overrun. They later watched as the remnants of the 22nd Division straggled past them in groups of 5 to 15. The retreating ARVN soldiers were carrying very few small arms and no crew-served weapons. Many of them had discarded their web gear and steel helmets. They were completely disorganized but displayed no panic. It was if they were out for a Sunday afternoon stroll.[19]

Immediately after the disasters at Tan Canh and Dak To II, Brigadier General Hill sent out three helicopters on search-and-rescue missions to find any advisers who were trying to evade capture. Lieutenant Colonel Stanislaus J. Fuesel, the II Corps artillery adviser, flew in one of those helicopters on three successive days. On 25 April, he rescued two US advisers fleeing Tan Canh and later picked up seven ARVN soldiers. On the first of these three days, John Paul Vann saw ARVN soldiers on one of the threatened FSBs still firing a 105-mm howitzer, and he ordered Fuesel to get the firing pin from that gun so it would not be immediately usable if the NVA captured it. There was a US artillery captain aboard Fuesel's helicopter, so Fuesel set him down on the FSB with a radio. The captain managed to take the firing pin, but extracting him was difficult because panicked ARVN soldiers mobbed the helicopter when it landed and then hung on to the skids as it took off.[20]

Following the loss of Dak To II, Tan Canh, and so many FSBs, a meeting was held in the ARVN conference room at II Corps to assess the situation. Lieutenant General Dzu wanted to use B-52s to bomb all the lost bases and even friendly villages. He called for "bombs, bombs, bombs!"[21] Mr. Vann attributed part of the 22nd Division's collapse to "years of very incompetent leadership and the defeatist attitude, particularly of General Trien [Major General Le Ngoc Trien], the former 22nd ARVN Division commander, who for two and a half years had made it one of his major objectives to convince all of his subordinates they could not defeat the NVA."[22]

ARVN FSBs 5 and 6 were the last remaining FSBs on Rocket Ridge. Lieutenant General Dzu now considered them untenable, and on 25 April he ordered them evacuated. The NVA soon occupied them and could then control Highway 14 by fire. They could also fire on the remaining ARVN-held FSBs to the south to hasten ARVN withdrawal from those bases.[23] There was no longer any significant ARVN force between the NVA and Kontum.

With the NVA threat to the FSBs and Border Ranger camps northwest of Kontum growing daily, Mr. Vann called for volunteers to augment the adviser teams in the threatened area. Americans serving in safer areas volunteered to go into isolated ARVN camps or FSBs and to stay there despite the danger because they knew that if the base were overrun, John Paul Vann would rescue them. They had that much confidence in him.[24]

Captain John E. "Jed" Peters was an artillery adviser in Binh Dinh Province when he volunteered to go as an adviser to the 72nd Border Ranger Battalion on FSB 5. The other American on FSB 5 was First Lieutenant James "Mack" Cloninger, who had been an adviser in Binh Dinh Province when he volunteered in February to go to the Highlands, where the action was. About 260 men from a variety of ethnic groups were on FSB 5. One entire company consisted of Khmer soldiers. Peters arrived in early April. Although the base never faced an NVA ground assault, it was subjected to sporadic artillery and rocket fire. With only one PRC-25 radio and tenuous contact with higher headquarters or aircraft, Peters put in air strikes and directed AC-130 gunships against the NVA. However, the ARVN artillery never fired a shot all the time he was there—probably because they did not have forward observers deployed who could identify targets and adjust fire.

FSB 5 was a good defensive position because the slopes on all sides were so steep that an infantry assault against it would be especially difficult. However, it was not an easy place to resupply. It was dangerous to fly into, out of, or even over because the NVA surrounded it with anti-aircraft weapons. This FSB could probably hold out as long as its ammo, food, and water held out, but if the NVA could cut it off and prevent resupply for long enough, the troops there would eventually be lost. When the order came to evacuate FSB 5, a chopper came for Peters, Cloninger, and some of the Yards. The others walked out.[25]

Although there was no time pressure, the FSB evacuation was

not well organized or methodical. Captain Peters was ordered to take the breechblocks from the six 105-mm artillery pieces on the FSB so the guns could not be fired if the NVA captured them. He told the artillery battery commander what he had to do, and the ARVN officer agreed somewhat reluctantly to give him the breechblocks. Just as the battery commander was handing him a heavy canvas bag, a helicopter landed to extract Peters, and he had no chance to check the contents of the bag before they landed in Pleiku. He found six M-12 panoramic telescope sights in the bag, but no breechblocks. He flew back to FSB 5 and told the battery commander he must have the breechblocks, all six of them. The ARVN officers and troops were resentful that the Americans were departing without them, and some of the troops were panicked with fear that they would be captured by the NVA. However, the battery commander finally gave Peters the six breechblocks, and Peters took them to Kontum.[26] Hooks (Chinooks) successfully extracted three of the six 105-mm howitzers on FSB 5, and late on the afternoon of 26 April US tactical air strikes destroyed the remaining three howitzers as well as two that had been abandoned to the enemy at Dak To District Town.[27]

As the South Vietnamese forces manning the FSBs on Rocket Ridge abandoned their positions or were driven off, in some cases they were ambushed near the base of the mountain. Most of the withdrawals were not well planned and executed, and after an ambush they degenerated into individuals or small groups trying to E&E the enemy. The paratroopers withdrew in better order, and most of them made it to Highway 14, where they were picked up and brought to Kontum.[28]

Thousands of Montagnard refugees fled southward from the fighting around Tan Canh and Dak To and made their way to Kontum City.[29] When the undisciplined 22nd ARVN Division soldiers fleeing Tan Canh and Dak To II and the troops from the abandoned or overrun FSBs arrived in Kontum, they were collected in the MACV compound. Master Sergeant Stevens said they defecated in the sinks, threw feces on the walls, and generally trashed the place.[30]

After the fall of Tan Canh and Dak To II, the 22nd Division units in Kontum Province were pulled back to Pleiku and later moved to Binh Dinh Province. The division was reorganized in Binh Dinh with replacements, 12 new battalion commanders, all new regimental commanders, and a new division commander, Colonel Phan Dinh Niem. Colonel Kaplan, his adviser, considered Niem a good officer. He was promoted to major general and remained in command of the 22nd Division until the end of the war.[31]

The loss of Tan Canh and Dak To II was an enormous setback for John Paul Vann.[32] When the ARVN defenders at Tan Canh and then Dak To were overrun and routed by the enemy's tank-led attacks, it seemed like a rerun of what had happened in I Corps. The II Corps headquarters "fell into a blue flunk." Morale sank, and a sense of defeatism set in. Then Captain Vaughan saw Mr. Vann quickly turn around the sense of impending doom. Vann assembled all the II Corps staff and advisers at the Daily Update briefing the next morning and "lit into them." He told them in no uncertain terms that, far from being overrun by the enemy, they were going to use Arc Lights and tactical air strikes to destroy three North Vietnamese divisions. He was like a football coach talking tough to his losing team at halftime. Vaughan thought it was the greatest pep talk he had ever heard and an outstanding example of Vann's strong personality and dynamic leadership.[33]

At An Khe, as we talked about the collapse of ARVN units in I Corps and the rout of the 22nd ARVN Division at Tan Canh and Dak To II, we wondered whether our own 44th Infantry Regiment troops would run or stand and fight if they were attacked by tanks. We were not encouraged by descriptions of how the 22nd Division troops threw down their weapons, abandoned their defensive positions, and fled in terror from the attacking Communist tanks. I knew exactly how my grandmother, the daughter of a Civil War soldier, would describe their conduct: "They skedaddled!"

11

A New Team
for the Defense

Anytime the wind is blowing from the north where B-52
strikes are turning the terrain into moonscape, you can tell
from the battlefield stench that the strikes are effective.
               —John Paul Vann speaking about the B-52 strikes
                                        around Kontum in May 1972

Tan Canh and Dak To II were now held by the enemy, and the 71st
and 95th Border Ranger Defense Battalions at Ben Het, the 90th at
Dak Seang, and the 88th at Dak Pek were suddenly behind enemy
lines. They could be resupplied only by air.[1]

Brigadier General John G. Hill Jr., Brigadier General Wear's
replacement, had graduated from West Point in 1946 and had
earned the Distinguished Service Cross and the Silver Star in Korea.
He was an experienced fighter, and Vann would need a fighter in
the battle ahead. Hill was also a qualified army aviator. General
Abrams told Hill he would be in command of the US troops, but
Vann would be in charge of II Corps. Hill and Vann had known
each other for years but were not close friends. They both had been
on the staff of a Reserve Officers' Training Corps summer camp,
in the same US Army headquarters in Germany, and in III Corps
as advisers to ARVN divisions in 1964–1965. At the beginning of
his current tour, Hill had served as deputy commanding general
of the 101st Airborne Division, and when the 101st went home, he
had been assigned to close down the big American base at Cam
Ranh Bay. Hill had that last job virtually running on autopilot by

the time Vann asked to have him assigned as his deputy. If Vann had asked Hill if he wanted to work for him, Hill would have said no. But he was not asked, and there was an important battle to be fought and won.[2]

Brigadier General Hill considered John Paul Vann abrasive and self-centered and saw him run roughshod over people. However, during the six weeks he spent with Vann he realized what a good fighting man he was. Vann never asked his subordinates to do anything he would not do himself, and Hill never knew any officer who got so much loyalty from his troops. Hill had more military experience than Vann but could not equal Vann's influence with the Vietnamese. Vann was the one American who came, stayed for a decade, and showed the Vietnamese he cared. This feeling and his good rapport with the Vietnamese enabled him to look them in the eye and say things like, "You really screwed that one up!"[3]

Hill arrived in Pleiku the day after Tan Canh and Dak To II fell. Vann, using his own helicopter, took his new deputy on a guided tour of the battlefield but gave him no specific instructions. During that initial tour and later, there was never any question about their ability to hold Kontum. Hill knew he could not inspire the Vietnamese the way Vann did, but he could get the battle organized. He moved quickly to accomplish three things. His first priority was to get the fire support organized and coordinated. His second priority was to cut the number of men in the DTOC. The G-3 and deputy senior adviser, Lieutenant Colonel Bill Bricker, was a key man, and Hill considered him a "battlewise guy." However, there were so many excess men in the DTOC that it was difficult for the essential staff members and their advisers to get at their own maps to do their jobs. He cleared the unnecessary staff out of the DTOC. Third and most urgent, Hill needed to develop a system to control all the aircraft already filling the airspace above Kontum.[4]

The US Army's Cobra gunships were providing fire support; US Army Hooks were transporting supplies into Kontum and taking refugees out; and slicks were providing C&C ships and tactical airlift for ARVN troops. The USAF FACs were in the air controlling air strikes by USAF, US Navy, and US Marine Corps fighter-bombers. USAF AC-130 Spectre gunships were attacking targets, and USAF C-130s were landing with supplies. VNAF C-123s were landing with supplies and taking out refugees; VNAF A-1s were making tactical air strikes; and VNAF fixed-wing "Spooky" gunships were attacking targets. ARVN L-19s were flying overhead to direct artillery fire. The sky was already crowded, and Brigadier General Hill knew it would get worse when the battle for Kontum started. He set up an "air boss," usually a lieutenant colonel or major, who would fly overhead in an OH-58 to serve as the "traffic cop" for all army, USAF, and VNAF aircraft coming into the area. Hill asked for and got Colonel John A. Todd, deputy commander of the 1st Aviation Brigade, to organize the US air cavalry and other US Army air assets. At the height of the Battle of Kontum, as many as 250 tactical air strikes and 50 B-52 strikes were made in one day, so Hill asked the USAF to provide an officer to help coordinate them, and he eventually obtained the services of Colonel Donald B. Swenholt, whom he considered an especially good officer.[5]

Vann and Hill also thinned out the US presence in the Highlands. The third-echelon aircraft maintenance was moved from Pleiku to Cam Ranh Bay. In a worse-case scenario, if Kontum was lost and the remaining ARVN troops and their advisers were defending Ban Me Thuot, at least they would still have helicopter maintenance available outside the battle area.[6] Brigadier General Hill's attitude toward aircraft maintenance was, "If the pilot breaks it today, I want the maintenance officer to fix it tonight so the pilot can break it again tomorrow."[7] Company D (a rifle company) from the US Army's 1st Battalion, 12th Cavalry, was placed under the operational control of the 17th Aviation Group to provide an immediate reaction force to defend the Pleiku area.[8]

There was never a strong bond or even a smooth and effective working relationship between Colonel Ly Tong Ba and his adviser. Colonel Keller did not hesitate to criticize Ba in public, which created ill will between them. Mr. Vann considered replacing Ba, but Brigadier General Hill pointed out that the 23rd Division commander had not been given an adequate chance to prove himself and that the possible replacements, including the other ARVN colonels still in Kontum, might not be any better. Hill thought the airborne commander especially was all talk and no fight. However, he told Vann that Keller had to go, and Vann agreed.[9]

After relieving Colonel Keller—and with a major battle about to start—Mr. Vann needed to find a replacement fast. Colonel R. M. Rhotenberry was scheduled to replace Keller at the end of the summer. However, when Vann asked to have him sent to Vietnam immediately, he learned that Rhotenberry was recovering from a medical problem and could not come for a month or two. As an interim replacement for Keller, Vann selected Colonel John O. Truby, the senior military adviser for Civil Operations and Revolutionary Development Support (CORDS) in II Corps. Truby was stationed in Nha Trang, where he served under Thomas Barnes, a State Department civilian who was in charge of CORDS in the corps area. As Barnes's military deputy, Colonel Truby had traveled all over II Corps, so he knew all the higher-ranking ARVN officers and their counterparts and was abreast of the current military situation. He also knew the territory. Truby had come to Vietnam in 1962 as part of the first large cohort of advisers ordered there on short notice by President John F. Kennedy. During that one-year tour, he had been the G-3 operations adviser at II Corps, so he was familiar with the II Corps area. Truby also knew what the NVA was trying to do and understood Vann's strategy. Vann needed Truby in his CORDS assignment, but he needed him more urgently in Kontum.[10]

John Paul Vann notified Colonel Truby about his new assignment and personally flew to Nha Trang to pick him up. During their flight into Kontum, Vann outlined the existing problems and gave Truby his mission. His first priority was to keep the airfield open. With the highways interdicted by the NVA, the airfield was going to be Kontum's lifeline. Vann insisted the B-52 strike planning must be done by the Americans alone and that the map showing where those strikes were planned must be kept covered and not shown to anyone else. He also wanted the other US air assets tightly controlled because they gave him leverage with the Vietnamese. One of the things Vann wanted to improve was information sharing with the ARVN staff, and he knew the status of Arc Lights was good trading material to get better information and coordination from the ARVN officers. Truby also understood that it was necessary for him to establish a good working relationship with Colonel Ba.[11]

Colonel Truby arrived in Kontum on 28 April and found the situation chaotic. As was the case with most ARVN divisions, from the time the 23rd Division's regiments had been formed, they had been deployed independently to cover wide areas of the division's area of operations. They had never been assembled so that all the regiments and support units would operate together as a complete division. And of course they had never conducted a division-size perimeter defense. A different problem for Truby was the large number of US Army NCOs who were the remnants of logistical units with no further mission in Kontum. The NCOs wanted to stay, but they all had logistics rather than combat arms experience. To retrain and organize them would take too long, so Truby sent them all to Pleiku. Colonel Truby inherited a good adviser staff in Kontum. They were efficient and reliable. His deputy and G-3 adviser, Lieutenant Colonel Bricker, was a mainstay who helped him a great deal. Bricker knew Vann and spent time encouraging him because Vann was edgy about how things were going.[12]

Colonel Truby's selection as the division's adviser at this critical time was fortunate for another reason. When he was selected to attend the Command and General Staff Course at Fort Leavenworth, Kansas, in 1956, he had been transferred there several months before his classes started. Truby's interim assignment was to write an academic exercise to teach how an infantry division should conduct a perimeter defense. Now, with the chips down and the stakes high in Kontum, he would have a chance to put that knowledge to good use.[13]

To start, Colonel Truby invited his South Vietnamese counterpart to walk the entire perimeter with him. They talked about coordinating the limiting points between units and how important it was to be certain adjacent units were tied in to form a tight perimeter so the enemy could not penetrate between them. Truby also emphasized the need to have the defensive fire coordinated to make it mutually supporting. Colonel Ba understood all this. The troops' foxholes were only 6 to 12 inches deep, so Truby explained why they should dig deeper to make their foxholes 4 to 5 feet deep so they could let a tank roll over them and then pop up to hit it from behind. As Ba visited his soldiers' positions, he would explain this on the spot to them while their officers took notes. Colonel Truby had a positive feeling about Colonel Ba and liked him. He thought that he was a good commander and that together "they could pull it off." Ba knew his soldiers lived in terrible conditions—constantly out in the field, always dog tired, and with only ten days' leave every year. Ban Me Thuot, the home of the 23rd Division, where most of the soldiers' families lived, was 250 kilometers south of Kontum on Highway 14. Seeing their families so seldom was bad for morale, so Ba emphasized the importance of winning the coming battle.[14]

Troops, ammunition, and supplies transported by truck from Qui Nhon farther down on the coast traveled 180 kilometers up Highway 19 to Pleiku, and those going on to Kontum traveled another 45 kilometers north on Highway 14 to Kontum. Much of this 225-kilometer route was steep and winding, and all of it was vulnerable to road mines and enemy ambushes. Before the NVA invasion started, the population of Kontum had been about 25,000, but tens of thousands of refugees passed through the city during the Easter Offensive. The Communists still blocked Highway 14 between Pleiku and Kontum, so the only way to resupply the city or evacuate refugees was by air. Anti-aircraft fire threatened the transports flying in and out of Kontum, and enemy artillery and rockets hitting the airfield made the transports' ground time hazardous. The 374th Tactical Airlift Wing stationed in Taiwan maintained 24 C-130Es at Tan Son Nhut for missions in Vietnam and Thailand.[15] Starting in late April, 15 C-130s landed at Kontum every day: 7 carried ammunition, 3 brought fuel, and 5 were loaded with rice. VNAF also made 15 landings a day.[16] On 24 April, the C-130 bladder birds of the 374th Tactical Airlift Wing brought 24,000 gallons of fuel into Kontum.[17]

Dien Binh, a village eight road miles southeast of Tan Canh on Highway 14, was the ARVN outpost to which a few of the 22nd ARVN Division's artillery pieces had been sent just before Tan Canh fell. ARVN airborne troops occupied the base there until 26 April, when they abruptly withdrew without a fight. The 141st NVA Infantry Regiment promptly occupied it.[18]

Even while the NVA was still consolidating its gains at Tan Canh and Dak To II as well as along Rocket Ridge and Highway 14, it was moving more artillery into position around Kontum for its attack on the city. Kontum airfield was under direct observation by NVA artillery forward observers, and various NVA weapons were registered on potential targets in and around the city, so flying in and out of Kontum was a risky mission.

On 26 April, Lieutenant Colonel Reed C. Mulkey flew a 374th Tactical Airlift Wing C-130, number 865, into Kontum. Here is what happened at the airfield, according to Mulkey:

> We descended through the clouds and picked up the field and landed. After I rolled out, [I] turned around on the runway to taxi back to the refueling pits. When we were about

halfway down the runway, a rocket exploded a thousand feet ahead of us. The tower called and told us the field was under attack and to get the hell out of there. There was not sufficient runway in front of us to even start to make a take off. Kontum is 2,000 feet above sea level, and it was a good 90 degrees outside, and my takeoff roll was 3,200 feet. The runway there is only 3,600 feet long. So I taxied back to the end and started my turn around to take off when we felt a bump. At this point, things start to run together.

The tower told us we had been hit and to abandon the airplane and run for the bunker straight ahead of us. I applied full power and started my takeoff roll. But number three engine, instead of going to full power, was dying. The engineer said we couldn't get off the ground on three engines. I knew that. I headed the airplane off the runway, across a taxiway, and onto an apron. I feathered all four engines, the engineer cut the battery, and within fifteen seconds (or fifteen years) the entire crew was out of the airplane and running for the bunkers that were at the side of the parking apron.[19]

The army picked them up later, and Mulkey called his unit on the high-frequency radio in the airfield tower. The additional 200 feet of hose needed to offload the fuel was brought in on an army CH-47. Mulkey, the loadmaster, the engineer, and two refueling specialists made the hose connections and offloaded the fuel. They were under sporadic mortar fire during the entire process, and the five of them were awarded the Bronze Star with "V" device (for valor) for that action.[20]

The crew flew out on another aircraft, and a replacement engine and maintenance crew were flown in two days later. The rocket attacks continued while the repair was under way, and a VNAF C-123 parked nearby was hit and caught fire. The USAF maintenance crew put out the fire and moved the C-123 a safe distance away from their own aircraft. Five days later the new engine was installed in number 865, and it was ready to fly again. Lieutenant Colonel Mulkey and a volunteer crew, including loadmaster Richard "Rick" Ivars, were flown into Kontum from Tan Son Nhut to take back the repaired aircraft. However, the new engine would not start. Artillery and mortar fire started falling on the airfield again. Rather than risk both the aircraft and the crew on the ground, Mulkey feathered that prop, taxied out, and took off on three engines. They made it out of Kontum and landed in Pleiku. It was a long time before this C-130 flew again. All four engines and both wings had to be replaced.[21]

There was one piece of good news. The ROK headquarters reported that An Khe Pass was finally cleared of the enemy, and Highway 19 was opened to traffic on the morning of 26 April.[22]

In a speech to the American people on the evening of 26 April, President Nixon said,

> Let us look at what the stakes are—not just for South Vietnam, but for the United States and for the cause of peace in the world. If one country, armed with the most modern weapons by major powers, can invade another nation and succeed in conquering it, other countries will be encouraged to do exactly the same thing—in the Mideast, in Europe, and in other international danger spots. If the Communists win militarily in Vietnam, the risk of war in other parts of the world would be enormously increased. But if, on the other hand, Communist aggression fails in Vietnam, it will be discouraged elsewhere, and the chance for peace will be increased. We are not trying to conquer North Vietnam or any other country in this world. We want no territory. We seek no bases. We have offered the most generous peace terms: peace with honor for both sides, with South Vietnam and North Vietnam each respecting the other's independence. But we will not be defeated. And we will never surrender our friends to Communist aggression.[23]

Newspapers and magazines were now publishing war maps with big enemy attack arrows pointed at Kontum. On 26 April, during my R&R in Hong Kong, the English-language newspaper *China Mail* reported under a banner headline on the front-page:

VIETNAM CRISIS—U.S. QUITS KEY CITY. American Army chiefs in the South Vietnamese town of Kontum have begun destroying secret documents as Communist forces close in. The Americans are preparing to evacuate Kontum and other bases in the Central Highlands.

Colonel Ba was having difficulty taking command of the defense of Kontum and getting it organized. The 53rd ARVN Regiment was the only unit from his own division and the only unit in Kontum whose commander would take orders from him. The 2nd Airborne Brigade, the 2nd and 6th Ranger Groups, and the Kontum Province RFs and PFs were ostensibly available for the defense of Kontum City, but the independent airborne and Ranger units had their own chain of command, and most of their superiors were not even in Kontum. The province chief, Colonel Long, continually tried to undermine Ba, and the commanders of the other nondivisional units would not cooperate with him or even attend vital planning meetings.[24] If Colonel Ba was going to defend Kontum successfully, he needed subordinates who would follow his orders.

The 6th Ranger Group was involved in heavy fighting in Hue before it was transferred to II Corps to replace the airborne troops departing on orders from Saigon. When the 6th arrived on 24 April, its CP as well as the 34th and 35th Battalions were positioned on FSB Lam Son, blocking Highway 14 north of Kontum. (The American name for Lam Son was probably "Lima.") They received sporadic enemy artillery and rocket fire over the next two days but sustained only light casualties. Nevertheless, on 27 April the group commander, Lieutenant Colonel De, used VNAF Hueys to move his CP south to FSB November four kilometers northwest of Kontum City. He left the two battalions—a major part of the group—to defend Lam Son. For a while after the CP moved, De had no contact with the troops he had left behind. The NVA continued to attack Lam Son by fire and with ground probes. During an attack on 1 May, the crews of four defending M-41s abandoned their tanks and fled. The NVA promptly appropriated those vehicles, but VNAF tactical air strikes and USAF Stinger gunships destroyed them. The 6th Group commander then pulled out his two battalions. The artillery crew, with no infantry or armor left to defend them on this FSB, were forced to join the withdrawal. The NVA quickly occupied Lam Son. On 4 May, Lieutenant General Dzu relieved the group commander for disobedience and disregarding orders.[25]

After the loss of FSB Lam Son, Lieutenant General Dzu revealed he planned to relieve Colonel Ba and replace him with a general because Ba was a colonel, and Dzu did not believe the colonels commanding the airborne, Ranger, and province forces would ever take orders from another colonel. Mr. Vann interceded to retain Ba as division commander, but this decision did not settle the question of who would be in overall command of the diverse units defending Kontum.[26] Vann wanted Dzu's deputy, Brigadier General Tran Than Phong, for that assignment. However, Phong's sister-in-law, the wife of the South Vietnamese prime minister, General Tran Thien Khiem, derailed the assignment. She considered Kontum too dangerous for her brother-in-law. This opening left Colonel Ly Tong Ba as the logical choice to be in overall command but also left unresolved the problem of achieving unity of command.

Mr. Vann and subsequently Lieutenant General Dzu became convinced that the best way to achieve unity of command in Kontum and to ensure that all the unit commanders would follow Colonel Ba's orders would be to replace the airborne brigade and the two Ranger groups with the 23rd Division's own 44th and 45th Regiments. The exchange would not result in any net loss of fighting strength. The 45th Regiment was ordered to move by convoy up Highway 14 from Pleiku to replace the 6th Ranger Group. The 44th Regiment at An Khe would be moved to Kontum by either vehicle or airlift.[27] The 44th's performance during the fighting in An Khe Pass had earned some well-deserved praise, and Mr. Vann said he told General Abrams that the 44th Regiment was the best regiment in II Corps.[28] After only a few months as the 44th's adviser, I could not claim much credit for that good reputation. The credit belonged to the Americans who had preceded me as advisers to the 44th and especially to Lieutenant Colonel Tran Quang Tien, an excellent officer who concentrated on fighting the war.[29]

General Cao Van Vien confirmed the importance of placing Brigadier General Ba in overall command in Kontum and of replacing the Ranger and airborne troops with Ba's own regiments: "The deployment of the 23d Division Headquarters to Kontum City and the replacement of the division commander was [sic] accomplished at the right moment. But the defense of Kontum could have faltered if the 23d Division organic forces had not replaced the heterogeneous defense units in time. This gave the division commander unity of command, absolute discipline authority, and morale cohesiveness which were the very elements of success at Kontum."[30]

When Colonel Ba assumed command of all ARVN forces in Kontum Province, he repositioned some units. The 22nd Ranger Battalion was sent to Polei Kleng to reinforce the Border Ranger battalion there. Blocking positions manned by four battalions of rangers were established at Vo Dinh and farther south along the Dak Poko River. A final blocking position was manned by the 2nd ARVN Ranger Group at FSB November on Highway 14, four kilometers in front of Kontum's main defensive line. The 53rd Regiment, reinforced by more Rangers, was responsible for Kontum City. Four 155-mm and forty-four 105-mm howitzers would provide fire support for the city's defense. Vann received priority on Arc Lights and used some to pound the abandoned bases on Rocket Ridge. However, that bombing campaign was somewhat hampered by the streams of refugees headed south, the 22nd Division soldiers still straggling toward Kontum, and the fact that some advisers were MIA. To avoid endangering those groups with Arc Lights but at the same time to hit identified NVA targets, more tactical air strikes by fighter-bombers were used. There were 180 tactical air strikes over the three days from 24 April to 26 April.[31]

With the entire 23rd ARVN Division assembling in Kontum and its commander, Colonel Ba, in overall command of the city's defense, it was necessary to send the division's support elements plus more staff officers, advisers, and equipment from division headquarters in Ban Me Thuot to establish a forward CP in Kontum. Most of the 23rd Division advisers traveled from Ban Me Thuot to Pleiku in an ARVN military convoy and were then airlifted into Kontum around the third week in April. However, some 23rd Division headquarters elements traveling by vehicle up Highway 14 from Pleiku to Kontum on 22 April were ambushed. The resulting loss of personnel and equipment made it difficult to get the DTOC in Kontum fully operational as soon as possible.[32]

Doctor (Captain) Giap Phuc Hai, who took command of the ARVN 230th Medical Company in Ban Me Thuot in March 1972, described his experience:

Around 23 April, elements of the 23rd Division moved north on QL 14 to Kontum. At 2:00 P.M. my company was cut off from the main convoy as we were ambushed [and] shelled and could not move forward because of destroyed trucks all over the road. Our company lost an ambulance carrying medical supplies along with the company typewriter and seal. It was hit by a direct 75-mm shell. My Jeep also was hit with shrapnel and 30-mm bullets. But it was drivable. My driver had to change a front tire. Other ambulance drivers had to do the same to their trucks under intense shelling coming from Chu Pao pass. It was terribly hot and at times wet by shower. Incredibly, there was no air cover with the exception of an L-19 circling above.

I had a PRC-25 radio, but I could not communicate with my boss. Then I heard a voice asking to talk to the ground commanding officer. There was no answer after repeat inquiries. I then picked up the handle and identified myself in Vietnamese as Delta Hotel (Doctor Hai). I did not know who was up in the sky, but he asked me to lead the troops back to Pleiku. The time was around 5:00 P.M. As we made the U-turn, I ordered all my drivers and medics to collect all the wounded along the road. At the same time I gave the hand signal to "follow me" to a very long convoy of Signals, Artillery, Engineers, MP [military police], and other support units. I took all the wounded to the Military Hospital in Pleiku. There I asked my friend, pharmacist Lieutenant Nguyen Tien Hoai, the CO [commanding officer] of the 722nd Pharmaco-Medical Supply Depot Annex, to allow the 23rd Medical Battalion (minus our CO) to bivouac inside his base for the night. Later that night, I was able to communicate with my boss, who safely made it to Kontum with his driver. He ordered me to take the next morning helicopter to Kontum.

The 2nd Field Hospital was completely empty, its staff gone. The next day, we moved to an old US Special Force camp (B5). I was assigned a very small, completely detached two-room "house" next to the tents of the 23rd Recon Co. Then, as the road was cleared, the troops came up, and we were able to build an underground bunker, with a "roof able to sustain 122-mm rockets" (according to my CO, also a self-proclaimed bunker expert from his days with the Vietnamese airborne). As we anticipated lots of casualties, we asked the artillery people to give us the wooden boxes to build "field hospital beds," and we right away befriended the Vietnamese air force liaison officer (which later on brought big dividends). Our company had the triage section, the ambulance section, the field hospital unit, and other support personnel. We had plenty of medical supplies, rice, water, and electricity from the Signal unit generator. My CO collected empty 155 shell canisters, and had them filled with water (just in case). We only temporarily were going to run out of gasoline once, but we received the gasoline "buffalo" container right away. We never ran out of blood, medications, IVs, or antibiotics. Staff at Ban Me Thuot base regularly sent me newspaper[s], coffee, and my salary whenever I asked. I also could call my wife directly from my bunker at night.

Civilians were flown out by Chinook helicopters. It was a mess at the city soccer field. I met the province public-health chief; he was the only civilian doctor in town, and as a brother and senior medical graduate, he was very kind to me. He offered us all the chicken[s] we could eat. But we could not take him up on his offer as we did not have the means to cook them.[33]

The first night in Kontum the leaders on the perimeter had trouble keeping their troops awake and ready to fight at night. When a Claymore antipersonnel mine set out for security was tripped in the dark, everyone assumed it was an enemy attack and fired toward it. The next morning they found the dead "enemy" was an Indo-Chinese tiger so big it took four men to carry it away on a pole. There were no more problems with the troops falling asleep when they were supposed to be on alert.[34]

The DTOC in Kontum was set up in a basement with a row of 55-gallon drums filled with dirt and covered with sand bags as a "roof." Despite all that overhead protection, when a 130-mm shell scored a direct hit on the DTOC, it killed the ARVN operations sergeant. The DTOC was then moved to a better basement closer to the northern front lines in the old 5th Special Forces Group B-24 Compound, where Highway 14 turned to the northwest. This site was about halfway between the vital airfield on the north side of town and the northwest defensive perimeter and thus closer to the NVA's likely avenues of approach. It would be closer to where the action was going to be.[35] To provide an offset to detonate any 130-mm shells or 122-mm rockets before they penetrated into the basement, timber and sandbags were placed on top of empty 55-gallon drums on the first floor of the building.[36]

As the NVA troops assembled to attack, they became a better target for air strikes. More than 3,400 American and VNAF sorties were flown against targets in II Corps during April. On 30 April, B-52s flew 28 Arc Light missions, more than were flown on any previous day during the Vietnam War. Half of those missions hit targets around Kontum. The North's infrastructure was also being bombed regularly. On 29 and 30 April, B-52s flew 700 missions over North Vietnam. By late April, US bombers were hitting targets in North and South Vietnam with 3,000 tons of munitions every day. That ordnance alone was costing at least $7 million a day.[37]

Colonel Stephen W. Bachinski, the Kontum Province senior adviser, summed up the local situation in his report for the period ending 30 April, noting that except for the Ben Het and Dak Sang (Seang) Border Ranger camps,

> effective control was lost with all the hamlets and military installations from Tri Do/Vo Dinh to the north. . . . The road from Kontum City to Pleiku has been cut effectively by the 95B Regiment since the beginning of the month. . . . Kontum City itself remains as an island in a NVA sea. Our present situation—as seen by the people—is one of misery, confusion, and pessimism; the poor performance by the 22nd ARVN Regiment at Tan Canh did anything but spark confidence; wild stories by the hundreds of stragglers from these units is causing a grave morale problem among the civilian population and the combined territorial and ARVN forces assigned to the defense of Kontum City.
>
> The NVA forces were successful beyond their wildest dreams. They are now repositioning themselves for their main attack on Kontum City. Hopefully, B-52 strikes on targets developed by these few units who will stand and fight and our B/17 Cav will cut down the total size of the forces to be used by the enemy. No artillery or heavy mortars have been used on the city as yet[;] however, daily doses of rockets have been used to minimize the amount of air traffic at our airfield.
>
> Soldiers accompanying families are reluctant to do anything until their families are evacuated from the city. . . . Civil servants charged with the handling of refugees . . . have been trying to get out themselves—and most have succeeded; the PDF (Popular Self-Defense Force) . . . has been halved due to departures; medical service has all but stopped, due

to the loss of doctors and staff personnel who left on choppers earmarked for the wounded. . . . A prolonged period of siege may result in serious outbreaks of disease due to inadequate sanitation . . . among the refugee population, numbering now about 8,000 on the official roll and an equal number being cared for by relatives or friends in the city.

Stories of VC atrocities continue to pour in from those Highland tribesmen who survived the long trek through the jungle from Dak To and points south: clergy murdered; village officials with throats slit; families of US employees killed and slogans posted over their homes; young boys and girls separated from their families and taken into the jungle; and refugees being held forcefully by the NVA in obvious ambush positions in order to avoid B-52 strikes. The situation in the city is critical but not hopeless. . . . The people are paying a heavy price for their government's tolerance of inept commanders. . . . When we match the NVA in motivation, discipline, and leadership, the war will end. . . . Our severe losses in this province can be attributed to a failure of leadership at all levels—especially at the top.[38]

Some of the ARVN regimental and division commanders in I and II Corps personally collapsed under the NVA attacks. They either ran or simply gave up. In contrast, Colonel Ba said he would stay and do his best to defend Kontum.

Colonel Ba believed that going after the enemy in the jungle and fighting on ground the enemy had chosen and prepared was like going into another man's house in the dark when the man is waiting for you with a gun. He wanted to let the enemy come to him. Then he could kill around 10 percent with tactical air strikes, another 10 percent with artillery, and—if he could target them—another 30 percent with B-52 strikes. Colonel Ba told a reporter, "First we had to organize our defensive posture completely. Now, we will move out and try to strike the enemy. We want to counterattack, get the enemy to come into our artillery fan and strike him before he comes to Kontum."[39]

During my R&R in Hong Kong, I had bought a paperback copy of Barbara W. Tuchman's new book *Stillwell and the American Experience in China, 1911-1945*. It would be my reading material during the trip back to An Khe. General Joseph W. Stillwell was so blunt, caustic, and critical that his nickname was "Vinegar Joe." He spoke fluent Chinese and liked the Chinese people and China. However, during World War II he was extremely critical of his Chinese counterpart, Generalissimo Chiang Kai-shek, the president of Nationalist China. In correspondence with his military superiors and President Franklin D. Roosevelt, Stillwell repeatedly complained there was no quid pro quo in the US relationship with China. The United States gave them vast amounts of cash, war materiel, and other aid but did not demand specific accomplishments from the Chinese in return. The same shortcoming existed in our relationship with South Vietnam.

As far as I knew when I returned from R&R on 10 May, the 44th Regiment was still at An Khe and would probably remain there indefinitely. I caught a flight from Saigon to Pleiku and signed up for a flight to An Khe. Some USAF pilots in the operations building at Pleiku airfield were talking about a new ground-to-air heat-seeking missile the enemy was using. They were justifiably concerned but continuing to fly their assigned missions. Just before dawn on the second day, I walked around outside to take a break from Stillwell and get some fresh air. Captain *Diem,* one of the company commanders in the 44th Regiment, walked up to me with a big grin. We shook hands, and I asked, "What are you doing here, Captain *Diem?*" He waved toward hundreds of ARVN troops sitting and lying on the ground nearby and said, "I go Kontum! Whole regiment go Kontum! You go Kontum, too!" So I was going to the embattled city currently featured in newspapers and magazines—the city with the big enemy attack arrows pointed at it. I cancelled my request for a flight to An Khe and arranged to fly to Kontum with the 44th Regiment troops waiting outside. My interpreter, Sergeant *Hao,* and my Jeep were there and would go to Kontum with me.

On the coast, II Corps was also being attacked where the 22nd ARVN Division's two regiments were stationed in Binh Dinh Province. Lieutenant General Ngo Quang Truong, I Corps commander, later described the situation there:

> While the enemy was gaining ground in the Central Highlands and preparing to push toward Kontum, in the coastal lowlands of Binh Dinh Province, the NVA 3d Division and VC local forces cut off Route QL-1 at Bong Son Pass and attacked the three isolated northern districts, Hoai An, Hoai Nhon and Tarn Quan. This forced the 40th and 41st Reg-

iments of the 22nd ARVN Division to abandon their two major bases, Landing Zones English and Bong Son, and other strong points in the area. Enemy attacks then spread out rapidly northward along Route QL-1 and southwestward along the Kirn Son River, engulfing the district towns of Tarn Quan and Hoai An in the process. In the face of the enemy's momentum, all defenses in the area crumbled rapidly.[40]

After five days of assaults, the Communists seized Quang Tri in I Corps on May Day. It was the first provincial capital to fall to the enemy. NVA tanks were now 27 miles south of the DMZ and driving for the old imperial capital of Hue, only 24 miles farther south. In addition to the enemy's rapid advances in the North and in the Central Highlands, they seized Loc Ninh and were besieging An Loc in the south.

Across South Vietnam, 350,000 refugees were on the move, mostly by road, desperately fleeing the Communist onslaught. Civilians fleeing Hue were offering $50 for the one-hour car trip to Danang. Some South Vietnamese officers were moving their own families and belongings south in well-polished Jeeps. An estimated 10,000 people, including military men, were evacuated from Kontum on the last two days of April.[41]

Kontum City was obviously the next major objective for the North Vietnamese invaders, and they would be counting on their tanks to achieve a swift and overwhelming victory. Terrified ARVN troops had fled from Tan Canh, Dak To II, and some of the Central Highlands FSBs when tanks attacked them, which did not bode well for Kontum. We needed something to tip the balance back in our favor.

The US Army ordered an experimental aerial antitank system deployed to Vietnam. At Fort Lewis, Washington, a team was evaluating the TOW antitank missile system: tube launched, optically tracked, and wire guided. The helicopter-mounted TOW system and its capabilities were described in detail in a March 1972 article published in the *US Army Aviation Digest,* so the Russians, Chinese, and North Vietnamese knew it existed and might be employed against Communist tanks in South Vietnam. The XM-26 TOW system carried three 50-pound missiles in a launch pod on each side of a UH-1B helicopter. The copilot/gunner used an inertial guidance–stabilized telescope sight to acquire the target. After he fired the missile, it appeared in the sight, and the gunner guided it by holding the crosshairs of the sight on the target until impact. Visibility had to be good enough for the gunner to acquire the target and keep it in sight until the missile hit. The two guidance wires were unreeled behind it in flight. Missiles were usually fired from an altitude of about 3,000 feet and slant range of 3,000 feet from the target. A TOW missile could travel the 3,000 feet in less than five seconds. In 1972, each missile cost $2,600, and each helicopter carried six missiles.[42]

Despite the testing already done, no American soldier had ever fired a TOW missile from a helicopter.[43] Sending the experimental TOWs to Vietnam would test this new weapons system against enemy tanks in combat—moving tanks that could shoot back and were often protected by heavy anti-aircraft fire. This test would be the toughest anyone could devise. However, with NVA tanks charging across South Vietnam, there was an urgent need for an airborne weapons system capable of stopping tanks dead in their tracks.

The 1st Combat Aerial TOW Team, Vietnam, arrived at Tan Son Nhut on 24 April. The two helicopters were reassembled; the TOW systems were mounted on them; and on 26 April they were sent to Long Binh, where they were placed under operational control of the 1st Aviation Brigade. As the team's name implied, this was the first time the US Army had deployed a TOW system mounted on aircraft in combat against enemy tanks. The team was assigned the radio call sign "Hawk's Claw." The army aviators received a cram course on the system, went through missile-tracking drills, and checked out cockpit procedures. Then each of them fired two missiles from their helicopters. This was the first time any of them had ever fired a live TOW missile.

Tan Canh and Dak To II fell the day the team arrived in Vietnam, and enemy tanks were moving toward Kontum, so on 28 April the TOW Team flew north to be stationed in Pleiku. The II Corps area was chosen in part because enemy anti-aircraft fire there was considered to be less intense and less accurate than in the I and III Corps areas. The TOW Team would have a better chance of surviving in II Corps. Also, it was obvious ARVN's next big test would be the impending NVA attack against Kontum.[44] Whether the city would hold or be overrun might depend on how many enemy tanks could be knocked out.

The 1st Combat Aerial TOW Team was first employed in combat on 2 May. It destroyed four M-41 tanks, a 105-mm artillery piece, and a 2.5-ton truck—all American-made equipment that ARVN had abandoned to the enemy at FSB Lam Son (Lima) the previous day. When WO Carroll W. Lain knocked out the first of those four M-41 tanks, he became the first American soldier to fire an American-made guided missile in combat.[45]

Aerial reconnaissance reported NVA troop and equipment movements from northwest to southeast on trails parallel to Highway 14. Throughout late April and early May, all FSBs and outposts in the Highlands came under increasingly heavy attacks by fire. The enemy moved closer to them and made probing attacks to test their defenses. Some isolated positions could be supplied only by parachute, and many of those bundles fell into enemy hands because VNAF flew too high for accurate delivery.

Except for Kontum City and a handful of isolated outposts, the Communists now controlled all of Kontum Province. Strong enemy forces controlled Highway 14 both north and south of Kontum City. The NVA also controlled the territory to the east and west of the city. Kontum was surrounded, and the enemy was going to hit it with everything he had.

In 1954, North Vietnamese general Vo Nguyen Giap had achieved his greatest victory by surrounding the French forces at Dien Bien Phu, capturing the stronghold, and thus ending the French occupation of Vietnam. First, he had cut the French supply lines and surrounded Dien Bien Phu. Then he had blocked aerial resupply or reinforcement by pounding their airfield with artillery fire from US 105-mm howitzers that had either been given to China during World War II or been captured by the Chinese in Korea. Giap's troops had dug caves in the hillsides so his artillery pieces could be rolled out to fire and then withdrawn into the caves to avoid French counter-battery fire. All the while, his infantry had dug their trenches closer and closer to the French lines, slowly but surely tightening the noose around Dien Bien Phu. Giap was now using some of the same tactics—and tightening the noose around Kontum.

12

Closing in on Kontum

> The poor display of will to fight by the 22nd Division at Tan
> Canh is discouraging and makes the defense of Kontum City
> difficult to foretell. . . . In light of this there is no basis for
> confidence that Hue or Kontum will be held.
> —General Creighton W. Abrams
> to Secretary of Defense Melvin Laird

After Tan Canh and the outposts fell, John Paul Vann thought his
reputation and his career were on the line. He had to win in Kontum or be sacked. That sort of pressure might have crushed a lesser
man, but Vann rose to the challenge. It brought out his strengths as
a commander, and he used his energy, drive, and personal involvement to ensure that Kontum would not fall.

During daylight, when an Arc Light struck north of Kontum,
the rising smoke and dust could be seen, the deep rumbling of
the explosions could be heard, and the vibrations could be felt in
the city. The bombs dropped by US and VNAF fighter-bombers
were less spectacular, but when the F-4s came streaking in to drop
napalm, the surging fireballs and black smoke were impressive to
watch. In Kontum City, a few of the remaining Honda owners rode
out to the northern perimeter, and some advisers and reporters
gathered on a veranda to watch the show while enjoying a cold
beer. They were wise to enjoy it while they could.[1]

M-72 LAWs were issued to the 23rd Division's units. Then several old tank hulls were set up as targets in open areas so they could
practice firing the M-72 and see the results on a tank's armor. Pic-
tures from An Loc and Quang Tri showing ARVN soldiers beside
the T-54 tanks they had knocked out with M-72s were used to con-

vince our troops that a single ARVN soldier really could destroy one of the dreaded monsters.[2] Colonel Ba also showed his troops some captured NVA soldiers to prove they were not supermen but just frightened teenagers.[3]

On 29 April, a high-level "troika" of American advisers was formed in Pleiku. They included John Paul Vann, the corps senior adviser; Brigadier General John G. Hill, Vann's deputy; and Colonel John A. Todd, the deputy commander of the 1st Aviation Brigade. Todd's inclusion acknowledged the important roll anticipated for US Army air assets. This group, in conjunction with the corps commander, Lieutenant General Ngo Dzu, would make the major decisions about defending the II Corps area.[4] This arrangement allowed Vann to spend more of his own time overseeing the use of Arc Lights and conferring with the ARVN officers.

Under the headline "Red Tanks, Troops Near Kontum," *Stars and Stripes* reported from Kontum, "This city is in danger of extinction. North Vietnamese tanks and troops are drawing closer from the north and south. Many of the city's 30,000 residents are packing to leave . . . as soon as the highway to Pleiku is opened."[5]

Air reconnaissance in early May discovered new NVA supply dumps and pioneer roads north of Kontum in the vicinity of Vo Dinh.[6] On the eve of the assault on Kontum, ARVN reported that the enemy forces closing in on Kontum consisted of the B-3 Front Headquarters with the 2nd and 320th Infantry Division headquarters commanding a total of 8 infantry regiments with a total of 29 infantry battalions, all supported by 2 tank battalions and an artillery regiment with 13 artillery battalions—a total of 19,900 men.[7] President Thieu sent a letter to the ARVN Corps commanders directing them to hold Quang Tri, Hue, and Kontum at all cost and to clear the enemy from An Loc and Highway 13 by 2 May.[8]

Summarizing the situation for Secretary Laird, General Abrams said,

> In MR2, the poor display of will to fight by the 22nd Division at Tan Canh is discouraging and makes the defense of Kontum City difficult to foretell. . . . I must report that as the pressure has mounted and the battle has become brutal, the senior military leadership has begun to bend and in some cases to break. In adversity it is losing its will and cannot be depended on to take the measures necessary to stand

and fight. The known exceptions to this are General Phu, 1st Division and General Truong, IV Corps commander. In light of this there is no basis for confidence that Hue or Kontum will be held.[9]

General Abrams also reported that the troop dispositions northwest of Kontum were two Border Ranger battalions at Ben Het, one at Dak Pek, and one at Dak Seang. The other friendly forces in the area consisted of 6 Ranger battalions, 4 infantry battalions, 2 airborne battalions, 48 tubes of artillery, and 18 tanks—all preparing to defend Kontum City. Abrams noted there was evidence of dissention among unit commanders "that may cause this sizeable combined force to cave-in in the early stages of any heavy enemy pressure." He added, "Enemy staying power is his most effective battlefield characteristic. It is based first on his complete disregard for the expenditure of resources, both men and materiel, and second on discipline through fear, intimidation, and brutality. An enemy decision to attack carries an inherent acceptance that the forces involved may be expended totally."[10]

In early May, General Abrams told Secretary of State Kissinger, "ARVN may have lost their will to fight and 'the whole thing may be lost.'"[11] About the same time, Nixon sent Kissinger a memorandum emphasizing his own determination:

We have the power to destroy his war-making capacity. The only question is whether we have the *will* to use that power. What distinguishes me from Johnson is that I have the *will* in spades. If we now fail it will be because the bureaucrats and the bureaucracy and particularly those in the Defense Department, who will of course be vigorously assisted by their allies in State, will find ways to erode the strong, decisive action that I have indicated we are going to take. For once, I want the military and I want the NSC [National Security Council] staff to come up with some ideas on their own which will recommend *action* which is very *strong, threatening,* and *effective.*[12]

Increased bombing of the North would have to be done with air assets diverted from the South, though, and General Abrams resisted sending the bombers, his only US reserve, "away hunting rabbits while the backyard was filled with lions."[13] By 1 May, the

United States had withdrawn from Southeast Asia: 95 percent of its infantry and armor battalions, 97 percent of its artillery battalions, and—important to those of us remaining in Vietnam—91 percent of its attack aircraft squadrons.[14]

The Americans wanted to prevent ARVN commanders from abandoning their posts, at least on US aircraft. General Abrams encouraged the Vietnamese commanders to stand and fight by issuing an order to all American commanders that said, "Effective immediately no Vietnamese commander will be airlifted out of a unit defensive position by US fixed-wing aircraft or helicopter unless such evacuation is directed personally by the RVNAF [Republic of Vietnam Armed Forces] corps commander. Inform your counterpart."[15] Some South Vietnamese officers, who realized American support was the key to their survival, threatened to prevent forcibly any evacuation of the American advisers from Kontum.[16]

On 2 May, enemy mortar and artillery fire on Kontum airfield damaged two C-130s.[17] The same day a collision with a helicopter on the congested airfield took several feet off the end of a C-130's wing. On 3 May, rockets damaged another bladder bird. Although Highway 14 from Pleiku was still closed, daylight fixed-wing aircraft landings at Kontum airfield were ended.[18]

According to an American newspaper report, by the end of May the US Command admitted to less than half-a-dozen aircraft lost to Strella missiles, but unofficial reports indicated many more had been destroyed. The South Vietnamese refused to discuss the subject. Most of the crewmen in planes hit by Strellas died instantly. One eyewitness said a Strella went right up the tailpipe of a helicopter and blew the aircraft to pieces. A US Army helicopter pilot said, "Once it gets on your tail, you're through." Two of the missiles were captured in I Corps and sent to experts for study. They said that the operator needed to hold a bead on the aircraft for seven and a half seconds before firing, that the missile traveled at 450 miles an hour, and that it had an extraordinary turning capability so it could pursue an aircraft trying to dodge it.[19]

In a personal meeting with President Thieu, General Abrams listened to Thieu's "big arrow" description of how the coming battle should be fought.

[Then I] described for him my conviction that the real problem for South Vietnam was the effectiveness of his field commanders. I described in some detail the ineffectiveness of individual commanders by name in northern MR1 [I Corps], the B-3 Front [II Corps] and MR3 [III Corps]. I told the president that it was my conviction that all that had been accomplished over the last four years was now at stake, and, at this stage, it was the effectiveness of his field commanders that would determine the outcome—either winning all or losing all. At this point President Thieu talked to his executive and directed that all corps commanders be called to the palace today. President Thieu then continued, advancing the view that if Hue and Kontum held for four days they would have won the battle. I told the president that no one should think in any less terms than six weeks more of heavy, bloody fighting and maybe more. This is a battle to the death, the Communists have planned it that way and will not quit until they have been totally exhausted. It was a very candid meeting, but at no time did President Thieu show either irritation, impatience, or disagreement.[20]

On 3 May, Mr. Vann reported to General Abrams, "Of the 24 battalions assigned to the 22nd and 23rd Divisions and MR II Ranger Command, 10 are rated ineffective: This includes the complete 40th and 42nd Regiments [of the 22nd Division in Binh Dinh]. 14 are rated as marginal. Several battalions have less than 200 soldiers. ARVN has lost 54 artillery pieces and 30 tanks. . . . There is a severe shortage of major items of equipment."[21]

MACV estimated enemy strength in South Vietnam at 236,000, with 80 percent of it in combat units. General Abrams summed up the fight and the importance of air power:

This government [of South Vietnam] would now have fallen, and this country would now be gone, and we wouldn't be meeting here today, if it hadn't been for the B-52s and the tac air. There's absolutely no question about it. . . . What you've got here, in my opinion, is a go-for-broke thing by the North Vietnamese. And they've thrown everything they've got in it. . . . It's just an all-out onslaught, and the losses on both sides—I mean, *he's* losing tanks like he didn't care about having any more, *and* people, *and* artillery, *and* equipment. The level of violence, and the level of brutality, in this whole thing right now is [*sic*] on a scale not before achieved in the war in Vietnam.[22]

In another attempt to clear the Kontum Pass and reopen Highway 14, the ARVN 45th Regiment moved north from Pleiku, and elements of the 2nd Ranger Group moved south from Kontum. H Troop of the 10th Air Cavalry Squadron provided reconnaissance and screening. On 5 May, both units got through the pass.[23] However, the day after a government spokesman declared Highway 14 south of Kontum open—after only one convoy had passed through from Pleiku to Kontum—the NVA closed it again. At the end of a day of heavy fighting, ARVN infantrymen were driven off Chu Pao Mountain, which dominates and thus controls the highway.[24]

A total of 350,000 South Vietnamese refugees fled their homes nationwide between the 30 March start of the Easter Offensive and 1 May.[25] Most of the refugees who arrived in Kontum said they had fled mainly to escape the American bombing rather than the NVA. One woman from Dak To said, "The Viet Cong come so the airplanes shoot and bomb and so we leave." Kontum's population of 27,000 was expected to double in another week unless an NVA attack stopped the refugee flow. With Highway 14 to Pleiku blocked by the NVA, there was no way out of Kontum for refugees except by air, and there were far too few flights to remove all of them. The Catholic bishop said, "Even those who do not completely recognize how Kontum is going to be destroyed know they are trapped. Even Asian resignation to fate does not offset this." A rice trucker, trapped in the town, said, "The North Vietnamese are like an ocean tide and will sweep over Kontum. The [South Vietnamese] army will not be able to stop them."[26]

A *New York Times* headline read "Thousands Flee Kontum in Panic as Enemy Nears." The article reported that 10,000 people were evacuated by plane or helicopter from Kontum, "a key city in the Central Highlands encircled by North Vietnamese forces. . . . Nuns, priests, military dependents, officials and many military men, including deserters, were among those leaving. All but a dozen Americans were evacuated. Reliable sources in Kontum said in reports telephoned to Saigon that residents were bribing South Vietnamese helicopter pilots the equivalent of $240 a person to make the 20 minute trip to Pleiku."[27]

A steady stream of refugees was flowing down Highway 14 and

into Kontum 24 hours a day. They were evacuated to Pleiku on VNAF Hueys and US Chinooks. The Chinooks, carrying 60 to 70 Vietnamese at a time, were making continuous, dawn-to-dusk flights loaded with refugees. Thirty percent of the 30,000 Montagnards in Kontum were evacuated by 4 May.[28] After Kontum airfield was closed, Master Sergeant Lowell W. Stevens was unable to fly with the Covey FACs, so he helped with the evacuation. The civilians were panicked and difficult to control. Stevens would organize them into groups of safe load size, but when the Chinook's loading ramp came down, the civilians mobbed the helicopter in a desperate effort to get out on that flight. Stevens finally had to arm his 14 US soldiers with baseball bats to beat them away and maintain order.[29]

As the evacuation progressed, Stevens noticed some of the VNAF helicopters were taking off with Honda motorcycles tied to the skids. At first, he thought VNAF must be taking out the refugees' vehicles for them. But he was tipped off to what was really happening when some refugees boarding a US CH-47 tried to pay the crew. Stevens questioned them and learned that VNAF was charging for the evacuation flights. Other refugees said VNAF would not evacuate them because they had no money or Hondas to pay for their passage. Stevens went over to the VNAF loading area with an interpreter and verified that VNAF pilots were indeed demanding money or motorcycles from their passengers. Here were VNAF pilots, trained by the Americans, flying helicopters given to their government by the Americans, flying with fuel obtained free from the Americans, and they were illegally charging Vietnamese civilian refugees to fly them out of extreme danger. Stevens was angry and disgusted to see the VNAF pilots take such unfair advantage of their own people. His reaction was, "For me, that was the straw that broke my back about Vietnam."[30]

When Gladiator 715 was shot down in flames and crashed after taking off from Dak To II on 24 April, it was assumed there were no survivors because the helicopter had reportedly exploded on impact. Three of the six advisers, including Major Carter and Lieutenant Jones, died. However, three other advisers, Major Warmath, Captain Keller, and Staff Sergeant Ward, survived, and so did the Huey's gunner, Specialist 4 Charles M. Lea. On 6 May, a FAC flying near Polei Kleng picked up a radio transmission from "Gladiator 715," and the survivors were finally rescued after evading enemy search parties during 13 days in the jungle.[31]

On 8 May, after conferring with the National Security Coun-
cil and his cabinet, Nixon told the US Navy to mine Haiphong
and six other ports and ordered resumed bombing of Hanoi and
Haiphong. He told his advisers, "I have the will in spades," and
vowed he would not lose the war or repeat his mistake of not bombing when his instincts told him he should. "Those bastards are
going to be bombed like they have never been bombed before,"
Nixon said as he kicked off Operation Linebacker. It was one of
the largest bombing campaigns in history and the first major use
of precision-guided "smart" bombs—as opposed to "dumb" grav-
ity bombs. Between April and the end of October, 155,548 tons of
bombs were dropped on North Vietnam.[32]

During the week before Nixon left for the Moscow summit, US
aircraft made more than 1,800 separate attacks on the North. They
cut the only two rail lines from China, cut the pipeline carrying
fuel to the NVA tanks in the South, and finally bombed down the
Paul Doumer Bridge over the Red River outside Hanoi. Some of
the successful bombing was attributable to the new 3,000-pound
smart bombs.[33]

The US flotilla of 60 ships offshore in the South China Sea and
farther north in the Gulf of Tonkin included six aircraft carriers
with almost 500 planes, cruisers, and destroyers; these ships could
and did bomb targets ashore. Although no incoming ships were
to be attacked on the high seas, if they attempted to move cargo
to shore on lighters, those smaller craft would be attacked. A few
freighters tried it, and the US Navy sank the barges.[34]

US Navy planes mined all of North Vietnam's seven major harbors and its working rivers and canals. Estimates indicating that 75
percent of North Vietnam's imports from Communist countries
arrived by sea and that 95 percent of those imports came through
Haiphong underscored the importance of mining this port. Prac-
tically all of the North's petroleum imports were pumped into
Haiphong.[35] Cutting off the fuel supply might leave some of the
NVA tanks headed our way out of fuel and dead in their tracks.

To defend Kontum, Colonel Ba had the three regiments of his
own division, two RF battalions from Kontum Province, some PF
soldiers, four 155-mm and forty-four 105-mm howitzers, and ten
tanks. There was also USAF and VNAF tactical air support and
the Arc Lights, which could strike out beyond artillery range. The
New York Times reported on 7 May, "Ten South Vietnamese battal-

ions totaling 5,000 men at the most now face a North Vietnamese attacking force of at least twice that size that is equipped with tanks and heavy antiaircraft weapons."[36]

Except for the problem that the RFs and PFs were controlled by the province chief, unity of command was achieved when the Ranger and airborne units were replaced by the 23rd Division's own regiments. Mr. Vann and Colonel Truby respected and had confidence in Colonel Ba, and they considered him a good commander. The situation was becoming more positive; the perimeter was being tightened and improved. Truby thought they would be able to defend Kontum successfully.[37]

Vann started coming to Kontum several times a day. Vietnam was his whole life, and after finally achieving a high rank in the American effort there, he did not want to jeopardize his career. He had lost a great deal of credibility when Tan Canh and Dak To II fell, and he could not afford to lose Kontum. Vann admitted that if Kontum fell, it would be difficult to defend Pleiku. He issued orders that if Kontum did fall, the ammunition dump was to be blown up to keep it out of enemy hands.[38]

Although both Vann and Brigadier General Hill thought Kontum should and could be defended, in early May Vann directed Hill to assemble all the advisers to answer individually the question "Do we fight for Kontum?" The advisers were told to answer just "yes" or "no," and any "yes, buts" were cut off. All of the advisers said we should fight for the city. So Kontum rather than Pleiku would be the decisive battle. If Kontum was lost, the 23rd Division would be lost, but the Highlands would not be abandoned. The remaining forces would fall back to Ban Me Thuot. They would hold whatever they could with whatever they could pull together.[39]

The shock of the enemy's aggressive attacks with armor, his easy defeat of strongly fortified ARVN bases, and the rapid collapse of the 22nd Division reverberated throughout South Vietnam. The NVA achieved the same type of psychological impact the German blitzkrieg had achieved in Poland and France early in World War II. American advisers wondered if the South Vietnamese would stand and fight to defend their own country, and the South Vietnamese wondered if it was possible for them to defend against massive assaults by North Vietnamese soldiers who attacked with tanks.

Those questions would be answered in Kontum.

The II Corps advisers and their ARVN counterparts at II Corps Headquarters in Pleiku in February 1972. *Front row, left to right:* Colonel Binh (chief of staff), Brigadier General Wear (deputy senior adviser), Mr. Vann (senior adviser), Lieutenant General Dzu (commanding general), Brigadier General Lam Son (deputy commanding general), Colonel Pizzi (chief of staff), Colonel Tuong (assistant commanding general, operations). *Second row:* Colonel Tho (corps artillery commander), Lieutenant Colonel Fuesel (artillery senior adviser), Colonel Pahl (G-2 adviser), Lieutenant Colonel Khuong (G-3), Lieutenant Colonel Goff (deputy G-3 adviser), Lieutenant Colonel Dick (G-4 adviser). *Third row:* Major Tu (corps surgeon), Colonel Otto (surgeon adviser), Lieutenant Colonel Kha (provost marshal), Lieutenant Colonel Falkenstein (provost marshal adviser), Lieutenant Colonel Hien (inspector general), Lieutenant Colonel Bennett (inspector general adviser), Lieutenant Colonel Kieu (G-1), Lieutenant Colonel McCoy (G-1 adviser). *Fourth row:* Colonel Huong (signal officer), Major Khieu (assistant G-4), Lieutenant Colonel Bates (corps engineer), Captain Thuy (headquarters commandant), Major Hollingsworth (adjutant general adviser), Major Smith (information officer). *Back row:* Major Richardson (secretary to the general staff adviser), Captain Lai (secretary to the general staff), Captain Tien (protocol officer), Lieutenant Colonel Roscoe (chaplain). (Photo courtesy of the US Army.)

Display of weapons captured during operation at Phu Nhon in November 1971. Lieutenant Colonel McKenna holding RPG warhead. (Author's collection.)

USAF B-52 in flight with bombs dropping. (Photo courtesy of the USAF.)

The Green House. The advisers' building at An Khe in early 1972. This 1871 French colonial mansion was at the end of the airfield runway. The US 1st Cavalry Division added the airfield control tower on the roof. (Author's collection.)

This Jeep hit a mine near Mang Yang Pass on Highway 19. Although badly hurt, the occupant survived. (Photo by James T. Vaughan.)

ARVN M-113 APCs on Highway 19 during fighting in An Khe Pass in April 1972. This view is just east of An Khe Pass and looking toward the east. (Author's collection.)

Lieutenant Colonel Tran Quang Tien, CO of the 44th ARVN Infantry Regiment, at an April 1972 display of enemy weapons captured in An Khe Pass. (Author's collection.)

Colonel Le Duc Dat, commander of the 22nd ARVN Infantry Division, with his adviser, Colonel Phillip Kaplan, at Tan Canh. (Photo by Matt Franjola, courtesy of the Library of Congress, Washington, DC.)

Two young NVA prisoners captured at Dak To II on 13 February 1972. (Photo by Stephen E. James.)

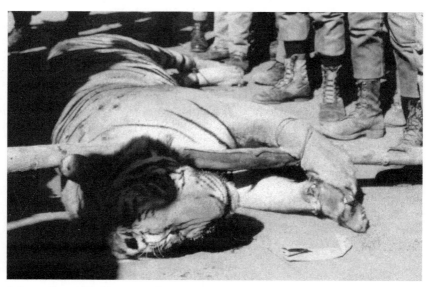

A large tiger killed by a mechanical ambush, probably a Claymore, on a small firebase on Highway 14 between Kontum and Pleiku. (Photo by James T. Vaughan.)

Kontum airfield in April 1972. A Huey is parked at the lower right, and the runway is in the distance. (Photo by Reed C. Mulkey.)

Kontum airfield on 28 April 1972. This VNAF C-123 has just been hit by enemy fire and is starting to burn. (Photo by Reed C. Mulkey.)

Ben Het Border Ranger Camp under attack on 9 May 1972. View from the command bunker with Montagnard soldiers on the front line in center and smoke from a burning PT-76 tank knocked out by Spectre 02 in the distance. (Photo from Mark Truhan.)

Ben Het Border Ranger Camp after the 9 May 1972 attack. Captains Mark Truhan and Robert Sparks on the PT-76 tank that Truhan "scared to death." (Photo from Mark Truhan.)

The 1st Combat Aerial TOW Team, Vietnam, with their helicopters. *Crew chiefs on top of helicopters (left to right):* Specialist 4 David W. Lehrschall, Specialist 5 Wayne Evans, Specialist 5 Ronald G. Taylor. *Middle row:* (in light shirts) Kenneth Blum, James M. Faulk, Dennis J. Camp, Thomas E. Zagorski; (in uniforms) Lieutenant Colonel Patrick L. Feore Jr., Hugh J. McInnish Jr. (civilian), Captain Roy Sudeck, Sergeant First Class Boyce A. Hartsell. *Bottom row:* (kneeling left of sign) CWO2 Caroll W. Lain, CWO2 Danny G. Rowe, CWO3 Lester M. Whiteis; (right of sign) CWO2 Edmond C. Smith, CWO2 Scott E. Fenwick, CWO2 Douglas R. Hixson Jr. (Photo from Hugh J. McInnish Jr.)

Three scout pilots by an LOH-6 Loach. *From left to right:* Captain Stephen James; Lieutenant Craig Smith, who was "shot down" by a tank; unknown captain from the Scalp Hunters. (Photo from Stephen James.)

Highway 14 looking north from FSB November north of Kontum on 13 May 1972. The Round Hill is just to the left of this point. (Photo by author.)

44th Regiment field CP in the jungle on FSB November. (Photo by author.)

An ARVN soldier and civilian engineer Hugh J. McInnish Jr. inspecting a T-54 knocked out by a TOW missile. (Photo from Hugh J. McInnish Jr.)

T-54 tank knocked out by the 44th ARVN Regiment on 14 May on display in the Kontum soccer stadium. (Photo by Richard Gudat.)

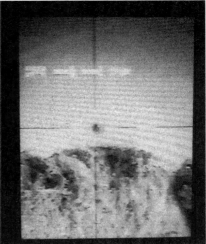

Gun camera photos from a TOW helicopter firing TOW missiles to destroy a tank disguised as an island in a river. (Video number 472.1, "XN26 Airborne TOW Combat Firing May 1972, Central Highlands, Republic of Vietnam." Courtesy of the National Archives, College Park, MD.)

USAF C-130 number 62-1854 destroyed by incoming fire on Kontum airfield on 23 May 1972. (Photo from Stephen James.)

Captains Raymond W. Hall and John R. Finch examining a captured Soviet 12.7-mm (.51-caliber) heavy machine gun. (Photo from Ly Tong Ba.)

In front of 44th ARVN Regiment's CP bunker after 26 May attack. *From left to right:* Major Wade B. Lovings; destroyed T-54 tank; ARVN soldiers in front-line positions. (Photo from Wade B. Lovings.)

South Vietnamese president Nguyen Van Thieu, in dark baseball cap, congratulates the victors in Kontum on 30 May 1972. Brigadier General Ly Tong Ba is on Thieu's right. Major General Nguyen Van Toan is to the right behind Thieu. (Government of South Vietnam photo from Ly Tong Ba.)

South Vietnamese president Nguyen Van Thieu and Major General Nguyen Van Toan, the II Corps commander, in Kontum on 30 May 1972. (Government of South Vietnam photo.)

The battered C-130 that pilot Lieutenant Colonel Reed C. Mulkey flew on the fateful mission into Kontum tells him it will not make that trip again. (Cartoon by SMS Davis published in *Det One Report: Yearbook Supplement for the People Who Fly and Support the C-130E Hercules Aircraft of the 374th Tactical Airlift Wing,* 4 July 1972. Courtesy of Rick Ivars.)

GIA ĐÌNH TRÔNG CHỜ BẠN TRỞ VỀ VỚI QUÂN ĐỘI VIỆT-NAM CỘNG-HÒA.

Chieu Hoi message, "Families are waiting for you to return to the Army of the Republic of Vietnam." Leaflets like this were air dropped in and around Kontum to encourage NVA soldiers to leave the NVA and come over to ARVN under the Chieu Hoi Program. (Leaflet from author's collection.)

French kilometer stone on Highway 14 north to Kontum. (Author's collection.)

13

Cut Off and Surrounded

Men, remember, there is no retreat from here. You must die
where you stand.
                —Sir Colin Campbell to the 93rd British Highlanders,
                                battle of Balaclava, 25 October 1854

Mr. Vann said that after the fall of Tan Canh and Dak To II the situation in Kontum was so serious and morale there was so low that
if the NVA had brought 50 battery-powered tape recorders to play
recordings of tank noises—grinding and clanking and motors rev-
ving up—over loudspeakers outside the city, the entire garrison and
population would have fled in panic.[1]

In early May, General Abrams told his commanders,

> In the last few weeks, in my conversations with General Vien,
> and with the President, I've said it straight, and called it for
> what it was worth. Just the other day General Vien was tell-
> ing me about some equipment they wanted, and I told him
> that we were doing everything we could to get this equip-
> ment to them and so on. But I then went on to tell him, I
> said, "Equipment is not what you need. You need men that
> will *fight*. And you need officers that will fight, and will lead
> the men." I said, "No amount of equipment will change the
> situation. It's in the hands of *men*, and if they'll fight, and
> their officers will lead them, you've got—even today—you've
> got all the equipment you need." I said, "That's the trouble."
> I said, "I don't think you've lost a tank to enemy fire. You lost
> all the tanks in the 20th because the men abandoned them,

led by the officers. You lost most of your artillery because it was abandoned and people wouldn't fight."[2]

On 7 May, Mr. Vann reported to General Abrams that his counterpart, Lieutenant General Dzu, had complained to him that he was being set up by President Thieu to be the scapegoat if Kontum fell. Dzu was certain he would be court-martialed when that happened. He went on to say that the coming losses would force Thieu to resign and that, in fact, Thieu's wife and children were already in Switzerland. He saw a cease-fire as the only hope for South Vietnam. Vann punched a number of holes in Dzu's theories but was unable to buck up his morale or attitude. However, after Polei Kleng, which was under assault at the time, held out through the night, Dzu became more positive and said that he would fend off the personal attacks by holding Kontum.[3]

Camp Le Khanh was a large, hilltop outpost about 22 kilometers west–northwest of Kontum on Highway 511. It was on a hill named "Polei Kleng," so the Americans called it by that name. In May 1972, the 62nd Border Ranger Battalion commanded by Major Buu Chuyen manned it. His advisers were Captain Geddes MacLaren and Lieutenant Paul McKenna.[4] US Special Forces had built Polei Kleng in June 1966, so it was well constructed and had an airfield. Ben Het, Dak Mot, Dak Pek, and Dak Seang, all farther northwest near the Cambodian border, were still holding out, and the NVA appeared to be bypassing them. However, the NVA had to take Polei Kleng because it controlled Highway 511, which the NVA needed for its attack on Kontum. From 24 April to 5 May, attacks by fire on the Ranger camps astride the NVA supply routes increased. The NVA moved anti-aircraft weapons close to Polei Kleng, and resupply or reinforcement by air became virtually impossible. Starting in early May the defenders were subjected to attacks by fire from 82-mm and 122-mm mortars.[5]

At 1530 on 5 May, the airborne TOWs were launched against T-54 tanks in the Polei Kleng area. The TOW crews sighted two enemy tanks from above but could not get a clear shot at them because, at the slant ranges from which they needed to fire, vegetation masked their view. Tactical air fighter-bombers were sent to bomb the tanks.[6] At noon on 6 May, the bombardment of Polei Kleng increased until more than 50 rounds fell in an hour and a half. US tactical air strikes stopped the enemy fire until the FAC had to leave at 1515. After he departed, the bombardment resumed, and 500 rounds fell on the base between then and 1900. The accuracy of the incoming rounds and the systematic manner in which they were destroying the ARVN bunkers told the advisers that an observer was adjusting the incoming fire. The bunker from which Captain MacLaren and Lieutenant McKenna were directing air strikes received several direct hits. At 1730 hours, another direct hit blew out an oak door and collapsed several walls. The advisers dug out of the rubble and moved into open foxholes near the perimeter.[7]

While MacLaren and McKenna watched, the enemy artillery methodically destroyed all aboveground buildings, all bunkers, and all radio antennas. The Rangers, who had withstood so many previous attacks, were demoralized by the intensity and accuracy of this attack by fire. At 1800, McKenna went looking for the battalion commander and discovered that he had already fled the compound. As the lieutenant returned to his foxhole, he saw the NVA using flashing red beacons to signal their infantry to attack. With the battalion commander gone, it was time for the advisers to go.[8] They called for extraction, and at 1900 hours an OH-6 piloted by Captain Jim Stein landed through heavy anti-aircraft and ground fire to pick up the two Americans. Stein tells how he rescued Captain Geddes MacLaren and Lieutenant Paul McKenna from Polei Kleng:

On May 6th we were released to return to camp Holloway when we were asked to extract two American Advisers from Polei Kleng. The base camp was involved in heavy fighting and it was looking like it would be overrun. John Paul Vann wanted his advisers extracted. The 361st Guns "Pink Panthers" would be providing gun coverage and guns from the 7/17th Cav "The Undertakers" would join them. Panther lead was running the operation and gave me a briefing of the situation. I told him we would descend to the ground and fly low level into the base camp approaching from the West. We would fly blacked-out except for one light on top. Gun lead confirmed and when we descended to the ground he confirmed his front seat had us sighted. As we approached Polei Kleng we could see flashes and explosions all over the camp. I noticed one of the gun ships was clearing a path in front of the aircraft using, I assumed, his 40mm.

As we entered the camp I could see silhouettes of soldiers, NVA or ARVN's running around from the explosions. I spotted a built up bunker covered with sand bags; figuring it was the command bunker, I headed for it. I believe we took a few of their communication antennas down as we flew to the bunker and landed on top. We could hear and feel bullets hitting the LOH. I told my observer to aim his M-60 at anyone coming our way and if the figure wasn't large, shoot it. I can't remember if I was in direct contact with the advisers, I believe I would have been, but can not confirm that. My observer spotted two larger figures moving our way and we decided they were the advisers. They jumped into the LOH and started firing their weapons. I have no idea how many ARVN's were wounded or killed by friendly fire. I checked my gauges and made my call to Panther lead; we had the advisers and were coming out the same way we entered. Lead just said "We got you." As we started to enter the perimeter of the camp low level, I again noticed explosions far enough out in front of our aircraft to clear a path. I asked the Advisers if they were in need of any medical care or could we go to Mr. Vann's headquarters. We landed at Mr. Vann's headquarters dropping off the advisers; flew over to Camp Holloway, took a shower, ate and again lost in Poker. Lucky in flying and a loser in Poker.[9]

Polei Kleng amazingly managed to hold out through three more days of attacks by fire and ground assaults by the 64th NVA Regiment. After the advisers were extracted, Spectre 03, an AC-130 gunship, arrived overhead and was able to attack by coordinating with an ARVN officer on the ground. The gunship fired all of its ammunition—including 96 rounds from the 105-mm gun. Spectre killed more than 350 enemy soldiers, and the attack was repulsed. Sixteen Arc Lights were employed around Polei Kleng during those three days. A Hoi Chanh said there were 40 KIA and many more WIA just in his company of 100 men.[10]

On 7 May, the bombardment of Polei Kleng increased from 2000 until midnight, then the enemy attacked from the east. Documents captured later revealed that 7 May had been chosen to commemorate the fall of Dien Bien Phu in 1954. The defenders held, and at 0600 the next morning the enemy withdrew to regroup. They left more than 300 dead behind.

Another tactical emergency was declared at Polei Kleng at 0800 on 8 May. VNAF tactical air responded with A-1s and A-37s. USAF Spectres and F-4s also responded. The weather worsened, but the VNAF and USAF FACs continued to work over the area as much as possible. However, at 0500 the next morning the enemy attacked again. After a heavy bombardment, the 64th NVA Regiment assaulted, with 20 tanks leading the way. The Rangers knocked out five tanks with M-72s and again beat back the enemy assault. Heavy incoming fire forced the defenders into bunkers and trenches. The soldiers' families, 300 Montagnard women and children, were crowded in with them. Women carried ammo and cared for the wounded. Lightly wounded men returned to the firing line. Most of the radio antennas were knocked out by direct fire from the surrounding hills, and the enemy began to destroy the remaining bunkers systematically one by one. Early on 9 May, Major Chuyen and his deputy, Captain Phan Thai Binh, decided to abandon the camp rather than be captured. The hundreds of wives and children were going to make withdrawal slow and difficult, but they could not be left behind.

At 0400 on 9 May, the Rangers used a Bangalore torpedo to blow a gap in the defensive wire, and Lieutenant Kchong, a Montagnard, led the 1st Company out into the darkness. He was followed by Major Chuyen and his CP group. They went east. Captain Binh with the remaining Rangers and the women and children left last and headed north. A VNAF L-19 contacted them by radio when it arrived over the camp, and they informed the pilot they were outside the camp and enemy tanks were now inside. The pilot managed to call in jets to bomb the camp before he was shot down and forced to bail out.

As Captain Binh and his group neared the Dak Poko River, they were almost surrounded. Firing while they retreated, they managed to fight their way to the river. The Rangers held off the enemy while the wounded, the women, and the children crossed the river to safety. The NVA then started mortaring the crossing site. One mother was killed, but her baby, attached to her in the typical Montagnard sling, continued to suckle. A Ranger cut the sling and carried the baby across the river, which was now running red with blood. Only 97 people reached the safety of the far bank, from where they were taken into Kontum. The others were killed, captured, or lost in the jungle. Major Chuyen was captured and then killed.[11]

Except for the camps near the border, Polei Kleng was the last strong point to the northwest of Kontum. Now the city was open to attack from that direction, and the enemy tanks could use Highway 511 as their avenue of approach. However, while overcoming Polei Kleng, the NVA suffered so many casualties that it postponed its attack on Kontum. This delay gave the city's defenders more time to prepare. John Paul Vann said, "In the brutal terminology of war, Polei Kleng has paid for itself in numbers of enemy dead."[12]

"Ben Het and loving it" was the adviser's sign and motto at Ben Het. It was a relic from the days when the US Army Special Forces had worked out of this camp only eight miles from the border with Cambodia and Laos. Highway 512 wound all the way from Bet Het back to Kontum. It was just a dirt track, but it was drivable—except for the danger of being ambushed. So Ben Het's resupply was by helicopter. At the height of Special Forces involvement, there had been 37 border camps in II Corps alone. By February 1972, there were only eight camps left and only two advisers in each camp. In the spring of 1972, Captain Stephen M. "Mark" Truhan was the adviser to the 95th Border Ranger Battalion, and Captain Robert C. Sparks was the adviser to the 71st Border Ranger Battalion, both at Ben Het.

Mr. Vann visited Ben Het a few days before the impending attack. After Captains Truhan and Sparks briefed him, Vann looked around and said, "I hope you get hit with a regiment. Ben Het is a strong camp." He was apparently counting on a lucrative Arc Light target when the NVA massed for their attack.[13] On the night of 6–7 May alone, there were 45 US tactical air sorties in the Highlands.[14] A USAF FAC crashed and burned while doing a victory roll after putting in successful tactical air strikes on the enemy assaulting Plei Mrong, a Border Ranger camp in Pleiku Province and about 22 kilometers south of Kontum.[15] In early May, Ben Het, Dak Pek, Dak Seang, and Plei Mrong were pounded by artillery and mortar fire. On 7 May, the NVA fired 160-mm mortar rounds into Ben Het. The 160-mm was a massive mortar round 6.24 inches in diameter. The NVA was using this weapon for the first time in II Corps. Then NVA tanks and troops were reported moving toward Ben Het.

At 0530 on 9 May, enemy troops from the 66th NVA Regiment and quite possibly one other regiment, plus a company of PT-76 tanks,[16] assaulted Ben Het. Two of the tanks attacked the main gate but were knocked out, as described more fully later. At 0730 hours, five PT-76 tanks attacked the eastern perimeter, and LAWs knocked out two of the tanks. The remainder of the tanks withdrew after the NVA infantry breached the eastern perimeter and seized about one-third of the camp. When the attack started, the defenders had six 105-mm and two 155-mm artillery pieces. During the fighting, all but one 105 was destroyed by incoming 122-mm or 130-mm artillery rounds. Only 3 of the 12 M-41 tanks sent toward Dak To II on 24 April survived the ambush en route by returning to Ben Het after one of them broke down. These three tanks were operable and should have participated in the defense of the camp. However, when the fighting started, their crews disappeared without firing a shot, and none of the other defenders knew how to operate a tank.

The Rangers spent the next two days ejecting the enemy and restoring the eastern perimeter. They were aided by 24 air strikes by USAF fighter-bombers and 4 air strikes by VNAF. During those two days, one Ranger battalion commander was completely ineffective. He just sat there throwing up. The attacking NVA forces lost 11 tanks and more than 100 KIA in their attempt to overrun Ben Het. They continued to harass Ben Het with attacks by fire and sporadic probes, but they did not make another major assault until fall.[17]

Captain Truhan later described how six different methods of killing a tank were employed at Ben Het—all against one enemy tank—and how he scared to death another PT-76 tank:

> We think at least a company, about 10 tanks, were in the initial assault. When the NVA opened fire on us that morning, the first thing we did was get on the radio and yell for help. . . . When Spectre arrived overhead, he already had some of the tanks picked out. One burst of his 40mm flamed a tank on the road to our northeast—about 200 meters outside the perimeter. Another burst disabled a tank about to roll through our main gate. . . . Even though he was disabled, the tank continued to roll forward and struck an anti-tank mine that blew off his left track. Now stationary, a Montagnard soldier dashed out of a bunker and put an M-72 LAW into him. Hit three times already, one of our damaged 155mm howitzers fired a bore-sighted HE round at him from less then 100 meters away and he burst into flames.

Hawks [*sic*] Claw . . . showed up about 1000, announcing themselves as "Claw." (We didn't have a clue who these guys were.) They declared they had tank killing ordnance on board, but before we could tell them we were fresh out of targets for the moment, the pilot yelled out "There's a tank at your main gate!" (Dead for about 4 hours, the tank had stopped burning by now.) Well, Claw rolled in before we could stop him and made a beautiful first round hit on the tank, which politely starting burning again. Now, that's the fifth hit on that hapless tank. We tried to tell Claw the tank had been dead for hours, but they wouldn't believe us . . . during the night of 9 May, NVA sappers snuck up to the dead tank at the main gate and blew its turret off. That's six hits.

We also accounted for one other tank right on our northeastern perimeter that I like to think I scared to death. The tank bogged down in soft ground, with miles of barbed wire and engineer stakes wound in his tracks. Try as he might, he just kept grinding in deeper. I took a LAW, crawled up to one of our partially destroyed perimeter bunkers and tried to knock him out from about 25 ft away, but the damned rocket wouldn't go off. I was desperately trying to remember my basic LAW misfire training when the tank picked me up on his co-ax machinegun and let loose a couple of bursts, and I ducked back into the bunker to ponder what to do next. Then, sneaking a peek outside the bunker, I saw the tank's hatch fly open and out tumbled the three-man crew, who were immediately shot. The only thing I can figure is the crew thought I'd go find a LAW that worked and try again, so they bailed out of the mired but undamaged tank, leaving the engine running. So, I scared it to death, sort of. Scratch three tanks. And this was by about 0530, just at first light.[18]

About 150 NVA were KIA inside the camp, and at least that many were left in the wire. Countless hundreds—even thousands—were killed by air strikes outside Ben Het. Montagnards who reached Ben Het in June said the NVA took hundreds and hundreds of their wounded from the Ben Het fight to Tan Canh for treatment.[19] Ben Het's example was encouraging to those of us expecting to be attacked in Kontum because it demonstrated that ARVN troops could and would kill enemy tanks, counterattack enemy penetrations, and successfully defend their positions.

In his "Daily Commanders Evaluation" to General Abrams for 8–9 May 1972, Mr. Vann wrote about the attack on Ben Het: "During the early morning of 9 May, the enemy used dogs to detonate mines in the perimeter wire." This dog tale was repeated in subsequent accounts. However, Captain Truhan says it did not happen, and it was just the advisers' own pet Montagnard mutt that had nimbly found his way through their wire and mines to go outside the perimeter and into the jungle at night. As he was returning before dawn on 9 May, the NVA followed him in through the defensive wire. Some of the Ben Het Montagnards saw this and started the dog story.

On 10 May, the NVA threw one of their own wounded soldiers out of a bunker they had captured and were still holding in the Ben Het compound. The defenders took him prisoner, and one of the Montagnards made the throat-slitting gesture to suggest how he should be handled. Fortunately, the ARVN officers interrogated him instead, and he showed them on a map where his unit was assembling for another attack the next morning. It was only a thousand meters away, which was pushing the minimum clearance needed for a B-52 strike. The advisers requested one anyway, and Mr. Vann radioed to ask, "How badly do you want this Arc Light?" Truhan and Sparks responded, "How badly do you want to hold Ben Het?" About 0230 the next morning, the NVA assembly area blew up in smoke and fire. There was no enemy assault that morning.[20]

Maintaining an adequate level of food, ammunition, and other supplies in Kontum while Highway 14 was blocked by the enemy meant the city was completely dependent on aerial resupply. Attempts to reopen Highway 14 were repeatedly defeated, but John Paul Vann was not entirely unhappy about that. He did not really want the pass opened until the battle for Kontum was over and said, "As long as the pass is closed, we have the cork in the bottle." If the pass were reopened, the ARVN forces in Kontum would have a clear route of retreat toward Pleiku. With the pass closed, they would have to stand and fight in Kontum.[21]

After the fall of Tan Canh, Lieutenant General Dzu went to see President Thieu in Saigon and then, in an agitated state, went to General Vien's home that evening. He told Vien that Thieu had ordered him to hold Kontum at all costs. Dzu said that both Kontum and Pleiku were indefensible and that he did not have the means to hold them. He wanted permission to withdraw from the Highlands. Vien disagreed and sent him back to Pleiku. Dzu started calling Thieu and Vien, even at night, and Thieu eventually called Vien to talk about their Dzu problem. They discussed relieving Dzu. Vien thought Dzu had lost his nerve and become a *défaitiste*. They could not leave a man like this in command of a corps.[22]

General Vien called four or five of his two- and three-star generals to offer them the command, but they all had excuses for not taking the job. Their health or their astrologer's advice or some other personal reason prevented them from accepting at that time. They obviously considered the situation in II Corps hopeless and did not want to risk their careers or their lives to become the commander of a lost cause. Vien decided he would need to find a major general who wanted to earn a third star and who also needed to redeem himself from some past problem to get that promotion. By process of elimination, he selected Major General Nguyen Van Toan, a two-star general who had previously been accused of corruption. A Hong Kong newspaper described Toan as "a large, jovial man whose dealing in the cinnamon business as 2nd Division commander several years ago was the subject of a formal investigation by the South Vietnamese government's anti-corruption inspectorate."[23] His reputation was also tarnished by an affair with a 15-year-old girl.

On the positive side, Major General Toan came with a good reputation as a fighting commander. He was the first ARVN general to be awarded the US Silver Star for valor. President Thieu relieved Lieutenant General Dzu and replaced him with Major General Toan on 10 May. Dzu's last major decision before leaving was to order the transfer of the entire 44th ARVN Regiment from An Khe to Kontum. He left his command in a happy mood, saying that even though he had been fired, at least he had not lost any province capitals. Mr. Vann immediately pressured Major General Toan to obtain quality replacements for some of the corps staff, whose daily briefings were based more on what the staff thought the commander wanted to hear than on what was really happening.[24]

Major General Toan was a big, burly man who looked like and was a strong leader. Colonel Truby got to know him well, considered him effective, and thought they were better off after he assumed command of the corps.[25]

Mr. Vann described the new corps commander at a 12 May MACV Commanders Briefing: "General Toan, 45 minutes after arrival, asked me to get him transportation and go with him to Kontum. And yesterday [he] went down and spent the night in Kontum City. Last evening we visited combat units until nearly midnight, and then began again at 6:30 this morning until we had visited *nearly* every battalion . . . in the Kontum area, where he inspected field positions and raised hell at nearly every place that he saw the field positions. Last night he also had assembled the entire province staff, earlier in the evening, and gave them a good pep talk and told them we were going to hold Kontum City."[26]

General Abrams gave his opinion of the advisers during this same commander's conference: "I just think that their performance has been magnificent. In fact it's probably the glue that's held this whole thing together. It's not only the heroics involved in it, but the real toughness and real ability. . . . And I want to tell you, if it wasn't for the advisers, none of us would be sitting here in Saigon today. We'd either be in a [POW] enclosure, dead, or have managed to escape by submarine, powerboat, or some other fucking thing! To Hong Kong. That's what advisers are!"[27]

Four artillery rounds hit Kontum airfield and destroyed a US Cobra gunship on 11 May.[28] On 12 May alone, there were more than 50 US and 28 VNAF sorties plus 25 Arc Light strikes in the Kontum area.[29] That same day, six 122-mm rockets hit Pleiku airfield, and several rounds of incoming fire came very close to a C-130 on Kontum airfield. The 7th Air Force stopped flying C-130s in and out of Kontum during daylight hours.[30]

After Kontum airfield became too dangerous for daylight landings, the C-130s started landing at night. The USAF Ground Control Team in Kontum used radar to bring them in on a ground-controlled approach with all lights out. Then, just before the C-130 hit the runway, the pilot would turn on the landing lights. Except for fuel bladders, all the cargo was rigged on pallets so a combat offload could be done. As the C-130s rolled down the runway, the pallets rolled off the lowered ramp door at the rear of the aircraft. They did not need to shut down the engines or even come to a complete stop. Using that method, their record was five pallets unloaded in 37 seconds.[31]

Late in the morning on 12 May, Lieutenant Craig Smith, a scout pilot from the "Scalp Hunters," was flying his OH-6 on a reconnaissance mission when he noticed a pile of bamboo that did not look quite right in the jungle three kilometers northeast of Vo Dinh. Hawk's Claw was knocking out enemy tanks left and right, so the enemy crews were trying to camouflage them. Smith hovered around and made a pass at the bamboo to get a better look. It was a tank, and the crew realized they were detected. He called in a FAC and marked the tank with a smoke round. However, the jungle was so thick that the FAC lost track of the target. Smith made four more passes at the tank, firing another smoke round each time. As Smith made his fifth pass in front of the tank crew, they fired both their main gun and their machine gun at him. This was probably the only time during the Vietnam War that an enemy tank fired its main gun at a helicopter in the air. If the round from that 100-mm gun had hit any part of the Loach, it would have destroyed it completely. By luck, it missed. However, the powerful muzzle blast blew the rotor blades off the helicopter, and it crashed. After escaping under fire and evading the enemy, Smith and his observer were promptly picked up.[32]

The Hawk's Claw team was sent after the tank but could not find it under the jungle canopy. Eight sets of USAF fighter-bombers were used to destroy most of the surrounding jungle before Hawk's Claw was able to get a clear shot at the target. They finally hit a tank—probably that one—and it burst into flames. There was evidence of other tanks being in the area, but none could be located for a TOW shot.[33]

POW interrogations, captured documents, and radio intercepts gave the ARVN officers and their advisers at division and corps level a good understanding of the NVA's battle plan. The 2nd NVA Infantry Division would not participate in the attack on Kontum, but the 320th NVA Infantry Division would attack us with two reinforced regiments.[34] This division had defeated the French at Dien Bien Phu in 1954 and was probably hoping to achieve a similar victory at Kontum. There were estimates that the two NVA divisions approaching us had already lost half their troops. Yet a news report said, "Few Allied commanders held much hope that the city of Kontum could hold against a determined enemy attack."[35]

The TOW systems mounted on helicopters were proving their worth in combat, but the tank threat to Kontum was increasing by the day. Moving under secret orders, probably because the US government did not want any publicity about any American ground troops going to Vietnam, some TOW missiles mounted on Jeeps were sent from the 82nd Airborne Division at Fort Bragg, North Carolina, to Vietnam. On 13 May, MACV headquarters approved sending three or four of the Jeep-mounted TOW teams into Kontum to be under operational control of the senior adviser to the 23rd ARVN Division.[36]

A Nixon aide summed up the president's mood: "Mr. Nixon is not going to back up one iota from his hard line with the Communists on Vietnam. He will risk the May 22 summit with the Russians, his re-election and everything else, but he won't take defeat in Southeast Asia. He is going right down to the mat with Moscow and Hanoi over this."[37]

The mission to defend Kontum was unlike anything in the 23rd Division's previous experience. This defense would be the first time all of its units were assembled in the same place to perform a common mission. Years of experience in guarding government installations and fighting small battles, mostly with lightly armed Communist units, had not prepared this division to defend a city that was already surrounded and would soon be attacked by the heaviest artillery in the Communist arsenal, human-wave assaults by battle-hardened NVA soldiers, and tanks.

The collapse of the ARVN's 22nd Division at Tan Canh and Dak To II, the NVA's successes, and ARVN's failures in other corps areas were in combination a severe blow to the morale of the South Vietnamese. The soldiers of the 23rd Division were no exception. They had more reason than anyone else to worry because they were in Kontum and next in line to be hit by the Communist juggernaut. The 22nd Infantry Division had operated in the Highlands for years, and they had frequently fought North Vietnamese soldiers. Yet when they were confronted with tanks, they folded. Could the 23rd Infantry Division, which was normally based in the southern part of II Corps and fighting mostly VC, be expected to stand and fight when confronted by the NVA and their tanks?[38]

14

Tanks Attacking!

This city [Kontum] is in danger of extinction. North
Vietnamese tanks and troops are drawing closer from the
north and south. Many of the city's 30,000 residents are
packing to leave . . . as soon as the highway to Pleiku is
opened.

—*Pacific Stars and Stripes,* 30 April 1972

Early on 13 May, I flew from Pleiku to Kontum sitting on the floor
of a USAF C-141 Starlifter with 490 ARVN soldiers and my Jeep,
which the air force loadmaster had tied down. The interior of the
airplane was rigged for cargo delivery, so there were no seats, seat-
belts, or other restraints. The number of passengers it carried
may have set a record for C-141s. When almost 500 ARVN soldiers
walked off the airplane, it reminded me of the circus act in which
a dozen clowns get out of one small car. It was 0520 on Saturday,
13 May, and I was seeing Kontum for the first time. Mountains
were visible in all directions. In the northeast and southeast, they
were more than 3,000 feet high, and to the north Ngok Linh was
8,524 feet high. A large mountain mass to the northwest was called
Rocket Ridge. Even though some of those mountains were 10 to 20
kilometers away, they seemed to loom over Kontum.

Major Wade B. Lovings, formerly the division artillery adviser,
met me at the airfield. He would be my new deputy, and I was
happy to have him with me, especially after having a series of
deputies assigned to my team for only a few weeks each to finish
their required time in Vietnam. We reclaimed our Jeep and drove
straight to the DTOC. I reported to the new 23rd Division senior
adviser, Colonel John O. Truby, who said, "Thank God the 44th

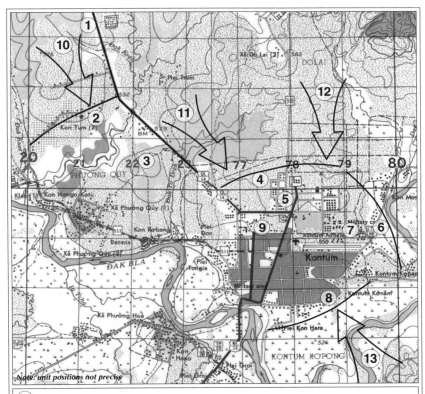

1. Outpost Nectar with 3rd Battalion (-), 44th ARVN Regiment.
2. General trace of frontline positions of 44th ARVN Regiment.
3. The Round Hill with CP of 44th ARVN Regiment and one battalion (-).
4. General trace of frontline positions of 45th ARVN Regiment.
5. CP of 45th ARVN Regiment with company of tanks from 1/8th Armored Regiment.
6. General trace of frontline positions of 53rd ARVN Regt. Other elements to the east, northeast, and southeast of here.
7. CP of 53rd ARVN Regiment.
8. General trace of frontline positions of Kontum RF and PF + battalion of 45th Regt.
9. The DTOC with 4th Battalion, 44th ARVN Regiment for security.
10. Attack by 48th NVA Regiment and tanks from the 297th NVA Tank Battalion.
11. Attack by 64th NVA Regiment with tanks from the 297th NVA Tank Battalion.
12. Attack by the independent 28th NVA Regiment of the B-3 Front.
13. Probing attacks by the 141st NVA Regiment of the 2nd NVA Division.

The attacks on Kontum, 14–16 May 1972.

Regiment is here." I was a bit surprised because I did not know our arrival meant the entire 23rd Division was now assembled in Kontum. Also, I did not realize how precarious the situation was until Colonel Truby briefed me. Then I could see how our one regiment could make a significant difference.

The 44th Regiment was relieving the 2nd Ranger Group, which included the 11th, 22nd, and 72nd Ranger Battalions on FSB November, about four kilometers north of Kontum. This FSB blocked the enemy's main avenue of approach along Highway 14. The Rangers' senior adviser was Lieutenant Colonel Thomas L. Stanford, a friend of mine from 1962 service in the 18th Infantry in Manheim, Germany. He oriented me on the area and the enemy situation. The relief in place had started two days earlier when the first 44th Regiment units had arrived in Kontum. The soldiers who arrived with me would complete the process. Our troops quickly moved into the prepared positions that the Rangers were leaving. An attack was expected at any time, so we did not have the option of changing the troop dispositions and preparing new defensive positions. However, we soon learned the enemy artillery knew exactly where the old ARVN positions were located.

There were no friendly forces between the 44th Regiment and the NVA juggernaut moving toward us. Farther northwest, near the Cambodian border, steadfast Ben Het, Dak Pek, and Plei Mrong were still holding out. However, it was all "Indian territory" between them and us.[1]

The initial dispositions around the perimeter placed the 44th Regiment on FSB November and the 53rd Regiment east of Highway 14 about two kilometers north of the city. Most of the 45th Regiment was in the north, but one battalion of the 45th was in the south, where it was manning part of the perimeter to serve as a reserve, and to put backbone into the Ruff Puffs holding the southern sector.[2]

At 0700 on 13 May, radio intercepts revealed the 320th NVA Division was in the final stage of attack preparations in its assembly area. This news confirmed air cavalry reports of a large buildup of enemy troops and tanks on Highway 14 just south of Vo Dinh.[3] When seven enemy tanks were spotted near Vo Dinh, they were hit by US and VNAF tactical air, and one tank was reported destroyed.[4] The same morning, an NVA supply truck driver gave a ride to a dozen Montagnard women but told them to stay out of that area in the future. Refugees from Polei Kleng said they saw a large Communist force of infantry with tanks following it moving toward Kontum City.

Colonel Tien, his executive officer (XO, second in command), Major Lovings, and I inherited what appeared to be a good, solid bunker, which had probably been built by US Army engineers. It was dug in about five feet and had two layers of large-diameter pine logs crossed over the top and under a couple feet of dirt. A bunker like this should hold up against anything but a direct hit. We set up our folding canvas cots inside, stashed our gear beside them, and then walked around to check out the troops' dispositions and preparations. The dominant feature on FSB November was the Round Hill just west of Highway 14. The 44th Regiment CP and one battalion would be there. Two of our battalions and one company of our 3rd Battalion would defend the perimeter in front of the Round Hill. The remainder of our 3rd Battalion was on Outpost Nectar almost two kilometers farther north on the west side of Highway 14. Our 4th Battalion was providing security around the DTOC in back in Kontum.

While we were not in our bunker, it received a direct hit, which destroyed it, so we moved the regimental CP to a position closer to the front lines and not already pinpointed by the NVA artillery. We were in a pine forest with some heavier jungle on the edges. The ARVN soldiers dug a nice, deep, two-man foxhole with overhead cover for us, and we set up our cots beside it and under a poncho tied between some trees. We kept only the necessary equipment and personal belongings in the field, moved our bags back to the DTOC, and stored them in a corner there.

Throughout the afternoon and evening of 13 May, reports of enemy activity kept coming in, including tank sightings, light contact with enemy units, and sporadic artillery and rocket fire on our positions. At 1750, heavy incoming fire started falling on FSB November. At 1915, Major Lovings relayed to the DTOC a report of two enemy tanks and two artillery pieces sighted north of us.

It was dark by the time Major Lovings and I finished checking troop positions, communications, and our own plans for doing all we could to ensure the regiment was ready to face an enemy attack. Then we talked over whether the troops would hold fast or cut and run if tanks attacked us. We knew this regiment was a far better one in a far better division than the units that had collapsed at Tan

Canh and Dak To II. Our regiment and division also had far better leaders. Nevertheless, it was prudent to make our own contingency plans in case we were overrun and had to E&E like Lieutenant Colonel Brownlee and Captain Carden. When we first arrived in Kontum, we were briefed on how to E&E to a helicopter pickup point in case Kontum was overrun. A two-part survival kit sealed in hard plastic containers that fit into the M-16 clip pouches on standard web equipment was issued to me in Ban Me Thuot months earlier. On one of our trips back to the DTOC, I acquired a "transponder," which would send out a signal to aircraft searching for advisers trying to E&E through the jungle. So we had some good equipment. Following our Ranger School training, we got under a poncho and used a flashlight to study our maps. We plotted a route we would try to follow to the pickup point and selected some rallying points where we would try to meet if we were separated. Then we settled in and hoped for the best.

At 1900 that evening, a radio intercept revealed that the 320th NVA Division was going to attack as soon as possible because it knew it had been detected and did not want to risk being bombed by B-52s. At 2020 on 13 May, an excited Colonel Ba entered the DTOC with an intercepted message from the 320th NVA Division artillery commander ordering his artillery units to support a division attack scheduled to begin at 0400 the next morning. The report of the message came from a US signal intercept element in Kontum. The element informed Mr. Vann and Colonel Ba, but Colonel Truby learned about it from his counterpart, Colonel Ba, who considered the message authentic. With so many indications of an impending attack, Colonel Truby was now convinced it would come the next morning. He immediately called Mr. Vann and the II Corps G-3 adviser to relay this latest information and to request air attacks on the enemy tanks at first light. The air assets were normally over Kontum around 0700, but Truby wanted them overhead at first light, by 0530. Vann was still not convinced a full-scale attack was coming because the NVA usually preceded its big attacks with an especially heavy artillery preparation, which had not happened yet. Although both Vann and the G-3 were still skeptical, Vann believed it was better to be prepared and told Truby he would get the air assets to him at first light.[5]

At 2140, the DTOC alerted the regimental advisers to "check with counterparts on possibility of enemy action tonight." At 2230, the 44th Regiment's front-line troops reported vehicle lights coming toward us down Highway 14. Major Lovings and I ran to a vantage point to see for ourselves. We were expecting the enemy to attack us in the night or at dawn with infantry and tanks, but here were vehicles driving down the highway toward us with their headlights blazing. Civilian vehicles were unlikely to be moving down this highway in the middle of the battlefield. Were NVA trucks boldly driving toward our lines with their headlights on? We did not know the Communists had driven with their tank headlights on when they attacked the 22nd Division at Tan Canh in the early-morning darkness, so what we were seeing seemed crazy and inexplicable to us. However, what we saw actually was the enemy's tanks, moving forward into their attack positions. The NVA was not experienced in maneuvering its tanks at night and probably decided it was more important to drive with the lights on and attack us at the scheduled time and place than to conceal its movement by driving with the lights off and risk getting lost in the dark.[6]

At 0400 on 14 May, the DTOC log recorded, "All defenses manned and ready." A Spectre gunship was ordered to expend its remaining ammo in support of the 44th Regiment before returning to base. The defenders were alert and waiting for the impending attack, but when 0400 came, there was no attack. Then the 23rd Division G-2, Lieutenant Colonel Tieu, brought in another intercepted message, which indicated a half-hour delay in the attack, to 0430. Tieu also pointed out that because these orders were coming from B-3 Front headquarters, the time given was probably Hanoi time—one hour earlier than the Saigon time the defenders used. This would mean an 0530 attack. Colonel Truby had just settled in for some much-needed sleep outside the DTOC bunker when he was awakened by the sounds of the attack commencing at 0530—right on schedule. The big test was starting. We would soon know how the 23rd Division troops would react to a tank attack.[7]

Starting at 0430, the volume of indirect fire on FSB November became increasingly heavy. The tempo of ground probes and attacks by fire increased, and a Spectre gunship used its minigun to hose down the enemy massing in front of us. After expending all its ammo, the Spectre departed.

At 0530, the incoming rounds suddenly increased. Enemy artillery and rocket rounds were falling on our positions every five to ten seconds. By 0600, we were fighting off a fierce ground assault by enemy tanks and infantry. The division artillery was responding to our calls for fire support, but Major Lovings told the DTOC, "The incoming enemy artillery fire is twice as strong as the friendly supporting fire." Colonel Hung, the division artillery commander and a graduate of the US Army Artillery School, massed all his artillery fire on the attacking enemy. This action separated the NVA infantry from their tanks and allowed our tank-killer teams to fire their M-72s at the enemy tanks.[8] We soon received the first report of an enemy tank knocked out by an M-72. We were too busy fighting for our lives to think about it at the time, but when that first plucky ARVN soldier crawled out of his hole and used a shoulder-fired rocket to destroy one of the oncoming iron monsters, it was an important turning point in the battle. The impact of that first kill was far greater than just one tank knocked out; it demonstrated to our troops—and probably to the enemy—that a single ARVN infantryman could kill a tank. This knowledge gave a big boost to our troops' morale and confidence. The first kill was quickly followed by another report of a T-54 knocked out by an M-72. (Our troops may have used captured RPGs rather than M-72s to kill some of the T-54s.) The 23rd Division operations adviser, Lieutenant Colonel Bricker, said, "They fought the tanks before daylight, before we could bring in tactical air, the Cobras, the gunships, or the TOW missiles."[9]

The initial attack was a fast fight. By 0625, the enemy assault was stopped, and I could report to the DTOC, "Seven enemy tanks destroyed and another three have fled." Gladiator 29 started hunting for those three fleeing tanks, but the T-54s soon revealed themselves by returning to attack our front line again. The DTOC called for air support, and a Covey FAC and VNAF A1s were scrambled to come to our assistance. The VNAF FAC and A1s would not arrive for another 40 to 45 minutes, but the DTOC reassured us that the "cavalry" was on the way. The Aerial TOW Team, anticipating they would be needed to help us deal with the enemy tanks, had already taken off from Pleiku. Hawk's Claw arrived at 0650, and we directed them to the three tanks attacking us. Our own artillery was now firing furiously at the attacking infantry and tanks, but this raised so much dust over the battlefield that the TOW gunners could not see the tanks. I readily called off the artillery because it was important to kill those T-54s, which were the main threat.[10]

By 0705, the tide had turned. However, incoming fire was increasing again, and we braced for a second attack. The Panther Cobra gunships would support us, and USAF tactical air was now overhead.[11] As other enemy tank, truck, and gun positions were detected during the day, Hawk's Claw and air strikes were used to destroy them.

The 23rd Division claimed ten enemy tanks were destroyed during this one day of fighting, and ARVN claimed that the enemy lost 35 percent of his men and equipment over the next seven days of constant combat.[12] We captured two POWs, who said they were from the 203rd NVA Tank Regiment.[13] I later described the action in a letter: "In the initial assault North West of the city that day at dawn, the NVA threw ten tanks into the battle. It was only about 20–30 minutes before Hawk's Claw, the TOW firing helicopter arrived from Pleiku. I directed him to the area by radio and he rapidly knocked out his first tank. The TOW got seven of the ten tanks that morning. One hit a mine and two were knocked out by our troops using an M-72 and a captured RPG."[14]

The NVA attacks on 13 and 14 May came on three major axes of advance. The 48th NVA Regiment of the 320th NVA Infantry Division and one company of the 297th NVA Tank Battalion attacked from the northwest down the west side of Highway 14 to assault the 44th Regiment on FSB November. The 64th NVA Regiment of the 320th NVA Infantry Division, also with a company from the 297th NVA Tank Battalion, attacked from the north–northwest on the east side of Highway 14 to assault the 45th ARVN Regiment. Farther east, the independent 28th NVA Regiment of the B-3 Front attacked the 53rd ARVN Regiment from the north. The 141st NVA Regiment of the 2nd NVA Division probed against the Ruff Puffs who were defending the southern sector of the perimeter. When the 320th NVA Division's 52nd Regiment had attacked Polei Kleng and seized it on 9 May, it had suffered so many casualties that it was held in reserve during the mid-May attacks on Kontum.[15]

Until the morning of 14 May, I knew virtually nothing about the TOW-firing helicopters other than seeing a photo of a US Army helicopter armed with antitank missiles in a publication I had read while on R&R in Hong Kong.[16] An American helicopter that could destroy a tank with one missile was an unpleasant surprise for the NVA tank crews. When a TOW missile hit a tank, it was like a bolt of lightning that burned a hole through the armor, exploded any ammunition in its way, and probably killed the entire crew. Most of the enemy tanks the Aerial TOW Team attacked did not take evasive action and thus were stationary when the missile hit them. Two T-54s attempting to cross the Dak Kuet River five kilometers northwest of Kontum on 14 May were a good example. The Aerial TOW Team rolled in and knocked out the lead tank, which was in the middle of the river. The second tank was still on the bank, but the crew bailed out and ran when they saw the fate of the lead tank. The TOWs then destroyed the abandoned tank.[17] The Aerial TOW Team had three big advantages over tactical air: they could operate in marginal weather with a low ceiling; they could fire multiple missiles on the same run toward the target if they saw the first missile was not enough; and they produced very little collateral damage to friendly troops or civilian structures.[18]

Although intermittent incoming rounds were still a hazard, there appeared to be a lull in the fighting. Mr. Vann and Major General Toan took advantage of it and choppered into town for lunch with Colonel Ba at the 23rd Division headquarters in Kontum. A *Los Angeles Times* reporter asked the corps commander what he had done since taking command, and Toan responded, "I have tried to raise the morale of the troops. I gave the order to fight in place—no retreat—and I let them know that if someone has some successes he will get recompense. I am ready with rank insignia, decorations, and $120 as reward for each destroyed tank." Vann admitted that until we successfully repelled the initial tank attack on Kontum, he had thought, "The chances [are] about 50–50" that we could hold. Now he was confident: "The line would be held." From 14 May on, John Paul Vann came to Kontum at least once in every 24-hour period.[19]

On 14 May, Colonel R. M. Rhotenberry arrived in Vietnam to become senior adviser to the 23rd ARVN Division. Vann had specifically requested Rhotenberry because he thought Rhotenberry had more combat experience than any other officer in the army. Rhotenberry was a highly decorated combat veteran who had earned the Distinguished Service Cross and a battlefield commission in Korea. This tour would be his fifth in Vietnam—possibly a record for the number of one-year tours served by one man who was not a pilot. Because he had served so many tours in Vietnam, some of the ARVN officers called him "the soldier of fortune." Especially significant for this assignment, he had served most of his previous tours as a MACV adviser, had worked with Ly Tong Ba during his 1962–1963 tour when Ba had been province chief of Binh Duong Province, and had worked closely with John Paul Vann from July 1966 to July 1967. Rhotenberry was the right man for the job.[20]

When Colonel Rhotenberry arrived at Tan Son Nhut on 14 May, Mr. Vann had a U-21 fixed-wing, propeller-driven airplane waiting to fly him to Pleiku. Vann was flying over the Kontum battlefield in his own helicopter that day, but as soon as he could, he flew Rhotenberry to Kontum. During the flight, Vann briefed him, described his mission, and emphasized how important it was. Rhotenberry remembered exactly what Vann said: "Here's what I want you to do. I want you to make sure that the 23rd Division holds Kontum. I don't care what you need. Let me know and I'll get it for you. You know, Rhot, this is very important to me. My credibility is at stake. At Tan Canh the troop disposition was mine. I said we could defend there if we disposed the troops the way they were disposed. And they didn't hold. My career is at stake because I've said we can defend Kontum. If you don't hold it, I no longer have any credibility or career."[21]

Colonels Truby and Rhotenberry had first met in 1962 when they were in the initial large group of advisers sent to Vietnam and went through adviser training together at Fort Bragg, North Carolina. They agreed Rhotenberry would stay in the background and let Truby continue to run things for a few days before taking over from him. Rhotenberry wanted to learn as much as possible as soon as possible about how the 23rd Division, II Corps, and the American and ARVN staffs in the DTOC were operating. He believed he could not influence anything until he was "hooked in" with the Vietnamese. He had had only a few hours of sleep since arriving in Vietnam and would now go without any sleep for the next two nights, staying up all night to listen to the tactical frequency on the DTOC radio, observing the operation of the DTOC, and asking questions. During this period, he ran on coffee and Camel cigarettes. Rhotenberry knew Lieutenant Colonel Bricker slightly, but the other members of Team 33 were strangers to him. He decided the Americans were running an independent TOC and needed to exchange information with the Vietnamese staff to compare, cross-check, and evaluate what they were receiving from US sources. The enemy pressure was continuous as Rhotenberry tried to figure out the tempo of the NVA attacks.

Colonel Rhotenberry's main concern was the division units' capabilities. Would they fight or flee? He also wanted to assess the advisers' qualifications. Assessing the tactical situation was important, but assessing the advisers was equally important. He thought the advisers in the DTOC were not sending information to II Corps, so he ordered them to start doing it. The air assets had been turned over to the regiments, and he brought them back under division control. He also wanted any adjustments in the air or fire support relayed back to him so he could cross-check that information with the ARVN staff. He decided that the information from the ARVN chain of command was more accurate than information received through the advisers.[22]

During the remainder of 14 May, most of Kontum City was hit with some intermittent incoming artillery and rocket fire. The perimeter defenses and the 44th Regiment's CP were hardest hit. Some of the incoming was silenced when the enemy batteries were located from the air and then hit with tactical air strikes. Important areas, such as the DTOC and the airfield, were hit in a manner indicating that the impacting rounds were being adjusted by enemy forward observers to pinpoint where heavy barrages should fall in conjunction with a future attack. Fierce, hand-to-hand fighting restored the 23rd Division's front lines by nightfall on the 14th. However, Colonel Ba was concerned that the enemy would get in behind the 44th Regiment on FSB November and occupy the graveyard between FSB November and the city. If NVA forces could seize and hold the graveyard, they would be in a position to smash the 44th between the "hammer" of their attacks on the front line and the "anvil" of their blocking position behind the regiment.[23]

While walking the line to check our positions after dark that night, I was surprised when an American sergeant from the 82nd Airborne Division reported to me. He was the leader of a Jeep-mounted TOW team. Sergeant *Thatcher* explained what the TOW could do, and we worked out where it could best be employed: just below the nose of the hill in a lightly wooded area where he could fire at any tanks guiding on Highway 14 to attack us. TOW gunner Private First Class Angel L. Figueroa was credited with knocking out a T-54 on the evening of 14 May. Firing through the woods, he hit several trees but then got a round through the trees and saw it hit the tank. Other tanks were driven back by incoming artillery before he could fire at them. Figueroa was probably the first American soldier to destroy an enemy tank in combat by firing a Jeep-mounted TOW missile at it.[24]

A total of 26 Jeep-mounted TOW teams from the US 82nd Airborne were sent to Vietnam on temporary duty. Maintenance contact teams, a Department of the Army missile-maintenance technician, and TOW instructors from the United States accompanied the TOW teams to Vietnam. After four days of training and practice firing at Bien Hoa, an enormous American base just north of Saigon, 23 TOW teams with 18 Jeep-mounted TOW systems were airlifted into Pleiku and Kontum. The other three TOW teams remained at Bien Hoa. In Vietnam, the TOW teams were assigned to the ad hoc Task Force Salvo with the mission "to provide timely anti-mechanized defense for the safety and evacuation of U.S. personnel." Salvo was composed of D Company of the 1st Battalion, 12th Cavalry Regiment; a "TOW company" made up of selected infantrymen from the Cavalry Brigade's maneuver battalions; a Ground Surveillance Radar Section from headquarters and Headquarters and Service Battery of the 1st Battalion, 21st Artillery; and 12 Jeep-mounted TOWs in a "brigade antitank platoon." The "brigade" designation was probably a cover to give the impression that this platoon was part of the 3rd Brigade (Separate) of the 1st Cavalry Division (Airmobile), which was still in Vietnam. The arrival of the TOW teams in Vietnam was classified, and the message from MACV headquarters to the corps advisers concerning the movement of these "3rd Brigade" troops to Pleiku was classified "Secret."[25]

When John Paul Vann asked General Abrams for authority to send some of the Jeep-mounted TOWs to Kontum under command of the senior adviser to the 23rd Division, Abrams approved it, saying, "Some of the people up there are very worried about tanks. But: my *real* reason is as long as those advisers are going to stay there, I want to—I think it improves their situation immensely. And that's what it's for. Also, they may get a chance to knock out some tanks, which will be also pretty good. . . . It's also reported to me that's [the TOW crews] a pretty fine bunch of men."[26]

Colonel Truby deployed two of the three Jeep-mounted TOW teams on FSB November because we faced the greatest threat of a tank attack. The third team was held in reserve near the DTOC, where it could also protect that facility.

At 2000 the night of 14 May, we were hit again. The enemy

infantry came in hard and fast, and some tanks came with them. This assault was more intense than the one we had fought off in the early morning, and the 53rd Regiment on our right flank, to the east, was hit equally hard. In the darkness, an NVA battalion managed to get in between the 44th and 53rd Regiments. Major Lovings and I realized we were fighting off three separate enemy battalions to our front, right flank, and rear. We were in a perilous situation, and Colonel Tien called for artillery fire on our own positions. A commander does this at great risk to his own troops and only as a last, desperate measure to prevent being overrun. If all goes well, the friendly troops will be safe in bunkers or foxholes with adequate overhead cover, but the attacking enemy infantry will be mowed down by the airbursts of artillery rounds with variable-time or proximity fuses (which would detonate at a set height above the ground). If only rounds with impact fuses are available, they can be used, but the risk to friendly troops is greater because a round that detonates only when it hits something can blow apart any foxhole or bunker it lands on. Colonel Tien's request for artillery fire on our positions was cancelled when a Spectre gunship arrived overhead and was allocated to us because we were being attacked from three directions and needed immediate help. Targets received from the front lines were relayed through Colonel Tien to Major Lovings, who told Spectre where to fire around our imperiled perimeter.[27]

At this point in the battle, Colonel Truby was concerned about the lack of an uncommitted division reserve. Colonel Ba had previously tentatively agreed to use the 45th Regiment's battalion positioned in the south as a reserve. However, now that the battalion was needed to counterattack the penetration, Ba would not move it through town in the dark. Also, he did not want to risk leaving only the Ruff Puffs to defend the vulnerable southern perimeter. Something needed to be done fast, or Kontum would fall before dawn. Colonel Ba agreed to move the 53rd's own reserve into position in front of the enemy forces' penetration to block them from driving deeper into the defenses.[28]

Without a division reserve to counterattack and with the situation rapidly worsening, Colonel Truby recommended a B-52 strike at the base of the penetration. Colonel Ba and Mr. Vann concurred, but less than an hour later they learned it was disapproved in Saigon because it was too close to a village just north of the penetration. One of the advisers commented that on a target like the closely massed NVA attacking force, an Arc Light would have almost the shock effect of a nuclear strike. This comment reminded Truby of a discussion at the Command and General Staff College 15 years earlier about how troops in contact could be withdrawn, a low kiloton tactical nuclear weapon could be used on the enemy, and then the friendly troops could attack to regain their position. (The army later realized the inadvisability of entering an area with high levels of radiation.) With this reminder, Truby realized the same tactic could be used with an Arc Light.[29]

Although the 53rd Regiment troops could temporarily pull back from the Arc Light strike box, the 44th Regiment would still be too close to it. Because the NVA held the streambed behind the Round Hill, the 44th could not be pulled back there. Colonel Truby called me on the landline between the DTOC and FSB November. He said that we were in a desperate situation and that drastic action was required to prevent us from being overrun that night. He proposed putting in an Arc Light dangerously close to our lines to catch the enemy in the open as they massed to attack us. He pointed out the danger of a B-52 strike so close to us and asked if I was willing to take the risk. We were already close to being overrun, and the worst was probably yet to come. We did need something extra to tip the odds in our favor. I agreed to have the Arc Light hit wherever the DTOC wanted to plot it. Captain John R. Finch plotted the nearest edge of the Arc Light box only 700 yards from our front-line troops. Such a close strike was a safety violation, but Finch thought—as I would have had I known it at the time—that taking this risk was better than being overrun.

Colonel Truby convinced Colonel Ba to pull the 53rd Regiment troops defending against the penetration 500 meters south so that a previously approved B-52 strike could be diverted 200 meters south into a previously used Arc Light box. Mr. Vann was hesitant to approve this plan because of its complexity. However, after talking to both Truby and Ba and with Ba's agreement, Vann approved it for lack of any feasible alternative. When the Arc Light request was phoned in, there were objections because it would go into an Arc Light box used previously. Colonel Truby got on the phone and pointed out that the attacking NVA was probably using the bomb craters from the previous Arc Light as cover and so hitting exactly the same area was likely to produce extra casualties. The ARVN troops were pulled back at the appointed time, and artillery fire into the penetration was increased to hold the NVA in place. The Arc Light struck at 0425, and the NVA attack was broken up shortly after it started.[30]

Just behind the front lines on FSB November, Major Lovings and I got into a good, deep foxhole and squeezed down into the bottom before the scheduled Arc Light. There was time to ponder how accurate the air force could be from 30,000 feet above us. If just one bomb bumped into another bomb as they tumbled out of the bomb bay, it might be thrown off course enough to hit us. When the Arc Light struck at 0425, there was a rumbling vibration that seemed to start from deep down in the center of the earth. We heard a long series of loud, shrill whistles as the sound of the falling bombs reached us. These whistles were intermixed with the long drum roll of explosions as the bombs detonated. When those hundreds of bombs came screeching down, it sounded as if they were all coming straight toward our foxhole. During a BDA the next day, the crater of one errant 750-pound bomb was found only 300 meters from our front lines. We may have been as close to the impact of an Arc Light bomb as any American soldiers ever were during the Vietnam War.[31]

After the Arc Light hit, the 53rd's own reserve was able to counterattack and eject the enemy from the penetration. Colonel Ba ordered limited offensives into the areas bombed the night of 14 May. So at first light the morning of 15 May, ARVN troops pushed out from our lines to find the enemy's new positions, develop new Arc Light targets, and count the carnage. Hundreds of bodies and many parts of bodies were found within the Arc Light box and half of them were in the old bomb craters. At least 200 dead NVA soldiers lay in front of the 44th Regiment's lines, and Major Richard O. Perry with the 53rd Regiment reported another 189. Our troops also picked up a couple hundred enemy weapons. While the 2nd Battalion, 53rd Regiment, was searching the B-52 strike area at 1000, they found 23 enemy KIA and one WIA. The wounded NVA soldier said they had just started their attack when the bombs fell on them. He revealed that even before the strike there were only 25 men left in his company. The air cavalry reported a big increase in enemy activity west, northeast, and southeast of Kontum City that day. The NVA buildup in the south, where the Ruff Puffs manned the perimeter, especially concerned the advisers. Many of the troops in those territorial forces lived in Kontum and were in the habit of going home for the night, leaving unmanned gaps in our defenses.[32]

Just after 1500, the 1st Battalion, 44th Regiment, west of Highway 14 on our left flank, received heavy mortar and machine gun fire from the northeast across Highway 14. That assault continued through the afternoon as the incoming fire increased all along the front.[33] The enemy sometimes scored a lucky hit with all that intermittent artillery, rocket, and mortar fire. In the late afternoon, one or more of their rounds struck the JP-4 aircraft-fuel storage at Kontum airfield and set it on fire.[34]

On the night of 14–15 May, sappers cut the fence around the POL storage area in Pleiku and used C-4 plastic explosives to destroy a storage tank containing 150,000 gallons of JP-4. They rigged other storage tanks for destruction, but the explosives did not detonate. This was a major loss of aviation fuel during a period when the refueling point at Pleiku was using 32,000 gallons a day. The sappers also destroyed the pumping station. Attacks by fire on the Pleiku airfield destroyed 330 tons of ammunition, including 97 tons of dynamite, 90,000 feet of detonating cord, 18,000 one-pound blocks of TNT, 90,000 fuses for the 105-mm shells, and various amounts of 40-mm, 57-mm, and smaller ammo. This explosion must have made one heck of a racket, and the sight and sound must have given the enemy a tremendous sense of accomplishment. The JP-4 operation was soon back in operation, but the total ammunition and POL losses were staggering, and replenishing them by truck up Highway 19 would always be dangerous and sometimes impossible for days on end.[35]

Captain Giap Phuc Hai described his experience in Kontum:

Soon all the three regiments of the 23rd Division were in place; the field command was unified, and on May 13th, 1972, my boss told me to be ready as the enemy was expected to launch the attack in the wee hours of next day morning. Indeed, they did. The shelling was intense; the division TOC was hit with delayed type 130-mm shells, [and] quite a few staff were killed or wounded as part of the bunker collapsed, especially the corner where the air force support section sat. The enemy also used captured 105/155 howitzers to shell us, and that was the first time I knew what a "fleshette" meant or looked like. I faithfully wore my flak jacket and helmet since.

On the radio, the front troops reported that enemy tanks were hit, but they did not know who did it and how they were destroyed. Our little house/triage area was hit by 90-mm shell from T-54 tank. It also hit the place where we collected guns and grenades from the wounded soldiers. The smoke grenades exploded, and very soon most of us were painted in different colors: purple, yellow, orange. No one was killed; many of us were slightly wounded. That day we counted over 400 WIA. The ambulances were moving nonstop. Calls [were] coming from all the places, and we managed to help out. The seriously wounded were flown out by choppers to Pleiku Military Hospital. Among them was the CO of the 45th Regiment, with his femoral artery severed. He survived and returned to visit us many months later, wearing new rank of Colonel. He brought us Ban Me Thuot coffee as a token of gratitude. Another night, the call for helicopter was answered right away for a severe case of chest wound. The VNAF helicopters *always came when we needed them*. My boss's friendship with the air force staff paid off very handsomely, and it was a lesson that I cherished and later applied during my brief military career. We parked 4 ambulances with parking lights on at 4 corners, and the chopper was able to land straight down in that area.

One day, a major, CO of a battalion of the 44th Reg., was sent to me because of severe malaria. He just wanted a quick IV with quinine; he did not want to leave his battalion. He was physically exhausted. I saw that his young wife accompanied him to Kontum from Song Mao. I forced him to stay, and I admitted him to my "quarter." I wanted him to have some much needed rest as well as some time with his wife. He was KIA a few weeks later by a shell which landed right over his tent. He was a graduate of our Dalat Military Academy.[36]

A crewman from one of the enemy tanks attacking us on 14 May was captured and told his story. Corporal Tran Van Minh said he was a tank gunner in the 2nd Company, 297th Tank Battalion, 203rd NVA Tank Regiment. He had been born 9 October 1952 in

Van Yen Village, Dai Tu District, Ac Thai Province; had graduated from high school; and had been a candidate for the University of Agriculture when he was drafted in August 1970. After training and service in various places, his tank battalion started to infiltrate down the Ho Chi Minh Trail in December 1971. After the long march south along the Ho Chi Minh Trail, the enemy rested, reequipped, and trained in base areas or secret zones they controlled. There were eight of those base areas within II Corps and another four adjacent to it across the western border with Laos and Cambodia.[37] They arrived in the Central Highlands in March 1972 and came down Highway 14 to attack Kontum.

On 13 May, Lieutenant Luyen (full name not known), their company commander, briefed them and said that, following an artillery barrage, they would attack at 0300 the next morning. Four tanks from their company would attack with the 3rd Battalion of the 48th Infantry Regiment and the 7th Infantry Battalion of the 64th Infantry Regiment. It would be a two-pronged attack, with 800 meters between the prongs and two tanks leading each infantry battalion. They were told there was a threat from M-72 "light anti-tank weapons," but the ARVN soldiers would probably run rather than use them. After they "rolled over" FSB November, they were to continue south to attack Kontum City.

Minh was the first POW to report that an NVA commander had admitted an attack might fail. He was told that if their attack did not succeed before dawn, they were to withdraw to the shelter of a banana grove, where engineers of the 14th Company of Engineers, which was attached to the 203rd Tank Regiment, had prepared positions. They were also told if the "Tay Nguyen Battlefield"—the western Highlands—was not liberated before the end of the dry season, the campaign must continue into the wet season to "succeed at any price."

At 0300, Minh's tank and the tank it was paired with drove onto Highway 14 and proceeded toward the right (western) side of their objective, FSB November. The other two tanks and the infantry battalion behind them were proceeding toward the left (eastern) side of the objective. Then Lieutenant Luyen ordered the two tanks on the right to join those on the left. All four tanks attacked, but Minh could not fire his main gun because of some mechanical difficulty. As his tank reached the first ARVN bunker, it was hit in rapid succession by the rounds from three LAWs and one captured RPG. All four of the attacking tanks were destroyed. Minh never learned the fate of the other crews, but he was the only survivor in his tank.

Minh said that at the NVA tank school they had received a lecture on coordinating tanks and infantry, but they did not know how to do it because they had never practiced. He thought a lack of coordination and their failure to rehearse their attack were the reasons they failed to overrun FSB November. This failure threw off the timetable for the attack on Kontum City.[38]

When the advisers and ARVN soldiers had inspected some of the tanks knocked out at An Loc, they had discovered that the Communist crewmen had been chained into their seats.[39] We never saw evidence of such extreme measures in NVA tanks captured or knocked out in Kontum.

The US Army's doctrine for employing tanks emphasizes armor's special strengths: shock action, firepower, and mobility. By the 1970s, the main guns on the major military powers' medium and heavy tanks were at least 90 or 100 millimeters, and their range and penetrating power made them deadly to any opposing vehicles, including enemy tanks. They could also destroy bunkers or blast through the walls of buildings. The NVA often drove their tanks down the roads when they should have sacrificed speed for safety by moving cross-country. Other times they moved slowly and cautiously when they should have gone "hell bent for leather" to overrun the ARVN defenders. On many occasions, they employed their tanks almost hesitantly by attacking with only a few tanks at a time rather than in overwhelming mass. Also, they failed to employ their tanks and infantry as a team. The infantry can protect tanks against individual enemy soldiers who can approach from the tanks' blind spots to disable or destroy them with a shoulder-fired rocket or an explosive charge. The tanks can protect their infantry and advance the attack by knocking out enemy armored vehicles or heavy-weapons positions in bunkers or buildings.

As the fighting and our bombing intensified, thousands of civilians were driven from their homes. The flow of refugees grew to a flood. Immediately after the disasters at Dak To and Tan Canh, about 30,000 civilians had fled from Kontum to the coastal regions and southern provinces. Between late April and mid-May, 20,000 refugees were evacuated from Kontum, but more refugees kept coming. Barefooted Montagnard men wearing loincloths and bare-breasted women carrying their babies in slings and their possessions in reed baskets streamed into Kontum, fleeing ahead of the NVA. By mid-May, there were still 15,000 Yards and 10,000 other refugees in the city. Weapons were issued to 2,500 of the Montagnard men, and they were assigned to the militia units defending the city. On 15 May, the airlift effort was increased to evacuate other refugees to the relative safety of Pleiku. At the same time that 14,000 refugees from Kontum and points north managed to reach Pleiku, 45,000 of Pleiku's own population of 60,000 fled the city.[40]

At a briefing with his field commanders, General Abrams said about the battle, "I *doubt* the fabric of this thing could have been held together without US air. But the thing that had to happen before that is the Vietnamese, some numbers of them, *had* to stand and fight. If they didn't do that, ten times the air we've got wouldn't have stopped them."[41]

15

Struggling to
Hold It Together

Under extended bombardment or bombing the nerve ends
are literally beaten. The ear drums are tortured by blast and
the eyes ache from the constant hammering.
                    —John Steinbeck, *Once There Was a War*

At 1950 on 15 May, the incoming fire increased in caliber and volume. Our regiment's front-line elements on the Round Hill were
being hit with direct fire from the NVA tanks' 100-mm main guns.
At 2016, four to six T-54s were spotted about a kilometer to the
northeast on the forward slope of a hill the other side of Highway
14. A Spectre gunship was on station and unsuccessfully attacked
the tanks with 40-mm cannon fire. The Jeep-mounted TOWs fired
at the tanks and thought they scored two hits. Both Spectre and a
USAF FAC later reported seeing a tank burning. Hawk's Claw was
launched from its laager in Pleiku, and the C-130 dropped flares
to illuminate the tanks for them. However, the TOW gunners were
unable to locate the tanks in their sighting systems. After firing one
missile at a suspected target, Hawk's Claw returned to Pleiku. The
tanks withdrew after a couple hours, but the gunship remained
on station to provide illumination and fire support. Our front-line
units reported receiving tank fire again at 0615 the next morning.[1]

John Paul Vann thought the enemy offensive would be stopped
at Kontum because B-52 strikes and artillery could break the siege
and destroy the bulk of the NVA in the Highlands. He said, "The
enemy has sufficient forces to be able to die for the next six to eight

weeks around Kontum. Whether or not Kontum is held is going to depend on how much steel there is in [South Vietnam's] soldiers and how much air power and airborne resupply we can provide to them."[2]

Scattered attacks continued across the Highlands over the next two days. At 0600 on 16 May, FSB 42 south of Kontum received indirect fire and a ground attack that penetrated the perimeter wire. The attack was beaten off, with 47 enemy and 23 ARVN KIA. Elements of the 44th, 45th, and 53rd regiments made contact with the enemy north of Kontum. Hawk's Claw confirmed an enemy tank destroyed by a mine west of our positions, and their TOW missiles destroyed two APCs, an ammo truck, and a 105-mm artillery piece. They also blew up an ammo dump five kilometers west of Vo Dinh. At 0325 on 17 May, sappers got into the Pleiku air base ammo dump and destroyed some 105-mm and other ammo. Sapper attacks also destroyed 1,500 tons of ammunition at Cam Ranh Bay. Mr. Vann advised Major General Toan to inflict and advertise the stiffest possible disciplinary actions for all such defensive failures.[3]

Colonel Ba decided he needed to eliminate the enemy penetrations, so on 16 May a battalion of the 44th Regiment attacked to drive the NVA out of the streambed behind our regiment's positions on the Round Hill. The 44th was unable to clear the enemy out of the streambed completely before dark, when it had to return to FSB November to man positions there during the night. Then the reserve from the 53rd Regiment counterattacked the enemy in a graveyard on the northwest, but that attack was also unsuccessful.[4]

The NVA continued its harassment and interdiction fire on Kontum City and refined its attacks on aircraft landing at the airfield. Every time a helicopter landed to refuel, up to 12 rounds of artillery or mortar fire would be fired at it. Enemy forward observers were adjusting this indirect fire. At 1515 on 16 May, three helicopters were damaged and a crewman wounded by incoming fire. Starting at 1740, another 50 rounds landed in 20 minutes. Two VNAF C-123s sitting on the parking ramp were systematically destroyed. One was loaded with ammunition, and when it exploded, shrapnel flew in every direction, and the runway was badly pitted. The airfield was closed until 0645 the next morning. Mr. Vann recommended to the corps commander that he direct the Kontum Province chief to use martial law authority to organize an airfield cleanup team of civilians to sweep the runways after future attacks by fire. The C-123s destroyed at Kontum were later bulldozed aside to make offloading space for other aircraft.[5] The division artillery, with its incoming ammo supply cut off while it was firing almost constantly, was dangerously low on some types of ammunition. A few artillery units were down to only 10 percent of their normal ammunition stock— not a comfortable level in the early stages of a big battle. It would be necessary to increase and maintain ammunition levels by flying more USAF C-130 and VNAF C-123 missions into Kontum despite the danger to aircraft and crews. At 2240, an enemy assault against the 53rd Regiment was stopped dead in its tracks when an Arc Light hit the attacking enemy force.[6]

Major General Toan and Mr. Vann spent the night of 16–17 May in Kontum at the 23rd Division DTOC to iron out arrangements and responsibilities for controlling and monitoring the airfield. Toan appeared to have reservations about Colonel Ba's ability to run the battle and was openly critical of his performance. Colonel Rhotenberry took over as Ba's adviser on 16 May, and Vann suggested—probably because of Rhotenberry's previous relationship with Ba as his adviser in 1962—that this change might strengthen the division commander's performance. After a month and a half in Kontum, Colonel Truby departed on the morning of 17 May and returned to his assignment in Nha Trang. Before he left, Colonel Ba assembled the American and Vietnamese staffs and presented Truby with the ARVN Gallantry Cross.[7]

Colonel Rhotenberry learned that Mr. Vann dealt directly with his "doers" in the field and did not go through his staff. He did not follow a routine or operate on normal hours. His Arc Light briefing could be at 0200. There was no working telephone landline between the DTOC in Kontum and II Corps headquarters in Pleiku. Communication by FM radio required a radio relay, such as an aircraft overhead, and Rhotenberry quickly gave up on that. So his voice contact with Vann and the other II Corps advisers was by single-sideband radio. It was not a secure means of communication, but Vann discussed everything over the radio, and he sometimes called three times during the night. Colonel Ba slept upstairs, above the DTOC, and Rhotenberry slept in the DTOC by the radio until around 5 June, when a small bunker was built next to the DTOC for him to live in. During this period, Vann wore slacks, a T-shirt, and a helicopter pilot's "chicken plate" or "bullet bouncer"—a carrier with front and back ceramic plates encased in fiberglass. Rhotenberry never wore a flak jacket, so he sometimes joked with Vann about his chicken plate.[8]

Brigadier General Hill thought Colonel Rhotenberry acted more in the capacity of a liaison officer than as an adviser and later said, "He was more Ba's man to us than he was our man to Ba. Perhaps he had known Colonel Ba too long but he failed to prod him, as a senior adviser should, to take actions like establishing outposts in front of the perimeter."[9] Hill also criticized Colonel Ba for not using his tanks. Colonel Rhotenberry said that on one visit Hill "really chewed Ba's ass," and Ba was understandably upset. On Vann's next visit, Rhotenberry took him aside and asked him to "get Hill off our ass. We have enough trouble with the enemy." From then on Hill came to Kontum only to ask if they needed anything.[10]

At a 17 May press conference in Pleiku, Mr. Vann answered questions and made a number of points on a variety of issues. He said that although 20,000 refugees had been evacuated from Kontum, they kept coming, and 30,000 more were waiting to be evacuated. During the rainy season, we could get air support only 50 percent of the time. B-52 strikes and bombing by tactical air had killed half the men in the 320th NVA Infantry Division. The 2nd NVA Infantry Division was 3 to 15 kilometers from Kontum. An NVA tank crewman who was captured the previous Sunday said he did not have a round chambered in his main gun when he entered Kontum because they were told the infantry had already seized the objective. Vann added, "The NVA are characterized by dogged determination. They will keep attacking as long as one man is left."[11] A Hoi Chanh from the 48th NVA Regiment said his regiment had been massing north of Kontum for an attack on us when they were hit by a B-52 strike and suffered extensive casualties.[12]

Artillery and mortar fire continued to pound the airfield on 17 May. At 1130, two Cobra gunships were damaged and a crewmember was wounded when a rocket landed nearby. My letter home on this day said, "Tonight, the U.S. Air Force will be flying in again all night. The U.S. Air Force has saved us so far. The South Vietnamese would be lost without it. One of the tanks we knocked out on 14 May was operable and it is now on display at the soccer field. Kontum is 90% evacuated."

On the third consecutive day of constant attacks against the 44th

Regiment, 17 May, the NVA were infiltrating around and behind us by using the streambed of the Dak To Dreh, which ran north–south behind the Round Hill where the 44th was positioned. The stream-bed was so deep and narrow that enemy movement could not be seen from the Round Hill on FSB November. The enemy was also infiltrating into the graveyard between the Round Hill and the city. This graveyard was important terrain because it had a command-ing view of the airfield and the city. Securing the graveyard was the responsibility of the 53rd Regiment, but if the enemy were to hold it, they would cut off the 44th Regiment from the rest of the defen-sive perimeter. Enemy infiltration into the graveyard increased during the night of 16 May and by morning of 17 May a reinforced enemy battalion was holding it, and the situation was serious.

Colonel Rhotenberry did not normally eat breakfast, but this morning he started eating all his meals, including breakfast, with Colonel Ba. It gave them a chance to talk without interruption or staff members listening in. Rhotenberry discussed their "grave" problem with Colonel Ba. When Mr. Vann came, Colonel Rhoten-berry told him we needed help and requested an Arc Light in the vicinity of the graveyard to hit after dark. He showed Vann where the Arc Light box should be positioned and admitted that some ARVN troops would be inside the required three-kilometer stand-off from the strike. Colonel Ba knew how desperately we needed the Arc Light and said that his troops would pull back to a safe dis-tance just before the strike. Neither Vann nor Rhotenberry said so, but they both knew those ARVN soldiers would not really make a move like that in the dark.[13] The Arc Light fortunately struck with-out any friendly casualties.

On 17 May, General Abrams briefed Vice President Spiro Agnew when Agnew stopped in Saigon en route to Bangkok. He told the vice president that the South Vietnamese needed good divisions rather than more divisions. When asked about weaponry, Abrams reassured the vice president that "the M48 tank will outdo any Soviet tank here" and noted that the 3rd and 22nd Divisions had folded from inept leadership rather than from inadequate or infe-rior weaponry. He said the ARVN troops were good soldiers when properly led; although there were some South Vietnamese gener-als who wanted to fight, only about ten of them were earning their pay. He added, "After this situation is finished, the Government of South Vietnam will know those who will fight and those who won't." Abrams also praised the US advisers as heroic, smart, and professional in every sense of the word and gave them credit for holding the situation together during the most critical times. He said it was too early to be certain, but he was "beginning to feel that the thing is turning."[14]

To the south of Kontum, just across the Dak Bla River, there were NVA forward observers who could call in artillery fire whenever they saw a target on the airfield. The ARVN would fire a few mortar rounds at the observers' probable locations when an aircraft was inbound, but Kontum airfield remained a dangerous place to be caught in the open. Major Richard C. Gudat, one of our Team 33 G-4 advisers, spent a great deal of time there supervising the unloading of aircraft and the disposition of cargo. At 1430 on 17 May, a C-130E from the 776th Tactical Airlift Squadron, 374th Tactical Airlift Wing, approached, and Gudat made radio contact with the pilot. Gudat directed, "Land and travel to the end of the field while unhooking your load as you go. At the end, turn quickly, and unass your load down the ramp as you take off." Unfortunately, the pilot moved too slowly. He turned around and started back toward takeoff with his cargo of ammo on pallets sliding down the open ramp as he rolled down the runway. Mortar rounds suddenly started falling around the C-130, and the pilot decided to take off immediately. The aircraft started climbing before the ramp—which was probably weighed down by the third and last pallet—was up, and sparks flew as it dragged on the runway. When the pilot started to climb and turn, the C-130's right wing hit a brick kiln at the end of the runway. Part of the wing was sheared off, the fuel tank ruptured, and the aircraft cartwheeled into a spectacular, fiery crash. The pallet of ammunition still onboard exploded.

Out on FSB November north of Kontum, we could hear the explosions and see a tall pillar of black smoke rising into the sky. Major Gudat suddenly interrupted a transmission on the adviser radio net to describe the destruction of the C-130. Seven crewmembers died in the crash. Two were taken from the wreckage, but one died from second-degree burns all over his body. Only the loadmaster survived, and he escaped death because the explosion blew him out through the open ramp door. The ammunition dump was nearby at the west end of the airfield on the south side of the runway. The fires and explosions quickly spread to the POL and ammunition-storage areas at the airfield. The JP-4 pumping station was destroyed, and the ammunition dump caught fire, with the result that 25,000 gallons of POL started burning, and more than 3,000 rounds of 105-mm artillery shells plus mortar rounds and small-arms ammunition started exploding. It was an impressive sight from FSB November. As the explosions grew larger and louder, it was like the grand finale of a Fourth of July fireworks display—with shrapnel added. At this time, it was more dangerous to be on the airfield than on the front line. The ammo dump burned for days. The incoming enemy rounds leading to this C-130 crash triggered more material destruction than any other NVA attack by fire during the entire battle. More incoming rocket fire in the evening closed the airfield through the night of 17–18 May. After this incident, fixed-wing flights into Kontum were limited to the hours of darkness.[15]

After all the accidents, explosions, and incoming artillery and rocket fire at Kontum airfield, debris—including unexploded ordnance—was a serious hazard to aircraft landing and taking off. The senior USAF officer in II Corps Direct Air Support Center (II DASC, located in Pleiku) pushed the Kontum Province chief to keep the runway, ramp, and taxiways clear all the time. He also suggested the riverbed to the south should be prepared and secured as a suitable drop zone in case resupply by paradrop became necessary. He was justifiably unhappy with ARVN's failure to take any offensive action to silence the NVA artillery, which obviously had the airfield under direct observation, and said, "Thus far, the favorite actions that the ARVN keep falling back on is [sic] an Arc Light in the suspected area followed by TACAIR [tactical air support]."[16]

Around 2200 hours on 17 May, we were hit with another ground attack. The fighting grew more intense until our defensive lines were penetrated around 0500. At 0515, Colonel Tien, my counterpart, informed the DTOC we were being overrun and called for variable-time artillery fire on our own positions. As reports went up the chain of command all the way to MACV headquarters in Saigon, General Weyand was very concerned about the situation in Kontum. We were saved when a preplanned Arc Light hit the enemy at 0530. They broke off the attack and withdrew. One of our companies counted 50 enemy KIA in front of their position.[17]

The 23rd Division did not collapse, and after beating back the big attacks on 14 and 15 May, it developed a great deal of confidence.[18] Nevertheless, if it became necessary to evacuate the advisers from Kontum, John Paul Vann did not want a repetition of the extractions under fire from Tan Canh and Dak To. Multiple lifts had been required there, and 22nd Division soldiers' clinging to the skids had caused one helicopter to crash. With those events in mind, Vann ordered the number of advisers staying overnight in the 23rd Division DTOC pared down to seven. This number was the max load one slick could carry in addition to its crew. The seven who stayed were Colonel R. M. Rhotenberry (senior adviser), Lieutenant Colonel Bill Bricker (deputy senior adviser and G-3 adviser), Major Edgar F. Burch (assistant G-3 adviser), Major Kenneth Fleisher (G-4 adviser), Major Harold D. Jones (USAF air liaison officer), Captain Raymond W. Hall (signal adviser), and Captain John R. Finch (G-3 air adviser).[19]

To separate the Americans from the ARVN soldiers who could hinder an emergency extraction, Vann devised a clock system and required each one of the overnight advisers to select a different direction in which they would go from the DTOC and to point out on Vann's map exactly where they would be waiting for pickup. Only Vann knew those locations, and the advisers were ordered not to tell anyone else where they were going. That way, if an adviser were captured and tortured, he could not reveal any other extraction points. The Huey picking them up would make just one pass, starting on the east and working its way around the seven pickup points. If someone was not there when the chopper came, he would be on his own to E&E back to Pleiku—or some other place away from the enemy onslaught. Captain Finch thought going south or southwest would be best, so he selected a sandbar in the Dak Bla south of town as his pickup point. The secret signal the advisers selected to implement their departure from the DTOC was "Nunc Imos."[20]

Whether the ARVN officers in the 23rd Division headquarters suspected or not that their advisers had an evacuation plan, it was well known that many other advisers had been extracted from collapsing ARVN units while their counterparts were left behind. In mid-May, Lieutenant Colonel Tieu, the division G-2, pointed a nicotine-stained finger at Captain Finch and warned him, "You try to leave, we kill you!"[21]

A POW from the 64th NVA Regiment, 320th NVA Infantry Division, captured on 13 May, indicated that his regiment had suffered about 1,200 casualties before its first attack on Kontum. (An NVA regiment's full, authorized strength was about 2,500.) Interrogation of five POWs from the 52nd NVA Infantry Regiment, 320th NVA Infantry Division, indicated that even after the regiment received replacements, its strength was only 1,000 to 1,400 men. This same regiment had overrun Polei Kleng, where at least one of their battalions was rendered combat ineffective. An NVA soldier who rallied by deserting from the independent 28th NVA Infantry Regiment on 18 May described the personnel strength in his regiment. The regiment received 1,000 replacements in February and another 100 in May. However, after suffering 900 casualties from B-52 strikes, ARVN artillery, and combat with ARVN troops near Kontum, only approximately 700 men were left in the entire regiment.[22]

Because Captain Finch's basic army branch was Military Intelligence, the G-3 adviser, Major Edgar F. "Bear" Burch, called him "Spook." Finch, the G-3 air adviser, worked in the DTOC, mostly at night, plotting where the B-52 strikes would go on a 1:50,000-scale map on a table. The map was covered to conceal it from visitors and the ARVN staff. Where the targets were plotted was a closely held secret among only those advisers who needed to know. The one-by-three-kilometer Arc Light target boxes were usually at angles to the map grid lines. To plot targets at an angle, Finch improvised a template of the correct scale by cutting a rectangle out of a C-ration box. He kept it in his pocket, wrapped in scrap plastic so it would not be warped by sweat and humidity. He used the template to plot hundreds of B-52 strikes. Millions of pounds of bombs were dropped around Kontum based on coordinates plotted with Finch's little piece of cardboard. American ingenuity![23]

Captain Finch shackled (coded) the map coordinates of the Arc Lights using a "whiz wheel" or a "one-time pad" and then sent them in the clear to II DASC in Pleiku by single-sideband radio. John Paul Vann also flew some target requests back to Pleiku in his OH-58, but time was always the key factor. The directive on how to order Arc Light strikes was two standard-size pages stapled together and marked "SECRET—NOFORN": no foreigners, including our ARVN allies, were allowed to see it. Finch always carried it in his right trousers pocket, which had two buttons. He never laid it down and was prepared to destroy it if necessary. Finch and USAF Major Harold D. Jones, the air liaison officer to the ARVN 23rd Infantry Division, learned that because what they did had such a devastating effect on the enemy, the NVA placed a piaster price equal to $2,000 each on their heads. So the NVA knew which American officers by name were involved in plotting and obtaining the B-52 strikes.[24]

Sergeant James N. Barker was a US Army language specialist who could read, write, and speak Vietnamese. In Kontum, Sergeant Barker had five or six ARVN soldiers who worked with him in a CONEX, a large, steel shipping container, where they were intercepting, transcribing, and translating enemy radio messages. On some days, Barker translated as many as 15 pages of intercepts into English. Their CONEX was only about 50 meters from the 23rd Division's DTOC in an area they knew the NVA called "Special Area 24." He also interrogated POWs and sent his reports to an intelligence group in Pleiku. The captured enemy soldiers were hungry and often suffering from diarrhea and malaria, but they felt an overwhelming sense of relief they were still alive. They told him that when the NVA had captured Tan Canh and Dak To, the soldiers had raced for the rice because they were starving. They all were draftees and told Barker that if they deserted, their families in the North would be harassed—or worse. One POW tank crewman said their tanks rolled into the ARVN lines without accompanying infantry because they were told their infantry had already secured the area.[25]

Light contact and intermittent incoming fire continued through 18 May. Hawk's Claw destroyed a tank at the Krong Poko River about 13 kilometers northwest of Kontum City. Two of the enemy's long-range 130-mm guns, protected by two twin-barreled 23-mm anti-aircraft guns, started firing at us from the southern end of Rocket Ridge, about 18 kilometers away. Hawk's Claw knocked out the anti-aircraft guns, and our gunships and tactical air had a field day attacking enemy artillery and troops moving in the open. Seven US servicemen were wounded and two VNAF transport planes destroyed by the intermittent bombardment of Kontum airport. The field was temporarily closed. John Paul Vann claimed the NVA losses, mainly due to Arc Lights, were 9,000 to 10,000 men during the offensive in the Central Highlands. ARVN losses were 3,000 to 4,000 men. Elsewhere, the Communists again cut Highway 19 from the coast to Pleiku by blowing up two spans of a highway bridge.[26]

Night landings resumed at Kontum airfield on 18 May when 12 dauntless C-130 crews made it through the NVA gauntlet of anti-aircraft fire to land and unload on a runway already pockmarked by the impact of hundreds of incoming rockets and artillery rounds. They delivered the food, ammunition, and other vital supplies we so desperately needed. Those aircraft were individually cleared for landing only after it was determined the situation on the ground would permit it.[27]

Evaluation of all the available intelligence indicated that the NVA intended to launch a major attack to seize Kontum City, but that its timetable was being disrupted by Arc Lights and tactical air strikes.[28] We expected a Communist attack to commemorate Ho Chi Minh's birthday on 19 May. On Thursday evening, 18 May, a couple hundred artillery and mortar rounds hit the city as the enemy registered their fires, recording the firing data they used to hit a target so they could hit exactly the same place again. The NVA usually did this did prior to an attack. Probing attacks started at 2200 and increased in intensity through the night. Early the next morning we were pounded by 105- and 155-mm artillery. As Major Lovings and I endured the intense bombardment, it was easy to identify the big 155-mm rounds. This artillery and probably most of the ammunition was made in America. Although some of the US-made artillery used by the NVA in Vietnam might have been sent to China during World War II or captured by the Chinese in Korea, much of it had been captured from the French or the South Vietnamese in Vietnam.

Following the artillery barrage, a couple thousand men from the 48th NVA Regiment launched five successive human-wave attacks on our northern perimeter. Six enemy tanks supported the NVA attacks with direct fire but did not move against us. The first wave of attackers suffered heavy casualties from the Claymore antipersonnel mines set out in front of our troops. The NVA pressed their attack, and there was hand-to-hand fighting as the enemy got close enough to throw hand grenades into the ARVN trenches. With the help of Cobra gunships launched from Camp Holloway in Pleiku and USAF AC-130 gunships, we were able to beat back most of them again and again. At dawn, USAF F-4s joined the fray.[29]

Despite all the firepower on our side, by 0500 on 19 May the enemy was in our forward positions. The division commander was close to calling for his own artillery to fire on his own positions in the penetration. By a fortunate coincidence, preplanned Arc Lights were hitting in the vicinity of the front lines every hour. At 0530, one of those B-52 strikes, parallel to our front and only one

kilometer away, hit the NVA troops assaulting to expand their penetration. The NVA troops broke off their attack and withdrew. Our
troops were able to kill many of them as they fled.[30]

Hourly Arc Lights close to our front lines, gunship support, and
prompt action by ARVN commanders defeated all the attacks on
19 May. Equal credit belongs to the infantry troops, who defended
their positions and then counterattacked to regain lost positions in
fierce close combat, with both sides lobbing hand grenades at their
opponents. In sharp contrast to Colonel Dat, cowering in his bunker at Dak To II, ARVN officers such as Colonel Tien and Colonel
Ba exercised personal leadership to lead and win the fight.

ARVN losses during the night of 18–19 May were reported as 16
KIA and 61 WIA versus NVA 151 KIA. This enemy casualty count
included bodies found while searching only about 10 percent of the
areas hit by the hourly Arc Light bombardments. Encouraged and
perhaps even emboldened by these results, the 23rd Division sent
forces probing outside the perimeter to the north and northwest. At
1100 on 19 May, VNAF helicopters lifted the 23rd Division's 60-man
Reconnaissance Company in an air assault on a suspected enemy
artillery position eight kilometers to the north–northwest. The 1st
Battalion, 45th Regiment, concurrently moved north to establish a
blocking position. The plan was for the Reconnaissance Company
to move south, driving any enemy troops against the blocking position. That scenario went as planned until the NVA encountered the
blocking position and attacked it. The 1st Battalion held its position, but its reaction force refused to counterattack the NVA. So
although the 23rd Division demonstrated its ability to move outside the Kontum perimeter to conduct a reconnaissance in force,
the NVA was not smashed between ARVN's "hammer and anvil."
The 2nd Battalion of the 45th also moved north, found 24 more
NVA soldiers KIA by Arc Lights, and killed another five while they
were about it. The 44th and 53rd Regiments sent two battalions
each just north of their line of contact but did not go far enough to
do a BDA of the main Arc Light target areas.[31]

The afternoon of 19 May the enemy probed the position of the
44th's 1st Battalion, and there was a brief exchange of small-arms
fire. Later in the day the NVA probed us again. This time they
used CS gas delivered by an unknown means. An Arc Light strike
hit ten kilometers north of the city at 1555. Twenty minutes later
the air cavalry was making a BDA of the target area when they saw

two guards in clean uniforms standing in front of an undamaged bunker. The guards appeared to be headquarters types who were guarding an enemy CP. The cavalry gunned down the guards, and an Arc Light was scheduled for early the next morning to destroy this bunker and some others not hit by the earlier Arc Light. Kontum airfield reopened at 2030 on 19 May, and 17 C-130s landed safely during the night. Another 15 made it on 20 May.[32]

By that date, MACV was estimating enemy infiltration into South Vietnam at 126,900 total since the start of the year. MACV also estimated that since the enemy's offensive had begun on 30 March, they had fired at least 1,173 SA-2 "Red SAMs" at US aircraft and had succeeded in knocking down 13 of them.[33]

Flying out of Kontum, C-130 pilot Captain Brian Sweeney saw signal mirror flashes, and when he circled around for another look, he spotted two Americans on the ground waving at him. He radioed their location back to Kontum, but before they could be rescued, he saw enemy soldiers grab them.[34]

Every night the enemy would attack us again and again. We would jump off our cots, put on our web equipment, flak jackets, and helmets, then grab our maps and flashlights and get into our foxhole. After a while, the attack would die down, and we would crawl out of our hole, unload, and try to get back to sleep. The whole cycle would soon start over again. Sometimes we would lie on our cots talking to a C-130 gunship by radio. The gunship would fire at the coordinates we got from the regimental staff right next to us. We would ask the Vietnamese to check with the front-line troops to see if the gunship's fire was hitting the right place and then adjust it if necessary. We were fighting the war from our beds, reading the map with a flashlight, and shouting back and forth with the Vietnamese. The US aircraft would eventually go back to Saigon for fuel or a crew change. We would tell them, "Good night, thanks for your help, good shooting." We learned to recognize some of the pilots' voices as the same ones from previous nights. But the man on the ground never met the man in the air, who went home to an air-conditioned room in Saigon. We were a bit envious of that but knew they could be blown out of the air by a Strella at any time— just as we could be blown to bits by an incoming round at any time.

Starting at 0345 on 20 May, the 53rd ARVN Regiment's left flank was hit with three successive assaults. The defending troops were worn out from weeks of heavy combat and lack of sleep. During the early daylight hours, the third assault pushed the 2nd Battalion of the 53rd off a company-size position. This enemy penetration between the 53rd and 44th Regiments was a serious threat to both regiments and could be exploited to strike into the heart of Kontum. It was imperative to eliminate it before dark. By 1645, the enemy entrenchments were within 20 meters of the nearest 53rd positions, which was too close to use tactical air against them, and Colonel Ba was reluctant to commit his armor to the counterattack. The 53rd repeatedly tried to eliminate the penetration, and several times it reported the job was done. After each of those reports, Colonel Rhotenberry sent an adviser up in the C&C chopper, and the adviser would report that the enemy still held the penetration and that the 53rd's reports were false. Finally, Mr. Vann and Major General Toan arrived, conferred with Colonels Ba and Rhotenberry, and persuaded Ba to commit his reserve, including nine tanks. At first, the tank commanders refused to attack, but Toan and Ba convinced them it would be in their best interest to follow orders. The nine M-41 tanks lined up and fired their 76-mm main guns directly into the enemy positions. With this fire support, the involvement of the corps commander, and Ba's personal command of the counterattack, the 53rd was finally able to retake its former positions. Although Major General Toan knew the 53rd had lied to him twice by falsely reporting that the positions had been retaken earlier in the day, he took no disciplinary action against the individuals responsible.[35]

During a limited objective attack from our lines out to the north on 20 May, the 1st and 3rd Battalions of the 44th Regiment reported killing 69 enemy soldiers and capturing a 60-mm mortar. The airfield was attacked with more than a dozen 122-mm rockets on this day, and one destroyed a VNAF C-123 on the ramp. The air cavalry spotted enemy troops in the open and in bunker complexes to the northeast of Kontum City. They were hit with tactical air strikes and gunships. It appeared that the NVA was now building up its forces in that area and that its likely avenue of approach would be a valley that led to Kontum City.[36]

The night of 20–21 May was relatively quiet until 0500 on 21 May, when our 3rd and 4th Battalions were hit with heavy incoming mortar fire. Under this covering fire, the 406th NVA Sapper Battalion and an NVA infantry battalion, probably from the 64th NVA Regiment, 320th NVA Infantry Division, seized a position between our 4th Battalion and the 1st Battalion of the 45th Infantry Regiment. That drove a wedge into our lines and cut Highway 14 three kilometers north of the city and behind us. At about the same time, another enemy force found a gap between the 45th's 4th Battalion and the 53rd's 2nd Battalion and recaptured the salient it had been ejected from just before dark the previous day. With our defenses penetrated in two places, the situation was serious, and those lost positions had to be retaken before the enemy could exploit them and overrun Kontum.

VNAF scrambled an AC-47 Spooky gunship from Pleiku. It arrived 30 minutes later, just as the enemy launched another assault on our forward defenses. Spooky started hosing down the attackers with its three 7.62-mm miniguns, and the assault was stopped and repulsed. Within the next two hours, the NVA launched two more assaults, but those attacks coincided with two of our prescheduled Arc Lights on their positions, and both failed.[37]

To deal with the enemy infantry and sappers next door, I requested an air strike. A USAF FAC with the call sign Covey 529 was passed to me on our FM fire-support radio net. I described where our troops were and where the enemy was located, and the FAC used his other radio to call for fighter-bombers. Then he called back:

COVEY 529: "OK, I have Fox Fours with CBU." ("Fox Fours" referred to US Navy F-4s, probably from an aircraft carrier in the South China Sea and armed with CBUs.)

SNAPPER 14 [me]: "No, we can't use CBUs. Too close."

COVEY 529: "Wait. All right, I have a pair of F-105s with thousand-pound bombs. How close are the friendlies?"

SNAPPER 14: "About 400 meters east."

COVEY 529: "That's too close. Within the minimum safe distance for thousand pounders. I can't put them in without somebody's initials."

I asked Colonel Tien about it, and he said, "No problem! My troops in bunkers." I gave the FAC my initials for the record, and I would be held responsible if those bombs killed ARVN soldiers.

SNAPPER 14: "OK. Tango, Papa, Mike. Put 'em in."

The jets dove in from out of sight, and with every pass they dropped two 1,000-pound bombs. The advisers in the DTOC were as impressed as I was by the size of the bombs. They recorded in the log, "Airstrikes in spt of LTC McKenna vic ZA230920 (1000 lb bombs!)."[38] Later that day, we watched while our 2nd Battalion swept through the area. They found 65 NVA bodies. There was too much else going on to keep track of how many air strikes I had called in since arriving in Kontum. So much was happening so fast, and we were so sleep deprived that the days and nights ran together. Everyone was exhausted, and tempers were short. The enemy shelled the same places again and again until the additional incoming rounds did not do much more than make the rubble bounce. However, the continuing bombardment did have a cumulative effect on us: it kept us awake, kept us tense, and kept us on the alert for the human-wave assaults that usually followed a heavy artillery barrage. It wore us down.

Colonel Tien moved quickly to counterattack the enemy penetration on Highway 14 by using his 3rd Battalion, 44th Regiment, to counterattack south along Highway 14 in coordination with an attack to the north by the 44th's 4th Battalion and the 45th's 1st Battalion. They were supported by US gunships and tactical air. After fierce fighting, the enemy was cleared out, and the two friendly forces linked up and secured the area. However, the NVA wedge driven between the 45th and 53rd Regiments remained and posed a serious threat. Colonel Rhotenberry was convinced that the 53rd Regiment had abandoned its positions shortly after dark and shortly after retaking them on 20 May had pulled back several hundred meters. He urged Colonel Ba to retake the positions, and a counterattack was planned.[39]

Starting at 1400 that afternoon, Colonel Ba personally commanded a well-coordinated counterattack against the enemy penetration between the 45th and 53rd Regiments. First, tactical air pounded the enemy in the penetration, and then two ARVN battalions supported by tanks attacked. The tanks were stopped by both direct and indirect enemy fire, and two of the light M-41s were 30 to 40 percent damaged. However, the enemy was driven out, and by 1500 the 45th and 53rd Regiments' positions were restored. Casualties were 28 ARVN KIA and 76 WIA versus 147 NVA KIA. Mr. Vann told General Abrams that Colonel Ba's presence at the front during the counterattacks was the decisive factor in the success. The corps commander personally congratulated Colonel Ba.

On 21 May, ARVN reported the casualties and tank losses for our previous seven days of fighting as: friendly 106 KIA and 440 WIA; enemy 1,035 KIA. Tank losses were nine enemy T-54s destroyed and our two damaged M-41s.[40]

After dark on 21 May, USAF C-130s started landing at Kontum airfield to resupply us. They were the first fixed-wing aircraft to land here in 48 hours. Twelve C-130 sorties carrying ammunition and cargo landed without incident. The two 10,000-gallon fuel bladders destroyed on 17 May were replaced, and the refueling point was fully operational by dawn. Then in the early-morning darkness, at 0115 on 22 May, Spare 622, a C-130E from the 21st Tactical Air Squadron, blew a tire when it made a hard landing with a heavy load. Except for one bladder bird, landings were suspended for the remainder of the night. The aircraft with a flat tire was parked on the east ramp, and II DASC requested a repair crew, which arrived at 0615 the next morning. The air cavalry was assigned to work over suspected enemy firing positions while repairs were made, but at 0815 six rounds landed on the airfield, and the aircraft being repaired was hit and started burning. The ARVN soldiers were indifferent to the blaze, but a US Army colonel used a large fire extinguisher to put it out. By that time, though, the aircraft was unfortunately destroyed beyond repair. With the airfield obviously under direct enemy observation and the NVA artillery able to hit it at will, any aircraft on it during daylight hours was a sitting duck.[41]

The intrepid USAF C-130 and VNAF C-123 crews earned my deepest respect, admiration, and thanks. They flew those dangerous missions into Kontum through heavy anti-aircraft fire to make nighttime landings and takeoffs at an airport with only very basic navigation aids, while artillery, mortar, rocket, and sometimes even small-arms fire was hitting the airfield. Without them, we would not have received enough food, ammunition, and other supplies to hold out, and we would have been overrun by the enemy.

Colonel Rhotenberry visited FSB November on his first day in Kontum and could see that the Round Hill was a key piece of terrain in the defense of Kontum City. If the enemy could seize and hold it, they could hit Kontum City with observed mortar and artillery fire and even direct fire from their tanks. However, he did not like the troop dispositions he had inherited and was especially concerned about the 44th Regiment on FSB November. Rhotenberry thought that it was too far out in front of the main defensive perimeter and that defending it overextended and created gaps in the perimeter. Worse yet, most of the 44th's 3rd Battalion was almost two kilometers farther out, defending outpost "Nectar" northwest of November. When asked about this, Colonel Ba said that the corps commander had refused him permission to abandon either Nectar or November.[42]

The 44th Regiment bore the brunt of the initial assaults on 14 and 15 May. During our ten days on FSB November, we were under continuous attacks by fire, ground probes, and repeated assaults by enemy infantry and tanks. The regiment suffered many casualties, and our troops were physically and mentally worn out. To give the 44th a respite, and to adjust and tighten the defensive perimeter, Colonel Ba decided to move the regiment from FSB November back to a former hospital compound inside the northern perimeter in Kontum City, where it would be in reserve. The 45th Regiment would replace us on FSB November. He discussed this plan with Major General Toan and Mr. Vann when they were in Kontum on 16 May, and they approved it.[43]

Starting on 22 May and over the next two days, the 45th Regiment replaced us on FSB November as we moved back into reserve in Kontum, behind the main perimeter manned by the 45th Regiment on the northwest and the 53rd Regiment north of us. Only two of the 44th's four battalions and a troop of tanks would remain around our CP and serve as a reserve. One of our battalions would provide security around the DTOC, and another would be in the southern part of the city with the Ruff Puffs.

Our new area had once been a French hospital, then an ARVN hospital, and next a US Army hospital. Most of the buildings in the compound were single story, built by the French, and some still had big red crosses painted on them. Although Kontum City was relatively flat, at 560 meters this area was the highest point in town. From on top of the earthen mound covering a bunker, we could look down on most of the city—including the DTOC to the south, the airfield to the southeast, and the logistics compound to the east where the 53rd Regiment's CP was located.

Major Lovings and I were assigned to a small building of our own. We set up our cots, arranged our equipment, and then drove our Jeep over to the DTOC. We picked up our mail and the available *Stars & Stripes* and went over the situation with the staff while looking at their maps. Not long after we returned to our building, artillery and mortar fire started falling in the hospital area. There was a small sandbag bunker in our hallway, so we took cover in it. An ARVN soldier staggered in with his arm almost severed and bleeding badly. A Vietnamese captain who was talking to us chewed him out for bleeding all over the floor. Major Lovings took the wounded man to the medics. After he returned, he went back outside two more times to save other wounded men. Incoming rounds were falling all around him while he did that. No ARVN soldiers lifted a hand to help him provide aid to their own soldiers. Wade Lovings was one of the bravest men I ever knew.

When the incoming changed from sporadic to intense, an excited Sergeant *Hao* came running into our building and announced, "Regimental commander say we move to bunker!" He meant right now, lock, stock, and barrel, and not temporarily. We moved all our gear out of our nice building and down into a windowless, underground, concrete bunker, which then became 44th Regiment's CP and operations center. When the US 2nd Field Hospital had been here, the US Army engineers had built this large, concrete underground surgical bunker for them. The 22nd ARVN Division later used it as a DTOC until the division moved to Tan Canh. The NVA may have assumed the 23rd Division DTOC was in the same place. If so, that would explain the enemy's persistent, heavy attacks by fire on this area and why it would be the main objective of so many enemy ground attacks.[44] We set up our cots at one end of the bunker. The bunker was dimly lighted and somewhat stuffy, and the only way out was a door at the top of a few stairs. However, it was much safer here than sleeping in the jungle with only a poncho above us. That night I slept with my boots off for the first time since arriving in Kontum.

When we next saw our adviser building and our Jeep, which was parked beside it, the building was a charred ruin and the Jeep was a burned-out hulk of scrap metal. This sight confirmed the wisdom of moving into the big bunker.

In addition to incurring heavy casualties, the NVA was already suffering from shortages of ammunition and food by the time it captured Tan Canh and Dak To II. All of the 160-mm mortars of the 40th NVA Artillery Regiment were damaged, and there was an acute shortage of ammunition. So the regiment took four 105-mm and three 155-mm howitzers that ARVN abandoned in usable condition to form an ad hoc artillery unit. Captured ammo for those guns was transported by bicycle, and this American-made artillery and ammunition were then used against us when the NVA attacked Kontum. After those guns ran out of captured ammo, they were withdrawn to Dak To District and hidden there.[45]

Either because the US radar equipment used to track incoming rounds and locate the enemy's firing position was too complicated to use or because it was not properly maintained—or both—throughout the Vietnam War, it never did what it was supposed to do. So we used a nontechnical method. By analyzing the crater where an artillery round explodes, and the spray pattern of the shrapnel it throws out, it is possible to determine—at least roughly—the direction and distance to the gun that fired the round. Every American soldier receives some basic training in crater analysis, and because Major Lovings was an artillery officer, he was especially expert at it. The NVA obviously fired one captured US 105-mm artillery piece at us repeatedly and very accurately. Lovings's analysis indicated that the howitzer shooting at us was on Rocket Ridge. However, pilots trying to find it could never pin down the exact location, so we concluded the NVA must be concealing it in a cave except when they rolled it out to throw a round or two our way. Hitting the mouth of a cave on a mountainside with counter battery fire is extremely difficult, and even a direct hit with an aerial bomb on the entrance might not get the gun if it is rolled way back into the cave. Our side had better luck on 24 May when smoke was observed coming from an enemy bunker about ten kilometers east–northeast of the city while artillery rounds were hitting Kontum. Midafternoon that day, Hawk's Claw fired a TOW missile right through the bunker's aperture and probably destroyed a large-caliber NVA artillery piece.[46]

Two Special Forces NCOs who were shell-reporting experts arrived on 24 May to analyze the craters and shell fragments to determine what weapons the enemy was using against us. The ARVN records were unfortunately not good enough for the NCOs to accomplish their mission, so Colonel Rhotenberry sent them away the next day. While they were at the chopper pad waiting to fly out of Kontum, one of them was killed in a firefight.[47] Somebody in Washington must have heard our pleas for help in locating the NVA artillery's firing positions, though. On 21 May, the US Army's Field Artillery School at Fort Sill, Oklahoma, sent teams to Vietnam to offer assistance on target acquisition.[48] When I made it

back to the DTOC bunker one day in late May, two artillery lieutenant colonels from Fort Sill were there. I took the opportunity to
complain about the lack of some type of radar or technical system
that could pinpoint the location of an enemy gun, like the one peri-
odically firing at us from Rocket Ridge.

The teams from Fort Sill concluded that the ARVN Artillery
School was teaching target acquisition, but also that the ARVN
artillery units in the field were not practicing it with any sense of
urgency, so they recommended better command supervision by
ARVN artillery officers and continuing follow-up from the advisers.[49] American advisers had been working on problems like this for
the past ten years, but now they were rapidly withdrawing, and time
was running out for ARVN to assume full responsibility for practicing what they had been taught and equipped to do.

Analysis by the Fort Sill teams also provided some interesting
insight into how the NVA artillery functioned. The artillery crews
were extremely capable and professional, generally fired at maximum range, and preferred to keep their tubes dispersed rather than
concentrated as the US Army and ARVN did. Their ability to mass
the fire from those widely separated tubes on a single target indicated that they surveyed their gun positions and had communications efficient enough to exercise centralized control of their fire.[50]
The scattered dispersal of their tubes must have made ammunition
resupply much more difficult, but it also presented less lucrative
targets to ARVN counterbattery fire and aerial bombing.

There was some action every day. The NVA artillery and rocket
attacks became part of our expected daily routine. The enemy
would probe our positions, and we would push out to probe theirs.
The 23rd Division's infantry companies were suffering a steady toll
of killed and wounded that was gradually reducing our strength
and our ability to defend our positions and retake lost ground.
However, all available intelligence—including POW interrogations—indicated that the NVA was suffering far more casualties
than ARVN. Most of the time we could not get an accurate count
of how many NVA were killed by air, but when our troops went into
an area recently hit by an Arc Light or tactical air strike, they usually found dozens of enemy bodies.[51]

We were tired, hungry, thirsty, and running on nervous energy
during this period. I kept rehashing in my mind, "What is the most
effective thing we can do now?" and "What should we be prepared

to do next?" As a commander, I could have ordered some immediate action, but as an adviser I could only recommend action. This was frustrating.

On 23 May, province forces received a Hoi Chanh from the 48th NVA Regiment who revealed the location of his regiment's CP. He said nearly every company in his battalion was down to only ten men as a result of casualties from B-52 strikes. Those strikes also destroyed so much of the supplies en route to their front-line units that artillery ammunition, malaria-prevention pills, and even food were in critically short supply.[52]

The monsoon rains were beginning to hamper the enemy's movement and resupply through the jungle, and the tactical air attacks and Arc Lights were taking a heavy toll on their troops and equipment. They needed either to seize Kontum or to withdraw, so they planned an all-out attack to achieve a decisive victory. The *New York Times* reported from Saigon, "In the Central Highlands the North Vietnamese have mounted a serious threat to the provincial capital of Kontum, and the loss of the city would surprise no one here."[53]

16

"Brother, This Is Going to Be It!"

Soldiers when in desperate straits lose the sense of fear. If there is no place of refuge, they will stand firm. If they are in the heart of a hostile country, they will show a stubborn front. If there is no help for it, they will fight hard.
—Sun Tzu, *The Art of War*

The *Washington Post* reported on 27 May 1972, "Kontum, once a pleasant town with abundant fruit trees and gentle climate, has been abandoned by more than 80 percent of the 30,000 people who lived there before the offensive."[1] Under the headline "Kontum Is Next—and It Knows It," *Stars and Stripes* said:

KONTUM, Vietnam (AP)—This city in South Vietnam's central highlands is living on borrowed time and a fervent hope that defenses which crumpled elsewhere will hold here. North Vietnamese forces, which have captured with ease almost every objective they sought in the highlands, are thus far content to probe at the nervous city's outer perimeter. Since the initial predawn attack on May 14, there has been no indication when a large-scale assault is likely against the city that many allied officials believe is a certain target in the next phase of Hanoi's general offensive.[2]

A sample of entries on the nine-page DTOC log for the 24 hours commencing at 0001 on 23 May gives an idea of the varied friendly and enemy activity:

C-130 landed. Unloading . . . Covey 550 directing air strike
. . . Spectre 01 orbiting "Truck Alley," engaging targets . . .
airfield took 1 round . . . C-130 is burning . . . Sappers
repelled outside of wire . . . tactical air strike requested on
.51 position . . . VNAF A1s going in . . . 4/53 still in contact
. . . MAJ Lovings—5 rounds incoming . . . VNAF strike going
in . . . Arc Light detonated . . . Bladder bird due in tonight . . .
Arc Light detonated . . . Airfield received 5 rounds . . . Tactical air strike requested . . . LTC McKenna reports his position received 3 rounds . . . Nail 43 put in strikes . . . Spectre
20 engaging truck . . . Spectre engaging bunkers.[3]

Although a few NVA tanks were detected during daylight hours
and destroyed by the TOWs, the NVA's typical pattern was to hide
its tanks in the dense jungle during the day and then attack again
in the night. If the NVA shifted its tanks to attack from a new
direction, our air cavalry scouts were usually able to detect their
movement and thus predict where the next nighttime attack would
strike.[4] There were about 38 tanks in every NVA tank battalion, yet
most of their tank attacks were made with only ten or fewer tanks.[5]
In addition to the enemy's inept use of the tanks they had, the
number of tanks available to them was declining because of maintenance problems and combat losses. On Wednesday, 24 May, Mr.
Vann said that so many enemy tanks were already destroyed, there
were only 15 to 25 left in the Kontum area.[6]

The 23rd ARVN Division launched some offensive operations
to the north and east on 24 May. Starting at 1045, VNAF helicopters were used to lift the 1st Battalion, 44th Regiment, for a combat assault on an area four kilometers north of our positions. The
objective was three kilometers back to the southeast. Two hours
later our 2nd Battalion made a similar combat assault one kilometer
east of the 1st Battalion and then attacked toward an objective three
kilometers to the southeast. Those two battalions attacked roughly
parallel to each other, and a blocking force was set up south of
their objectives. About a kilometer south of that blocking force, two
battalions of the 53rd Regiment attacked to the east toward three
successive objectives, the last of which was a village occupied by the
NVA on 22 May. The 45th Regiment also participated by sending
one battalion north to operate west of Highway 14. By 1800, all of
the objectives were under ARVN control. The 1st Battalion of the

45th returned to its normal defensive positions, but the other units remained on their final objectives through the night of 24–25 May. Total casualties for the day were reported as 86 enemy KIA, and ARVN losses were at 9 KIA and 31 WIA.[7]

The operations north of our defensive perimeter on 24 May were a good way to find the enemy and to keep him off balance. They also helped to build confidence and improve the morale of the ARVN and RF troops who were able to go on the offensive after taking a terrible battering from enemy artillery and ground attacks for so long.

In this period, the C-130s supporting us flew out of Tan Son Nhut. It was just a one-hour flight to Kontum, but our airfield was challenging. It was only about 3,200 feet long, right at the edge of a C-130's limit. To line up for landing, pilots came over the gap in a mountain to the south. Only two C-130s were allowed on the ground at the same time, so sometimes as many as 10 to 15 were stacked up, orbiting above at 2,000-foot intervals until it was their turn to land. After 12 May, when daylight landings were stopped because of observed enemy artillery and mortar fire on the airfield and anti-aircraft fire from the plateau to the west, the C-130s landed at night by radar-assisted ground-controlled approach. They descended with everything, including the cockpit, blacked out. Day or night, there was usually intermittent enemy fire on the airfield, and there sometimes were firefights between ARVN and the NVA right at the edge of the airfield. Landing at Kontum was tense and required an experienced crew. One C-130 pilot made seven attempts to land but finally gave it up and returned to Saigon.[8]

Despite the loss of aircraft to incoming artillery and rocket fire on Kontum airfield, the USAF flew in the vital supplies necessary to defend Kontum. Although the C-130 pilots considered night landings and takeoffs under fire at Kontum "a dicey operation," they kept coming. Eight delivered their cargo on the night of 22–23 May, and another 30 made it in and out over the next two nights. On the night of 23–24 May, they flew 13 C-130 sorties into Kontum to deliver the 105-mm howitzer ammunition we needed to replace the rounds destroyed in the ammunition dump explosion. They brought in 147 skids (pallets that could be quickly unloaded) with 3,758 rounds of 105-mm HE, 26 skids with 628 illumination 105-mm rounds, and 29 skids with 16,700 fuses for the 105-mm rounds. Additional sorties were scheduled but then cancelled because security measures slowed down the operation. The JP-4 deliveries were switched from bladder birds carrying two 4,500-gallon bladders—which needed to be pumped out while the aircraft sat parked on the airfield—to 500-gallon blivets on pallets for quick offloading. During the night of 24–25 May, 17 C-130 sorties landed with 136.4 tons of ammo, 45.2 tons of rations, and one bladder of JP-4, and there were 3 sorties with other POL. The C-130 resupply missions into Kontum were accomplished with Spectre gunships flying escort. These gunships could suppress anti-aircraft fire, and their presence overhead discouraged NVA artillery and rockets.[9]

Enemy attacks by indirect fire escalated early and continued through the day of 24 May. The heaviest concentrations—around 60 rounds an hour—hit the airfield, division artillery positions, and the DTOC. Some of it was coming from US-made 105- and 155-mm pieces. It was extremely accurate, indicating good forward observation by the NVA or even adjustment by infiltrators inside the city.[10] Another example of the enemy's accurate, adjusted fire occurred in the 53rd Regiment's area. After two 105-mm howitzers were destroyed by enemy fire, Lieutenant Colonel Norbert J. Gannon, the new senior adviser to the 53rd Regiment, insisted that the division artillery battery in his area move to its secondary position. However, as soon as that move was completed, the next incoming round landed only five meters from the new position. It was followed by a six-round barrage that destroyed another 105-mm howitzer.

Midafternoon on 24 May, heavy 105- and 155-mm artillery fire started falling on our positions in the former hospital area. We were supposedly in reserve, but the intensity of the bombardment warned us that the enemy would soon make another major assault. We did not have long to wait.

At midnight on 24 May, the 53rd Regiment reported hearing tanks. The reports of increased attacks by fire, enemy infantry probes, and the sound of tanks continued to pour in. By 0330 on the morning of 25 May, Colonel Rhotenberry said, "Brother, this is going to be it!" He called Vann, who asked, "What's up?" Rhotenberry joked, "Oh, I was just sitting here with nothing to do, so I thought I'd call." He then described the situation to Vann and said, "This is it. I recommend that when you come in the morning, you bring everything you can get." Vann said, "Right!" and hung up.[11]

On this morning, our one division of three regiments was

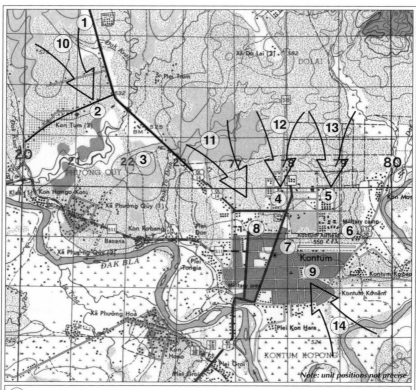

1. Outpost Nectar manned by 3rd Battalion (-), 45th ARVN Regiment.
2. General trace of frontline positions of two battalions (+) of 45th ARVN Regiment.
3. CP and a battalion (+) of 45th ARVN Regt. on The Round Hill at FSB November.
4. CP and 1st and 3rd Battalions of 44th ARVN Regiment in hospital area.
5. Two battalions of 53rd ARVN Regiment.
6. CP and 2nd Battalion of 53rd ARVN Regiment.
7. West end of the airfield runways.
8. The DTOC with 4th Battalion, 44th ARVN Regiment for security.
9. RF & PF of Kontum Province plus 2nd Battalion, 44th ARVN Regiment.
10. 64th NVA Regiment plus tanks.
11. 52nd NVA regiment plus tanks.
12. 1st NVA Regiment, 2nd NVA Division, plus a sapper battalion and tanks.
13. The independent 66th NVA Regiment of the B-3 Front plus tanks.
14. 141st NVA Regiment, 2nd NVA Division, plus 304th & 400th NVA Sapper Battalions.

The attacks on Kontum, 25 and 26 May 1972.

attacked by five NVA regiments, three sapper battalions, and almost a battalion of tanks—and they came at us from three directions. The 64th Regiment of the 320th NVA Division attacked from the north–northwest along the west side of Highway 14, and the 52nd Regiment of that same division attacked along the east side of Highway 14. The 1st Regiment of the 2nd NVA Division, a sapper battalion, and a tank company launched the main attack from the north into the former hospital area where our 44th Regiment CP and 1st and 3rd Battalions were located. The 44th's 2nd Battalion was still attached to Kontum Province to reinforce the Ruff Puffs in the southern sector, and its 4th Battalion was providing security around the DTOC. The independent 66th NVA Regiment of the B-3 Front and a tank battalion also attacked from the north into the 53rd ARVN Regiment's positions on the northeast side of the defensive perimeter.[12]

The NVA found a gap between the 45th and 53rd Regiments and drove a wedge into it, and the North Vietnamese troops flooded in. It continued its attack to hit the 44th Regiment, which was in reserve, and made major penetrations into our positions. The NVA also turned to hit the 45th and 53rd from the rear, and it looked as if those two regiments might be cut off.[13]

Starting at 0200 on 25th May, heavy attacks by fire hit the airfield and the southeastern part of the city. The Ruff Puffs manning the defenses in the southern sector shortly afterward reported that the enemy was crossing the Dak Bla River south of them. At 0300 hours, the 141st NVA Regiment, augmented by the 304th and 400th NVA Sapper Battalions, infiltrated through the Ruff Puffs' positions in the southeast portion of Kontum City and attacked from that direction into the city and toward the airfield. Prior reconnaissance had revealed to the NVA what the US advisers already knew: some of the Ruff Puffs had left gaps in the defenses at night when they abandoned their defensive positions to go home to their families in Kontum City. The infiltrating enemy force moved in small squad-size units. Some of these soldiers were disguised as civilian refugees, and others wore ARVN uniforms captured from the 22nd ARVN Division. Infiltrators already inside the city aided them.[14]

The enemy sappers occupied the built-up area south of the airfield and soon held a Catholic compound that enclosed a cathedral, a nunnery, an orphanage, Lasan School, a seminary, the home of Monsignor Paul Seitz, and American doctor Pat Smith's hospital for Montagnards. Five hundred civilians, including about 200 Montagnard civilian patients, were captured and held there. However, unlike during Tet 1968 when the VC had shot women and children patients in the legs and threw hand grenades at them, this time the NVA soldiers did not harm the civilians. Doctor Smith, known to the Yards as "Big Grandmother of Medicine," had already evacuated to Pleiku with most of her patients.

The DTOC first learned there was a major penetration in the south when Captain Hall radioed from the airfield to say he was pinned down there by enemy small-arms fire from the south. This was the first major attack from the south, and if this enemy force could seize the airfield and link up with the Communist forces attacking from the north, Kontum would be cut in half.[15]

The sappers who attacked into the southeastern part of the city probably had as their objective a linkup with their forces coming from the north or west. A combination of ARVN units—including the 53rd Regiment, the 2nd Battalion of the 44th Regiment, and the remnants of a battalion of the 42nd Regiment from the 22nd Division—finally stopped the enemy attack only 100 meters from the airfield by holding firm at the bunkers forming the airfield's final defensive line. Failure to hold there could result in the loss of Kontum.[16]

In the early-morning darkness of 25 May, a C-130 piloted by Captain Felix Courrington and with Rick Ivars as loadmaster was ready to start its ground-controlled approach into Kontum when the USAF controller at Kontum airfield radioed, "Our house is closed! Don't land!" The NVA had seized the eastern end of the runway in a night attack, and the two-man Combat Control Team and the five-man Aerial Port Team at the airfield were fighting off an NVA ground attack. The pilot could hear small-arms fire on the radio, but he told the air force teams on the ground, "We are coming in. Be at the end of the runway in ten." The C-130 landed, and the USAF ground personnel ran up the opened ramp, still firing their individual weapons at the enemy soldiers who were pursuing them. Small-arms fire from three directions was hitting the aircraft, and incoming artillery and rocket rounds were hitting the runway as they took off. The entire aircraft crew received the Distinguished Flying Cross for that daring rescue. This incident was the last of the night landings at Kontum airfield. US Army and VNAF Chinooks would fly cargo into the soccer field until C-130 airdrops could be started.[17]

At daylight on 25 May, the enemy surprised the defenders with a .51-caliber machine gun they managed to get up into a water tower north of the airfield. Those towers were heavily reinforced concrete, built like a pillbox on stilts. This gun could cover a wide area with deadly fire, so it had to be taken out. The ARVN artillery used direct fire from 200 meters away and eventually silenced it. However, the enemy quickly replaced it with another .51 caliber, and we had to start all over again. After other weapons were tried, a TOW missile fired by Hawk's Claw finally blasted into the tower and killed the crew. The NVA also positioned about a dozen anti-aircraft guns only 100 meters east of the 44th Regiment's compound and less than a kilometer from the airfield. Both artillery and tactical air strikes were required to destroy them. At 0925, a Ruff Puff company attacked an enemy unit southwest of the airfield, captured one sapper, and killed 20 more who were firing 60-mm mortars at the airfield.[18] A VNAF FAC reported five enemy tanks headed for the 53rd Regiment at 0930, and Hawk's Claw was sent after them.[19]

A US Huey C&C ship making a visual reconnaissance was hit by small-arms fire coming from a bunker complex in the southern sector of the city. It went down just northwest of town and burned. The rotor blade decapitated the pilot as he exited the aircraft, and the other four Americans on board were injured. About the same time, an RPG shot down an OH-6A. The two crew members were killed when it crashed and burned. At 1300 on 25 May, Brigadier General Hill declared a tactical emergency, which gave Kontum top priority for all available tactical air and gunship support in South Vietnam. Shortly afterward, the DTOC was hit by an incoming round and damaged. By 1515, the NVA's rate of fire had doubled to one round every 30 seconds. A crater analysis by Major Lovings confirmed that it was big 155-mm rounds hitting us. The enemy bombardment pinned the division artillery crews in their bunkers and also destroyed their guns and ammunition. By 1900, only fourteen 105-mm and two 155-mm howitzers were still able to support us. The VNAF ground team at the airfield was rendered ineffective, the airfield was closed, and by 1700 all nonessential US personnel were evacuated from Kontum.[20]

The enemy consolidated their gains southeast of Kontum, and the ARVN troops and RFs there could barely contain the penetration. However, this area would be the NVA's high-water mark in that part of the city. The enemy was able to reinforce its positions in both the northern and southern penetrations. South Vietnamese casualties for 25 May were 42 KIA and 142 WIA.[21]

It was impossible to get enough sleep during this period. We were constantly pounded by artillery rounds and rockets, any one of which could kill us. We never knew when we would be hit by another enemy ground attack with tanks. My mind was constantly running over a mental checklist of things we needed to do. Was there anything I forgot to check on? Anything else I could do to strengthen our defenses? We needed to make periodic radio checks with the DTOC, and we constantly monitored the adviser radio channel. The ARVN staff had their own radios operating, and they were chattering and sometimes shouting. Major Lovings and I tried to take turns sleeping, but it was hard to turn off enough of the noise and stress to doze off.

C-130 night landings were still cancelled, so the 23rd Division was left without any resupply for 24 hours.[22] With the battle at its height and the possibility of having to E&E to an extraction point increasing, the DTOC advisers ran out of M-16 ammunition. There was a Ruff Puff headquarters nearby with an arms room full of World War II–era weapons, all standard Ruff Puff armament until recently, so the advisers raided it and armed themselves with M-1 rifles, M1A2 carbines, and even old Thompson submachine guns—all with plenty of ammo.[23]

On 25 May, Mr. Vann told a reporter that 304 enemy bodies had been found around Ben Het and that 1,150 NVA soldiers had been killed within a two-mile radius of Kontum during the previous week.[24] SRAG published classified procedures for extracting all US personnel from Artillery Hill in Pleiku, if it became necessary. The publication included instructions to destroy the artillery's radar equipment and the Jeep-mounted TOWs stationed there.[25]

After enduring nine hours of continuous rocketing by the NVA on 25 May, Sergeant Barker, the Vietnamese-language specialist, was evacuated to Pleiku for the night. Before he left that day, he translated a radio intercept saying there would be "concentrations of heavy rocket fire on Special Area 24 [the DTOC area] in Kontum." He would be back in Kontum the next morning for what he would remember as his longest day.[26]

17

"You Are Going to Be Overrun!"

Here lie the bones of Lieutenant Jones,
A graduate of this institution.
He died last night in a firefight,
Victim of the approved solution.
—Graffito at the Infantry School,
Fort Benning, Georgia, 1953

Kontum was surrounded by around 5,000 enemy troops with tanks.[1] We were being constantly pounded by intermittent artillery and rocket fire, and at 0100 on 26 May the tempo picked up. As we lay on our cots in the CP bunker, Major Lovings looked at his watch and started counting. An enemy artillery round was hitting us every 30 seconds. Nearly a thousand artillery and rocket rounds hit Kontum that night.[2]

At 0300 hours, the enemy launched human-wave attacks from the north against the positions of the 44th and 53rd Regiments. The enemy artillery continued pounding us, while their infantry and tanks broke through our front-line positions. The 44th Regiment was hit with an enemy infantry regiment and about 20 tanks.[3] Possibly because the NVA thought the division CP was there—or because this position was the highest point in the city—its main attack was against the 44th Regiment, and it assaulted directly toward our regimental CP. With only two of our four battalions with us in the hospital area, we were hard pressed to hold off the much stronger assaulting force. The NVA's secondary attack was against the 53rd Regiment to the northeast of the 44th. It also assaulted our forces in other areas of the city.[4] Our troops endured a terrible battering even before dawn. The area around our CP was mostly rubble and burned-out buildings. The intensity of the fighting outside the bunker increased. We could hear the *knuck, knuck, knuck* of enemy AK-47s firing just outside and knew a sapper could toss a big satchel charge into our bunker at any minute.

Then Major Lovings and I heard something neither of us had ever heard before, but we knew instantly what it was: the extra loud, sharp CRACK! of an enemy tank firing its main gun directly at us. Major Lovings ran to the bunker entrance to see for himself. An enemy tank with a battle streamer flying from its turret was only 50 yards away. From one of the nearby bunkers, an ARVN officer fired an M-72 at the tank, and the sound of its impact could be heard above the other battle noise. It made a hole in the turret, and the tank engine stopped. Seeing the lead tank destroyed, the next T-54 turned to move away. Another ARVN soldier took advantage of the broadside shot and knocked it out with an M-72.[5]

Colonel Tien was standing near the bunker door, surrounded by his staff, and shouting rapidly into his radio. Our situation was critical, and his voice and manner conveyed a sense of urgency. I stood nearby with Sergeant *Hao* and told him to translate what the CO was saying. *Hao* frequently gave only the briefest summary: "He ask battalion commander what is situation." It was like the old foreign movies with subtitles where an Italian would talk for five minutes and the English subtitle would summarize it all as, "Somebody stole my bicycle."

Our 3rd Battalion was the main element defending our own positions. So many soldiers were coming down into the bunker that we began to wonder how many were still manning the perimeter. We got word that the 3rd Battalion had broken and run. Then their battalion commander himself came into our bunker.

Major Lovings slung our radio onto his back, picked up his rifle, and said, "We're in deep shit, Colonel." I nodded my agreement and slammed a magazine into my M-16. Colonel Tien looked my way, said, "We go," and headed for the door, followed by his entourage. As we started after him, I radioed the DTOC with a last message, "My counterpart is leaving the bunker!" Colonel Rhotenberry asked, "What are you going to do?" I said, "We're going with him." He responded, "We'll try to get you out of there." Lovings and I exchanged a quick glance. We knew there was no way for anyone to extract us from the middle of such an intense firefight. We would have to fend for ourselves. We would come out shooting, but this gunfight would probably end like the climax of *Butch Cassidy and the Sundance Kid*. Nevertheless, we would rather die that way than be blown to bits by a satchel charge tossed into our bunker.

Colonel Tien continued shouting into his radio as he moved slowly toward the bunker door. He suddenly stopped. Perhaps he realized we would not get far outside the bunker, or perhaps this was when he learned that only one company of the 3rd Battalion had cut and run while the other two companies were holding firm. But we were still in bad trouble. In the old cowboy movies, just when things looked hopeless for the pioneers, the US cavalry would save them by galloping in with flags flapping and bugles blowing the charge. This morning the "bugle" was Brigadier General Hill calling on our radio. The "cavalry" coming to save us was a pair of Cobra gunships and the TOW helicopters he brought with him. General Hill saved our lives that day.

Brigadier General Hill had been certain there would be another enemy attack on the morning of 26 May, so he had alerted the crews of the TOW helicopters and their Cobra escorts to be ready to take off at 0515. The old UH-1B Hueys with the TOWs could not keep up with the new, fast Cobras, which arrived over Kontum just before daylight. By then, the 53rd Regiment, the front-line regiment, had already been overrun, and our 44th Regiment, the reserve regiment, was partially overrun. Brigadier General Hill radioed that he could see six enemy tanks driving toward us across the open area at the north of our compound and enemy infantry advancing through the buildings in our compound. Major Lovings told him that our northern line of defensive bunkers ran along map grid line 90 and that anything north of there was a free-fire zone. The Cobras immediately made a strafing run, firing their rockets and machine guns to separate the NVA tanks and troops. After a loud, fast radio conversation, my counterpart told me—with much agitation—that the fire from the Cobras was too close. Some of it was hitting his troops and causing casualties. I relayed this information to Brigadier General Hill. From his vantage point in the air, he could see that the situation was worse than we realized and told me we had to make a choice: "If we hold fire, you are going to be overrun in about three minutes." I told him to let the Cobras continue

attacking. As the strafing Cobras separated the NVA infantry from their tanks, two of the T-54s tried to hide by driving into deserted buildings. This effectively removed them from the fight for the time being as Hawk's Claw destroyed the other attacking tanks.[6]
Brigadier General Hill described the action:

> In the attack on Kontum at the end of May, the NVA launched its attack at approximately 0400, penetrated an infantry regiment's position, and with tank-infantry teams started overrunning the reserve regiment. We responded from the airfields at Pleiku and at first light, 0600, had a command and control aircraft and a set of guns in the area. The guns engaged the tank-infantry force. Our people on the ground complained that the fire from the rockets was too close and hitting among them. But when it was pointed out that the alternative was to be overrun, they agreed to successive runs. On these runs fire was held to the turret so it could be more accurately placed. This fire, however, was sufficient to drive to cover the infantry elements of the tank-infantry teams. The tankers, in turn, being concerned about penetrating built-up areas in the city without infantry support, stopped to regroup. Successive runs by the Cobras delayed the regrouping and suppressed 12.7 machine guns that were accompanying the force. The TOWs, lumbering up on the B models, arrived approximately 0625 and in the next hour destroyed the tanks of the entire attacking force. By 0730 the battle had been decided, although there was considerable mopping up remaining to be done by the infantry on the ground, and this took days.[7]

Hawk's Claw turned the tide in this early morning battle, but the 44th Regiment's troops got some of the T-54s with M-72s. One ARVN soldier fired an M-72 at a tank and knocked off its left track. The tank could still turn to the left using just its right track, but it could not move in a straight line. Other ARVN soldiers moved in on the crippled tank and knocked it out with M-72s.[8] The enemy forces seized two-thirds of our compound and were only minutes away from overrunning us completely. We finally stopped them, but the two enemy tanks knocked out only a stone's throw from our bunker door showed how close we came to being overrun.[9] Tactical air strikes started at 0730, and they smashed the enemy attacks. Spectre killed one tank with its 105-mm gun, and either a mine or an M-72 killed another one. Hawk's Claw reported destroying six NVA tanks and three abandoned ARVN M-41s.[10]

The T-54 burns about a gallon of fuel per mile, and as the British counterinsurgency expert Sir Robert Thompson said, "You cannot refuel T-54 tanks with gasoline out of water bottles carried on bicycles. It has got to come down in trucks, and trucks in quite large numbers."[11] Thompson was partially wrong on that last point. The North Vietnamese had built a pipeline all the way from North Vietnam to send fuel down the Ho Chi Minh Trail. But from the end of the pipeline, the fuel still needed to be trucked to their tanks in the field. After the firing died down, Major Lovings climbed up on an enemy tank standing motionless not far from our bunker. The crew compartment was empty, so he lowered himself into the driver's seat for a look at the interior. After experimenting with the various switches and gauges, he discovered that the fuel tank was empty. This is what had stopped it dead in its tracks. President Nixon's orders to mine the ports in North Vietnam and to bomb fuel-storage facilities and transportation networks paid off in the battle for Kontum when this tank ran out of fuel just short of our bunker. Thank you, President Richard Milhous Nixon!

Over Kontum, the TOW Team flew and fired through smoke and dust while threatened by anti-aircraft fire. Their ability to hit pinpoint targets saved many civilian structures and prevented friendly casualties, which would have occurred in tactical air strikes on the same targets. Their finest hours were in the early morning of 26 May. When the TOW Team arrived, they fired 21 missiles and destroyed five T-54 tanks, five PT-76 tanks, a truck, a bunker, and two successive machine guns in a water tower. The two TOW helicopters relieved each other on station and flew three sorties each that morning. CWOs Edmond C. Smith and Danny G. Rowe were one crew, and CWOs Douglas R. Hixson and Lester F. Whiteis were the other crew. They returned the next morning to kill two more tanks. All the tanks were knocked out while they were stationary. None of them took evasive action or fired on the TOW aircraft.[12]

In the afternoon of 26 May, Colonel Ba ordered the division reserve, a battalion of the 44th Regiment reinforced by eight of his M-41 tanks, to counterattack the penetration between the 44th and 53rd Regiments. This attack did stop and contain the penetration but did not retake the lost ground. It was the same story in all parts of the city: our forces were able to limit the NVA gains but were unable to eject the enemy and restore the defensive perimeter. The tactical situation remained stabilized for the remainder of the day, but the air cavalry sighted large enemy forces moving to reinforce their penetrations.[13] Brigadier General Hill thought the situation was so bad because Colonel Ba had allowed the enemy to get in on top of him rather than detecting them and breaking up their attacks by using outposts 500 meters or more in front of the perimeter.[14]

The airfield was still closed to fixed-wing aircraft, so all resupply missions were flown by Chinook helicopters landing on the soccer field. These helicopters also evacuated refugees and seriously wounded ARVN soldiers. However, many lightly wounded ARVN soldiers tried to use these flights to escape the beleaguered city. Armed American security guards were placed on the Chinooks to stop them from boarding.[15] By afternoon, even helicopter flights into the soccer field were curtailed because of the tactical situation. The G-4 staff started planning airdrops of critical supplies. In Pleiku, Colonel Joseph J. Pizzi, the II Corps chief of staff adviser, signed the "Daily Commanders Evaluation" to General Abrams on 26 May. He noted, "Mr. Vann, BG Hill, and the corps commander are in the Kontum battle area."[16]

After dark on 26 May, indirect fire on the 45th and 53rd Regiments' CPs increased. Three battalions of the 64th NVA Regiment, 320th NVA Infantry Division, then assaulted the 45th Regiment, penetrated between the 45th and 53rd, and cut off the 45th. All available air support was diverted to the embattled regiment. Lieutenant Colonel John C. Grant, the senior adviser to the 45th Regiment, conferred with Colonel Rhotenberry, who agreed to divert two scheduled B-52 strikes to hit the NVA troops assaulting the 45th. The Arc Light struck at 0230 on 27 May and broke up the enemy attack. Spectre gunships fired in support of the 53rd through the night as Grant relayed targets from the front lines.[17]

UPI reporter Arthur Higbee reported that Kontum "is a constant explosion" from the bombs, rockets, mortars, and artillery of both sides.[18]

The *Chicago Tribune* summed up the action of 26 May:

The defenders of Kontum fought off a second day of North Vietnamese attacks today, claiming a dozen tanks knocked out and 1,000 enemy troops killed or pushed back. . . . It was feared that if the enemy could hold out until dark it could bring in reinforcements for a renewed assault on the provincial capital.

American military advisers in Kontum described the situation as under control and said the enemy had been contained. . . . The North Vietnamese first penetrated the city early yesterday, pounded it with some 800 rounds of rockets and artillery. They strengthened their attack force today. Two battalions of North Vietnamese, many of them in South Vietnamese uniforms, were reported to have infiltrated the city and to have attacked at dawn with tank fire backing them up.

South Vietnamese headquarters in Pleiku claimed 157 enemy killed in and around Kontum today but gave no report on its own casualties. American sources said 12 enemy tanks were destroyed by United States wire-guided missiles, government artillery, and hand-carried, single-shot light antitank weapons. The sources said three of the tanks were U.S.-built M-41s captured from South Vietnamese troops by the North Vietnamese earlier in the day.

U.S. forces are using special helicopters and Jeeps armed with armor-piercing missiles to combat the recent influx of tanks for use in the North Vietnamese offensive. The correspondent said the Kontum province chief and his U.S. adviser, Col. Stephen Bachinski, were shot down in a helicopter yesterday but escaped unhurt. They were back in the air today to direct U.S. Cobra helicopter gunships firing rockets into Montagnard huts near the Kontum airstrip. North Vietnamese troops were believed holed up in the area.[19]

Although NVA accounts are generally overblown, one of them is partially accurate:

On the nights of 24 and 25 April [the correct dates are 25 and 27 May, the writer possibly confusing this action with the fall of Tan Canh and Dak To II in April] the 2nd Division and the 209th Companies of the Cong Tum City unit together with a tank unit, made power thrusts at the city where enemy defenses showed weak spots. They seized the southern section of the provincial administrative center, the airfield area, the 44th Regiment headquarters, Supply Depots 40 and 41, the field hospital, and two-thirds of Special Zone 24.[20]

In his "Daily Commanders Evaluation" sent to General Abrams on 27 May, John Paul Vann was realistic and somber but also confident about eventual victory:

> The overall situation in Kontum City is critical but not at all hopeless. However, it is extremely doubtful that the former perimeter will be restored or that the present penetration will be eliminated in the near future. I expect that Col Ba will consolidate his forces within that area of the city still under his control and that future fighting will closely resemble that which has taken place in An Loc. U.S. air support will continue to be vital to a sustained defense of the city, and the increasingly bad weather conditions will dictate making maximum use of sky spots and Loran controlled drops. In this connection, my 7th AF liaison officer states that this support cannot be brought closer than 700 meters to friendlies although the corps commander has stated that they want the support into 500 meters and will assume responsibility for the consequences.[21]

At dawn on 27 May, the situation was still critical. The NVA penetrations from the north and the southeast were close to linking up and splitting the defending forces.[22] The action started early that day when NVA infantry and tanks attacked all three of the 23rd Division's regiments. The enemy was consolidating positions already seized and attacking from all sides, pushing hard to expand their penetrations. Two NVA tanks were destroyed by M-72s, and at 0730 Hawk's Claw attacked two more tanks just north of the city. The Claw fired only one missile at each vehicle, and the T-54s exploded. USAF and VNAF air strikes, gunships, and the air cavalry also supported us. With all that air support and the front-line soldiers' continuing efforts, by 1000 the defenders were able to stop the enemy's attempts to advance. However, they were still unable to restore the original perimeter by ejecting the Communists from positions they already held.[23]

At 0715 on 27 May, an enemy mortar round hit the main ammo dump one kilometer north of the airfield. The ammo started exploding and ignited a fire in a large POL dump. The burning POL emitted a big cloud of black smoke, which limited visibility for the aircraft overhead. Sixty percent of the ammunition in the dump, including 10,000 rounds of artillery ammunition—brought in at great risk to the cargo aircraft carrying it—was destroyed. The division artillery was down to only 3,500 rounds before it was resupplied.[24]

The enemy continued to push us throughout the day, and by noon they held scattered areas behind the ARVN positions all across the city's northern front.[25] In the afternoon, a VNAF FAC located a large enemy troop concentration and requested a VNAF air strike on it. No aircraft were immediately available, so he contacted the ARVN ground commander, who requested and received a US air strike. It killed 60 of the enemy. Near the embattled 53rd Regiment positions north of the airfield, two NVA .51-caliber machine guns were firing at every aircraft within range, especially the fighter-bombers. Two daring VNAF A-1E pilots made pass after pass in the face of a deadly crossfire and finally took out those two weapons. They also destroyed a 23-mm anti-aircraft gun when it revealed itself by firing at them.[26]

The airfield was still closed, and supplies could not be parachuted in until a drop zone could be secured, so our only source of resupply was by US Army CH-47s landing on the soccer field. During one 24-hour period, those valiant Chinook crews brought in 100 tons of supplies and took out more than 200 wounded on the return trip to Pleiku. At 1800, VNAF helicopters began shuttling supplies from the soccer field to the regiments. To avoid landing at each regiment's CP, the VNAF crews kicked the supplies out the door as their helicopters made low passes over the CPs. In the 53rd Regiment's area, Lieutenant Colonel Gannon, the senior adviser to the 53rd, organized ARVN troops into teams to retrieve supplies from the drop zone. The enemy artillery was firing constantly on the teams while they worked. As Gannon was moving back to his bunker, he was wounded in the upper leg. He was evacuated but returned to duty after a few days.[27]

The attacks on the 25th and 26th emphasized the urgency of changing our troop dispositions. The NVA could have cut off the 45th on FSB November and then cut off the 53rd. The situation continued to deteriorate as the NVA reinforced its attack near the airfield. The night of 25–26 May Colonel Rhotenberry and Brigadier General Ba had a heart-to-heart talk about the troop dispositions. Rhotenberry pushed Ba to withdraw from outpost Nectar, but Ba again said that the corps commander had ordered him to hold it. Rhotenberry considered the situation at Nectar to be serious but not critical. When Major General Toan and Mr. Vann arrived on 27 May, Colonel Ba briefed them and showed them the penetrations. In regard to tightening the perimeter, Toan said, "No withdrawal! If you do withdraw, you demoralize the troops."[28]

Colonel Rhotenberry had a 1:12,500-scale map of the city covered with acetate, and he used grease pencils to draw our troop dispositions on it in black and the enemy penetrations in red. He marked the 45th Regiment's position on the Round Hill in the northwest, just west of Highway 14. The 44th Regiment's positions in the hospital area were marked with an A, and between them he drew a big enemy penetration and wrote "Regt" to indicate an NVA regiment was there. East of the 44th, he labeled the 53rd Regiment's areas B and C and wrote "Regt" to indicate another NVA regiment attacking them. In the southeast, Rhotenberry wrote "Regt" again where the reserve and the Ruff Puffs were pushed up against the southern edge of the airfield by another enemy regiment. The DTOC location was shown with a flag symbol in the middle of the city. This picture was a startling depiction of how bad our situation was. The enemy held almost half of Kontum City. Worse yet, the penetrations in the northeast and southeast were close to seizing the airfield and linking up to split our defenses in two. The only thing preventing those penetrations from joining was ARVN's stubborn defense of the airfield's final defensive line of bunkers. Those bunkers were only 100 meters from the runway, and they ran parallel to it on both the north and south sides.[29]

Colonel Rhotenberry used this map to brief Mr. Vann on the situation and recommended contracting to reduce the perimeter, "or we may lose the city," he warned. Vann took the map and went upstairs where Toan and Ba were talking. Vann showed Toan the map and said, "This is where we stand right now. A two-battalion force, a regiment, has penetrated here, a regiment has penetrated here, and a regiment coming from the south has almost seized the airfield and linked up with the force coming from the north. They have the ability to reinforce these penetrations. If we don't establish a concentrated defensive position, we could lose the city."

Major General Toan asked Colonel Ba, "What do you think about this plan?" Ba agreed it was a good plan. Toan ordered that it be implemented. Rhotenberry thought Toan's asking Ba for his opinion was Toan's attempt to cover his own posterior if the changes he approved did not save the city. Rhotenberry did not consider Toan professionally competent, and Vann once told Rhotenberry, "Toan was the only man I could get."[30]

With the airfield closed and the NVA still controlling most of the eastern half of Kontum, airdrops would be vital to our defense. C-130E(I)s with all-weather airdrop capabilities were rushed to Thailand from Pope AFB, North Carolina, and Little Rock AFB, Arkansas, to supplement the C-130s of the 374th Tactical Airlift Squadron of the Tactical Airlift Wings. These special operations C-130E(I)s were equipped with the All Weather Airdrop System that used an onboard computer rather than visual references to determine the release point. They could drop bundles without slowing down and without outside guidance.[31] A drop zone was established near the river in the southwest corner of the city, and airdrops started on 27 May. The next day 64 bundles were dropped, and 50 were recovered. Over the next four days, C-130s parachuted 19 loads into the drop zone. The ground-radar, high-velocity method was used for all these drops.[32]

The NVA still controlled the graveyard between the 45th Regiment troops on FSB November and the 44th Regiment in the hospital area. ARVN attacks would grind the enemy down, but the enemy would then send in a fresh battalion. Troops from the 23rd Division must have counterattacked this graveyard eight to ten times. Air strikes, ground attacks, and counterattacks destroyed all the tombstones.[33]

At one point, the NVA captured an ARVN M-113 APC. When the TOW helicopters were attacking targets in Kontum, this vehicle was pointed out to them, and it was knocked out with a broadside shot. The TOW missile left a big hole in the side, destroying the vehicle and the enemy inside.[34] During this one day, 27 May, a total of 137 air strikes by US and VNAF fighter-bombers hit enemy positions on the north and northwest sides of the city. After dark, we could see fires burning in the enemy-occupied areas.[35]

The NVA infantry and sappers remained firmly entrenched in the hospital compound where the 44th Regiment was located. They were only 40 meters from our forward positions. We received the usual small-arms fire and a few incoming mortar rounds, but the evening passed without major incidents. Spectre, Spooky, and Stinger gunships supported us that night.[36]

Colonel R. M. Rhotenberry's map showing the situation in
Kontum on the morning of 27 May 1972.

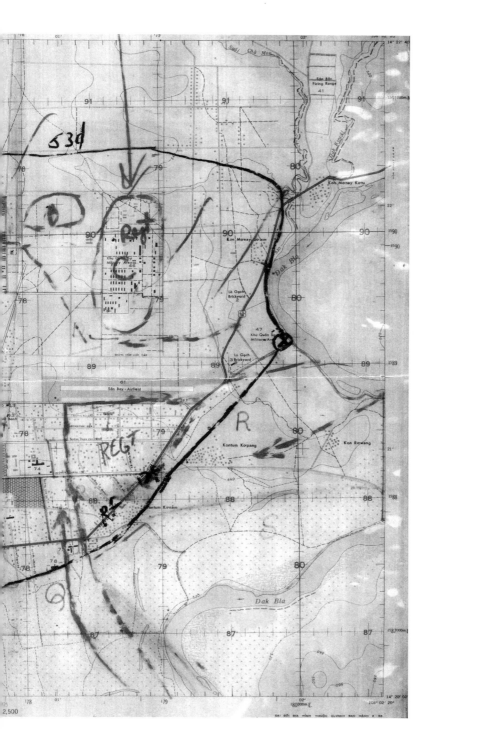

The outpost on Nectar was finally pulled in and positioned to guard the streambed behind the Round Hill.[37] South of Kontum, the effort to open Highway 14 slowly ground on with close combat and casualties on a daily basis. The corps commander questioned the wisdom of continuing that road-clearing operation, and President Thieu suggested that the forces tied down there might be better used to reinforce Kontum.[38]

The 250-pound bombs dropped by the B-52s were sometimes so close to Kontum that they broke windows and knocked the advisers' coffee cups off their worktables in the DTOC bunker.[39] John Paul Vann once remarked, "Anytime the wind is blowing from the north where B-52 strikes are turning the terrain into moonscape, you can tell from the battlefield stench that the strikes are effective."[40]

UPI reporter Matt Franjola said the situation "looks pretty grim," but he reported that 19 waves of B-52s plus tactical air strikes were causing heavy Communist casualties. On 27 May, gunships, TOW helicopters, and ARVN infantrymen knocked out 8 more enemy tanks for a total of 18 tanks destroyed in two days.[41]

We were now in worse danger than ever before. The airfield was still closed, so the only resupply or medical evacuation was by helicopter, and enemy anti-aircraft fire threatened every aircraft flying over, into, or out of Kontum. Most of the ammo dumps had been blown up by enemy artillery or mortar fire. Each of the 23rd Division's infantry battalions was supposed to have 826 men, but because of combat losses and desertions, they were hard pressed to put more than 300 each in the field. One of the battalions in the 44th Regiment was down to 200 men. Some of the ARVN soldiers could not take it any longer. During the heaviest fighting, Major Burch, whose job was working in the DTOC as assistant G-3 adviser, went out with an interpreter to stop ARVN soldiers who were trying to flee to the rear. The American captain in charge of the helicopter resupply operation at the soccer field sent refugees out on the helicopters bringing ammo in. He said that the only way he could hold off ARVN soldiers who were trying to escape Kontum with the refugees was to threaten to shoot them.

18

The Dirty Job of Killing

Sometimes it just gets down to the dirty job of killing until
one side or the other cracks.

—General Dwight D. Eisenhower

Before dawn on 28 May, we were hit with around 400 rounds of
mortar fire but the attacks by fire tapered off and there was no
major ground attack against the 44th Regiment. During the day,
about 100 large-caliber rounds hit inside the city. They were apparently fired indiscriminately rather than aimed at the airfield and
other military targets. One round hit the Highway 14 bridge over
the Dak Bla River south of the city and slightly wounded an American adviser.[1]

The II Corps advisers knew air support would be needed in
Kontum before dawn on 28 May. However, early-morning darkness was certain, and bad weather was predicted, so tactical air
strikes would not be available to hit pinpoint targets. The defenders turned to Combat Sky Spots, a type of air support that could
bomb even in the dark by using "smart bombs" guided to the target
with laser beams. It was similar to the system used for Arc Lights. A
series of Combat Sky Spots on preplanned targets along the battle-
front were scheduled for every 20 minutes between 0350 and 1230.
The USAF radar station in Pleiku would control the Sky Spots, and
the radar in Danang would take over the Arc Lights scheduled for
that period.

At 0500, sappers attacked elements of the 53rd Regiment
defending the former 14th Armored Cavalry Regiment compound
on the northern perimeter. Positions of the 44th Regiment to the

west were attacked shortly afterward. Elements of the 44th and 53rd Regiments, supported by tanks from the 8th Armored Cavalry Regiment, later attempted to dislodge the enemy from the northern compounds. When the weather improved, VNAF A-37s and US Cobra gunships supporting the 53rd troops reduced the compounds to rubble. In hand-to-hand combat throughout the day, the enemy attempted to link up their penetrations near the airfield. At the same time, the Ruff Puffs were engaged in heavy fighting in the southern area of Kontum, where the NVA was still holding a school and some houses at the southern edge of the airfield.[2]

Under pressure from Mr. Vann, Major General Toan finally agreed to withdraw what Vann called "the rather useless FSB November," thus permitting better utilization of Arc Lights north of the city. On 28 May, Toan also agreed to pull the 45th and 53rd Regiments back enough to tighten the perimeter. Withdrawing even a short distance while in contact with the enemy without having it turn into a rout is an extremely difficult military maneuver. Vann acknowledged, "It is going to be ticklish."[3] At 1100 on 28 May, 45th Regiment forces started their withdrawal from FSB November by attacking to the southeast to eliminate pockets of enemy resistance and to move into their new positions within the new, smaller defense perimeter. They encountered an entrenched NVA battalion, and it was not until the next day that the entire regiment was able to close into the city's defensive ring.

Colonel Rhotenberry wanted to put in an Arc Light northwest of FSB November late that day. The minimum clearance from the edge of the target box to friendly forces had to be 1,000 meters, but the clearance for this one was only 700 meters from the nearest friendly forces. ARVN commanders would probably approve the reduced clearance, but 18 Americans were included in those friendly forces: two Jeep-mounted TOW squads who were positioned to cover a gap in the perimeter with their antitank missiles and soldiers from the US Army's Company D, 1st Battalion, 12th Cavalry Regiment, who were providing close-in security for the TOWs.

When Mr. Vann visited Kontum late in the day, he said he could not approve a strike so close to friendly troops. Rhotenberry told him the ARVN and TOW troops would be pulled back to the 45th Regiment's CP on FSB November before the Arc Light hit. This strategy seemed to satisfy Vann. However, by the time Rhotenberry talked to the adviser on FSB November, the adviser told him that because it was already dark and the mechanical ambushes were already set out, the friendly troops could not be moved.

Rhotenberry really wanted that strike, and he wanted it right where he had plotted it, so he told the adviser on November, "Monitor the radio, and when I say 'Duck!' they [the troops] need to duck." An assistant G-3 adviser at II Corps called to question the safety limits. He acknowledged that Mr. Vann had approved the strike but cautioned Rhotenberry, "If anything happens to those Americans, it will be your personal responsibility." Rhotenberry thought the G-3 was trying to cover Vann's posterior without Vann's knowing about it. The Arc Light went in when and where Rhotenberry wanted it, and there were no friendly casualties. It did not hurt the NVA as much as Rhotenberry was hoping, but at least the 45th Regiment was able to withdraw from FSB November without being attacked.[4]

Units of the 23rd Division launched limited attacks to eject the enemy from the northern compounds and around the airfield, but no significant progress was made despite support from tactical air and Cobra gunships. The increased combat activity meant increased use of ammunition. US and VNAF gunships fired more than 3,000 rockets on 28 and 29 May. The weather was good enough for 53 tactical air sorties around the city. Some of them were used, along with Cobra gunships, to attack an estimated 100 enemy troops the air cavalry had found one kilometer northwest of town. Troops from the 53rd Regiment swept the area afterward and found 70 NVA bodies. Two NVA trucks were knocked out just north of FSB November after the 45th Regiment pulled back from there. Taking their trucks so close to the front lines may have been just the truckers' mistake. However, it might also have indicated that the Communist commanders were confident that they would soon take Kontum.[5]

In the 28 May *Stars and Stripes,* an article about knocking out enemy tanks with TOW missiles revealed that some were fired from Jeeps and that "jeeps and American personnel from Ft. Bragg, NC" had come to Vietnam.[6] On Sunday, May 28, 50 B-52s dropped 1,250 tons of bombs around Kontum. Some of the strikes were within two miles of the city. Troops from the 23rd Division recaptured the school and orphanage in the south, but NVA forces remained entrenched in other parts of both the northern and the southern sectors of Kontum.[7]

Late on 28 May, the Kontum District headquarters completed an orderly withdrawal, bringing all their vehicles, 105s, ammo, and 500 troops into the new defensive perimeter. During the afternoon, the 3rd Battalion, 47th Regiment, arrived at the soccer field in US Chinooks. They came from Camp Inari south of Pleiku, where they had been reorganized, retrained, and reequipped after their ignominious defeat at Dak To II in April.[8]

The two TOW-firing Hueys were an important part of our US Army air support, but they were only part of it. During the heavy fighting in April and May, the normal daily aircraft commitment for the 17th Aviation Group (Combat) was to provide 41 Hueys (including the C&C ship our Team 33 received every day), 8 Hooks, 7 OH-58 Kiowa scouts, and a separate gun company of 14 Cobra gunships. In addition, there was an air cavalry troop working around Kontum every day, and another troop could be diverted to Kontum when needed. H Troop of the 17th Air Cavalry Squadron worked for the II Corps G-2 air but was sometimes placed under the 23rd Division senior adviser for operational control. Their daily commitment was four Hueys, four Cobras, and four Loachs. The air cavalry located enemy supply dumps and infiltration routes and provided most of the intelligence we used for planning tactical air or Arc Light strikes.[9]

Correspondent Matt Franjola reported from Kontum on Sunday, 28 May:

VIETS TAKE MOST OF KONTUM
AS REDS APPEAR IN RETREAT

KONTUM (UPI)—We felt a lot more secure walking around Kontum Sunday, even though we were pinned down for about 20 minutes by machine gun fire.

Last week half the town was in North Vietnamese hands. Now most of those areas are secure. The South Vietnamese soldiers and a U.S. senior province adviser said the NVA appear to be pulling out of Kontum to the northeast.

A group of South Vietnamese soldiers, some of them Regional Forces militiamen, others ARVN regulars from the 23rd Div.'s 44th Regt., told UPI photographer Jeff Taylor and me:

"As we move up, we see NVA running away. NVA afraid of us. We come, they run away."

Taylor and I flew to Kontum aboard a US Army CH47 Chinook helicopter airlifting supplies into the city. As we approached, we saw fires burning in the former 22nd ARVN Div. headquarters compound.

We landed at the soccer field in the center of town, where 60 South Vietnamese soldiers with minor wounds were awaiting helicopter evacuation.

We walked down to the La San School which was held by the NVA last week. It was clear now, but an orphanage 500 yards to the south was still in Communist hands.

South Vietnamese M-41 tanks were firing cannon and machine guns into the NVA positions. The Communists were firing back with AK47 rifles and light machine guns.

The NVA opened up with rifles and a light machine gun at us, and we dived into a ditch. They kept us pinned down for 20 minutes. Finally we made a break for it and ran for shelter behind a stone wall a few yards away.

The ARVN soldiers said they think there is an NVA battalion headquarters in a house in a bamboo grove just east of the La San School. The soldiers said they had it surrounded on three sides.

In the center of town civilians were milling about, selling or buying food and soft drinks. A few girls were selling cans of rations. There didn't seem to be any food shortage.

Despite the fighting, 95 per cent of the business district seems to be intact.

The NVA still are holding an area just north of the airfield but Taylor and I made it to within 150 yards of the runway and 300 yards from the Air Vietnam terminal.

We watched South Vietnamese A1 Skyraiders making strikes but we couldn't tell whether they were hitting the Communist targets. The airfield remained closed.[10]

Mr. Vann gave the VNAF bomber pilots a well-deserved compliment. Major Gordon E. Bloom, a USAF adviser to VNAF, recalled,

John Paul Vann came in just elated at the VNAF performance. They were getting right down on the deck and putting their butt right on the line. There was murderous fire there, because the NVA had brought down numerous 51 cal quad 50's: they had even 23mm AAA guns up there and those guys were going right down the barrel . . . John Paul Vann came in so excited and said: That's the best damn bombing I've seen in my 11 years over here! That was his estimation of the VNAF. I don't think you need any more testimony than that. In the defense of Kontum the VNAF has been magnificent, absolutely magnificent.[11]

All the advisers held the VNAF fighter-bomber pilots in high esteem. Unfortunately, the VNAF helicopter pilots seldom earned similar praise.

Captain Roy Sudeck was flying his Huey low over the muddy water of a twisting, turning river in Kontum Province when he saw an island he did not remember from previous reconnaissance missions. It was a small island about 20 feet out from the riverbank. He turned around and came back for a better look. On either bank, there was a trail leading to a ford, and the new island was in the shallow water of the ford. His suspicions were confirmed by fresh tank tracks on one of the trails leading into the water. Another closer look revealed that the "island" was a T-54 tank covered with sand bags and well camouflaged. He reported this target, and the Aerial TOW Team was launched. When the TOW Hueys arrived, Sudeck marked the target with smoke, and the TOW pilot, CWO2 Douglas R. Hixson Jr. made an initial pass over the target so his gunner, CWO3 Lester Whiteis, could get a good fix on it. Hixson then made an attack run, and Whiteis guided a missile into the target's center of mass. The missile blew away all the sand bags and camouflage but did not destroy the tank. They made another pass and fired a second missile. It hit the tank turret dead on and started a fire. The tank exploded moments later. Whether the NVA was testing a new method of hiding tanks or this tank broke down in four feet of water while fording the river is immaterial. The result was, "Scratch one enemy tank!"[12]

After firing accurately on only military targets for weeks, the enemy artillery switched to an indiscriminate pattern late on 28 May, which soon caused more than 100 civilian casualties. By that night, the situation remained critical; the NVA still held the same areas it had held at the beginning of the day. Again, the 23rd Division's only accomplishment during a day of hard fighting was to contain the penetrations in the northern compounds and the southern area.[13]

Every NVA soldier had started the battle with three belts filled with cooked rice. Transportation units were supposed to keep them resupplied with food and ammunition. However, continuing air strikes had forced the NVA to stockpile their supplies far from the front lines. Our bombing also disrupted their telephone communications and hindered the movement of their transportation units. Unable to resupply their front-line troops adequately—especially those who were holding the penetrations in Kontum—the enemy was forced either to seize Kontum soon or to withdraw to resupply, rearm, and reorganize their exhausted troops. The defenders were also feeling the pinch of inadequate resupply. However, they had resources the enemy did not. On one day, American C-130s had airdropped a total of 64 tons of ammunition, and three-quarters of it was recovered.[14]

As the fighting continued day after day and on through the nights, and as the artillery and rocket bombardment became more intense, my counterpart, Colonel Tien, became more and more bunker bound. When there was a lull in the fighting, I would suggest that we should go out to check on the troops. Just showing he was there and interested in how they were doing would improve their morale and increase their resolve to hold out. It would also give us a chance to see if their positions needed to be rebuilt or improved and if they had adequate food and ammo as well as to thank them for the fighting they had done and the courage they had demonstrated. Colonel Tien would agree that it would be a good idea to leave the bunker to visit his troops, but he would not follow through to do it. He was certainly one of the best ARVN regimental commanders and basically a "hands on" officer who would go check on things himself rather than just relying on reports, so now it was discouraging to see him physically and mentally withdrawing into the bunker. We all have our breaking point, and he had been fighting this war many years before I arrived.

19

All Over but the Shooting?

If Kontum City holds, the North Vietnamese will be defeated in II Corps.

—John Paul Vann, May 1972

Enemy activity tapered off on 29 May. The previous night was the first one since arriving in Kontum that we were not bombarded and then hit with major ground assaults supported by tanks. However, the front line was still only 100 meters from our bunker door. The perimeter was being pulled in so it would be easier to defend and to prevent enemy infiltration. It seemed to be the smart thing to do, but it could also be viewed as a tightening of the NVA noose around us. The relief force pushing up Highway 14 was not making much progress, and the airfield was still closed. All our supplies were coming in by Hook or by parachute. Pockets of enemy soldiers were holding out all over town, and just driving back to the DTOC was an adventure. Some days we could not get there at all. That meant no mail, *Stars and Stripes,* or personal contact with the other advisers. We were lucky to have food and water. Major Lovings and I had two cases of beer, and we heard the local ice plant was still operating, so we might even have cold beer someday. However, as we watched VNAF bombers striking an area right in front of us, I tried to think of ways we were better off than Dien Bien Phu.[1]

There were only sporadic sniper shots, and only 30 artillery, mortar, or rocket rounds landed in the city on this day. A Loach from B Troop, 7th Squadron, 17th Cavalry, was shot down seven kilometers north of the city. There were no survivors. Almost an entire NVA regiment was in the streambed behind FSB November. Pulling the 45th Regiment off FSB November had probably saved it from being cut off. Moving back into the city, the 45th Regiment linked up with the 53rd Regiment. Both regiments then withdrew into the new, tighter perimeter to strengthen our defenses. The 45th Regiment would be available as a reserve to counterattack penetrations.[2] By 1000, approximately 60 tactical air sorties had hit targets in and around Kontum. Fourteen of them struck in the northeast, where they destroyed 39 bunkers and other structures. The 44th Regiment attacked enemy positions in the hospital compound but made little progress despite heavy fighting. Those entrenched NVA soldiers were fighting for their lives. Also, the VNAF tactical air support for our attacks was 90 minutes late arriving, allegedly because of a weather hold in Pleiku. This excuse did not sit well with Major General Toan because the US fighter-bombers and helicopters were on station continually starting at 0600. At the end of the day, the enemy still held his positions in the north and southeast of Kontum. What we had was essentially a stalemate.[3]

In his "Daily Commanders Evaluation" written 29 May, Mr. Vann told General Abrams, "The consensus is that Arc Light results greatly exceed kills by all other means. My personal synthesis of all available information indicates that most enemy infantry units are at 50 percent or less of their entry strength in early 72. Nearly all PW and Hoi Chanh reports indicate average company strength of around 20–25. An exception to this was a report from a PW from the 28th NVA Regiment, who stated the recent arrival of 200 replacements for the regiment had raised the company strength up to 60 men."[4]

The American advisers at higher levels said that if we could hold out another seven days, the NVA would give up and go home. I was dubious. From my previous trips to Pleiku and passing through Saigon to go on R&R, I knew the Americans' optimism about the war increased in direct proportion to their distance from the front lines. Being on the front lines, I was mostly pessimistic and slightly hopeful at best.[5]

The enemy attacked the 44th Regiment through the night of 29–30 May. At 0100 on 30 May, the 44th and 53rd Regimental CPs were hit with heavy mortar fire, which continued until dawn. One Stinger and two Spectre gunships were on station and fired on the suspected mortar locations. The NVA then launched a ground attack against the 53rd Regiment. At dawn, we found two NVA battalions across the street to the east of our compound. We hit them with everything we had all day long. The 23rd Division again launched attacks to push the enemy out of the city. In the hospital area, the 44th Regiment attacked the enemy strongholds, including heavily constructed underground bunkers. We killed 103 of the enemy and took 3 POWs against our own losses of 13 KIA and 41 WIA but did not take our objective. The 3rd Battalion of the 47th Regiment and the 14th ARVN Cavalry moved to eject the enemy from the former 14th Cavalry compound near the northeastern perimeter but were stopped at 0725 when a stray mortar round hit the remains of the ammunition dump between the ARVN and NVA forces. The resulting fire and explosions caught the enemy in the open and may have killed or wounded many of them. Despite this unexpected assistance, the ARVN troops were not able to seize all their objectives. In the southeast, the 2nd Battalion of the 44th and the Ruff Puffs attacked the area south of the airfield and after five hours of fighting managed to seize their objective by 1530. The ground TOW team was credited with destroying a .51-caliber position in a bunker.[6]

When Colonel Ba obtained the concurrence of the II Corps commander to tighten the perimeter by pulling the 45th Regiment back from FSB November, that maneuver also allowed tactical air and Arc Light strikes closer to the new, tightened perimeter. The effectiveness of our air strikes was thus increased, and the NVA forces besieging Kontum and those already inside the city were deprived of vital supplies. By the morning of 30 May, the enemy troops' performance was suffering from their lack of food, ammunition, and other supplies. The 23rd Division's soldiers were now fighting bunker by bunker and building to building, using tear gas and hand grenades to dislodge the enemy. The fighting was bloody, brutal, and often hand to hand. In the rubble of the hospital area, bunkers were gradually destroyed or captured, and two T-54 tanks were destroyed by M-72s. By noon, the NVA held only a few scattered positions. As the 44th Regiment troops moved forward, they saw large groups of enemy soldiers moving away toward the northeast. FACs and the US air cavalry confirmed that the NVA was withdrawing from the battlefield.[7]

Across the street from our compound, the enemy held an area with rows of one-story buildings. Our artillery was pounding them, and most of the buildings were on fire. "Sage Street," the "air boss," called me on the tactical radio net. I keyed the handset and answered, "Snapper 14, over." He said, "I've got a pair of snakes here with rockets, but they have only 12 minutes left on station. If you don't have a target right now, I'll have to send them home." Looking through my field glasses, I saw eight or ten enemy soldiers—about a squad—run out from between two of the burning buildings. They wore brown uniforms, and some of them were bareheaded. One was carrying a machine gun, and the others had AK-47s. They were darting back and forth like scared rabbits, trying to find a way to escape. I told "Sage Street," "OK, I have a target for you," and identified it for him. The Cobras rolled in, one after the other, and the entire enemy squad disappeared in exploding rockets, smoke, and fire. I vividly remember that scene. When the division reconnaissance company pushed in there late in the day, they found 122 enemy bodies in and around those buildings.[8] The stench of rotting corpses was almost overwhelming. In positions where the smell was the worst, some of our troops were wearing their gas masks.[9] Mr. Vann said at least one-fifth of all the NVA soldiers whose bodies were found in Kontum Province had tattoos saying "Born in the North to die in the South."[10]

The G-3 adviser, Lieutenant Colonel Bricker, later described the use of the Chieu Hoi (Open Arms) Program, which encouraged the enemy soldiers to desert and rally (switch over) to the South Vietnamese side:

> We found early on the enemy was very young, just kids, and led by an experienced Communist officer who controlled the rice and the location of his force. The troops obviously did not want to fight, but were forced to. They had been brainwashed and believed they were going to fight Americans and free their country from our control. Knowing this, we put a max Chieu Hoi program into operation. A leaflet was quickly produced which told them . . . with a map . . . how to reach Chieu Hoi locations and that we had plenty of chow. The entire area of operations . . . was covered with leaflets. It worked so well we had to call in more MPs to control them. The info obtained from these [Hoi Chanh] helped us direct more bombs and artillery on their lines.[11]

The 23rd Division lost its chance to gain more Hoi Chanhs when some were slain while attempting to come into the ARVN lines.[12] In a letter home, I described what happened on the morning of 30 May:

> Bad incident this morning. We were attacked again and again through the night (and we are supposed to be behind the lines in reserve!). At daybreak there was a good-sized NVA force opposite the gate to our compound. Wade went out to look and said the ARVN troops were calling to them to surrender and then shooting them down when they tried [to surrender]. Wade took off his equipment, stepped out in front of the lines, and had the interpreter tell them through a loud speaker that they should surrender and that he, the American adviser, would guarantee their safety. Five NVA came forward with their hands up and the ARVNs shot them down.
>
> Wade said . . . not only the front line troops but all the cooks, clerks, and the colonel's houseboy were all out there shooting. If they [the enemy] had been allowed to surrender, their whole outfit might have followed them and we would not have to go dig them out.
>
> Wade came back in the bunker completely disgusted and said, "I've had it! I want out!" Col. Tien and the other Vietnamese officers came up with all sorts of excuses; the NVA leaders were shooting at their own men to keep them from surrendering, the NVA were shooting at our lines & we needed to return fire, and a previously ordered artillery round landed nearby. All of which is true but none of those things killed the men trying to surrender.
>
> I went out to see what was happening and two more NVA came forward with their hands up. They made it across to friendly lines, but we think it was only because Wade and I were watching.
>
> We told them [the Vietnamese] to get one of the two prisoners to talk to his NVA friends with the loudspeaker, tell them he had received medical treatment & food, and encourage them to surrender too. Instead they put in a VNAF air strike before trying any psywar [psychological warfare]. After one big pass by the bombers, suddenly the front line opened up. Probably some more NVA were trying to surrender. Part of the VNAF strike fell short and napalm & cluster bomb units fell on our lines. They are still counting casualties.

President Thieu, accompanied by an entourage of South Vietnamese military and congressional leaders, visited II Corps from 1130 to 1600 that day. John Paul Vann described the president's trip to Kontum:

> The president responded to a suggestion at lunch that he fly to Kontum City for a briefing and to promote several officers. He agreed, and at General Toan's request, the president's flight in and out was handled with U.S. helicopters and gunships to maximize safety. Other personnel in the party flew in a VNAF chopper. We rounded up all available press, got them to Kontum City ahead of the president, and then flew him in. An enemy shelling attack occurred during his visit, with three 122-mm rockets landing within 300 meters of the president. Additionally, long range sniper fire whistled overhead as the president walked throughout the area, shaking hands and chatting leisurely with the soldiers. Subsequently he received a briefing from the division commander and then promoted the following officers:
>
> A. Col Ly Tong Ba, 23rd division commander, to BG.
> B. LTC Tran Van Cha, 45th regimental commander, to COL.
> C. CPT Tran Van Le, Kontum district chief, to major.
>
> Throughout the visit, the president was in high spirits, talking freely to newsmen, posing for TV shots and interviews, and repeatedly expressing confidence that the enemy drive would be defeated. . . . Overall, it was an extremely impressive performance and a great morale boost to the forces in Kontum City.[13]

A later South Vietnamese government publication about the battle and President Thieu's visit published a photo of my counterpart and the corps commander with the caption, "A prize of 50,000 piasters [approximately $100] is presented to the commander of the 44th Infantry Regiment for the destruction of each enemy tank. The money will be divided among the troops in recognition of their gallant efforts."[14] We will never know how much of the money got down to the individual ARVN soldiers who bravely stood their ground and fired the missiles to knock out those tanks.

Every day I burned the previous day's codes and put the new ones in my code wheel. As I went through the days of May—14, 15 . . . 25, 26 . . . 29, 30—I was just glad to have lived through another one. The night of 30 May was relatively quiet. It was good not to be attacked again and again all through the night.[15]

20

Finishing the Job

You will kill ten of our men and we will kill one of yours, and
in the end it will be you who tire of it.

—Ho Chi Minh

John Paul Vann was elated. He was vindicated. His plan had
worked. The Arc Lights and tactical air killed tens of thousands
of the enemy, destroyed their supplies, and broke up their attacks.
The USAF, VNAF, and the Hooks brought in our necessary supplies. Colonel Rhotenberry and the other advisers did their jobs,
and Brigadier General Ba and his 23rd Infantry Division had held.
Kontum was saved. Although some pockets of enemy resistance
remained, around noon on Wednesday, 31 May, Mr. Vann declared
that the main battle for Kontum was over. At a press conference in
the Team 21 mess hall in Pleiku, Vann said the big test had been
on 14 May, when the first NVA tanks were destroyed in Kontum. He
said the battle was "characterized by the failure of the North Vietnamese to achieve any objectives." The NVA needed replacements
and resupply for its battered forces, and those forces were now
retreating from Kontum City, leaving nearly 4,000 of their dead
behind on the battlefield. Most had been killed by air strikes and
artillery. In clearing out the last of the NVA in the city, 23rd Division troops killed 237 enemy soldiers and found another 128 bodies
in a mass grave on the northern outskirts of Kontum.[1] In the evening, the 3rd Battalion of the 53rd was on a search mission three
kilometers northeast of Kontum when it found approximately 100
NVA bodies in destroyed bunkers and foxholes.[2]

As of 31 May, the Communists physically controlled all but

four hamlets in Kontum Province, and government control over those four was either marginal or inadequate.[3] The main supply route from Pleiku to Kontum, Highway 14, remained closed. Kontum airfield was also closed, so the only resupply was by Hook or parachute. As for the enemy, the province senior adviser recorded: "Reports from Hoi Chanh, POWs, and line crossers confirm that the enemy is critically short of ammunition and food; malaria and infected wounds are serious problems; death of many small unit leaders is resulting in aimless wanderings; after having been told that they were coming into Kontum as an occupying force, they expressed great surprise at the ferocious reception they received."[4]

When the monsoon season started, ground combat slowed down. As the enemy activity to our front slackened, the 23rd Division concentrated on eliminating the last strongpoints of enemy resistance within the city. The last day of May was the seventh day of intense, close-in fighting in Kontum. Reopening the airfield—at least to night operations—was a top priority, but we first needed to clear out all the NVA holdouts. The enemy-held areas in the southeastern part of the city were reduced to about four square blocks. However, the fighting between the 44th Regiment and the enemy in the hospital area was hard, bunker-to-bunker, house-to-house, and often hand-to-hand combat with a tough enemy who was determined to hold the buildings and bunkers he occupied. Our progress was slow and costly. There was heavy cloud cover most of the day, but when there were breaks in the ceiling, we used tactical air strikes a few hundred meters in front of our attacking troops.[5]

By the end of May, after two months of fighting, the Communists controlled enough territory to rule over half a million South Vietnamese, but that was 3 percent of the entire population of 18.9 million.[6] The enemy paid a terrible price in casualties for the territory and population seized. The NVA troops surrounding Kontum were in especially bad shape. Their repeated attacks against our defenses and our air attacks against them inflicted heavy casualties. Captured message logs revealed that the C6, C7, and C8 Companies of the 5th Battalion, 141st Regiment, 2nd NVA Division, were down to 20, 12, and 60 men, respectively. The 60 men in C8 Company included battalion headquarters and mess personnel. This battalion, with a normal strength of about 600, was now down to only 92 men. It was also short of ammo and radio batteries and had difficulty evacuating its wounded.[7]

An American journalist reported that ARVN soldiers monitoring NVA radio nets heard Communist units requesting permission to withdraw to the north because of severe casualties and the need to refit. Those requests were always refused—with threats of punishment. The journalist suggested that the NVA was using the Prussian model for discipline in combat: "The soldiers obey orders because they know that death is possible from up front but absolutely certain from behind."[8]

Although the NVA ended the battle for Kontum on a defiant "We'll be back!" note, its own official history admitted it was not able to take Kontum City: "On 14 and 25 May, we launched two assaults into Kontum city, but our forces were unsuccessful and suffered losses. Our units were ordered to pull back to regroup and prepare for a new assault."[9]

On 31 May, 102 tons of supplies were parachuted into Kontum, and 92 tons were quickly recovered. US CH-47s flew another 78 tons, including 20 tons of rice for refugees, into the soccer field. The stocks of ammo, POL, and other supplies expended during the battle and lost through destruction of the ammo and POL dumps were still low. Rebuilding them with airdrops and helicopters was much slower than using C-130s landing at the airfield would have been. Even delivery by C-130s and C-123s resulted in less volume at a much higher cost than delivery by trucks up Highway 14 from Pleiku. However, for the time being, delivery by air was the only option available. The operation to clear Highway 14 south of us was still moving forward, but at a very slow pace.[10]

A strange thing happened early on 31 May and played out over the course of the day. Our 44th Regiment's XO was talking on the ARVN radio net when a faint voice broke in and said, "We want to surrender." The XO asked who was speaking and where they were, and he was told there were 100 NVA soldiers with weapons who wanted to give up. The NVA soldier gave his location and said they were trapped behind our 45th Regiment's lines and wanted to surrender. Colonel Tien passed the message to the commander of the 45th Regiment, who started negotiations with the caller. Artillery fire and air strikes on that area were stopped while negotiations were conducted. Radio communication was lost around 1000 when the enemy soldier said he was afraid he was being monitored by one of his higher headquarters. Four men subsequently came toward our lines with their hands up but stopped about 300 meters away. Brigadier General Ba maintained a cease-fire in that area while he broadcast to them with a loudspeaker, but the surrender never happened. An ARVN officer said it was probably just a trick to allow this group of NVA soldiers to escape after being caught behind our lines.[11]

Wednesday, 31 May, turned into a beautiful day. It felt like Sunday or a holiday back home. The sun broke through the overcast for a while, there was virtually no incoming fire, and we had beaten back the enemy's best efforts to take Kontum. The 44th Regiment was preparing to attack some buildings still held by the invaders. Major Lovings and I decided it would be a good chance to visit the DTOC bunker. We drove our replacement Jeep and got our first look in days at the destruction caused by the recent fighting. Some buildings were still smoldering, and we had to weave past shell holes in the streets. A naked doll lying face up in the street caused me to wonder what happened to its little owner. At the DTOC, we talked to the other advisers, discussed what was happening and what was planned, and picked up our mail and some copies of *Stars and Stripes*. One of the advisers working in the DTOC told us that the Kontum Province advisers compound southwest of the airfield was relatively undamaged and that the showers there were still working. We looked at each other and at our own filthy fatigues and flak jackets and decided the other adviser was trying to tell us something. We got our toilet kits, towels, and clean underwear, socks, and fatigues out of our B-4 bags stored in the DTOC bunker and headed for the showers.

The compound's former occupants must have evacuated in a hurry, and Vietnamese scavengers had probably hit the place immediately afterward. The screen door was banging in the breeze. Old correspondence and other papers were scattered around the floor, and there was a heavy layer of dust over everything. It was a shock to see evidence that the Americans had been forced to flee in such disorder. At least the showers were working, though, and we took our time enjoying them. After I put on clean clothes and laced up my boots, I started to put on my flak jacket but stopped because it was so filthy. This did not seem like a dangerous day, so I decided to toss it into our Jeep rather than wear it.

We then drove back to the hospital compound. As we reached the gate, Mr. Vann came out, driving a Jeep with a civilian sitting beside him. He chided me, "Well, McKenna, I bring a famous war correspondent to see some real soldiers, and you are out sightsee-ing!" Vann introduced us to the correspondent, who climbed into our Jeep. We drove back to our bunker, parked the Jeep, and took him on a walking tour of the front. After describing the recent fighting and showing him a few dead NVA tanks—some intact, but most charred hulks—we reached the place where our troops were starting to assault some buildings held by the NVA. The side of one building was blasted away, so we could see the ARVN troops moving through it. They were wearing gas masks and using tear gas grenades to flush out the enemy. Suddenly there was the heavy CRUMP! CRUMP! CRUMP! of mortar rounds landing around us. The enemy was responding to our ground attack. Major Lovings and the correspondent ran in one direction, and I ran in another. I was looking for a building, a bunker, or a foxhole—any place for cover from what was becoming an intense mortar barrage. My flak vest was still in the Jeep back near our bunker.

WHAMP! A giant fist slammed me to the ground. Mortar rounds were falling all around me. When I tried to stand up and run, something was wrong inside my chest, and there was blood on the front of my fatigues. I had a bad pain in my chest and difficulty breathing. I was hit and did not feel like moving but knew it was necessary to get out of the mortar fire and to do it fast. With great difficulty, I stood up and started walking—staggering—to get away from the mortars. I passed a few ARVN soldiers in individual fox-holes too small for me to fit into beside them. None of them moved to help me even though they could see I was wounded. Once out of the mortar impact area, I had only another 100 meters or so to go to our bunker, where there would be help. I finally reached the bunker, made it down the steps, and collapsed on my cot. Sergeant *Hao* was shocked by my appearance. He used our radio, set on the adviser's radio net, to call the DTOC for help.

Major Richard C. Gudat was in our area and heard the radio message. He came to our bunker, helped me up the stairs to his Jeep, and drove to a place where a helicopter could land. A Huey, Gladiator 51 from the 57th Assault Helicopter Company, came in to pick me up. Its crew got me into one of the seats and fastened my seat belt. Lying down on the deck was what I wanted to do, but leaning way back eased the pain. We lifted off and up, up, up out of Kontum, out of the war, and into the cool air. It was impossible for me to tell how serious my wound was, but I knew a chest wound could be fatal. What mattered most right then was trying to find a less painful position for sitting while strapped into the canvas heli-copter seat.[12] Half an hour later I was in the emergency room of the 67th Evacuation Hospital in Pleiku. The helicopter medevac sys-tem and the excellent medical care available close to the front saved many lives in Vietnam—including mine.

At the hospital, the medical staff cut off my bloody fatigue jacket, X-rayed my torso, and then sat me on an examination table. A corpsman on each side held me in the upright sitting position. The lead doctor was a short, muscular major, a surgeon. He didn't explain what he was going to do, which was probably just as well. After giving me a numbing shot between the ribs on my right side, but before it took effect, he used a scalpel to slice a hole between my ribs. Another doctor and another medic joined the corpsmen on either side to hold me down. The surgeon took a long, stainless steel tube with holes in it—sort of like a piccolo—and worked it in between my ribs, around various organs, and deep into my chest. It was probably only six to eight inches long, but it felt like more than a foot long to me. Now I understood why four men were hold-ing me down. They attached a rubber hose to the "piccolo" and attached a vacuum machine to the hose. My chest was full of air, blood, and other unwanted fluids, and the machine was going to suck them out.

The surgeon later stood beside my bed with the X-ray and my records. He told me there were multiple shrapnel wounds in my upper torso, and one piece had punched a hole in my lung, which had then collapsed and was probably the main source of my pain. He said, "That piece of shrapnel is still embedded in the wall of your lung. I thought about removing it but have decided to leave it there. You can live with it." Remembering a magazine article by a man whose sternum was cut in half with a circular saw before his ribs were spread apart for an open chest operation, I assured the doctor his decision was just fine with me. He also told me I would be sent home for recuperation. For the first time in weeks, it looked like I might not die in Vietnam. At least the odds were now in my favor. In total, 61 lieutenant colonels from all services were killed in Vietnam.[13]

The patient ward was a long room in a one-story building. A chest-high partition ran down the middle, and on either side of it was a row of beds with their heads against it. The head of my bed was against that partition. Rows of beds also stood against each of the outside walls. In the night, I could hear a loud, eerie, spine-tingling wailing. It combined pain and extreme anguish and came from just the other side of the partition, but the source was out of my sight. The corpsman told me it was an old Montagnard woman whose stomach had been sliced open by artillery shrapnel up near Kontum. She had walked all the way to Pleiku, carrying her intestines in her hands, and came to the 67th Evac. The US Army hospitals were not supposed to accept Vietnamese patients—not even ARVN or VNAF military patients—but the hospital commander decided he could not turn her away, in part because she was going to die soon.

A couple times a day one of the corpsman removed the dressings and cleaned her wound. He wore a nose mask while doing it because the smell was so bad. The patients just held their noses until the procedure was over. Every night we heard her weird wailing. She must have been calling on all the ancient Montagnard gods of the mountains to save her—or to put her out of her misery. She died a few days later.

I was able to make a Military Affiliate Radio Station (MARS) telephone call home to my wife. Of course, she wanted to know how seriously I was wounded, so I told her what I knew. The US Army MARS operator in Vietnam was listening and broke in to rebuke me for giving those details over an insecure radio transmission. He threatened to cut us off.[14] The corpsman who retrieved the phone heard my conversation with the MARS operator and told me about a recent patient whose legs had been amputated above the knee. Talking to his family during a MARS call, he had told them, "They had to cut off about four feet of my legs."

The evening of 31 May, Mr. Vann and Brigadier General Hill came to see me. Although I had talked to Brigadier General Hill on the radio many times, this was the first and only time I ever saw him. After thanking him for bringing the gunships and TOW helicopters that saved us from being overrun on the morning of 26 May, I said, "You saved our lives." He responded, "Just doing my job."

In a spot report of all the day's activities sent to General Abrams, Mr. Vann said, "Fighting north of the airfield is still heavy, however, and my 44th RCAT adviser, LTC McKenna was wounded with shrapnel thru the lung about 1300 hours, and will be evacuated to the U.S. This is the second regimental adviser to be wounded and evacuated this past week from the 23rd."[15]

By 2 June, I was propped up on a couple pillows but still had the piccolo in my chest, was on a drip, and was breathing with a machine to pump up and exercise my lung. All those connections prevented me from walking around or even sitting up on the edge of the bed, so my view was restricted to a few beds on either side of mine and a few opposite me across the aisle.

In the afternoon, four new patients were moved from the emergency room into the ward. They were the crew and passengers of Gladiator 12, a Huey from the 57th Assault Helicopter Company, flown by CWO2 Bruce E. Delau. It had been shot down by heavy anti-aircraft fire just before 1000 as it had taken off after picking up passengers near the Rock Pile south of Kontum. It went down in flames, crashed, and burned. The copilot, Captain Joe W. Eubanks, died in the fire, and two of the US passengers and all three of the ARVN passengers were mangled and badly burned.[16]

The two worst burn victims were wrapped with bandages so that they looked like mummies and were unrecognizable. Seeing them made me feel very lucky. My own wounds were light compared to theirs. One was placed in the bed to my right. When a corpsman said the wounded man's name, I realized it was Captain Ray Hall, our Team 33 signal adviser. He had second- and third-degree burns over 50 percent of his body and was heavily sedated. Only a few days earlier Hall had been showing his friend Captain Finch a piece of shrapnel that had hit him in the chest but did not penetrate his flak jacket. He told Finch, "Well, Jack, they've had their chance. I'm gonna make it." Although he did make it, he was severely burned. Finch had the sad duty of gathering up Hall's belongings to ship home and writing "the Letter" to his wife.[17]

The other badly burned casualty was placed in a bed across the aisle from me. It was USAF major Harold D. Jones, our air liaison officer. He had second- and third-degree burns over 60 percent of his body and a traumatic amputation of his right leg. Jones had arrived in Vietnam at the end of February, and I had met him for the first time in Kontum. He was a muscular man with short hair. The last time I had seen him we were outside the DTOC, and he was standing by his Jeep talking on the big air force radio mounted in it, coordinating the air support so vital to our survival. I was standing nearby talking with other advisers and looking at maps.

Almost continuous artillery and rocket fire had been falling near us. It would be an exaggeration to claim that the army advisers were completely cool, calm, and collected, but we were more accustomed to so much incoming fire. Major Jones was obviously out of his element, though, and visibly shaking. It had occurred to me at the time that if I were riding in his jet fighter-bomber during a bomb run through heavy anti-aircraft fire, I would be doing more than shaking. He was a courageous man for continuing to do his duty while obviously worried about being killed by flying shrapnel.

A special evacuation flight was scheduled to come as soon as possible to take the burn victims directly to Brooke Army Medical Center at Fort Sam Houston, Texas, the burn center for all the US Armed Forces. Captain Hall left on that flight, but Major Jones died in the 67th Evacuation Hospital the day after the crash.

The other two casualties were the pilot of the helicopter, CW2 Bruce E. Delau, and the crew chief, Sergeant David M. Millard. Both were seriously injured and burned. They were in beds out of my sight, and I never talked to either of them. Millard had only ten days left in Vietnam when he had taken off on that fatal flight. They had expected the mission to be a routine "ash and trash" run from Camp Holloway in Pleiku, north to the Kontum area of operations, where they would make pickups and deliveries of personnel and munitions. Late in the morning they had landed near Highway 14 in the vicinity of the Rock Pile, where they picked up Major Jones, Captain Hall, and three ARVN soldiers to take them back into Kontum.

Later that night in the hospital, when the lights were low and the ward was quiet, Sergeant Millard told someone near him what had happened after they took off from the Rock Pile. He was out of my sight, but I heard every word he said. His voice was full of anguish, and he was suffering as much from his inability to save Captain Eubanks as he was from his own injuries. Here is Dave Millard's unforgettable story:

> After loading, we took off to the south and sucked for altitude. Banking hard right to set course for K-town, we were ripped open by 51 fire and God knows what else. We lost antitorque [and cyclic] and went in on fire; nose down, on the starboard [right] side, from perhaps 150 to 200 feet. I was ejected from the aircraft to the right somehow. My Nomex

trousers were soaked in JP4 and on fire, and my back was broken at T12. My gunner, [Specialist Fourth Class] William (Billy) Chlebowski of Reading, Pa., also survived the crash and somehow appeared around the rear of the wreckage and threw himself on me to smother the flames on my legs. He then dragged me toward the front of the chopper and away from the growing fire aboard. At this point I saw our aircraft commander, Bruce Delau, stagger from around the port [left] side of the chopper and toward myself and Billy. At this juncture Billy heard the screams of Major Jones and ran to assist him, doing all he could to put out the fire that was consuming his jungle fatigues and his flesh. After doing all he could, he left the still smoldering and screaming Major Jones to assist the ARVN soldiers as they attempted to extract themselves from the crash and growing conflagration.

At or about this same time it became apparent to me that Captain Eubanks was trapped in the chopper and was in immediate danger of burning also. The chin bubble on [his] side . . . was broken out and driven deep enough into the earth that there was no access to the cockpit thru it . . . the bird had collapsed enough to effectively pin Joe into place in his seat. . . . [His] armored seat had broken loose and pinned him very close to the windscreen. I remember picking up something, possibly a chunk of wreckage or something off the ground, and repeatedly trying to break the Plexiglas windscreen to help free Joe. As the flames grew hotter and higher and Joe's pleas grew into screams of agony, out of sheer frustration I repeatedly threw myself bodily at the windscreen trying to dive or crash thru it if possible to get to Joe and pull him out. At this time Billy came back around the front of the bird and saw what I was doing and had the sensibility to recognize the impending flashover and explosion of the wreckage, grabbed me and forced me back away from my vain attempts to save Joe moments before the whole aircraft blew up. He once again helped put out the JP4 fires on my Nomex that had reignited during my struggle to save Captain Eubanks, and we sat down together in shock, forced to watch as Joe died in the flames.

I remember looking at Billy and seeing him with his flight suit covered with burnt human flesh and melted jungle fatigue. His Nomex gloves all covered with dirt, caked blood, and strips of skin. His eyebrows and eyelashes were gone, burned away, and his face bright red and filthy. I have no idea how long it was, and we heard the muttering sound of another inbound chopper then the Thump, Thump, Thump of heavy MG [machine gun] fire and small arms. Neither Billy nor I was in possession of a weapon, [so] we just became very small, figuring our troubles had just begun. The approaching chopper veered away. Unknown to us at the time, its pilot, Captain Fredric Suttle of H 1/10 Cav, was killed in the fusillade of 51 fire that reached out for his chopper as he lined up to come in and extract us from a very bad situation. Eventually an ARVN patrol made it to us and secured the crash site. We were moved out to QL 14 and laid out next to a Jeep and a deuce-and-a-half [two-and-a-half-ton truck] and waited there while the ARVN cleaned out the area and silenced that heavy gun, allowing a Dustoff to come in and pull us out. I remember one of the ARVN that helped drag me out brought Billy and I a pan full of water and a couple of old green army towels as we sat so we could clean the dirt out of the burns. As I looked down into the pan of water to wring out the towel, I remember seeing my reflection and not knowing who it was. I looked over at Billy and told him to be careful not to look into the water at his reflection because the person he probably expected to see there was gone forever.

My pilot, and friend, was trapped in the wreckage and despite everything we tried and did, he was lost to the fire as I wept. The date was 2 June 1972. My pilot was Captain Joe Eubanks. After 35 years I still can close my eyes and see Joe like he just handed me the logbook and walked away down the apron. Some great men are immortalized in print or art. The greatest are held forever in the hearts of their friends and Brothers-in-Arms.[18]

Epilogue

The End of the Fight

Television brought the brutality of war into the comfort
of the living room. Vietnam was lost in the living rooms of
America—not on the battlefields of Vietnam.
—Marshall McLuhan, *Montreal Gazette*, 16 May 1975

Mr. Vann came to Kontum every day in early June, and every day
he would complain to Colonel Rhotenberry about the NVA troops
still in the city, "Hey, Rhot, haven't you gotten this goddamned city
cleared yet?" Starting around 2 June, the weather was bad enough
to ground tactical air support. So the ARVN soldiers had to clear
out the remaining enemy with more days of bunker-to-bunker
fighting. Finally, the last NVA holdout in the city was killed on 5
June 1972, and the next day Brigadier General Ba declared the city
free of enemy soldiers. When Vann came to visit on 6 June, Rhotenberry again showed him his 1:12,500-scale Kontum City map on
which he used colored grease pencils to draw the defensive perimeter, the attacks, and the penetrations. He told Vann the last penetrations had been cleared out that morning. This news was a high
point for Vann because then he knew for certain that the Battle of
Kontum was over and we had won. After Tan Canh and Dak To
had fallen, Vann had thought his entire career in Vietnam and his
reputation were on the line, so he was subdued and working under
a great deal of pressure to succeed. Now he was vindicated and
triumphant.

After the enemy was finally ejected from the city, a better drop
zone became available in northwest Kontum. Sixty-eight airdrop
missions were flown during the first week of June. The USAF

recorded, "A prolonged airlift to battered Kontum rivaled in significance and drama the An Loc resupply. Demanding night-landing techniques, airdrop methods lately worked out at An Loc, and adverse-weather aerial delivery system equipment were all used at Kontum." Finally, night landings at Kontum airfield—with only one plane at a time on the ground—were resumed on the night of 8–9 June. The first C-130 touched down at 2337. Five more sorties followed it. During the landings, ARVN artillery shot into the NVA lines to suppress anti-aircraft fire and fired flares to attract any Strella missiles launched at the landing planes. On 13 June a C-130 avoided a Strella in the only recorded Strella attack around Kontum.[1] In all of South Vietnam, by the end of May 1972 Strella missiles had knocked down seven Allied aircraft, including one fast mover, a US Marine Corps A4 Skyhawk hit on 26 May.[2]

After the battle, at least eight destroyed aircraft lay on Kontum airfield: a VNAF A-1 Skyraider that had made an emergency landing and was then destroyed by incoming fire; two USAF C-130s; three VNAF C-123s; a Cobra gunship; a VNAF Hook; and a VNAF Huey hit by the Hook when the Hook had a mechanical failure.[3] Kontum was littered with artillery shell casings, ammo boxes, and all the other trash combat generates. There were great heaps of garbage. In places, it looked like a city dump. Most of the fighting and thus most of the destruction were around the defensive perimeter and in the military areas of Kontum City. There was much less damage to the civilian areas. However, the province chief's house and the post office had been destroyed.[4]

During the Easter Offensive, the number of Arc Light sorties authorized per month was increased from 1,000 in January to 3,150 in June. The latter number was the peak for the entire war.[5] Arc Light missions in II Corps paralleled the tempo of the overall Easter Offensive. There were 136 in March, 229 in April, 334 in May, and 175 in June for a total of 874 during those four months. Between 14 May and 8 June alone, there were 300 Arc Lights in II Corps, most of them in support of Kontum's defenders. At about 100,000 tons of bombs per three-plane mission, 300 missions, and 2,000 pounds per ton, B-52 bombers alone dropped around 60 million pounds of bombs around Kontum during those 25 days.[6] Tactical air fighter-bombers dropped additional millions of pounds of bombs both inside and outside the city.

Brigadier General John Hill was going home. On 9 June, he

and Mr. Vann flew to Saigon, where General Abrams awarded Hill the Legion of Merit. Colonel Robert C. Kingston, who was on the promotion list to brigadier general, would be Hill's replacement, and he accompanied them back to Pleiku. Vann bragged that since the battle had started on 14 May, he had visited Kontum every day. He did not want to break that record. After a farewell dinner for Brigadier General Hill, Vann left around 2100 to fly into Kontum to spend the night. He gathered up an unopened bottle of wine and some fresh fruit and rolls to take to Colonel Rhotenberry and Brigadier General Ba.[7]

Mr. Vann's regular pilot was CWO Robert Richards, a skilled and brave pilot. But Vann literally wore him out by taking so many risks. Richards needed a rest. Vann's new pilot, First Lieutenant Ronald Doughtie, would fly that night, and there was room in the little OH-58 for one more passenger—anyone who wanted to go along for the ride. Doughtie asked Lieutenant Bart Engram, who worked in G-2 Targeting, if he wanted to go, but Engram still had work to do. He needed to brief Vann on potential Arc Light targets before he left and then pass the decisions to the G-3 air. Captain John P. Robertson, the officer responsible for the Team 21 compound, was known for being cautious. For the first few months after he arrived, he would not go into Pleiku at all, and he still would not go there without wearing his flak jacket. But Robertson was interested in becoming a pilot, and when Doughtie asked if he wanted to take the night flight into Kontum with him and Vann, Robertson accepted his offer. They never made it to Kontum. Everyone on board was killed when Vann's helicopter crashed near the Kontum Pass between Pleiku and Kontum.[8]

Although the Communists claimed credit for shooting down John Paul Vann, there was no evidence to support their claim. Vann radioed Rhotenberry for a weather report when they were 15 minutes from Kontum, but it was not possible from this call to determine if he was flying. Colonel Rhotenberry said they flew into the only patch of tall trees for 1,000 meters in any direction. ARVN soldiers reached the crash site before any Americans did, and they stole Vann's wallet, watch, and Rutgers class ring.[9]

Vann died at the peak of his career, just after destroying two North Vietnamese divisions and winning the Battle of Kontum. He did not know everything he accomplished in Vietnam was being given away in Paris. If he had lived to see South Vietnam defeated by the Communists and America's ignominious, forced withdrawal, he might have become a depressed and bitter man who thought all his effort and all his years in Vietnam were wasted. Referring to the timing of Vann's death, his biographer Neil Sheehan wrote, "He did not miss his exit. He died believing he had won his war."[10] John Paul Vann posthumously received the Medal of Freedom, the highest civilian award our nation can bestow, and the US Army's Distinguished Service Cross, second only to the Medal of Honor.[11]

Between 30 April 1972 and 11 January 1973, the two UH-1B TOW helicopters fired 162 missiles in combat. Of that total, 151 were reliable, and 124 hit the target.

Various sources differ on how many tanks, trucks, APCs, and other targets the aerial TOW Tam destroyed. There may be some double counting in all of these sources, but the records of the TOW Team's parent unit, the 17th Aviation Group (Combat), probably contain the most reliable count for the period covered. From 2 through 28 May, the team's results were recorded as: 11 T-54s, 7 PT 76s, 7 M-41s, 6 trucks, 3 APCs, and 3 artillery pieces or rocket launchers destroyed. The team also made hits on bunkers, buildings, ammo and POL dumps, machine guns in water towers, and suspected tank locations.[12]

The 1st Combat Aerial TOW Team, Vietnam, was engaged in combat until 20 June 1972.[13] Its deployment to Vietnam was always intended to be temporary and not the beginning of a normal one-year tour. By 22 June, the team was gone—but certainly not forgotten. Of the first 85 TOW missiles fired, 71 were hits. Twenty-one of the tanks destroyed were knocked out by two men: CWO Danny G. Rowe, with 12, and CWO2 Hixson, with 9. CWO3 Lester Whiteis, also a tank "ace" with the Aerial TOW Team, said, "My definition of a confirmed kill is when you leave the tank in flames."[14] Before departing, team members trained replacement crews from the 17th Aviation Group's Cobra gunship units and turned the TOW aircraft over to them. Those TOW-armed helicopters remained in Vietnam until January 1973.[15]

The Aerial TOW Team never went out without a pair of snakes for gun cover and support.[16] We did not want the enemy to capture the crews and the technology and did not want to lose even one of the TOW helicopters because we desperately needed these tank killers. Although the NVA had a vast array of the most sophisticated anti-aircraft weapons, the TOW helicopters never took a single hit from ground fire—mainly because they did not have to fly nap-of-the-earth, where they would be more vulnerable, but could fire from an altitude of 3,000 feet and a slant range of 3,000 feet from the target. Equally important to their survivability, the team developed good operating procedures and teamwork with the crews in the other aircraft they worked with on every mission; the 7th Air Cavalry Squadron's dedicated UH-1 C&C aircraft and the 361st Aerial Weapons Company's Cobra gunships. Those other aircraft and the Loachs, FACs, and fighter-bombers worked closer to the targets and drew most of the enemy's fire. Fortunately, the NVA did not use the Strella heat-seeking, ground-to-air, anti-aircraft missile against the old UH-1B TOW helicopters.[17]

Who should receive credit for knocking out any specific enemy tank was often difficult or even impossible to determine, especially when the battle was intense and visibility was poor. When an enemy tank was spotted, everybody with an antitank weapon tried to kill it, so there was some double counting. The NVA's tanks could be destroyed if they ran over a mine laid by ARVN soldiers or were hit by an M-72 or RPG fired by an ARVN soldier. They could be knocked out by direct fire from ARVN artillery firing HEAT rounds or by 106-mm recoilless rifle fire. However, there is no record of any tank kills by recoilless rifles in Kontum Province during the Easter Offensive. Three 106-mm recoilless rifles allegedly fired at oncoming T-54s during the final assaults on Polei Kleng but did not stop the oncoming tanks.

It would be unlikely for a tank destroyed by a TOW missile to be hit again from the ground. However, unless there was major damage visible from the air, a tank hit first from the ground might be hit again from the air. Hawk's Claw, a tactical air strike, or an AC-130 firing HEAT rounds would probably assume that any enemy tank that didn't look damaged was still operational even if it was not moving. So an already "dead" tank might be hit again and again from the air and counted as a new kill every time. If an enemy tank beyond the range of ARVN's shoulder-fired weapons and still moving was hit from the air, the kill should definitely be credited to that aircraft. Enemy tanks hit in an Arc Light strike could be destroyed by the bombs, but an accurate count of tanks destroyed in this manner would have to be made by a BDA immediately after the Arc Light. The NVA captured and used a few ARVN M-41s, so, depending on the circumstances, an M-41 could be counted as an enemy tank. Many permanently dead-lined (inoperable) ARVN M-41s were parked on the northern edge of Kontum City to be used as pillboxes (bunkers from which to fire), so some of the "enemy" tanks reported destroyed in the city and from the air may have been a case of mistaken identity.[18]

The NVA forces in the Central Highlands probably had the ability to retrieve and repair their own tanks. So even a tank we "destroyed," its entire crew killed, might be repaired to fight again another day—and perhaps be killed again and counted again as another enemy tank destroyed.

The enemy had a numerical advantage in almost every fight in Kontum Province, but they often wasted their infantry in repeated human-wave attacks that were defeated by Arc Lights, gunships, or tactical air strikes with heavy losses. The NVA also had numerical superiority in tanks, and their tanks had the ARVN tanks outgunned. ARVN's light M-41s armed with a 76-mm main gun were no match for the thick armor plate and 100-mm main guns of the T-54s. More important, although a few of the smaller Communist PT-76 tanks were used in earlier attacks, the Easter Offensive was the first time ARVN soldiers had ever faced battalions of the big T-54s, so the NVA had a big psychological advantage. The surprise and shock the Communists could achieve with a tank attack was demonstrated by their victories at Tan Canh and Dak To II. However, they failed to exploit the tanks' advantages of shock action, firepower, and mobility and thus failed to achieve optimum results. One of the most effective ways a commander can use his tanks is to support the infantry attack by direct fire and then attack with his reserves and massed tanks to exploit a breakthrough. If that succeeds, he can then make an armored thrust deep into the enemy's rear area to destroy artillery, headquarters, and support installations and to spread panic. However, the NVA commanders often committed their tanks piecemeal and employed them timidly rather than massing them to strike aggressively and deeply into the ARVN defenses.

Interrogation of NVA prisoners revealed that at least 3,000 of the NVA's tank crewmen fighting in the Easter Offensive had graduated from the Russian tank school in Odessa only four or five months earlier.[19] The NVA tank officers must have also received training from the Soviets. The enemy's inept use of tanks may have resulted from the fact that the NVA tank units were operating under the control of infantry commanders who did not understand—or at least had not practiced—how to coordinate their infantry and tanks so that they attacked in a mutually supporting manner. Even when the NVA infantry forces were not driven away from their tanks by gunships or ARVN artillery, their tanks often attacked alone—or ended up alone—without infantry to protect them from individual ARVN soldiers with shoulder-fired rockets.[20]

Stopping and in some places pushing back the NVA invasion deprived the North Vietnamese of complete victory in 1972 and left them in a weaker negotiating position because their army had suffered so many defeats in the field. However, in Washington the defeat of the Communists' Easter Offensive seemed to be viewed mainly as an opportunity to get an acceptable peace agreement in Paris while the North Vietnamese needed time to rebuild their army in the South and to recover from our bombing of the North.

Approximately 63,500 American ground troops were still in Vietnam during the Easter Offensive, but only about 6,000 were in US Army ground combat units, and virtually none of those units were involved in the fighting. Only 2,480 of the 63,500 were US Army advisers. Ninety-four Americans were killed in Vietnam between 1 January and 30 May 1972.[21]

In Kontum Province and in all of South Vietnam during the Easter Offensive, both sides suffered staggering losses of men and materiel. The surviving troops were exhausted, and many were wounded or sick—or both.

During 1972, the 23rd ARVN Division suffered heavy casualties, both KIA and WIA, about half of them in Kontum.[22] Between 1 April and 10 June 1972, the South Vietnamese regular forces nationwide suffered 23,059 total casualties: 4,400 KIA, 16,750 WIA, and 1,909 MIA. The Ruff Puffs reported almost 15,000 total casualties: 3,668 KIA, 9,622 WIA, and 1,573 MIA. Ammunition and other supplies were depleted, and equipment was suffering from overuse and lack of maintenance.[23] In II Corps, ARVN's admitted losses were 382 KIA, 1,621 WIA, 32 MIA, 3 tanks destroyed, 4 tanks one-third damaged, 4 crew-served and 47 small-arms weapons lost, and 6 radios lost.[24]

Through June, the South Vietnamese nationwide lost massive amounts of weapons and equipment, including $28 million worth of tanks, $8.5 million worth of artillery pieces, 25,196 M-16s, plus trucks, APCs, and more than 4,000 radios. The total replacement cost would be about $28 million.[25] In II Corps alone, the ARVN lost more than 100 artillery pieces, mostly in Binh Dinh Province. By the fall of 1972, all lost equipment and weapons were replaced.[26]

The advisers could not completely verify the number of NVA casualties, but the ARVN II Corps claimed that from 14 May to 6 June the Battle of Kontum cost the enemy 5,688 KIA, 34 POWs, 8 Hoi Chanhs, 38 tanks destroyed, 353 crew-served and 862 small-arms weapons captured, and 29 radios captured.[27] A much higher number of NVA casualties was given at a 23 October 1972 MACV command briefing when it was estimated the NVA suffered 16,000 casualties, killed and wounded, during the Battle of Kontum.[28]

ARVN claims regarding the number of NVA soldiers captured and the number who defected to ARVN are probably accurate. How many NVA soldiers were wounded was impossible to know, and how many NVA were killed is an estimate at best because the number probably includes double counting and possibly was inflated for propaganda purposes. The number of ARVN soldiers wounded is probably accurate, but the actual number killed is probably higher than what was officially admitted because a higher number would be bad for morale and would reveal their remaining strength to the enemy.

Some NVA units fought on until there were only 400 or 500 men left in regiments that had entered combat 2,500 strong and that may have received replacements during the battle.[29] During just three months, from the start of the Easter Offensive on 30 March through the end of June, the NVA suffered more than 100,000 casualties—probably 40,000 of them killed—out of their 200,000-man invasion force. Most of their tanks and half of their heavy artillery pieces were destroyed. Because the Easter Offensive fell so far short of the North's expectations, and the losses were so great, General Giap was eased out of his position as North Vietnam's defense minister. It took the Communists three years to recover enough to mount their final offensive in 1975.[30]

The North Vietnamese launched the Easter Offensive in the spring of 1972 because they thought Vietnamization was succeeding, because Nixon and Kissinger were forging agreements with Russia and China that might curtail the support North Vietnam received from its Communist patrons, and because 1972 was an election year for the American president. The 1968 Tet attacks had been a major factor in Lyndon Johnson's decision not to run again, and the North Vietnamese hoped an even stronger conventional attack would mean the end of Richard Nixon's presidency.[31] However, they underestimated his will to win. They also underestimated the ARVN troops' willingness to fight when surrounded and when supported by American advisers and air power. Nixon was willing to give the South Vietnamese whatever moral and material support they needed, and he sent enough US air assets back to Southeast Asia to defeat the NVA in the field. The NVA gambled that US airpower would not return, and when it did return with a vengeance, the NVA was probably surprised at the intensity and persistence of the American bombing of North Vietnam, the mining of its ports, and the impact on its troops and tanks in the field. USAF B-52s, fighter-bombers, and gunships flew 18,000 combat sorties against the attacking NVA during May and June 1972.[32] This support was crucial to blocking the North Vietnamese invasion.

The NVA made a major blunder by attacking in the spring of 1972 rather than waiting even one year. By then, virtually all American troops and advisers would have departed, and it probably would have been politically impossible for the American president to send American forces—even aircraft—back to Southeast Asia to counter a Communist invasion.

The NVA made another big mistake when it split its effort and attacked on three fronts. Its thrusts across the DMZ and from the west into I Corps, into the Central Highlands toward Kontum and in Binh Dinh Province on the coast in II Corps, and toward An Loc in III Corps were so widely separated that they were not mutually supporting. If the NVA had not split its forces, it would have had reserves adequate to exploit its successes. Also, the Communist command and control and logistics were badly stretched by that dispersion of their forces. The Saigon government had to deal with three different thrusts, but it had the advantage of operating on interior lines. The South also had airlift to move its forces, as when the airborne units and the Ranger groups were flown out of Kontum to reconstitute a national reserve and when the 44th Regiment was flown into Kontum. Launching a single, major thrust to cut South Vietnam in half during the Easter Offensive might have achieved in 1972 what that same tactic did achieve in 1975.

After the swift and easy victories at Tan Canh and Dak To II, the NVA probably could have seized Kontum with equal ease by immediately charging down Highway 14 General Patton style. Or if it had bypassed Tan Canh, Dak To II, and the other bases to attack Kontum as fast as possible, it might have been able to seize Kontum, push on to Pleiku, and then drive down Highway 19 to the coast to win the war in the spring of 1972. Instead, it spent nearly three weeks reorganizing, replenishing, and capturing—or trying to capture—all the scattered ARVN bases between the triborder area and Kontum.[33] The enemy apparently decided it was better to try seizing Tan Canh, Dak To II, the Border Ranger camps, and the FSBs on Rocket Ridge than to bypass them and have its rear area and main supply route threatened while it attacked Kontum. However, as the NVA troops massed to attack those ARVN forward positions, they became good targets for Arc Lights. Our bombs killed thousands of enemy soldiers and destroyed tanks and other weapons they could have used against Kontum. Equally important, the three-week break between the attacks on Tan Can and Kontum gave the defenders of Kontum time to assemble the entire 23rd Division in a unified command, establish a coordinated defense, and plan fire support for the battle. It also allowed the USAF to redeploy additional aircraft back to Southeast Asia, which enabled the air force to inflict heavy casualties on the Communists as they approached and finally attacked Kontum. All these actions strengthened Kontum's defenses enough to defeat the attack when it finally came.

One of the reasons the NVA failed to follow up with an attack on Kontum immediately after Tan Canh fell was that its logistics "tail" was inadequate to support its attacking "teeth." The Easter Offensive was North Vietnam's first big, mechanized war. It employed hundreds of thousands of troops and required that vast quantities of food, fuel, and other supplies be constantly moved forward to supply the attacking forces. The North Vietnamese logistics system had been adequate for their infantry and some vehicles in the South before 1972, but it was not up to the job of supporting 13 divisions—virtually the entire army—serving in the field in South Vietnam, Laos, and Cambodia during months of almost continuous action.

The US mining of ports and destruction of bridges and rail lines in the North contributed to the critical shortages at the end of the NVA's supply line. Chinese overland shipments were reduced from 160,000 to 30,000 tons a month. Virtually all of the North's POL storage facilities were destroyed.[34] Many of the supplies that did reach the Communist army in the field were then destroyed by tactical air operations and Arc Lights. During the offensive, the NVA committed thousands of tanks and other vehicles, all burning up fuel at a rate their army's logistics system could not sustain. The T-54 required about a gallon of diesel per mile, and when it ran dry, it was a sitting duck. In the attack on An Loc, the NVA tanks attacked without external fuel drums, and some ran out of gas before they ran out of ammunition.[35] The T-54 that ran out of gas just before it reached our bunker is my favorite example of how our bombing in the North produced results on the front lines.

The Communists made an all-out effort to achieve total, final victory in the spring of 1972, but they failed. If we consider their terrible losses during their attempts to take Kontum and An Loc, it is obvious that seizing those cities was one of their primary objectives. However, they were unable to take Kontum or An Loc or to hold major cities in I Corps. They did gain and retain control of millions of South Vietnam's citizens and some of its territory. They effectively eliminated the 17th parallel as the border between North and South Vietnam, and they pushed ARVN back from the Ho Chi Minh Trail and its bases on Vietnam's western border.

Speaking about the 23rd ARVN Division, General Abrams said, "They have been victorious. They *know* it. And they beat the best."[36]

Lieutenant General David R. Palmer later observed about the Easter Offensive:

Although American troops did not participate in the ground combat, advisers fought with their units. The conflict had come full circle—it was an advisory war again. Actually, it had never stopped being an advisory war. Ever since the first combat death in January 1961, Americans had been fighting and dying with South Vietnamese units. Their sacrifices and achievements had simply been monumentally overshadowed by the more newsworthy operations of US combat units after they entered in 1965. Advisors [*sic*] fought a largely ignored war. But they had always been there, the steel reinforcing rods keeping the concrete from crumbling. . . . Somehow it seemed almost nostalgic that, although America fighting elements had departed, advisers were still at work.[37]

During a briefing at MACV headquarters in Saigon, a senior American officer was asked what would have happened if US air support had not been available during the Easter Offensive. He responded, "We would be meeting in some other place today."[38]

We won the Battle of Kontum. Some might say we won by not losing. However, we also won by killing so many enemy soldiers and destroying so many of their tanks, weapons, and supplies that the NVA was forced to withdraw from the battlefield.

The American advisers; the US Army, Air Force, Navy, and Marine aviators; the VNAF aviators; and the helicopter and Jeep-mounted TOWs were essential to our victory at Kontum. However, in the end everything depended on the individual ARVN soldiers, their officers, and their NCOs. It was those men on the ground who withstood almost continuous artillery, rocket, and mortar fire and repeated assaults by enemy infantry and tanks. They also counter-attacked again and again to regain lost ground. Another key factor in our victory was the personal leadership of men such as John Paul Vann and Brigadier General Ly Tong Ba. Unlike Colonel Le Duc Dat at Tan Canh, Brigadier General Ba took an active role in the fighting and provided his troops with the leadership they needed to win the battle. The 23rd ARVN Division took a terrible battering at Kontum, but they held against all the bombardments, the human-wave assaults, and the enemy tanks—and that is why they were victorious.

In 1975, US Army colonel Harry G. Summers said to an NVA colonel, "You know you never defeated us on the battlefield."

To which the Communist colonel responded, "That may be so, but it is also irrelevant."[39]

Acknowledgments

Special thanks go to Lieutenant Colonel (Ret.) John G. Heslin, who launched his Battle of Kontum Web site (http://www.thebattleofkontum.com) on the 30th anniversary of the start of the Easter Offensive. Many of the people I interviewed found me through this Web site, and it serves as a continuing, growing collection of information and memories about the battle. His own book *Reflections from the Web* will be a permanent record of individual postings on his Web site.

Dale Andradé's *Trial by Fire: The 1972 Easter Offensive, America's Last Vietnam Battle* is the first account of the Easter Offensive throughout Vietnam; it and the newer version, *America's Last Vietnam Battle: Halting Hanoi's 1972 Easter Offensive,* are still the best accounts of the offensive. Andradé motivated me to write my own account by saying, "The advisers have not really told their own story." At the time, marine colonel G. H. Turley's *The Easter Offensive: The Last American Advisors* [*sic*], *Vietnam, 1972* was probably the only published book written by a former adviser. Dale Andradé also made helpful suggestions for my own research.

I also owe thanks to Neil Sheehan, author of *A Bright Shining Lie: John Paul Vann and America in Vietnam,* who donated more than 250 boxes of his own research materials and collected information to the Library of Congress. Using these materials, I was able to listen to hours of his recorded interviews with two of the most important participants in the battle, Brigadier General John G. Hill and Colonel R. B. Rhotenberry—who died before I was able to interview them—and to read or hear descriptions by others who were speaking while their memories of the battle were still fresh. Maps prepared during or immediately after the battle by Colonel Rhotenberry and Colonel Phillip Kaplan as well as other valuable documents given to Sheehan were available to copy at the Library of Congress.

Merle Pribbenow gave me English translations of important

North Vietnamese accounts of the battle. They provided information on which North Vietnamese army units participated in various attacks and an interesting Communist perspective on the battle.

Staff members at the following repositories were knowledgeable and especially helpful: Modern Military Records of the National Archives at Archives II; US Army Center of Military History; US Army Heritage and Education Center; Library of Congress; Library of the US Army Command and General Staff College; US Marine Corps Historical Center; and US Air Force Historical Research Agency.

Some of the most important and interesting parts of this book came from interviews with 35 men. They gave their own firsthand accounts (most to me, but a few to Sheehan) and in many cases lent me photos, maps, and documents to copy and use. I thank all these men, whether still living or now deceased: Ly Tong Ba, James N. Barker, James W. "Bill" Bricker, James M. Cloninger, William A. Duck, Bart J. Engram, John R. Finch, Stanislaus J. Fuesel, Richard C. Gudat, Giap Phuc Hai, Raymond W. Hall, John G. Heslin, John G. Hill, Richard Ivars, Stephen James, Phillip Kaplan, Martin S. Kleiner, Wade B. Lovings, James R. McClellan, Hugh J. McInnish Jr., David M. Millard, Reed C. Mulkey, William B. Page, John E. "Jed" Peters, John L. Plaster, R. M. Rhotenberry, Christopher E. Scudder, James E. Stein, Lowell W. Stevens, Brian Sweeney, John O. Truby, Stephen M. Truhan, James T. Vaughan, Cao Van Vien, and George E. Wear. (Complete information about the interviews can be found in the notes and the bibliography.)

Glossary

Abbreviations and Military Jargon

AFB	air force base
AFN	Armed Forces Network, which broadcast American music, news, and features to the Americans in Vietnam
air liaison officer	USAF officer, usually a fighter-bomber pilot, attached to an army unit to coordinate air support
AK-47	Soviet-designed assault rifle used by most Communist armies and many other armies or irregular forces
APC	armored personnel carrier; the US M-113 in the case of US and ARVN forces in Vietnam
Arc Light	a three-aircraft B-52 strike in South Vietnam
armor	the steel protecting tanks and/or APCs; also those vehicles themselves and the military units that have them
ARVN	Army of the Republic of Vietnam; also used like "GI," as in "An ARVN was killed" or "The ARVNs attacked."
ASCH	Assault Support Helicopter Company
attack by fire	an attack by artillery, rocket, or mortar rounds or direct tank fire
AWOL	absent without leave
BDA	bomb damage assessment; an inspection by air or preferably on the ground after a bombing to determine the results achieved
blivet	a rubberized bladder, in this case holding 500 gallons or more, used to transport or store JP-4 jet fuel
C-4	composition 4, relatively stable, plastic explosive with a consistency similar to modeling clay

C&C	command and control; in Vietnam, usually meaning airborne operations centers in helicopters
caliber	the largest diameter of the round fired, expressed either in millimeters, as in "12.7-mm round," or in hundredths of an inch, as in ".51 caliber"
CBU	cluster bomb unit; antipersonnel munitions dropped by air
Chieu Hoi Program	an effort to induce enemy soldiers to desert and switch sides
Chinook	CH-47, also known as "a Hook"; large twin-rotor US Army helicopter used to move troops and supplies
chopper	any helicopter, but in Vietnam most often a UH-1 Huey
chopper pad	a landing area designated for helicopter use
CIA	US Central Intelligence Agency
CO	commanding officer
Cobra	AH-1G US Army helicopter gunship; also called a "snake"
CORDS	Civil Operations and Revolutionary Development Support; the US organization for "nation building" in Vietnam
corps	multidivision-size army unit; in Vietnam, also the four South Vietnamese military and civil regions, which were, from north to south: I Corps, II Corps, III Corps, and IV Corps
corpsman	an enlisted man in the Medical Corps
CP	command post; where the unit's headquarters is located and established by units of any size
CWO	chief warrant officer
dak	"river" in Vietnamese
DASC	Direct Air Support Center, as in "II DASC" for the one in II Corps
direct fire	when the projectile—for example, a rifle bullet or artillery round—follows a line-of-sight path to the target; *see* indirect fire
district	political and military subdivision within Vietnamese provinces
DMZ	Demilitarized Zone; a supposedly neutral area delineating the border between North Vietnam and South Vietnam
DTOC	Division Tactical Operations Center
dustoff	US Army helicopter medical evacuation mission
E&E	escape and evade; to escape from or avoid capture and to evade enemy attempts to (re)capture

FAC	forward air controller; a pilot, often an experienced fighter pilot, in a small aircraft who coordinates air strikes and other air support
fatigues	US Army's green field uniform; the special design for Vietnam sometimes called "Jungle Jims"
fixed-wing aircraft	propeller or jet-propelled aircraft, as opposed to rotary-wing (helicopter) aircraft
flak vest	an armored vest. The word *flak* is a contraction of *Fliegerabwehrkanone,* for World War II German anti-aircraft guns, and used to describe anti-aircraft fire or the shrapnel from any exploding munitions.
FM radio net	The PRC-25 radios used by both ARVN and the American advisers for tactical communications were FM, "frequency modulated." Within a "net" used for a specified purpose, such as fire control, all stations (users) were talking on the same frequency. The AFN in Vietnam used FM to broadcast news and entertainment.
forward CP	a command post with only the personnel and equipment necessary to direct combat operations
friendlies	Americans, South Vietnamese, and other allied forces
FSB	fire-support base; a fortification, usually on a hilltop and manned by troops with artillery, from which observers could see the surrounding area and control it with artillery fire or air strikes they called in
G-3	operations and training officer at division, corps, or higher level
gunship	helicopter armed with machine guns or missiles or both; a USAF AC-130 with miniguns and sometimes a 105-mm howitzer or a VNAF AC-47
HE	high explosive, as in "HE artillery rounds"
HEAT	high-explosive antitank ammunition that could penetrate a tank's armor and could be fired by artillery pieces, tanks, or recoilless rifles
Hoi Chanh	VC or NVA soldier who switched sides and joined the South Vietnamese under the Chieu Hoi Program
Ho Chi Minh Trail	a tangle of 12,000 miles of foot trails, vehicle roads, and bypasses that was the NVA's infiltration route into and through Laos, Cambodia, and South Vietnam

Hook	*See* Chinook.
Huey	UH-1 utility helicopter. *See* slick.
indirect fire	when the projectile—for example, an artillery round—is fired high and drops onto the target
JP-4	jet propulsion fuel used by US military aircraft in the 1970s
KIA	killed in action
LAW	light antitank weapon, specifically the US M-72
Loach	light observation helicopter (LOH); in Vietnam, usually the LOH-6 Cayuse
LOH	*See* Loach.
MACV	Military Assistance Command, Vietnam
MARS	Military Affiliate Radio Station
medevac	medical evacuation, usually by helicopter in Vietnam
MIA	missing in action
MiG	Russian-designed jet fighter-bomber used by North Vietnam
military regions	regions coinciding with the four South Vietnamese corps boundaries
minigun	multibarreled 7.62-mm machine gun
Montagnard	member of one of the various ethnic groups—such as Bahnar, Jarai, Koho, Manong, and Rhade—inhabiting the Central Highlands
NCO	noncommissioned officer; sergeants, corporals, or specialists
NLF	National Liberation Front
NVA	North Vietnamese army
PFs	Popular Forces or "Puffs"; local village militias
POL	petroleum, oil, and lubricants
POW	prisoner of war
PRC-25	US Army FM field radio used by both ARVN and the advisors in 1972
R&R	rest and recreation; usually a one-week vacation outside Vietnam in a place such as Hawaii or Thailand
RCAT	Regimental Combat Assistance Team; the advisers assigned to assist ARVN combat arms regiments
recoilless rifle	antitank weapon with a dangerous back blast to prevent recoil; US models used by ARVN were 75 mm and 106 mm
RFs	Regional Forces, or "Ruffs"; province troops that seldom left their home province
RF/PFs	Regional and Popular Forces together; the "Ruff Puffs"
ROK	Republic of Korea, whose troops and divisions in Vietnam were called "ROKs" (Rocks)

rotary-wing aircraft	A helicopter is a rotary-wing aircraft, as opposed to a fixed-wing jet or propeller-driven aircraft.
round	one shot from an artillery piece, mortar, rifle, or machine gun, as in "ten rounds fired"
RPG	rocket-propelled grenade; a Soviet or Chinese shoulder-fired weapon used against vehicles, bunkers, or personnel; several versions used by the NVA in Kontum Province—for example, the RPG2/Type 56/B-40
SA-7	*See* Strella.
SAC	Strategic Air Command. SAC B-52s flew the Arc Light missions in South Vietnam and bombed North Vietnam.
SAM	surface-to-air missile used by the North Vietnamese
skids	rigid supports below a helicopter that the helicopter sits on when it lands; also wooden pallets loaded with cargo to be dropped by parachute or unloaded out the rear ramp of a cargo aircraft
slick	Huey helicopter with door guns but no weapons mounted on the exterior
small arms	rifles, machine guns, or other small-caliber weapons one or two men can carry (Whether a .50- or .51-caliber machine gun is "small arms" depends on whether it is shooting at you.)
snake	Cobra AH-1G helicopter gunship
SOG	MACV's Studies and Operations Group, which ran secret missions into Laos and Cambodia
sortie	one mission by one aircraft whether alone or with other aircraft
Spectre	USAF AC-130 gunship with two 20-mm Vulcan machine guns, a 40-mm Bofors machine gun, and a 105-mm gun firing HE or HEAT rounds
Spooky	call sign of VNAF AC-47 gunships armed with three 7.62-mm miniguns
SRAG	Second Regional Assistance Group; so designated under John Paul Vann, a civilian rather than a military commander, as opposed to the Second Regional Assistance Command, under a military officer
strategic bombing	bombing an enemy's homeland to destroy his infrastructure, factories, and war-making ability
Strella	Soviet-made, hand-held, heat-seeking, SAM missile that could destroy aircraft flying up to 10,000 feet high

T-54	Soviet medium tank used by many Communist armies
T-59	also "Type 59"; an unlicensed, slightly modified Chinese copy of the T-54
tactical air	fighter-bombers of any US service or VNAF and their bombing missions
Tet	Vietnamese lunar New Year celebration lasting three days starting at the first full moon after 20 January; also the Communist offensive launched at this time in 1968
TOC	tactical operations center
TOW	tube-launched, optically tracked, wire-guided missile
triborder area	where the borders of Vietnam, Laos, and Cambodia meet northwest of Kontum City in II Corps
tube	barrel of a mortar or artillery piece but often used to mean the entire piece, as in "six 155-mm tubes captured"
USAF	United States Air Force
VC	Vietcong, the indigenous Communist insurgents in South Vietnam
VNAF	South Vietnamese Air Force
white phosphorus	also "WP" or "Willie Peter"; packed in bombs, artillery shells, and hand grenades; burns when exposed to the air and so used to mark targets, start fires, or destroy equipment
WIA	wounded in action
WO	warrant officer; a specialist rank above noncommissioned and below commissioned officers
XO	executive officer; the second in command who takes command in the absence of the commander

Notes

Preface

1. Stanley Karnow, *Vietnam: A History* (New York: Viking, 1983), 641.
2. Brigadier General George E. Wear, senior military adviser and commander of US Forces in II Corps, telephone interview by the author, 14 Sept. 2004.
3. Bruce Palmer Jr., "How Bright, How Shining? Sheehan's Portrait of Vann and Vietnam," *Parameters* (U.S. Army War College) 19, no. 2 (June 1989), 23.
4. Captain (Lieutenant Colonel, Ret.) John R. Finch, email to author, 20 June 2006.
5. James G. Lowenstein and Richard M. Moose, *Vietnam: May 1972,* a staff report prepared for the use of the Committee on Foreign Relations, US Senate, 1972 June 29 (Washington, DC: US Government Printing Office, 1972), 9.

Prologue. Kontum: Now and Then

1. Hand-written questions by Neil Sheehan and 30 Sept. 1972 answers by Captain Christopher E. Scudder, undated notes by Neil Sheehan from his interview with Captain Christopher E. Scudder, air operations adviser, II Corps Headquarters, Neil Sheehan Papers, Container 122, Folder 19, Manuscript Division, Library of Congress, Washington, DC.
2. George D. Moss, *Vietnam: An American Ordeal* (Upper Saddle River, NJ: Prentice Hall, 1998), 386.
3. *Annex K, Kontum: The NVA Buildup,* annex to *United States Military Assistance Command Vietnam (MACV), Command History, January 1972-March 1973,* vol. 2 (Saigon: Military History Branch, Office of the Secretary, Joint Staff, MACV, 1973), K-11.
4. James K. Moore, "Giap's Giant Mistake," *Vietnam* (Feb. 1992), 28.

1. Autumn in the Highlands

1. Brigadier General George E. Wear, senior military adviser and commander of US Forces in II Corps, email to the author, 22 and 23 Jan. 2005.
2. Bruce Palmer Jr., *U.S. Intelligence and Vietnam,* special issue of *Studies in Intelligence* 28 (1984), 91–92.
3. Ibid., 91.

4. Lewis B. Sorley, *Remembering Vietnam* (pamphlet produced from lecture) (Washington, DC: National Archives, 30 Apr. 2002), 2.

5. James K. Moore, "Giap's Giant Mistake," *Vietnam* (Feb. 1992), 27.

6. Lester A. Sobel, ed., *South Vietnam: U.S.-Communist Confrontation in Southeast Asia,* vol. 6: *1971* (New York: Facts on File, 1973), 233.

7. William S. Turley, *The Second Indochina War: A Short Political and Military History, 1954-1975* (Boulder, CO: Westview Press, 1986), 130.

8. George C. Herring, *America's Longest War: The United States and Vietnam, 1950-1975* (New York: Wiley, 1979), 18.

9. "Vietnamization: A Policy Put to the Test," *Newsweek,* 17 Apr. 1972.

10. Quoted in Lewis Sorley, *A Better War: The Unexamined Victories and Final Tragedies of America's Last Years in Vietnam* (New York: Harcourt Brace, 1999), 183.

11. "The U.S. Army in Vietnam: From Tet to the Final Withdrawal, 1968-1973," in *American Military History,* rev., edited by Richard W. Stewart, Army Historical Series (Washington, DC: US Army Center of Military History, 2005), 341, available at http://www.history.army.mil/books/AMH-42/AMH%20V2/chapter 11.htm.

12. Ngo Quang Truong, "The Tactical Adviser," in *The U.S. Adviser,* by Cao Van Vien, Ngo Quang Truong, Dong Van Khuyen, Nguyen Duy Hinh, Tran Dinh Tho, Hoang Ngoc, and Chu Xuan Vien, Indochina Monographs (Washington, DC: US Army Center of Military History, 1980), 73–74.

13. "Hanoi's High-Risk Drive for Victory," *Time,* 15 May 1972.

14. Thomas Buckley, "The ARVN Is Bigger and Better, but—," *New York Times Magazine,* 12 Oct. 1969.

15. Bart King, "John Paul Vann's Reluctant Tiger," *Vietnam* (Oct. 2001), 20–21.

16. "Hanoi's High-Risk Drive for Victory."

17. Gordon L. Rottman, *North Vietnamese Army Soldier 1958-75* (London: Osprey, 2009), 13, 17–19.

18. Ibid., 11.

19. "Letter of Instructions to the Director, Second Regional Assistance Group (DSRAG)/Senior Adviser, II Corps and MR 2 (SA II Corps and MR 2)," 18 Nov. 1971, in *U.S. Army Build-up and Activities in South Vietnam, 1965-1972,* edited by Robert Lester, Vietnam War Research Collections (Bethesda, MD: University Publications of America, 1989), no page numbers.

20. A. P. Serong, *The 1972 Easter Offensive,* special issue of *Southeast Asian Perspectives,* no. 10 (Summer 1974), 41.

21. Brigadier General George E. Wear, email to the author, 22, 23, and 24 Jan. 2005.

22. Ibid., 30 Jan. 2005.

23. Donald E. Heap, lieutenant colonel, USAF, air liaison officer, 23rd ARVN Division, End of Tour Summary, 11 Jan. 1972, RG 472, National Archives, College Park, MD.

24. "1972 Orientation Edition," *The Observer* (MACV), 2 June 1972; Tom

Carhart, *Battles and Campaigns in Vietnam, 1954-1984* (New York: Crescent, 1984), 169.

25. "1972 Orientation Edition"; Carhart, *Battles and Campaigns in Vietnam,* 169.

26. Stanley I. Kutler, *Encyclopedia of the Vietnam War* (New York: MacMillan, 1997), 106; "Kontum Province," downloaded 12 June 2006 from http://www.vietnam-tourism.com/vietnam_gov/e_pages/hanhchinh/64info/kontum.htm.

27. Author's cassette tape from Ban Me Thuot, Vietnam, to family and friends, 16 Dec. 1971.

28. Ibid.

29. Brigadier General George E. Wear, email to the author, 28 Jan. 2005.

30. Ibid., 5 Feb. 2005.

31. Author's cassette tape from Ban Me Thuot, Vietnam, to family and friends, 16 Dec. 1971.

32. Herbert P. LePore, "The Role of the Helicopter in the Vietnam War," *U.S. Army Aviation Digest* (July–Aug. 1994), 36.

33. John F. Ross, "Landing Party," *Smithsonian* (Nov. 2004), 40.

34. Author's cassette tape from Ban Me Thuot, Vietnam, to family and friends, 16 Dec. 1971; 17th Aviation Group (Combat) Pleiku, Operations Report, Lessons Learned (ORLL), Pleiku, for the period 1 May 1972–31 Oct. 1972, p. 19, NND927622, RG 472, National Archives, College Park, MD.

35. Author's cassette tape from Ban Me Thuot, Vietnam, to family and friends, 16 Dec. 1971.

36. Harry G. Summers Jr., *The Vietnam War Almanac* (New York: Ballantine, 1985), 55.

37. Lewis Sorley, ed., *Vietnam Chronicles: The Abrams Tapes, 1968-1972* (Lubbock: Texas Tech University Press, 2004), 693.

2. Fighting in Phu Nhon

1. John L. Plaster, *Secret Commandos: Behind Enemy Lines with the Elite Warriors of SOG* (New York: Simon and Schuster, 2004), 340–42; Staff Sergeant (Major, Ret.) John L. Plaster, former SOG Covey rider, email to the author, 21 July 2005.

2. More than three decades later, when I opened a box at the National Archives and took out the DTOC logs from Phu Nhon, the top page was covered with red dust.

3. Author's cassette tape from Ban Me Thuot, Vietnam, to family and friends, 16 Dec. 1971.

4. Ibid.

5. Ibid.

6. Brigadier General George E. Wear, senior military adviser and commander of US Forces in II Corps, telephone interview by the author, 14 Sept. 2004.

7. David E. Ott, "1972 Enemy Offensive," *Field Artillery Journal* 45, no. 1 (Jan.–Feb. 1977), 42.

8. James K. Moore, "Giap's Giant Mistake," *Vietnam* (Feb. 1992), 32.

9. Brigadier General George E. Wear, telephone interview by the author, 14 Sept. 2004; Brigadier General George E. Wear, emails to the author, 22 Jan. and 3 Feb. 2005.

10. Brigadier General George E. Wear, email to the author, 22 Jan. 2005.

11. Ibid., 28 Jan. 2005.

3. A Hundred Tons of Bombs

1. Lieutenant Colonel (Ret.) Stanislaus J. Fuesel, former artillery adviser to ARVN II Corps, telephone interview by the author, 27 June 2005.

2. Edgar C. Doleman Jr., *The Vietnam Experience: Tools of War* (Boston: Boston Publishing, 1985), 48–50, 96–97; James K. Moore, "Giap's Giant Mistake," *Vietnam* (Feb. 1992), 29; Edgar Ulsamer, "Airpower Halts an Invasion," *Air Force Magazine* (Sept. 1972), 63; Lloyd C. Briggs, former artillery officer, email to the author, 18 Dec. 2006; Alden C. Walsh, "Soviet Artillery Weapons," *Field Artillery* (July 1962), 36.

3. Lawrence M. Greenberg, "'Spooky': Dragon in the Sky," *Vietnam* (Apr. 1990), 28.

4. 17th Aviation Group (Combat) Pleiku, Operations Report, Lessons Learned (ORLL), for the period 1 May 1972–31 Oct. 1972, p. 19, NND927622, RG 472, National Archives, College Park, MD.

5. First Lieutenant (Lieutenant Colonel, Ret.) James R. McClellan, forward air controller, Covey 507, telephone interview by the author, 20 July 2005.

6. Ibid.

7. Donald J. Mrozek, *Air Power and the Ground War in Vietnam: Ideas and Actions* (Maxwell Air Force Base, AL: Air University Press, 1988), 139–40, downloaded 1 Dec. 2006 from http://www.pbs.org/wgbh/amex/vietnam/trenches/language.html.

8. "B-52 Arc Light Operations," in *The U.S. Air Force in Southeast Asia, 1961-1963,* edited by Carl Berger (Washington, DC: Office of Air Force History, 1982), 150.

9. Paul Novak, "Fondly Called the BUFF (Big Ugly Fat Fellow) in Vietnam, the B-52 Stratofortress Still Plays a Vital Role in Today's Air Force," *Vietnam* (Aug. 2005), 10–11.

10. "B-52 Arc Light Operations," 149.

11. Major William A. Duck, B-52 navigator, telephone interview by the author, 1 Mar. 2006; "B-52 Arc Light Operations," 149–50.

12. Captain (Major, Ret.) Christopher E. Scudder, air operations adviser, II Corps headquarters, telephone interview by the author, 27 Feb. 2006; Captain (Lieutenant Colonel, Ret.) John R. Finch, email to the author, 20 June 2006.

13. Ulsamer, "Airpower Halts an Invasion," 62–63.

14. Finch, email to the author, 20 June 2006.

15. Scudder, telephone interview by the author, 27 Feb. 2006.

16. Warrant Officer 1 (Warrant Officer 4, Ret.) Larry Brassel, telephone interview by the author, 29 Jan. 2006.

17. Lieutenant (Lieutenant Colonel Ret.) Bart J. Engram, email to the author, 26 Apr. 2005.

18. Lewis Sorley, ed., *Vietnam Chronicles: The Abrams Tapes, 1968-1972* (Lubbock: Texas Tech University Press, 2004), 120, 763.

19. Quoted in Peter A. W. Liebchen, *Kontum: Battle for the Central Highlands, 30 March-10 June 1972*, USAF Southeast Asia Monograph Series, vol. 2, monograph 3, USAF Project Contemporary Historical Examination of Current Operations Report (Washington, DC: USAF, Oct. 1972), 34.

4. The Looming Threat

1. Michael Clodfelter, *Vietnam in Military Statistics: A History of the Indochina Wars, 1772-1991* (Jefferson, NC: McFarland, 1995), 197.

2. A. H. S. Candlin, "The Spring Offensive in Vietnam," *Army Quarterly and Defense Journal* (July 1972), 412.

3. Ngo Quang Truong, *The Easter Offensive of 1972*, Indochina Monograph Series (Washington, DC: US Army Center of Military History, 1980), 81.

4. Although the 203rd NVA Tank Regiment was repeatedly identified in intelligence reports as being in the Central Highlands during the Easter Offensive, other reliable sources say it was not there but was instead fighting in I Corps. When formed in 1971, the 203rd Tank Regiment included the 171st, 198th, and 297th Tank Battalions. The 297th Battalion was still organic to the 203rd Regiment during the ARVN invasion of Laos in February 1971, so when the 297th was identified in the Central Highlands in the spring of 1972, intelligence analysts may have assumed the headquarters and other battalions of the 203rd Tank Regiment were there also. By the spring of 1972, the 297th Tank Battalion was probably no longer organic to or was at least detached from the 203rd Tank Regiment. Why POWs captured in the Highlands claimed they were from the 203rd NVA Tank Regiment is unknown.

5. *Annex K, Kontum: The NVA Buildup*, annex to *United States Military Assistance Command Vietnam (MACV), Command History, January 1972-March 1973*, vol. 2 (Saigon: Military History Branch, Office of the Secretary, Joint Staff, MACV, 1973), K-1, K-4; Ngo, *The Easter Offensive of 1972*, 81.

6. *Annex K, Kontum*, K-4; Military Region 2 Weekly Intelligence Update, Headquarters, SRAG, 7 Apr. 1972, RG 472, National Archives, College Park, MD.

7. Lewis Sorley, ed., *Vietnam Chronicles: The Abrams Tapes, 1968-1972* (Lubbock: Texas Tech University Press, 2004), 696.

8. Lewis B. Sorley, *A Better War: The Unexamined Victories and Final Tragedies of America's Last Years in Vietnam* (New York: Harcourt Brace, 1999), 315–16.

9. SRAG, "Policy Guidance and Information Memorandum Number 1," quoted in "Senior Adviser's Notes #16," Advisory Team 22, 21 Dec. 1971, RG 472, Reference Paper Files, 201–7, Box 1, National Archives, College Park, MD.

10. Sorley, ed., *Vietnam Chronicles*, 730–31.

11. Captain (Lieutenant Colonel, Ret.) John R. Finch, former G-3 air adviser, 23rd ARVN Division, telephone interview by the author, 29 Mar. 2006.

5. The Year of the Rat

1. George Donaldson Moss, *Vietnam: An American Ordeal* (Upper Saddle River, NJ: Prentice Hall, 1998), 375.

2. Lewis Sorley, ed., *Vietnam Chronicles: The Abrams Tapes, 1968-1972* (Lubbock: Texas Tech University Press, 2004), 760.

3. Lewis B. Sorley, "Courage and Blood: South Vietnam's Repulse of the 1972 Easter Invasion," *Parameters* (U.S. Army War College) 29, no. 2 (1999), 39.

4. "1972 Vietnam Counteroffensive," chap. 7 of *RB-100-2,* vol. 1 of *Reference Book: Selected Readings in Tactics* (Fort Leavenworth, KS: US Army Command and General Staff College, April 1974), 7-1, 7-2.

5. William S. Turley, *The Second Indochina War: A Short Political and Military History, 1954-1975* (Boulder, CO: Westview Press, 1986), 138–39.

6. Sorley, ed., *Vietnam Chronicles*, 739–40, 745.

7. Mike Sloniker, "The Easter Offensive of 1972 to the War's End," in *Vietnam Helicopter Pilots Association Membership Directory* (Grapevine, TX: Vietnam Helicopter Pilots Association, 1999), 16:258.

8. Brigadier General George E. Wear, senior military adviser and commander of US Forces in II Corps, email to the author, 3 Feb. 2005.

9. *Annex K, Kontum: The NVA Buildup,* annex to *United States Military Assistance Command Vietnam (MACV), Command History, January 1972-March 1973,* vol. 2 (Saigon: Military History Branch, Office of the Secretary, Joint Staff, MACV, 1973), K-1.

10. Bernard F. Halloran, "Soviet Armor Comes to Vietnam," *Army* (Aug. 1972), 18, 23.

11. Sorley, ed., *Vietnam Chronicles*, 756.

12. Ibid., 758.

13. "U.S. May Up Air War to Hit North," *Stars and Stripes*, 7 Apr. 1972.

14. Sorley, "Courage and Blood," 42.

15. Ly Tong Ba, interviewed by Neil Sheehan, 14 June 1973, Neil Sheehan Papers, Container 58, Folder 11, RGA 6492–93, Manuscript Division, Library of Congress, Washington, DC.

16. General Cao Van Vien, chief, (South Vietnamese) Joint General Staff, notes of unrecorded interview by Neil Sheehan, 26 June 1973, Neil Sheehan Papers, Container 96, Folder 4, RGA 6492–93.

17. Ly Tong Ba, typed summary by Neil Sheehan of his first taped interview, Neil Sheehan Papers, Container 120, Folder 5, RGA 6492–93.

18. Master Sergeant Lowell W. Stevens, telephone interview by the author, 13 June 2005; "Province Report, Kontum Province," May and June 1972, RG 472, National Archives, College Park, MD.

19. "Infantry Units as of 16 July 1972," SRAG, General Records, 601-091 II Corps Strength Summary, RG 472, Box 1, National Archives.

20. Giap Phuc Hai, MD, former 23rd ARVN Division surgeon, email to the author, 9 Apr. 2005.

21. Neil Sheehan Papers, Container 2, RGA 6492–93.

22. 17th Aviation Group (Combat) Pleiku, Operations Report, Lessons Learned (ORLL), for the period 1 Nov. 1971–30 Apr. 1972, pp. 3–5, NND927622, RG 472, National Archives.

23. Lewis B. Sorley, *A Better War: The Unexamined Victories and Final Tragedies of America's Last Years in Vietnam* (New York: Harcourt Brace, 1999), 290.

24. Sorley, ed., *Vietnam Chronicles,* 777, 779.

25. Brigadier General George E. Wear, email to the author, 28 Jan. 2005.

26. 17th Aviation Group (Combat) Pleiku, ORLL, for the period 1 May 1972–31 Oct. 1972, pp. 18, 33.

27. *Annex K, Kontum,* K-4.

28. Sorley, ed., *Vietnam Chronicles,* 781.

29. "1972 Vietnam Counteroffensive," 7-17.

30. Lieutenant Colonel Thomas P. McKenna, letter to commanding officer, 44th Infantry Regiment, 10 Mar. 1972, Adviser Team 33, RG 472, National Archives.

31. Daily Intelligence Review, Intelligence and Security Division, MACV Deputy Chief of Staff, Operations (DCSOPS), 17 Mar. 1972, Box 3, Folder 12, Glen Helm Collection, Vietnam Archive, Texas Tech University, Lubbock.

32. John C. Burns, *XM-26 TOW: Birth of the Helicopter as a Tank Buster* (Quantico, VA: Marine Corps Command and Staff College, 1994), 29.

33. Military Region 2 Weekly Intelligence Update, Headquarters, SRAG, 7 Apr. 1972, RG 472, National Archives.

34. *Annex K, Kontum,* K-5; "1972 Vietnam Counteroffensive," 7-18.

35. Harry G. Summers Jr., *The Vietnam War Almanac* (New York: Ballantine, 1985), 55.

36. Military Region 2 Weekly Intelligence Update, 10 Apr. 1972.

37. Burns, *XM-26 TOW,* 24.

6. The North Vietnamese Invasion

1. John Colvin, *Giap, Volcano under the Snow* (New York: Soho Press, 1996), 267.

2. A. H. S. Candlin, "The Spring Offensive in Vietnam," *Army Quarterly and Defense Journal* (July 1972), 412.

3. "Waiting for Another Tet," *Time,* 31 Jan. 1972.

4. *The Nguyen Hue Offensive,* Military Assistance Command Direc-

torate of Intelligence Study 73-01 (Saigon: Intelligence Support Liaison Branch, Intelligence Production Division, Directorate of Intelligence, USMACV, 12 Jan. 1973), E-4.

5. Quoted in "Vietnamization: A Policy under the Gun," *Time,* 17 Apr. 1972.

6. Lewis Sorley, ed., *Vietnam Chronicles: The Abrams Tapes, 1968-1972* (Lubbock: Texas Tech University Press, 2004), 820; Dave R. Palmer, *Summons of the Trumpet: U.S.-Vietnam in Perspective* (San Rafael, CA: Presidio Press, 1978), 247–48; Brian M. Jenkins, *Giap and the Seventh Son* (Santa Monica, CA: Rand Corporation, 1972), 2; Dale Andradé, "Why Westmoreland Was Right," *Vietnam* (Apr. 2009), 32.

7. Ngo Quang Truong, *The Easter Offensive of 1972,* Indochina Monograph Series (Washington, DC: US Army Center of Military History, 1980), 9; BDM Corporation, *A Study of Strategic Lessons Learned in Vietnam,* vol. 6: *Conduct of the War,* report submitted to Department of the Army (9 May 1980), 4-74.

8. Palmer, *Summons of the Trumpet,* 249–50.

9. George Donaldson Moss, *Vietnam: An American Ordeal* (Upper Saddle River, NJ: Prentice Hall, 1998), 386; Clark Dougan and Stephen Weiss, *The American Experience in Vietnam: The Complete History with Eye-witness Accounts* (New York: W. W. Norton, 1988), 275.

10. Walter J. Boyne, "The Easter Halt," *Air Force* 81, no. 9 (Sept. 1998), 61; "The Flow of Red Arms U.S. Is Trying to Halt," *U.S. News & World Report,* 22 May 1972.

11. Jack S. Ballard, *Development and Employment of Fixed-Wing Gunships, 1962-1972* (Washington, DC: Office of Air Force History, 1982), 231; Boyne, "The Easter Halt," 61; John D. Howard, "They Were Good Ol' Boys! An Infantryman Remembers An Loc and the Air Force," *Air University Review* 26, no. 2 (Jan.–Feb. 1975), 34; Carl Otis Schuster, "North Vietnam's Light Anti-Aircraft Artillery," *Vietnam* (Oct. 2007): 21–22; Carl Otis Schuster, "The SA-7 Grail: Man-Portable Missile Packs a Punch," *Vietnam* (Feb. 2010): 15; Ian Ward, "Why Giap Did It: Report from Saigon," in *North Vietnam's Blitzkrieg: An Interim Assessment,* edited by Brian Crozier (London: Institute for Study of Conflict, Oct. 1972), 6.

12. John A. Doglione, *Airpower and the 1972 Spring Invasion* (Washington, DC: Office of Air Force History, 1985), 59; "The Flow of Red Arms U.S. Is Trying to Halt."

13. *The 1972 Quang Tri Offensive Campaign (Secret)* (Hanoi: Military Art Faculty of the Military Science Institute, 1976), appendix 9, 152.

14. Bob Baker, "Battle of the Bulge vs. Eastertide Offensive, Lessons Learned," *Vietnam* (Apr. 1999), 36.

15. Simon Dunstan, *Vietnam Tracks: Armor in Battle, 1945-1975* (Novato, CA: Presidio Press, 1982), 185.

16. Boyne, "The Easter Halt," 61; Philip D. Chinnery, *Vietnam: The Helicopter War* (Annapolis, MD: Naval Institute Press, 1991), 161.

17. Ray L. Bowers, *Tactical Airlift: The U.S. Air Force in Southeast Asia* (Washington, DC: Office of Air Force History, USAF, 1983), 559.

18. "The U.S. Army in Vietnam: From Tet to the Final Withdrawal,

1968-1973," in *American Military History,* rev., edited by Richard W. Stewart, 333-64, Army Historical Series (Washington, DC: US Army Center of Military History, 2005), available at http://www.history.army.mil/books/AMH-42/AMH%20V2/chapter 11.htm.

19. "1972 Vietnam Counteroffensive," chap. 7 of *RB-100-2,* vol. 1 of *Reference Book: Selected Readings in Tactics* (Fort Leavenworth, KS: US Army Command and General Staff College, April 1974), 7-2.

20. "The War That Won't Go Away," *Newsweek,* 17 Apr. 1972.

21. Bruce Palmer Jr., *U.S. Intelligence and Vietnam,* special issue of *Studies in Intelligence* 28 (1984), 93 n. 37.

22. Tran Van Hien, "The Communist Assault on Quang Tri," in *Vietnamese Marine Corps History,* part III: *1972,* formerly available online, copy in the author's files, 1.

23. Ward, "Why Giap Did It," 3-4; Michael Clodfelter, *Vietnam in Military Statistics: A History of the Indochina Wars, 1772-1991* (Jefferson, NC: McFarland, 1995), 198.

24. BDM Corporation, *Operational Analyses,* 4-74 to 4-115.

25. Bruce Palmer Jr., *The 25-Year War: America's Military Role in Vietnam* (Lexington: University Press of Kentucky, 1984), 119.

26. Moss, *Vietnam,* 378.

27. Donald J. Metcalf, "Why Did the Defense of Quang Tri Province, SVN Collapse?" student essay, US Army War College, Carlisle Barracks, PA, 1972, 31.

28. *Annex K, Kontum: The NVA Buildup,* annex to *United States Military Assistance Command Vietnam (MACV), Command History, January 1972-March 1973,* vol. 2 (Saigon: Military History Branch, Office of the Secretary, Joint Staff, MACV, 1973), K-4; Bowers, *Tactical Airlift,* 561.

29. David E. Ott, "1972 Enemy Offensive," *Field Artillery Journal* 45, no. 1 (Jan.-Feb. 1977), 43.

30. Quoted in G. H. Turley, *The Easter Offensive: The Last American Advisors [sic], Vietnam, 1972* (Novato, CA: Presidio Press, 1985), 142-52.

31. Ibid.

32. Quoted in Dale Andradé, *America's Last Vietnam Battle: Halting Hanoi's 1972 Easter Offensive* (Lawrence: University Press of Kansas, 2001), 89.

33. Baker, "Battle of the Bulge versus Eastertide Offensive," 37.

34. Brigadier General George E. Wear, senior military adviser and commander of US Forces in II Corps, email to the author, 30 Jan. 2005.

35. Lewis Sorley, ed., *Vietnam Chronicles: The Abrams Tapes, 1968-1972* (Lubbock: Texas Tech University Press, 2004), 809.

36. Ward, "Why Giap Did It," 3-4.

37. A. P. Serong, *The 1972 Easter Offensive,* special issue of *Southeast Asian Perspectives,* no. 10 (Summer 1974), 26-27.

38. Ward, "Why Giap Did It," 6.

39. James H. Willbanks, *The Battle of An Loc* (Bloomington: Indiana University Press, 2005); Ward, "Why Giap Did It," 4.

40. John D. Howard, "The War We Came to Fight: A Study of the Bat-

tle of An Loc, April–June 1972," unpublished student paper, US Army Command and General Staff College, Fort Leavenworth, KS, 1974.

41. *Annex K, Kontum,* 52; Clodfelter, *Vietnam in Military Statistics,* 198–99.

42. Author's cassette tape from An Khe, Vietnam, to family, c. 11 Apr. 1972.

43. "Recommendation for Decoration for Valor or Merit, Colonel Phillip Kaplan, MACV Adviser Team 22," Second Regional Assistance Command Awards Files, RG 472, National Archives, College Park, MD.

44. Boyne, "The Easter Halt," 64–65.

45. Incoming Messages, Jan.–June 1972, 201–7, Adviser Team 33, Senior Adviser, Weekly Staff Summaries, Box 1, Background Files, RG 472, National Archives.

46. Larry Berman, *No Peace, No Honor: Nixon, Kissinger, and Betrayal in Vietnam* (New York: Free Press, 2001), 126.

47. Arnold R. Isaacs, *Without Honor: Defeat in Vietnam and Cambodia* (Baltimore: Johns Hopkins University Press, 1983), 19.

48. Doglione, *Airpower and the 1972 Spring Invasion,* 63.

49. "The Harrowing War in the Air," *Time,* 1 May 1972.

50. Brigadier General Wear, email to the author, 31 Jan. 2005.

51. William S. Turley, *The Second Indochina War: A Short Political and Military History, 1954-1975* (Boulder, CO: Westview Press, 1986), 141–42.

52. David Burns Sigler, *Vietnam Battle Chronology: U.S. Army and Marine Corps Combat Operations, 1965-1973* (Jefferson, NC: McFarland, 1992), 130.

53. Bowers, *Tactical Airlift,* 561.

54. Boyne, "The Easter Halt," 64–65.

55. "*Midway,* on the Job Early, Aids Defenders of An Loc," *Pacific Stars and Stripes,* 7 May 1972.

56. Dougan and Weiss, *The American Experience in Vietnam,* 273.

57. General Cao Van Vien, chief, (South Vietnamese) Joint General Staff, interviewed by Neil Sheehan, 26 June 1973, Sheehan's notes, Neil Sheehan Papers, RGA 6492-93, Container 96, Folder 4, Manuscript Division, Library of Congress, Washington, DC.

58. Henry Kissinger, *The White House Years* (Boston: Little, Brown, 1979), 1111–12.

7. Attacking in An Khe Pass

1. Peter A. W. Liebchen, *Kontum: Battle for the Central Highlands, 30 March-10 June 1972,* USAF Southeast Asia Monograph Series, vol. 2, monograph 3, USAF Project Contemporary Historical Examination of Current Operations Report (Washington, DC: USAF, Oct. 1972), 36.

2. Military Region 2 Weekly Intelligence Update, Headquarters, SRAG, 10 Apr. 1972, RG 472, National Archives, College Park, MD.

3. 17th Aviation Group (Combat) Pleiku, Operations Report, Lessons Learned (ORLL), for the period 1 Nov. 1971–30 Apr. 1972, pp. 3, 29, NND927622, RG 472, National Archives.

4. Stanley R. Larson and James L. Collins Jr., *Vietnam Studies: Allied Participation in Vietnam* (Washington, DC: Department of the Army, 1975), 130; Recommendation for Decoration for Valor or Merit for Lieutenant Colonel Thomas P. McKenna, 18 July 1972, Second Regional Assistance Command Awards Files, RG 472, National Archives.

5. Author's cassette tape from An Khe, Vietnam, to family, c. 11 Apr. 1972.

6. Quoted in "Both Sides of Debate over Vietnam Bombing," *U.S. News & World Report,* 1 May 1972.

7. Brigadier General George E. Wear, senior military adviser and commander of US forces in II Corps, telephone interview by the author, 14 Sept. 2004.

8. William E. Le Gro, *Vietnam from Cease-Fire to Capitulation* (Washington, DC: US Army Center of Military History, 1981), 9.

9. James G. Lowenstein and Richard M. Moose, *Vietnam: May 1972,* a staff report for the Committee on Foreign Relations, US Senate, June 29 (Washington, DC: US Government Printing Office, 1972), 5–6.

10. Paul Kasper, "Arsenal: The M-132 Mounted Flamethrower Produced Devastating Battlefield and Psychological Effects," *Vietnam* (Oct. 2004), 14, 62.

11. Dale Andradé, "Tigers, Blue Dragons, and White Horses," *Vietnam* (Dec. 1989), 53.

12. John A. Doglione, *Airpower and the 1972 Spring Invasion* (Washington, DC: Office of Air Force History, 1985), 67.

13. Le Gro, *Vietnam from Cease-Fire to Capitulation,* 9.

14. Recommendation for Decoration for Valor or Merit for Lieutenant Colonel Thomas P. McKenna, 18 July 1972.

15. "Red Drive Slowed in Viet Highlands," *Pacific Stars and Stripes,* 28 Apr. 1972; "ROK Casualties Higher," *Pacific Stars and Stripes,* 29 Apr. 1972.

16. Lowenstein and Moose, *Vietnam,* 5.

17. 17th Aviation Group (Combat) Pleiku, ORLL, for the period 1 Nov. 1971–30 Apr. 1972, pp. 3–4.

18. Brigadier General George E. Wear, email to the author, 30 Jan. 2005.

8. Our Firebases Fall

1. Lieutenant Colonel (Ret.) Stanislaus J. Fuesel, former artillery adviser to ARVN II Corps, telephone interview by the author, 27 June 2005; BDM Corporation, *A Study of Strategic Lessons Learned in Vietnam,* vol. 6: *Conduct of the War,* report submitted to the Department of the Army (9 May 1980), 4-74 to 4-115.

2. Neil Sheehan, *A Bright Shining Lie: John Paul Vann and America in Vietnam* (New York: Random House, 1988), 754–55.

3. "1972 Vietnam Counteroffensive," chap. 7 of *RB-100-2,* vol. 1 of *Reference Book: Selected Readings in Tactics* (Fort Leavenworth, KS: US Army Command and General Staff College, April 1974), 7-18.

4. *Annex K, Kontum: The NVA Buildup,* annex to *United States Military Assistance Command Vietnam (MACV), Command History, January 1972-March 1973,* vol. 2 (Saigon: Military History Branch, Office of the Secretary, Joint Staff, MACV, 1973), K-5.

5. Ibid., 51.

6. Military Region 2 Weekly Intelligence Update, Headquarters, SRAG, 10 Apr. 1972, RG 472, National Archives, College Park, MD.

7. 17th Aviation Group (Combat) Pleiku, Operations Report, Lessons Learned (ORLL), for the period 1 May 1972-31 Oct. 1972, p. 33, NND927622, RG 472, National Archives; Intelligence and Security Division, MACV Deputy Chief of Staff, Operations (DCSOPS), Daily Intelligence Review, 5 Apr. 1972, pp. 1–2, Folder 12, Box 03, Glenn Helm Collection, Vietnam Archive, Texas Tech University, Lubbock.

8. Intelligence and Security Division, DCSOPS, Daily Intelligence Review, 5 Apr. 1972, pp. 1–2.

9. Ian Ward, "Why Giap Did It: Report from Saigon," in *North Vietnam's Blitzkrieg: An Interim Assessment,* edited by Brian Crozier (London: Institute for Study of Conflict, Oct. 1972), 3.

10. "The First Large-Scale Strategic Offensive in the Highlands Theater," in *History of the Central Highlands People's Armed Forces in the Anti-U.S. War of Resistance for National Salvation,* translated by the US Government Foreign Broadcast Information Service (Hanoi: People's Army Publishing House, 1980), 2.

11. First Lieutenant Gary Swingle, interviewed by Neil Sheehan, 26 Sept. 1972, RGA 8004, #7000, Side A, Recorded Sound Reference Center, Library of Congress, Washington, DC.

12. Lieutenant Colonel (Ret.) Stanislaus J. Fuesel, former artillery adviser to ARVN II Corps, telephone interview by the author, 27 June 2005.

13. 17th Aviation Group (Combat) Pleiku, ORLL, for the period 1 May 1972-31 Oct. 1972, p. 22.

14. Captain (Ret.) James E. Stein, former scout pilot, B (and H) Troop, 7th Battalion, 17th Air Cavalry, interviewed by the author, 19 Apr. 2008, Denver.

15. 17th Aviation Group (Combat) Pleiku, ORLL for the period 1 Nov. 1971-30 Apr. 1972, p. 6.

16. Captain (Colonel, Ret.) Martin S. Kleiner, telephone interview by the author, 28 June 2005; Kleiner mentioned the *Stars and Stripes* report but did not know the specific date.

17. Ibid.

18. "1972 Vietnam Counteroffensive," 7-19.

19. Ibid., 7-19; Daily Staff Journal, item nos. 3 and 16, from 0001, 22 Apr. 1972, to 2400, 22 Apr. 1972, MACV, SRAG, Pleiku, Vietnam (for Kontum Province), RG 472, National Archives.

20. Brigadier General (Ret.) George E. Wear, senior military advisor and commander of US Forces in II Corps, email to the author, 31 Jan. 2005.

21. Lewis Sorley, ed., *Vietnam Chronicles: The Abrams Tapes, 1968-1972* (Lubbock: Texas Tech University Press, 2004), 820.

22. Brigadier General Wear, telephone interview by the author, 14 Sept. 2004.

23. Transcript of Neil Sheehan's notes on his interview with Brigadier General John G. Hill, Neil Sheehan Papers, Container 68, Folder 2, RGA 6492-93, Manuscript Division, Library of Congress, Washington, DC.

24. Military History Institute of Vietnam, *Victory in Vietnam: The Official History of the People's Army of Vietnam, 1954-1975,* translated by Merle L. Pribbenow, foreword by William J. Duiker (Lawrence: University Press of Kansas, 2002), 293-94.

25. Message from John Paul Vann to General Creighton Abrams, "Daily Commanders Evaluation for 24 Hours from 1000H 20 April 1972," RG 472, National Archives.

9. The Collapse at Tan Canh

1. Neil Sheehan's typed transcript of his taped interview with Colonel Phillip Kaplan, Neil Sheehan Papers, Container 69, Folder 8, RGA 6492–93, Manuscript Division, Library of Congress, Washington, DC.

2. Colonel (Major General Ret.) Phillip Kaplan, former senior adviser, 22nd ARVN Division, telephone interview by the author, 5 Oct. 2004.

3. "Narrative," Recommendation for Decoration for Valor or Merit, Colonel Phillip Kaplan, MACV Adviser Team 22, Second Regional Assistance Command Awards Files, RG 472, National Archives, College Park, MD.

4. Quoted in "Waiting for Another Tet," *Time,* 31 Jan. 1972.

5. Kaplan, interviewed by the author, 5 Oct. 2004.

6. Colonel Phillip Kaplan, senior adviser, 22nd ARVN Division, interviewed by Neil Sheehan, Sept. 1972, Neil Sheehan Papers, Container 69, Folder 8.

7. *Annex K, Kontum: The NVA Buildup,* annex to *United States Military Assistance Command Vietnam (MACV), Command History, January 1972-March 1973,* vol. 2 (Saigon: Military History Branch, Office of the Secretary, Joint Staff, MACV, 1973), K-4.

8. Kaplan, interviewed by Sheehan, Sept. 1972.

9. Kaplan, interviewed by the author, 5 Oct. 2004.

10. Plot of ARVN positions at Tan Canh given to Neil Sheehan by Colonel Phillip Kaplan, Sept. 1972, Neil Sheehan Papers, Container 96, Folder 10.

11. Ngo Quang Truong, *The Easter Offensive of 1972,* Indochina Monograph Series (Washington, DC: US Army Center of Military History, 1980), 87.

12. General Cao Van Viên, chief, (South Vietnamese) Joint General Staff, unrecorded interview by Neil Sheehan, 26 June 1973, Sheehan's notes, Neil Sheehan Papers, Container 96, Folder 4.

13. Kaplan, interviewed by Sheehan, Sept. 1972.

14. Military Region 2 Weekly Intelligence Update, Headquarters,

SRAG, 10 Apr. 1972, RG 472, National Archives; "1972 Vietnam Counteroffensive," chap. 7 of *RB-100-2*, vol. 1 of *Reference Book: Selected Readings in Tactics* (Fort Leavenworth, KS: US Army Command and General Staff College, April 1974), 7-18; *Annex K, Kontum,* K-10, K-11.

15. Recommendation for Decoration for Valor or Merit, Colonel Phillip Kaplan, MACV Adviser Team 22, Second Regional Assistance Command Awards Files, RG 472, National Archives.

16. "1972 Vietnam Counteroffensive," 7-19.

17. Kaplan, interviewed by Sheehan, Sept. 1972; Neil Sheehan, "Working Files, Book VII, JPV Stays, the Climax, Kontum, Finale, and Crash," 1986, Neil Sheehan Papers, Container 24.

18. Kaplan, interviewed by the author, 5 Oct. 2004.

19. Kaplan, interviewed by Sheehan, Sept. 1972.

20. Ibid.; Recommendation for Decoration for Valor or Merit, Colonel Phillip Kaplan; Daily Staff Journal, 23 Apr. 1972, 1940 hours entry, "Tan Canh Log," from 0001, 23 Apr. 1972, to 2400, 23 Apr. 1972, MACV SRAG, Pleiku, Vietnam, RG 472, National Archives.

21. Daily Staff Journal, item no. 1, from 0001, 23 Apr. 1972, to 2400, 23 Apr. 1972.

22. Donn A. Starry, *Armored Combat in Vietnam,* Vietnam Studies (Washington, DC: Department of the Army, 1978), 212–13.

23. *Annex K, Kontum,* K-6; Kaplan, interviewed by the author, 5 Oct. 2004; Kaplan, interviewed by Sheehan, Sept. 1972.

24. Kaplan, interviewed by Sheehan, Sept. 1972.

25. Ibid.

26. Message from MACSR-GB, 12 Jan. 1973, secret, declassified 19 Oct. 2004, Neil Sheehan Papers, Container 87.

27. Simon Dunstan, *Vietnam Tracks: Armor in Battle, 1945-1975* (Novato, CA: Presidio Press, 1982), 187.

28. *Annex K, Kontum,* K-8.

29. Kaplan, interviewed by Sheehan, Sept. 1972.

30. "1972 Vietnam Counteroffensive," 7-20.

31. *Annex K, Kontum,* K-8.

32. Kaplan, interviewed by Sheehan, Sept. 1972.

33. Ibid.

34. Ibid.

35. *Annex K, Kontum,* K-8.

36. English version/translation of undated ARVN 23rd Infantry Division script for briefing visitors after the Battle of Kontum, Neil Sheehan Papers, Container 96, Folder 4.

37. "1972 Vietnam Counteroffensive," 7-21.

38. "The First Large-Scale Strategic Offensive in the Highlands Theater," in *History of the Central Highlands People's Armed Forces in the Anti-U.S. War of Resistance for National Salvation,* translated by US Government Foreign Broadcast Information Service (Hanoi: People's Army Publishing House, 1980), 9.

39. Kaplan, interviewed by Sheehan, Sept. 1972.

40. Captain (Lieutenant Colonel, Ret.) James T. Vaughan, adviser to ARVN 19th Armored Cavalry Regiment and duty officer at II Corps Tactical Operations Center, telephone interview by the author, 20 Feb. 2006.

41. Kaplan, interviewed by Sheehan, Sept. 1972.

42. Kaplan, interviewed by the author, 5 Oct. 2004.

43. Quoted in "U.S. Advisers Saved in Daring Rescue," *Louisville Courier-Journal,* 25 Apr. 1972.

44. Kaplan, interviewed by Sheehan, Sept. 1972.

45. Kaplan, interviewed by the author, 5 Oct. 2004.

46. Kaplan, interviewed by Sheehan, Sept. 1972.

47. Kaplan, interviewed by the author, 5 Oct. 2004.

48. Kaplan, interviewed by Sheehan, Sept. 1972.

49. Daily Staff Journal, item no. 2, from 0001, 25 Apr. 1972, to 2400, 25 Apr. 1972, MACV SRAG Pleiku, Vietnam.

50. Vaughan, interviewed by the author, 20 Feb. 2006.

51. Kaplan, interviewed by Sheehan, Sept. 1972.

52. Cable, 1972 May 25 PM 12:19, Mohr editorial note to Greenfield, forwarded to Neil Sheehan by Bob Rosenthal, the *New York Times,* 15 Oct. 1973, Neil Sheehan Papers, Container 51, Folder 11.

53. Transcript of a tape made by war correspondent Matt Franjola of a John Paul Vann press conference, Neil Sheehan Papers, Container 51, Folder 9.

54. "The First Large-Scale Strategic Offensive in the Highlands Theater," 9.

55. Military History Institute of Vietnam, *Victory in Vietnam: The Official History of the People's Army of Vietnam, 1954-1975,* translated by Merle L. Pribbenow, foreword by William J. Duiker (Lawrence: University Press of Kansas, 2002), 294.

56. Daily Staff Journal, item nos. 9 and 10, from 0001, 25 Apr. 1972, to 2400, 25 Apr. 1972, MACV SRAG, Pleiku, Vietnam.

10. A Debacle at Dak To

1. Map of ARVN positions at Tan Canh (Dak To II and other bases in that area), drawn by Colonel Phillip Kaplan, Sept. 1972, Neil Sheehan Papers, Container 96, Folder 10, Manuscript Division, Library of Congress, Washington, DC.

2. Colonel Phillip Kaplan, senior adviser, 22nd ARVN Division, interviewed by Neil Sheehan, Sept. 1972, Neil Sheehan Papers, Container 69, Folder 8.

3. Military Region 2 Weekly Intelligence Update, Headquarters, SRAG, 10 Apr. 1972, RG 472, National Archives, College Park, MD.

4. *Annex K, Kontum: The NVA Buildup,* annex to *United States Military Assistance Command Vietnam (MACV), Command History, January 1972-March 1973,* vol. 2 (Saigon: Military History Branch, Office of the Secretary, Joint Staff, MACV, 1973), K-6.

5. Quoted in "Scared S. Viets Refused to Fight at Hoai An—Adviser," *Pacific Stars and Stripes,* 22 Apr. 1972.

6. "The First Large-Scale Strategic Offensive in the Highlands The-

ater," in *History of the Central Highlands People's Armed Forces in the Anti-U.S. War of Resistance for National Salvation,* translated by US Government Foreign Broadcast Information Service (Hanoi: People's Army Publishing House, 1980), 7–10.

7. Ibid., 7; "1972 Vietnam Counteroffensive," chap. 7 of *RB-100-2,* vol. 1 of *Reference Book: Selected Readings in Tactics* (Fort Leavenworth, KS: US Army Command and General Staff College, April 1974), 7-21.

8. *Annex K, Kontum,* K-10.

9. Warrant Officer 1 (Warrant Officer 4, Ret.) Larry Brassel, telephone interview by the author, 29 Jan. 2006.

10. *Annex K, Kontum,* K-10; Mark Truhan, former adviser to the 95th Border Ranger Battalion, telephone interview by the author, 28 Aug. 2004.

11. *Annex K, Kontum,* K-10.

12. Colonel Brownlee was never seen again and was listed as a casualty in October 1978. He was on the promotion list to colonel and was promoted while in MIA status (see "Report of Board of Inquiry: Colonel Robert W. Brownlee, 493-26-2250," Second Regional Assistance Command, MACSR-GC, 11 Feb. 1973, Inspector General, Reports of Investigations, Box 8, RG 472, National Archives). Captain Yonan was never reported as a POW and was declared dead on 15 Aug. 1979. His body was eventually recovered and buried at West Point (see *Annex K, Kontum,* K-7).

13. "The First Large-Scale Strategic Offensive in the Highlands Theater," 10.

14. John A. Doglione, *Airpower and the 1972 Spring Invasion* (Washington, DC: Office of Air Force History, 1985), 66.

15. "The First Large-Scale Strategic Offensive in the Highlands Theater," 12.

16. Daily Staff Journal, MACV Command Center, from 1601Z, 24 Apr. 1972, to 1600Z, 25 Apr. 1972, RG 472, NND 913661, National Archives.

17. Quoted in Doglione, *Airpower and the 1972 Spring Invasion,* 66.

18. Sergeant James N. Barker, US Army Vietnamese language specialist, telephone interview by the author, 17 June 2006.

19. *Annex K, Kontum,* K-13.

20. Lieutenant Colonel (Ret.) Stanislaus J. Fuesel, former artillery adviser to ARVN II Corps, telephone interview by the author, 27 June 2005.

21. Ibid.

22. Lewis Sorley, ed., *Vietnam Chronicles: The Abrams Tapes, 1968-1972* (Lubbock: Texas Tech University Press, 2004), 844.

23. Ngo Quang Truong, *The Easter Offensive of 1972,* Indochina Monograph Series (Washington, DC: US Army Center of Military History, 1980), 90; *Annex K, Kontum,* K-11, K-12.

24. Brigadier General (Major General, Ret.) John G. Hill, deputy senior adviser, II Corps, sound recording by Neil Sheehan at Fort Hood, Texas, 6 July 1976, Vann/Sheehan Collection, RGA 6492–93, Library of Congress, Washington, DC.

25. Lieutenant (Major, Ret.) James M. Cloninger, telephone interview by the author, 26 July 2005.

26. Captain (Lieutenant Colonel, Ret.) John E. Peters, former adviser to 72nd Border Ranger Battalion, telephone interview by the author, 11 July 2005, and email to author, 16 Jan. 2006.

27. Daily Staff Journal, MACV (MACJ3-08), Command Center, item no. 29, from 1601Z, 25 Apr. 1972, to 1600Z, 26 Apr. 1972, p. 10, RG 472, National Archives.

28. 17th Aviation Group (Combat) Pleiku, Operations Report, Lessons Learned (ORLL), for the period 1 May 1972–31 Oct. 1972, p. 34, NND927622, RG 472, National Archives.

29. Waller B. Booth, "The Montagnards of Vietnam, Tragic Warriors of the Highlands," *Army* (May 1975), 50.

30. Master Sergeant Lowell W. Stevens, telephone interview by the author, 13 June 2005.

31. Colonel (Major General, Ret.) Phillip Kaplan, former senior adviser, 22nd ARVN Division, telephone interview by the author, 5 Oct. 2004.

32. Colonel John O. Truby, former senior adviser, 23rd ARVN Division, email to the author, 5 Aug. 2004.

33 . Captain (Lieutenant Colonel, Ret.) James T. Vaughan, adviser to ARVN 19th Armored Cavalry Regiment and duty officer at II Corps TOC, telephone interview by the author, 20 Feb. 2006.

11. A New Team for the Defense

1. *United States Military Assistance Command Vietnam (MACV), Command History, January 1972–March 1973,* vol. 1 (Saigon: Military History Branch, Office of the Secretary, Joint Staff, MACV, 1973), 51.

2. Brigadier General (Major General, Ret.) John G. Hill, deputy senior adviser, II Corps, sound recording by Neil Sheehan at Fort Hood, Texas, 6 July 1976, Vann/Sheehan Collection, RGA 6492–93, Library of Congress, Washington, DC.

3. Ibid.

4. Ibid.

5. Ibid.

6. Ibid.

7. John G. Hill, William J. Maddox Jr., and James H. Patterson, "Discussions of Combat Use of Helicopters," *U.S. Army Aviation Digest* 22, no. 3 (Mar. 1976), 4.

8. 17th Aviation Group (Combat) Pleiku, Operations Report, Lessons Learned (ORLL), for the period 1 Nov. 1971–30 Apr. 1972, p. 5, NND927622, RG 472, National Archives, College Park, MD.

9. Hill, sound recording by Sheehan, 6 July 1976.

10. Colonel John O. Truby, former senior adviser, 23rd ARVN Division, email to the author, 5 Aug. 2004.

11. Ibid.; Colonel John O. Truby, former senior adviser to 23rd ARVN Division, interviewed by Neil Sheehan, date unknown, typed transcript, Vann/Sheehan Collection, Container 122, Folder 35, RGA 6492–93.

12. Truby, interviewed by the author, 5 Aug. 2004.

13. Ibid.

14. Ibid.; Ly Tong Ba, interviewed by Neil Sheehan, 14 June 1973, Neil Sheehan Papers, Container 58, Folder 11, Manuscript Division, Library of Congress, Washington, DC.

15. Ray L. Bowers, *Tactical Airlift: The U.S. Air Force in Southeast Asia* (Washington, DC: Office of Air Force History, USAF, 1983), 560.

16. Ibid., 566–67.

17. *Det One Report: Yearbook Supplement for the People Who Fly and Support the C-130E Hercules Aircraft of the 374th Tactical Airlift Wing* (Tan Son Nhut Air Base, Vietnam: 374th Tactical Airlift Wing, 4 July, 1972), 2.

18. English version/translation of undated ARVN 23rd Infantry Division script for briefing visitors after the Battle of Kontum, Neil Sheehan Papers, Container 96, Folder 4.

19. Lieutenant Colonel Reed Mulkey (Ret.), email to the author, 28 July 2005.

20. Ibid.

21. More than 30 years later, C-130 number 865 was still flying for the USAF. Master Sergeant Richard Ivars (Ret.), former C-130 loadmaster with 21st Tactical Air Squadron, telephone interview by the author, 18 July 2005; Mulkey, email to the author, 28 July 2005; *Det One Report,* 2–3.

22. Daily Staff Journal, MACV (MACJ3-08), Command Center, item no. 28, from 1601Z, 25 Apr. 1972, to 1600Z, 26 Apr. 1972, p. 10, RG 472, National Archives.

23. Quoted in "The President's Report to Nation on Vietnam," *U.S. News & World Report,* 8 May 1972.

24. Colonel John O. Truby, former senior adviser, 23rd ARVN Division, interviewed by Neil Sheehan, date unknown, Neil Sheehan Papers, Container 88, Folder 9.

25. "1972 Vietnam Counteroffensive," chap. 7 of *RB-100-2,* vol. 1 of *Reference Book: Selected Readings in Tactics* (Fort Leavenworth, KS: US Army Command and General Staff College, April 1974), 7-22.

26. Truby, typed transcript of Sheehan interview.

27. "1972 Vietnam Counteroffensive," 7-22, 7-23.

28. Letter, author to family, 22 May 1972.

29. "1972 Vietnam Counteroffensive," 7-22, 7-23.

30. Cao Van Vien and Đông Van Khuyên, *Reflections on the Vietnam War,* Indochina Monograph Series (Washington, DC: US Army Center of Military History, 1980), 106.

31. "1972 Vietnam Counteroffensive," 7-22.

32. Captain (Lieutenant Colonel, Ret.) John R. Finch, former G-3 air adviser, 23rd ARVN Division, telephone interview by the author, 29 Mar. 2006; Captain (Lieutenant Colonel, Ret.) John R. Finch, former G-3 air adviser, 23rd ARVN Division, personal notes written in late May and early June 1972.

33. Giap Phuc Hai, MD, email to the author, 7 Nov. 2005.

34. Colonel (Ret.) James W. Bricker, email to the author, 6 Mar 2005.

35. Truby, interviewed by the author, 5 Aug. 2004.

36. Finch, interviewed by the author, 29 Mar. 2006, and email to the author, 14 July 2006.

37. John A. Doglione, *Airpower and the 1972 Spring Invasion* (Washington, DC: Office of Air Force History, 1985), 67; Edward W. Knappman, ed., *South Vietnam*, vol. 7: *U.S.-Communist Confrontation in Southeast Asia, 1972-73* (New York: Facts on File, 1973), 71; "The Air War Grows," *Newsweek*, 24 Apr. 1972; David Burns Sigler, *Vietnam Battle Chronology: U.S. Army and Marine Corps Combat Operations, 1965-1973* (Jefferson, NC: McFarland, 1992), 130.

38. Colonel Stephen W. Bachinski, *Province Report, Kontum Province, Period Ending 30 April 1972* (1 May 1972), 2–3, RG 472, National Archives.

39. Ly Tong Ba, interviewed by Sheehan, 14 June 1973; "Battle for City Looms / They 'Have to Get Out' of Imperiled Kontum," *Pacific Stars and Stripes*, 13 May 1972.

40. Ngo Quang Truong, *The Easter Offensive of 1972*, Indochina Monograph Series (Washington, DC: US Army Center of Military History, 1980), 91.

41. "350,000 Refugees on Move," *Pacific Stars and Stripes*, 3 May 1972; "Red Barrage Turned the Tide," *Pacific Stars and Stripes*, 4 May 1972; Knappman, ed., *U.S.-Communist Confrontation*, 71.

42. Bob Hubbard, "Testing TOW under Fire," *Army Logistician* (Mar.–Apr. 1973), 11–13; Philip D. Chinnery, *Vietnam: The Helicopter War* (Annapolis, MD: Naval Institute Press, 1991), 162; "Knock Out 26 Tanks, Army's New TOW Choppers Bat .802," *Pacific Stars and Stripes*, 29 June 1972.

43. Hugh J. McInnish Jr., "Germany Tests Airborne TOW," *U.S. Army Aviation Digest* (Mar. 1972): 10–13.

44. Mike Sloniker, "The Easter Offensive of 1972 to the War's End," in *Vietnam Helicopter Pilots Association Membership Directory* (Grapevine, TX: Vietnam Helicopter Pilots Association, 1999), 16:259.

45. Ibid. Other sources credit a USAF Stinger AC-130 gunship and VNAF tactical air strikes with destroying those four tanks. See, for example, Hubbard, "Testing TOW under Fire," 13–14.

12. Closing in on Kontum

1. Jacques Leslie, "S. Vietnam Troops Turn Back Red Attack at Kontum," *Los Angeles Times*, 15 May 1972.

2. "1972 Vietnam Counteroffensive," chap. 7 of *RB-100-2*, vol. 1 of *Reference Book: Selected Readings in Tactics* (Fort Leavenworth, KS: US Army Command and General Staff College, April 1974), 7-23.

3. Phan Vu, "The Vietnam War: A Free Vietnamese's Viewpoint," 23, unpublished manuscript, copy in author's files.

4. John G. Heslin, *Combat Power: An Ontological Approach* (Newport, RI: US Naval War College, 1978), 60.

5. "Many Will Flee, Others Vow to Fight / Red Tanks, Troops near Kontum," *Pacific Stars and Stripes*, 30 Apr. 1972.

6. Ngo Quang Truong, *The Easter Offensive of 1972*, Indochina Mono-

graph Series (Washington, DC: US Army Center of Military History, 1980), 95.

7. English version/translation of undated ARVN 23rd Infantry Division script for briefing visitors after the Battle of Kontum, Neil Sheehan Papers, Container 96, Folder 4, Manuscript Division, Library of Congress, Washington, DC.

8. Message from General Creighton Abrams to Secretary of Defense Melvin Laird, 1601Z, 1 May 1972, Center of Military History, Fort Leslie J. McNair, Washington, DC.

9. Ibid.

10. Ibid.

11. Larry Berman, *No Peace, No Honor: Nixon, Kissinger, and Betrayal in Vietnam* (New York: Free Press, 2001), 126.

12. Quoted in Henry Kissinger, *The White House Years* (Boston: Little, Brown, 1979), 1199, emphasis in original.

13. BDM Corporation, *A Study of Strategic Lessons Learned in Vietnam*, vol. 6: *Conduct of the War*, report submitted to the Department of the Army (9 May 1980), 4-90.

14. Lewis Sorley, ed., *Vietnam Chronicles: The Abrams Tapes, 1968-1972* (Lubbock: Texas Tech University Press, 2004), 777.

15. Message from Abrams to multiple addressees, 0452Z, 2 May 1972, MAC 04040, Center of Military History.

16. Jeffrey J. Clarke, *The U.S. Army in Vietnam, Advice and Support: The Final Years, 1965-1971* (Washington, DC: US Army Center of Military History, 1988), 484.

17. Peter A. W. Liebchen, *Kontum: Battle for the Central Highlands, 30 March-10 June 1972*, USAF Southeast Asia Monograph Series, vol. 2, monograph 3, USAF Project Contemporary Historical Examination of Current Operations Report (Washington, DC: USAF, Oct. 1972), 42.

18. Ray L. Bowers, *Tactical Airlift: The U.S. Air Force in Southeast Asia* (Washington, DC: Office of Air Force History, USAF, 1983), 567.

19. "Pilots Fear Reds' New Portable Rocket," *Cleveland Plain Dealer*, 28 May 1972.

20. Message from Abrams to Laird, 0443Z, 2 May 1972, Center of Military History.

21. Message from John Paul Vann to General Creighton Abrams, "Daily Commanders Evaluation for 24 Hours from 1000H 3 May," RG 472, National Archives, College Park, MD.

22. Sorley, ed., *Vietnam Chronicles*, 833–34, emphasis in original.

23. 17th Aviation Group (Combat) Pleiku, Operations Report, Lessons Learned (ORLL), for the period 1 May 1972-31 Oct. 1972, p. 32, NND927622, RG472, National Archives; Liebchen, *Kontum*, 37.

24. "Highlands Fighting Flares over Vital Highway Link," *Pacific Stars and Stripes*, 7 May 1972 and 8 May 1972.

25. Message from Abrams to Laird, 1601Z, 1 May 1972, Center of Military History.

26. Both quoted in Michael Parks, "Trapped Refugees at Kontum Pack and Await Attack," *Baltimore Sun*, 30 Apr. 1972.

27. Malcolm W. Browne, "Thousands Flee Kontum in Panic as Enemy Nears," *New York Times*, 1 May 1972. The sentence stating that "all but a dozen Americans were evacuated" must be a misinterpretation of the policy of sending all but 12 advisers to Pleiku overnight to reduce the number who might need to be evacuated from Kontum in the dark.

28. "Refugees Moved to Pleiku," *Pacific Stars and Stripes*, 4 May 1972.

29. Master Sergeant Lowell W. Stevens, telephone interview by the author, 13 June 2005.

30. Ibid.

31. "5 Safe after 2 Weeks in Jungle: A Most Dangerous Game of Hide-and-Seek," *Pacific Stars and Stripes*, 9 May 1972; Charles Lea (as told to Phil Powell), "Downed in the Jungle," *Vietnam* (Oct. 2002), 26–32.

32. Berman, *No Peace, No Honor,* 130–32.

33. "Message to Nixon: U.S. Moves Are Blunting Hanoi's Drive," *U.S. News & World Report*, 29 May 1972.

34. "Vietnam—Why the Standoff," *U.S. News & World Report*, 19 June 1972.

35. "Showdown over Vietnam," *U.S. News & World Report*, 22 May 1972.

36. Craig B. Whitney, "Government to Remove 30,000 Civilians Still in Kontum," *New York Times*, 7 May 1973.

37. Colonel John O. Truby, former senior adviser, 23rd ARVN Division, email to the author, 5 Aug. 2004.

38. Colonel John O. Truby, former senior adviser to 23rd ARVN Division, interviewed by Neil Sheehan, date unknown, typed transcript of interview, Vann/Sheehan Collection, Container 122, Folder 35, RGA 6492–93, Manuscript Division, Library of Congress, Washington, DC.

39. Brigadier General (Major General, Ret.) John G. Hill, deputy senior adviser, II Corps, sound recording by Neil Sheehan at Fort Hood, Texas, 6 July 1976, Vann/Sheehan Collection, RGA 6492–93.

13. Cut Off and Surrounded

1. Lewis Sorley, ed., *Vietnam Chronicles: The Abrams Tapes, 1968-1972* (Lubbock: Texas Tech University Press, 2004), 844.

2. Quoted in Lewis B. Sorley, "Courage and Blood: South Vietnam's Repulse of the 1972 Easter Invasion," *Parameters* (U.S. Army War College) 29, no. 2 (1999), 51–52, emphasis in original.

3. Message from John Paul Vann to General Creighton Abrams, 0726Z, 7 May 1972, RG 472, National Archives, College Park, MD.

4. This Lieutenant Paul McKenna is not related to the author.

5. Kieu My Duyen, *Chinh Chien Dieu Linh* (N.p.: n.p., 1994), downloaded 25 Mar. 2007 from http://www.bietdongquan.com/article1/rgr62 .htm; *Annex K, Kontum: The NVA Buildup,* annex to *United States Military Assistance Command Vietnam (MACV), Command History, January 1972-March 1973,* vol. 2 (Saigon: Military History Branch, Office of the Secretary, Joint Staff, MACV, 1973), K-14.

6. Message from John Paul Vann to General Creighton Abrams, 0650Z, 5 May 1972.

7. *Annex K, Kontum,* K-14.

8. Ibid.

9. Captain Jim Stein's account of this rescue downloaded 13 Mar. 2007 from the Battle of Kontum Web site at http://www.thebattleofkontum .com/memories/27.html.

10. *Annex K, Kontum,* K-14.

11. Kieu My Duyen, *Chinh Chien Dieu Linh.*

12. Quoted in "N. Viet Tanks, Troops Open Attack on Kontum," *Washington Post,* 14 May 1972.

13. Captain (Lieutenant Colonel, Ret.) Stephen M. (Mark) Truhan, former adviser to the 95th Border Ranger Battalion, telephone interview by the author, 28 Aug. 2004.

14. Peter A. W. Liebchen, *Kontum: Battle for the Central Highlands, 30 March-10 June 1972,* USAF Southeast Asia Monograph Series, vol. 2, monograph 3, USAF Project Contemporary Historical Examination of Current Operations Report (Washington, DC: USAF, Oct. 1972), 38.

15. Captain (Ret.) James E. Stein, former scout pilot, B (and H) Troop, 7th Battalion, 17th Air Cavalry, interviewed by the author, 19 Apr. 2008, Denver.

16. These PT-76 tanks were probably from the 16th Amphibious Tank Company, an independent unit attached to the 2nd NVA Division.

17. Truhan, interviewed by the author, 28 Aug. 2004; *Annex K, Kontum,* K-14; Mark Truhan, "The Battle of Ben Het—May 1972," downloaded Jan. 2005 from the Battle of Kontum Web site at http://www.tohebattleofkontum .com/memories/27.html; "Reds Squeezed Out of Ben Het; 11 Tanks Blasted," *Pacific Stars and Stripes,* 11 May 1972.

18. Truhan, "The Battle of Ben Het—May 1972."

19. Mark Truhan, notes to the author, Jan. 2008.

20. Truhan, "The Battle of Ben Het—May 1972."

21. Brigadier General (Major General, Ret.) John G. Hill, deputy senior adviser, II Corps, sound recording by Neil Sheehan at Fort Hood, Texas, 6 July 1976, Vann/Sheehan Collection, RGA 6492–93, Library of Congress, Washington, DC.

22. General Cao Van Vien, chief, (South Vietnamese) Joint General Staff, unrecorded interviewed by Neil Sheehan, 26 June 1973, Sheehan's notes, Neil Sheehan Papers, Container 96, Folder 4, Manuscript Division, Library of Congress, Washington, DC.

23. Laurence Stern, "Vann Calls the Shots in the Skies over Kontum," *Hong Kong Standard,* 14 June 1972.

24. General Cao Van Vien, Sheehan's notes from 26 June 1973 interview; message from John Paul Vann to General Creighton Abrams, "Daily Commanders Evaluation for 24 Hours from 1000H 10 May," RG 472, National Archives.

25. Colonel John O. Truby, former senior adviser, 23rd ARVN Division, email to the author, 5 Aug. 2004.

26. Sorley, ed., *Vietnam Chronicles,* 845, emphasis in original.

27. Quoted in Lewis B. Sorley, *A Better War: The Unexamined Victories*

and Final Tragedies of America's Last Years in Vietnam (New York: Harcourt Brace, 1999), 336.

28. Message from Vann to Abrams, "Daily Commanders Evaluation for 24 Hours from 1000H 11 May," RG 472, National Archives.

29. John G. Heslin, *Combat Power: An Ontological Approach* (Newport, RI: US Naval War College, 1978), 81.

30. Liebchen, *Kontum,* 42.

31. Richard Ivars (Master Sergeant, Ret.), former C-130 loadmaster with 21st Tactical Air Squadron, telephone interview by the author, 18 July 2005.

32. Stephen James, former Huey helicopter pilot, "Pallbearer 32," B Troop, 7th Squadron, 17th Air Cavalry Regiment, email to the author, 17 Jan. 2006; Warrant Officer 1 (Warrant Officer 2, Ret.) Larry Brassel, telephone interview by the author, 29 Jan. 2006.

33. Heslin, *Combat Power,* 79–81, 87; message from Vann to Abrams, "Daily Commanders Evaluation for 24 Hours from 1000H 12 May," RG 472, National Archives.

34. Colonel R. M. Rhotenberry, senior adviser, ARVN 23rd Infantry Division, sound recording by Neil Sheehan at Pleiku, Vietnam, 29 Sept. 1972, and during Jeep tour of Kontum battlefield, 2 Oct. 1972, Vann/Sheehan Collection, RGA 7662–70.

35. "Message to Nixon: U.S. Moves Are Blunting Hanoi's Drive," *U.S. News & World Report,* 29 May 1972.

36. Message from General Creighton Abrams to John Paul Vann, 1025Z, 13 May 1972, Center of Military History, Fort Leslie J. McNair, Washington, DC.

37. Quoted in "South Vietnam in the Balance," *U.S. News & World Report,* 15 May 1972.

38. First Lieutenant Gary Swingle, interviewed by Neil Sheehan, 25 Sept. 1972, RGA 8005, #7000, Side A, Vann/Sheehan Collection, Recorded Sound Reference Center, Library of Congress.

14. Tanks Attacking!

1. Colonel R. M. Rhotenberry, senior adviser, ARVN 23rd Infantry Division, sound recording by Neil Sheehan at Pleiku, Vietnam, 29 Sept. 1972, and during Jeep tour of Kontum battlefield, 2 Oct. 1972, Vann/Sheehan Collection, RGA 7662–70, Library of Congress, Washington, DC.

2. Colonel John O. Truby, former senior adviser, 23rd ARVN Division, telephone interview by the author, 24 Aug. 2004.

3. *Annex K, Kontum: The NVA Buildup,* annex to *United States Military Assistance Command Vietnam (MACV), Command History, January 1972-March 1973,* vol. 2 (Saigon: Military History Branch, Office of the Secretary, Joint Staff, MACV, 1973), K-15.

4. Peter A. W. Liebchen, *Kontum: Battle for the Central Highlands, 30 March-10 June 1972,* USAF Southeast Asia Monograph Series, vol. 2, monograph 3, USAF Project Contemporary Historical Examination of Current Operations Report (Washington, DC: USAF, Oct. 1972), 42–43.

5. *Annex K, Kontum,* K-15; Colonel John O. Truby, former senior adviser, 23rd ARVN Division, interviewed by Neil Sheehan, date unknown, Neil Sheehan Papers, Container 88, Folder 9, Manuscript Division, Library of Congress, Washington, DC; Colonel John O. Truby, former senior adviser to 23rd ARVN Division, interviewed by Neil Sheehan, date unknown, typed transcript, Vann/Sheehan Collection, Container 122, Folder 35, RGA 6492–93.

6. Message from John Paul Vann to General Creighton Abrams, "Daily Commanders Evaluation For 24 Hours From 1000H 13 May," RG 472, National Archives, College Park, MD.

7. Truby, interviewed by the author, 5 Aug. 2004; Daily Staff Journal, 23rd ARVN DTOC, U.S. Special Forces Compound, Kontum, Republic of Vietnam, item no. 11, 0001–2400, 14 May 1972, RG 472, National Archives; *Annex K, Kontum,* K-15.

8. "1972 Vietnam Counteroffensive," chap. 7 of *RB-100-2,* vol. 1 of *Reference Book: Selected Readings in Tactics* (Fort Leavenworth, KS: US Army Command and General Staff College, April 1974), 7-24.

9. Quoted in Liebchen, *Kontum,* 43.

10. Jacques Leslie, "S. Vietnam Troops Turn Back Red Attack at Kontum," *Los Angeles Times,* 15 May 1972.

11. Daily Staff Journal, 23rd ARVN DTOC, Kontum, Republic of Vietnam, item nos. 11 and 29, 0001 to 2400, 14 May 1972, RG 472, National Archives.

12. English version/translation of undated ARVN 23rd Infantry Division script for briefing visitors after the Battle of Kontum, Neil Sheehan Papers, Container 96, Folder 4.

13. Daily Staff Journal, 23rd ARVN DTOC, Kontum, Republic of Vietnam, item no. 152, 0001 to 2400, 14 May 1972, RG 472, National Archives.

14. Letter, author to Hugh McInnish, TOW Project officer, Redstone Arsenal, Huntsville, AL, 18 Apr. 1973.

15. *Annex K, Kontum,* K-15; "1972 Vietnam Counteroffensive," 7-24; *The Nguyen Hue Offensive,* Military Assistance Command Directorate of Intelligence Study 73-01 (Saigon: Intelligence Support Liaison Branch, Intelligence Production Division, Directorate of Intelligence, USMACV, 12 Jan. 1973), 19; map, 1:50,000 overlay, made by Lieutenant Colonel James W. Bricker, G-3 adviser, soon after the battle, copy in author's files.

16. Letter, author to family, 16 May 1972.

17. 17th Aviation Group (Combat) Pleiku, Operations Report, Lessons Learned (ORLL), for the period 1 May 1972–31 Oct. 1972, p. 46, NND927622, RG 472, National Archives.

18. John C. Burns, *XM-26 TOW: Birth of the Helicopter as a Tank Buster* (Quantico, VA: Marine Corps Command and Staff College, 1994), 55–56.

19. Leslie, "S. Vietnam Troops Turn Back Red Attack at Kontum"; Rhotenberry, sound recording by Sheehan at Pleiku, 29 Sept 1972, and Kontum battlefield, 2 Oct. 1972.

20. Truby, interviewed by the author, 5 Aug. 2004; Rhotenberry, sound recording by Sheehan at Pleiku, 29 Sept. 1972, and Kontum battlefield, 2 Oct. 1972.

21. Colonel R. B. Rhotenberry, interviewed by Neil Sheehan, undated typed transcript of tape, Neil Sheehan Papers, Container 75, Folder 8.

22. Rhotenberry, sound recording by Sheehan at Pleiku, 29 Sept. 1972, and Kontum battlefield, 2 Oct. 1972.

23. *Annex K, Kontum,* K-15; Rhotenberry, interviewed by Sheehan, undated typed transcript.

24. Angel L. Figueroa (former private first class), interviewed by the author, 9 Oct. 2010, and email to the author, 10 Oct. 2010.

25. The "After Action Report—Task Force Salvo (TOW Missile Systems)" has no unit heading, no date, and no signature, and it was classified only "Confidential."

26. Lewis Sorley, ed., *Vietnam Chronicles: The Abrams Tapes, 1968-1972* (Lubbock: Texas Tech University Press, 2004), 851.

27. *Annex K, Kontum,* K-17.

28. Truby, interviewed by the author, 24 Aug. 2004.

29. Colonel John O. Truby, former senior adviser, 23rd ARVN Division, email to the author, 13 Sept. 2004.

30. Truby, interviewed by the author, 5 Aug. 2004.

31. Letter, author to family, 24 May 1972; Captain (Lieutenant Colonel, Ret.) John R. Finch, email to the author, 18 Apr. 2009.

32. Truby, interviewed by the author, 5 Aug. 2004; *Annex K, Kontum,* K-17, K-18.

33. Message from Vann to Abrams, "Daily Commanders Evaluation for 24 Hours from 1000H 15 May," RG 472, National Archives.

34. Liebchen, *Kontum,* 42–43.

35. Message from Vann to Abrams, "Daily Commanders Evaluation for 24 Hours From 1000H 15 May"; message from Vann to Abrams, "Daily Commanders Evaluation for 24 Hours from 1000H 17 May," RG 472, National Archives; Liebchen, *Kontum,* 45–46.

36. Giap Phuc Hai, MD, email to the author, 7 Nov. 2005.

37. "II CTZ (Corps Tactical Zone) Major Road Net and Airfields," 1:2,000,000-scale map with enemy base areas drawn in by Lieutenant Colonel Stanislaus J. Fuesel, former artillery adviser to ARVN II Corps; original in author's files.

38. Minh's narrative is in "POW Interrogation Report Dated 21 May 1972," transcription by Neil Sheehan, Neil Sheehan Papers, Container 96, Folder 2.

39. "Tells How Reds Died: Chained Inside of Tanks," *Pacific Stars and Stripes,* 18 Apr. 1972.

40. "Kontum Readies for Fight, Families Flown to Safety," *Pacific Stars and Stripes,* 17 May 1972; *Annex K, Kontum,* K-18; Liebchen, *Kontum,* 46.

41. Sorley, ed., *Vietnam Chronicles,* 826, emphasis in original.

15. Struggling to Hold It Together

1. John G. Heslin, *Combat Power: An Ontological Approach* (Newport, RI: US Naval War College, 1978), 88–89; *Annex K, Kontum: The NVA Buildup,*

annex to *United States Military Assistance Command Vietnam (MACV), Command History, January 1972-March 1973*, vol. 2 (Saigon: Military History Branch, Office of the Secretary, Joint Staff, MACV, 1973), K-18; message from John Paul Vann to General Creighton Abrams, "Daily Commanders Evaluation for 24 Hours from 1000H 15 May," RG 472, National Archives, College Park, MD.

2. Quoted in "N. Viet Tanks, Troops Open Attack on Kontum," *Washington Post*, 14 May 1972.

3. Message from Vann to Abrams, "Daily Commanders Evaluation for 24 Hours from 1000H 16 May," RG 472, National Archives.

4. Colonel R. M. Rhotenberry, senior adviser, ARVN 23rd Infantry Division, sound recording by Neil Sheehan at Pleiku, Vietnam, 29 Sept. 1972, and during Jeep tour of Kontum battlefield, 2 Oct. 1972, Vann/Sheehan Collection, RGA 7662-70, Library of Congress, Washington, DC.

5. Message from Vann to Abrams, "Daily Commanders Evaluation for 24 Hours from 1000H 16 May"; Ray L. Bowers, *Tactical Airlift: The U.S. Air Force in Southeast Asia* (Washington, DC: Office of Air Force History, USAF, 1983), 568.

6. Peter A. W. Liebchen, *Kontum: Battle for the Central Highlands, 30 March-10 June 1972*, USAF Southeast Asia Monograph Series, vol. 2, monograph 3, USAF Project Contemporary Historical Examination of Current Operations Report (Washington, DC: USAF, Oct. 1972), 45-46; *Annex K, Kontum*, K-18.

7. Message from Vann to Abrams, "Daily Commanders Evaluation for 24 Hours from 1000H 16 May"; Colonel John O. Truby, former senior adviser, 23rd ARVN Division, email to the author, 5 Aug. 2004.

8. Rhotenberry, sound recording by Sheehan at Pleiku, 29 Sept. 1972, and Kontum battlefield, 2 Oct. 1972.

9. Brigadier General (Major General, Ret.) John G. Hill, deputy senior adviser, II Corps, sound recording by Neil Sheehan at Fort Hood, Texas, 6 July 1976, Vann/Sheehan Collection, RGA 6492-93.

10. Rhotenberry, sound recording by Sheehan at Pleiku, 29 Sept. 1972, and Kontum battlefield, 2 Oct. 1972.

11. John Paul Vann's comments at a 17 May 1972 press conference in Pleiku as described by Matt Franjola, correspondent and photographer, sound recording by Neil Sheehan, 24 May 1972, Vann/Sheehan Collection, RGA 6295-96.

12. Message from Vann to Abrams, "Daily Commanders Evaluation for 24 Hours from 1000H 17 May," RG 472, National Archives.

13. Rhotenberry, sound recording by Sheehan at Pleiku, 29 Sept. 1972, and Kontum battlefield, 2 Oct. 1972.

14. Message from General Creighton Abrams to Spiro Agnew, 1034Z, 17 May 1972, Center of Military History, Fort Leslie J. McNair, Washington, DC.

15. Major Richard C. Gudat, email to Captain (Lieutenant Colonel, Ret.) John R. Finch, 4 Apr. 2006, copy forwarded to the author and in the author's files; message from Vann to Abrams, "Daily Commanders Evalua-

tion for 24 Hours from 1000H 17 May"; message O 1709452 May 1972 from 374 TAW Det 1 Tan Son Nhut AB RVN to PACAF and multiple addressees, "Initial Loss Report," in *374th Tactical Airlift Wing History, 1 Jan.-30 June 1972,* vol. 2 (Maxwell Air Force Base, AL: Department of the Air Force, Air Force Historical Research Agency, 1972); Liebchen, *Kontum,* 46; Captain (Ret.) Ray W. Hall, interviewed by the author, 18 Apr. 2008, Denver.

16. Quoted in Liebchen, *Kontum,* 47.

17. Rhotenberry, sound recording by Sheehan at Pleiku, 29 Sept. 1972, and Kontum battlefield, 2 Oct. 1972; Colonel R. B. Rhotenberry, interviewed by Neil Sheehan, undated typed transcript of tape, Neil Sheehan Papers, Container 75, Folder 8, Library of Congress, Washington, DC.

18. Letter, author to family, 16 May 1972.

19. Captain (Lieutenant Colonel, Ret.) John R. Finch, former G-3 air adviser, 23rd ARVN Division, telephone interview by the author, 29 Mar. 2006.

20. Ibid.

21. Ibid.

22. "POW Interrogation Report Dated 21 May 1972," transcription by Neil Sheehan, Neil Sheehan Papers, Container 96, Folder 2.

23. Finch, interviewed by the author, 29 Mar. 2006.

24. Ibid.

25. Sergeant James N. Barker, US Army language specialist, telephone interview by the author, 17 June 2006.

26. "Viets Push Open Highlands Link," *Pacific Stars and Stripes,* 19 May 1972; message from Vann to Abrams, "Daily Commanders Evaluation for 24 Hours from 1000H 18 May," RG 472, National Archives; "Adviser Reports B52 Helped Cripple 2 NVA Divisions," *Pacific Stars and Stripes,* 18 May 1972; "Viets Push Close to An Loc," *Pacific Stars and Stripes,* 20 May 1972.

27. "B-52 Arc Light Operations," in *The U.S. Air Force in Southeast Asia, 1961-1963,* edited by Carl Berger (Washington, DC: Office of Air Force History, 1982), 177, 182.

28. Message from Vann to Abrams, "Daily Commanders Evaluation for 24 Hours from 1000H 19 May," RG 472, National Archives.

29. *Annex K, Kontum,* K-19.

30. Message from Vann to Abrams, "Daily Commanders Evaluation for 24 Hours from 1000H 18 May"; Liebchen, *Kontum,* 48 (based on Liebchen's interview of Rhotenberry); "B-52 Arc Light Operations," 182.

31. Message from Vann to Abrams, "Daily Commanders Evaluation for 24 Hours from 1000H 19 May"; Heslin, *Combat Power,* 91.

32. Message from Vann to Abrams, "Daily Commanders Evaluation for 24 Hours from 1000H 19 May"; Liebchen, *Kontum,* 49.

33. Lewis Sorley, ed., *Vietnam Chronicles: The Abrams Tapes, 1968-1972* (Lubbock: Texas Tech University Press, 2004), 857, 859.

34. Captain (Lieutenant Colonel Ret.) Brian Sweeney, C-130 aircraft commander, telephone interview by the author, 24 Feb. 2006.

35. *Annex K, Kontum,* K-19; Heslin, *Combat Power,* 91.

36. Message from Vann to Abrams, "Daily Commanders Evaluation for 24 Hours from 1000H 20 May," RG 472, National Archives.

37. *Annex K, Kontum,* K-20.

38. Daily Staff Journal, 23rd ARVN DTOC, U.S. Special Forces Compound, Kontum, Republic of Vietnam, item no. 11, 0001–2400, 21 May 1972, RG 472, National Archives.

39. Message from Vann to Abrams, "Daily Commanders Evaluation for 24 Hours from 1000H 21 May," RG 472, National Archives; *Annex K, Kontum,* K-19; TWX (message) from Vann to Abrams, 0355Z, 21 May, RG 472, National Archives.

40. Message from Vann to Abrams, 1128Z, 21 May 1972, RG 472, National Archives; message from Vann to Abrams, "Daily Commanders Evaluation for 24 Hours from 1000H 21 May."

41. Message from Vann to Abrams, "Daily Commanders Evaluation for 24 Hours from 1000H 21 May"; *Annex K, Kontum,* K-20; Liebchen, *Kontum,* 50.

42. Rhotenberry, sound recording by Sheehan at Pleiku, 29 Sept. 1972, and Kontum battlefield, 2 Oct. 1972.

43. *Annex K, Kontum,* K-18.

44. Rhotenberry, sound recording by Sheehan at Pleiku, 29 Sept. 1972, and Kontum battlefield, 2 Oct. 1972.

45. "POW Interrogation Report Dated 9 Dec. 1972," transcription by Neil Sheehan, Neil Sheehan Papers, Container 96, Folder 2.

46. Lieutenant Colonel (Ret.) Stanislaus J. Fuesel, former artillery adviser to ARVN II Corps, telephone interview by the author, 27 June 2005; message from General Creighton Abrams to corps senior advisers, 0946Z, 16 May 1972, Center of Military History, Fort Leslie J. McNair, Washington, DC; message from Hill to Abrams, "Daily Commanders Evaluation for 24 Hours from 1000H 24 May," RG 472, National Archives.

47. Rhotenberry, sound recording by Sheehan at Pleiku, 29 Sept. 1972, and Kontum battlefield, 2 Oct. 1972.

48. David E. Ott, "1972 Enemy Offensive," *Field Artillery Journal* 45, no. 1 (Jan.–Feb. 1977), 46.

49. Ibid.

50. Ibid.

51. Message from Vann to Abrams, "Daily Commanders Evaluation for 24 Hours from 1000H 22 May," RG 472, National Archives.

52. *Annex K, Kontum,* K-21.

53. Ngo Quang Truong, *The Easter Offensive of 1972,* Indochina Monograph Series (Washington, DC: US Army Center of Military History, 1980), 101; article title not known, *New York Times,* 22 May 1972.

16. "Brother, This Is Going to Be It!"

1. "Kontum Hit from 3 Sides," *Washington Post,* 27 May 1972.

2. David J. Paine, "Kontum Is Next—and It Knows It," *Pacific Stars and Stripes,* 26 May 1972.

3. Daily Staff Journal, 23rd ARVN DTOC, US Special Forces Compound, Kontum, Republic of Vietnam, 0001–2400, 23 May 1972, RG 472, National Archives, College Park, MD.

4. John G. Hill, William J. Maddox Jr., and James H. Patterson, "Discussions of Combat Use of Helicopters," *U.S. Army Aviation Digest* 22, no. 3 (Mar. 1976), 29.

5. Brigadier General (Major General, Ret.) John G. Hill, deputy senior adviser, II Corps, sound recording by Neil Sheehan at Fort Hood, Texas, 6 July 1976, Vann/Sheehan Collection, RGA 6492–93, Library of Congress, Washington, DC.

6. "Kontum Hit from 3 Sides," *Washington Post*, 13 May 1972.

7. Message from Hill to Abrams, "Daily Commanders Evaluation for 24 Hours from 1000H 24 May," RG 472, National Archives; *Annex K, Kontum: The NVA Buildup*, annex to *United States Military Assistance Command Vietnam (MACV), Command History, January 1972–March 1973*, vol. 2 (Saigon: Military History Branch, Office of the Secretary, Joint Staff, MACV, 1973), K-21.

8. Captain (Lieutenant Colonel, Ret.) Brian Sweeney, C-130 aircraft commander, telephone interview by the author, 24 Feb. 2006.

9. Messages from Brigadier General John G. Hill to General Creighton Abrams, "Daily Commanders Evaluation for 24 Hours from 1000H 23 May" and "Daily Commanders Evaluation for 24 Hours from 1000H 24 May," RG 472, National Archives; Peter A. W. Liebchen, *Kontum: Battle for the Central Highlands, 30 March-10 June 1972*, USAF Southeast Asia Monograph Series, vol. 2, monograph 3, USAF Project Contemporary Historical Examination of Current Operations Report (Washington, DC: USAF, Oct. 1972), 50.

10. Ngo Quang Truong, *The Easter Offensive of 1972*, Indochina Monograph Series (Washington, DC: US Army Center of Military History, 1980), 102.

11. Colonel R. M. Rhotenberry, senior adviser, ARVN 23rd Infantry Division, sound recording by Neil Sheehan at Pleiku, Vietnam, 29 Sept. 1972, and during Jeep tour of Kontum battlefield, 2 Oct. 1972, Vann/Sheehan Collection, RGA 7662–70.

12. *The Nguyen Hue Offensive*, Military Assistance Command Directorate of Intelligence Study 73-01 (Saigon: Intelligence Support Liaison Branch, Intelligence Production Division, Directorate of Intelligence, USMACV, 12 Jan. 1973), 19; English version/translation of undated ARVN 23rd Infantry Division script for briefing visitors after the Battle of Kontum, Neil Sheehan Papers, Container 96, Folder 4, Manuscript Division, Library of Congress, Washington, DC; overlay of 1:25,000 map made by Lieutenant Colonel James W. Bricker, G-3 adviser, shortly after the battle, copy in author's files. (These contemporary sources differ on the identity of enemy regiments and their routes of attack.)

13. Colonel R. B. Rhotenberry, interviewed by Neil Sheehan, undated typed transcript of tape, Neil Sheehan Papers, Container 75, Folder 8.

14. *Annex K, Kontum*, K-22; Ngo, *The Easter Offensive of 1972*, 99.

15. Rhotenberry, sound recording by Sheehan at Pleiku, 29 Sept. 1972, and Kontum battlefield, 2 Oct. 1972.

16. Ibid.

17. Master Sergeant Richard Ivars (Ret.), former C-130 loadmaster with 21st Tactical Air Squadron, telephone interview by the author, 18 July 2005; Ray L. Bowers, *Tactical Airlift: The U.S. Air Force in Southeast Asia* (Washington, DC: Office of Air Force History, USAF, 1983), 68.

18. *Annex K, Kontum,* K-22.

19. Rhotenberry, sound recording by Sheehan at Pleiku, 29 Sept. 1972, and Kontum battlefield, 2 Oct. 1972; Captain (Lieutenant Colonel, Ret.) John R. Finch, email to the author, 20 June 2006.

20. *Annex K, Kontum,* K-22; message from Hill to Abrams, "Daily Commanders Evaluation for 24 Hours from 1000H 24 May"; message from Colonel Joseph Pizzi to General Creighton Abrams, "Daily Commanders Evaluation for 24 Hours from 1000H 25 May," RG 472, National Archives; Stephen James, Huey pilot, "Pallbearer 2," B Troop, 7th Cavalry, 17th Air Cavalry Regiment, email to the author, 17 Jan. 2006.

21. Message from John Paul Vann to General Creighton Abrams, "Daily Commanders Evaluation for 24 Hours from 1000H 26 May," RG 472, National Archives.

22. *Annex K, Kontum,* K-22.

23. Finch, interviewed by the author, 29 Mar. 2006.

24. "U.S. Adviser: Red Offensive 'Major Blunder' by N. Viets," *Pacific Stars and Stripes,* 26 May 1972.

25. "Letter of Instruction Number 3-72," SRAG, 25 May 1972, RG 472, Box 3, Historian, Background Files, National Archives.

26. Sergeant James N. Barker, US Army language specialist, telephone interview by the author, 17 June 2006.

17. "You Are Going to Be Overrun"

1. Matt Franjola, "Smart Bombs Wreck Key N. Viet Bridge," *Pacific Stars and Stripes,* 29 May 1972.

2. Message from Colonel Joseph Pizzi to General Creighton Abrams, "Daily Commanders Evaluation for 24 Hours from 1000H 25 May," RG 472, National Archives, College Park, MD; "Foe's Thrust into Kontum Is Repulsed," *Washington Post,* 26 May 1972.

3. Arthur Higbee, "N. Viet Tanks Sweep Down on Kontum; 7 Knocked Out," *Pacific Stars and Stripes,* 28 May 1972; message from John Paul Vann to General Creighton Abrams, "Daily Commanders Evaluation for 24 Hours from 1000H 26 May," RG 472, National Archives.

4. Colonel R. M. Rhotenberry, senior adviser, ARVN 23rd Infantry Division, sound recording by Neil Sheehan at Pleiku, Vietnam, 29 Sept. 1972, and during Jeep tour of Kontum battlefield, 2 Oct. 1972, Vann/Sheehan Collection, RGA 7662-70, Library of Congress, Washington, DC.

5. *Annex K, Kontum: The NVA Buildup,* annex to *United States Military Assistance Command Vietnam (MACV), Command History, January 1972-March*

1973, vol. 2 (Saigon: Military History Branch, Office of the Secretary, Joint Staff, MACV, 1973), K-22, K-23.

6. Brigadier General (Major General, Ret.) John G. Hill, deputy senior adviser, II Corps, sound recording by Neil Sheehan at Fort Hood, Texas, 6 July 1976, Vann/Sheehan Collection, RGA 6492–93; *Annex K, Kontum,* K-23.

7. John G. Hill, William J. Maddox Jr., and James H. Patterson, "Discussions of Combat Use of Helicopters," *U.S. Army Aviation Digest* 22, no. 3 (Mar. 1976), 29.

8. Captain (Lieutenant Colonel, Ret.) John R. Finch, former G-3 air adviser, 23rd ARVN Division, telephone interview by the author, 29 Mar. 2006.

9. Letter, author to Hugh McInnish, TOW Project officer, Redstone Arsenal, Huntsville, AL, 18 Apr. 1973.

10. Message from Vann to Abrams, "Daily Commanders Evaluation for 24 Hours from 1000H 26 May."

11. Sir Robert Thompson, no title, in *The Lessons of Vietnam,* edited by Scott W. Thompson and Donaldson D. Frizzell (New York: Crane, Russak, 1977), 104.

12. 17th Aviation Group (Combat) Pleiku, Operations Report, Lessons Learned (ORLL), for the period 1 May 1972–31 Oct. 1972, Enclosure 10, p. 46, NND927622, RG 472, National Archives; Philip D. Chinnery, *Vietnam: The Helicopter War* (Annapolis, MD: Naval Institute Press, 1991), 162–63.

13. *Annex K, Kontum,* K-22; message from Vann to Abrams, "Daily Commanders Evaluation for 24 Hours from 1000H 26 May."

14. Hill, sound recording by Sheehan, 6 July 1976.

15. *Annex K, Kontum,* K-22.

16. Message from Pizzi to Abrams, "Daily Commanders Evaluation for 24 Hours from 1000H 25 May."

17. *Annex K, Kontum,* K-22.

18. Higbee, "N. Viet Tanks Sweep Down on Kontum."

19. "S. Viets Battle for Kontum; Report Reds Lose 12 Tanks," *Chicago Tribune,* 27 May 1972.

20. "The First Large-Scale Strategic Offensive in the Highlands Theater," in *History of the Central Highlands People's Armed Forces in the Anti-U.S. War of Resistance for National Salvation,* translated by US Government Foreign Broadcast Information Service (Hanoi: People's Army Publishing House, 1980), 12.

21. Message from Vann to Abrams, "Daily Commanders Evaluation for 24 Hours from 1000H 26 May."

22. "Province Report," Kontum Province, Province Senior Adviser's Monthly Reports, Semi-Annual Review, 1 July 1972, Lieutenant Colonel Willard B. Esplin, RG 472, National Archives.

23. Message from Vann to Abrams, "Daily Commanders Evaluation for 24 Hours from 1000H 26 May"; *Annex K, Kontum,* K-23.

24. Message from Vann to Abrams, "Daily Commanders Evaluation for 24 Hours from 1000H 26 May"; message from Vann to Abrams, "Daily

Commanders Evaluation for 24 Hours from 1000H 27 May," RG 472, National Archives; Rhotenberry, sound recording by Sheehan at Pleiku, 29 Sept. 1972, and Kontum battlefield, 2 Oct. 1972.

25. Message from Vann to Abrams, "Daily Commanders Evaluation for 24 Hours from 1000H 27 May."

26. *Annex K, Kontum,* K-23.

27. Message from Vann to Abrams, "Daily Commanders Evaluation for 24 Hours from 1000H 26 May"; message from Vann to Abrams, "Daily Commanders Evaluation for 24 Hours from 1000H 27 May"; *Annex K, Kontum,* K-23.

28. Rhotenberry, sound recording by Sheehan at Pleiku, 29 Sept. 1972, and Kontum battlefield, 2 Oct. 1972.

29. Topographic map of Kontum City, Vietnam, map, 1:12,500 scale, with acetate covering and friendly (black) and enemy (red) positions drawn on it by Colonel R. B. Rhotenberry, senior adviser to ARVN 23rd Infantry Division in late May 1972, Neil Sheehan Papers, Container 96, Folder 3, Manuscript Division, Library of Congress, Washington, DC.

30. Rhotenberry, sound recording by Sheehan at Pleiku, 29 Sept. 1972, and Kontum battlefield, 2 Oct. 1972.

31. Sam McGowan, email to the author, 14 June 2006.

32. Message from Vann to Abrams, "Daily Commanders Evaluation for 24 Hours from 1000H 27 May"; Ray L. Bowers, *Tactical Airlift: The U.S. Air Force in Southeast Asia* (Washington, DC: Office of Air Force History, USAF, 1983), 574.

33. Rhotenberry, sound recording by Sheehan at Pleiku, 29 Sept. 1972, and Kontum battlefield, 2 Oct. 1972.

34. Ibid.

35. Message from Vann to Abrams, "Daily Commanders Evaluation for 24 Hours from 1000H 27 May."

36. *Annex K, Kontum,* K-24.

37. Rhotenberry, sound recording by Sheehan at Pleiku, 29 Sept. 1972, and Kontum battlefield, 2 Oct. 1972.

38. Message from Vann to Abrams, "Daily Commanders Evaluation for 24 Hours from 1000H 27 May."

39. Colonel (Ret.) James W. Bricker, email to the author, 1 Mar. 2005.

40. Quoted in C. James Novak, "Linebacker II," *The Retired Officer Magazine* (Nov. 1992), 41.

41. Franjola, "Smart Bombs Wreck Key N. Viet Bridge."

18. The Dirty Job of Killing

1. Message from John Paul Vann to General Creighton Abrams, "Daily Commanders Evaluation for 24 Hours from 1000H 28 May," RG 472, National Archives, College Park, MD.

2. Message from Vann to Abrams, "Daily Commanders Evaluation for 24 Hours from 1000H 27 May," RG 472, National Archives; *Annex K, Kontum: The NVA Buildup,* annex to *United States Military Assistance Command*

Vietnam (MACV), Command History, January 1972-March 1973, vol. 2 (Saigon: Military History Branch, Office of the Secretary, Joint Staff, MACV, 1973), K-24.

3. Message from Vann to Abrams, "Daily Commanders Evaluation for 24 Hours from 1000H 27 May."

4. Colonel R. M. Rhotenberry, senior adviser, ARVN 23rd Infantry Division, sound recording by Neil Sheehan at Pleiku, Vietnam, 29 Sept. 1972, and during Jeep tour of Kontum battlefield, 2 Oct. 1972, Vann/Sheehan Collection, RGA 7662–70, Library of Congress, Washington, DC; Colonel R. B. Rhotenberry, interviewed by Neil Sheehan, undated typed transcript of tape, Neil Sheehan Papers, Container 75, Folder 8, Library of Congress, Washington, DC.

5. Rhotenberry, sound recording by Sheehan at Pleiku, 29 Sept. 1972, and Kontum battlefield, 2 Oct. 1972.

6. Arthur Higbee, "N. Viet Tanks Sweep Down on Kontum; 7 Knocked Out," *Pacific Stars and Stripes,* 28 May 1972.

7. "Reds Batter An Loc Relief Column," *Pacific Stars and Stripes,* 31 May 1972.

8. Message from Vann to Abrams, "Daily Commanders Evaluation for 24 Hours from 1000H 28 May."

9. John G. Hill, William J. Maddox Jr., and James H. Patterson, "Discussions of Combat Use of Helicopters," *U.S. Army Aviation Digest* 22, no. 3 (Mar. 1976), 1–5, 28–29; 17th Aviation Group (Combat) Pleiku, Operations Report, Lessons Learned (ORLL), for the period 1 May 1972–31 Oct. 1972, pp. 6, 31, NND927622, RG 472, National Archives.

10. Matt Franjola, "Viets Take Most of Kontum as Reds Appear in Retreat," *Pacific Stars and Stripes,* 31 May 1972.

11. Quoted in Peter A. W. Liebchen, *Kontum: Battle for the Central Highlands, 30 March-10 June 1972,* USAF Southeast Asia Monograph Series, vol. 2, monograph 3, USAF Project Contemporary Historical Examination of Current Operations Report (Washington, DC: USAF, Oct. 1972), 83.

12. "Sharp-Eyed Pilot Leads Cobras to NVA Tank," *The Observer* (MACV), 16 June 1972.

13. *Annex K, Kontum,* K-24.

14. Ibid., K-24.

19. All Over but the Shooting?

1. Letter, author to family, 22 May 1972.

2. Colonel R. M. Rhotenberry, senior adviser, ARVN 23rd Infantry Division, sound recording by Neil Sheehan at Pleiku, Vietnam, 29 Sept. 1972, and during Jeep tour of Kontum battlefield, 2 Oct. 1972, Vann/Sheehan Collection, RGA 7662–70, Library of Congress, Washington, DC.

3. Message from John Paul Vann to General Creighton Abrams, "Daily Commanders Evaluation for 24 Hours from 1000H 29 May," RG 472, National Archives, College Park, MD.

4. Message from Vann to Abrams, "Daily Commanders Evaluation for 24 Hours from 1000H 28 May," RG 472, National Archives.

5. Letters, author to family, 29 and 30 May 1972.

6. Message from Vann to Abrams, "Daily Commanders Evaluation for 24 Hours from 1000H 30 May," RG 472, National Archives; letter, author to family, 31 May 1972; *Annex K, Kontum: The NVA Buildup,* annex to *United States Military Assistance Command Vietnam (MACV), Command History, January 1972-March 1973,* vol. 2 (Saigon: Military History Branch, Office of the Secretary, Joint Staff, MACV, 1973), K-24.

7. Ngo Quang Truong, *The Easter Offensive of 1972,* Indochina Monograph Series (Washington, DC: US Army Center of Military History, 1980), 103; *Annex K, Kontum,* K-24, K-25.

8. Letter, author to family, 31 May 1972.

9. Ibid.

10. Colonel John O. Truby, former senior adviser, 23rd ARVN Division, interviewed by Neil Sheehan, date unknown, Neil Sheehan Papers, Container 88, Folder 9, Manuscript Division, Library of Congress, Washington, DC; Colonel John O. Truby, former senior adviser, 23rd ARVN Division, interviewed by Neil Sheehan, date unknown, typed transcript, Vann/Sheehan Collection, RGA 6492–93.

11. Lieutenant Colonel (Colonel, Ret.) James W. Bricker, email to the author, 13 Mar. 2005.

12. Captain (Lieutenant Colonel, Ret.) John R. Finch, former G-3 air adviser, 23rd ARVN Division, personal notes written in late May and early June 1972 and shared with the author.

13. Message from Vann to Abrams, "Daily Commanders Evaluation for 24 Hours from 1000H 30 May."

14. *Chien Thang Kontum,* tu 14-4-72 den 7-72, 22, Neil Sheehan Papers, Container 96, Folder 3.

15. Letters, author to family, 30 and 31 May 1972.

20. Finishing the Job

1. *Annex K, Kontum: The NVA Buildup,* annex to *United States Military Assistance Command Vietnam (MACV), Command History, January 1972-March 1973,* vol. 2 (Saigon: Military History Branch, Office of the Secretary, Joint Staff, MACV, 1973), K-25; transcript of an audio tape of Vann's press conference recorded by Matt Franjola, Neil Sheehan Papers, Container 51, Folder 9, Manuscript Division, Library of Congress, Washington, DC; "Phantoms Down 2 MiGs," *Pacific Stars and Stripes,* 3 June 1972.

2. Daily Staff Journal or Duty Officer's Log, SRAG, 0001, 31 May 1972, to 2400, 31 May 1972, RG 472, National Archives, College Park, MD.

3. "Mass before and after," Neil Sheehan Papers, Container 96, Folder 5.

4. "Province Report," Kontum Province, Province Senior Adviser's Monthly Reports, 1 June 1972, Stephen W. Bachinski, RG 472, National Archives.

5. Message from John Paul Vann to General Creighton Abrams, "Spot

Reports Following Up Today's Ops Summary," 1014Z, 31 May 1972, RG 472, National Archives; message from Brigadier General John G. Hill to General Creighton Abrams, "Daily Commanders Evaluation for 24 Hours from 1000H 31 May," RG 472, National Archives.

6. "Over Half Million under Red Control as Drive Continues," *Pacific Stars and Stripes,* 31 May 1972.

7. Translation of captured NVA message logs, 19 Mar. to 3 June 1972, Report no. 6 028 0474 72, dated 2 Oct. 1972, Reference DIRM 1D, 1D1, 1D2, item no. 2131909038, Texas Tech University Virtual Vietnam Archives, available online at http://www.vietnam.ttu.edu/virtualarchive/.

8. Taki Theodoracopulos, "What Makes Charlie Run?" *National Review,* 7 July 1972, 743.

9. Military History Institute of Vietnam, *Victory in Vietnam: The Official History of the People's Army of Vietnam, 1954-1975,* translated by Merle L. Pribbenow, foreword by William J. Duiker (Lawrence: University Press of Kansas, 2002), 294.

10. Message from Hill to Abrams, "Daily Commanders Evaluation for 24 Hours from 1000H 31 May."

11. Message from Vann to Abrams, "Daily Commanders Evaluation for 24 Hours from 1000H 30 May," RG 472, National Archives; message from Vann to Abrams, "Spot Reports Following Up Today's Ops Summary," 1014Z, 31 May 1972; "Saigon Forces Recover Some Parts of Kontum," *Washington Post,* 1 June 1972.

12. Letter, author to family, 1 June 1972.

13. Shelby L. Stanton, *Vietnam Order of Battle* (New York: Galahad Books, 1986), 347.

14. Letter, author to family, 1 June 1972.

15. Message from Vann to Abrams, "Spot Reports Following Up Today's Ops Summary," 1014Z, 31 May 1972.

16. Message from Vann to Abrams, "Daily Commanders Evaluation for 24 Hours from 1000H 2 June," RG 472, National Archives.

17. Captain (Lieutenant Colonel, Ret.) John R. Finch, former G-3 air adviser, 23rd ARVN Division, email to the author, 14 July 2006.

18. Dave Millard, email to the author, 14 June 2005.

Epilogue. The End of the Fight

1. Ray L. Bowers, *Tactical Airlift: The U.S. Air Force in Southeast Asia* (Washington, DC: Office of Air Force History, USAF, 1983), 559, 570.

2. "New Missiles Hit Hard in Vietnam," *Pacific Stars and Stripes,* 3 June 1972.

3. Colonel R. M. Rhotenberry, senior adviser, ARVN 23rd Infantry Division, sound recording by Neil Sheehan at Pleiku, Vietnam, 29 Sept. 1972, and during Jeep tour of Kontum battlefield, 2 Oct. 1972, Vann/Sheehan Collection, RGA 7662–70, Library of Congress, Washington, DC; message from John Paul Vann to General Creighton Abrams, "Daily Commanders Evaluation for 24 Hours from 1000H 8 June," RG 472, National Archives, College Park, MD.

4. Colonel R. M. Rhotenberry, interviewed by Neil Sheehan, undated typed transcript of tape, Neil Sheehan Papers, Container 75, Folder 8, Library of Congress, Washington, DC; Rhotenberry, sound recording by Sheehan, Pleiku, 29 Sept. 1972, and Kontum battlefield, 2 Oct. 1972.

5. Lewis B. Sorley, "Courage and Blood: South Vietnam's Repulse of the 1972 Easter Invasion," *Parameters* (U.S. Army War College) 29, no. 2 (1999), 42.

6. Hand-written questions by Neil Sheehan and 30 Sept. 1972 answers by Captain Christopher E. Scudder, and Captain Christopher E. Scudder, air operations adviser, II Corps Headquarters, interviewed by Neil Sheehan, undated notes by Sheehan, Neil Sheehan Papers, Container 122, Folder 19.

7. Neil Sheehan, *A Bright Shining Lie: John Paul Vann and America in Vietnam* (New York: Random House, 1988), 785–86; Rhotenberry, interviewed by Sheehan, undated typed transcript of tape.

8. Lieutenant (Lieutenant Colonel, Ret.) Bart J. Engram, email to the author, 26 Apr. 2005.

9. Rhotenberry, interviewed by Sheehan, undated typed transcript of audio tape; Sheehan, *A Bright Shining Lie,* 786, where Sheehan describes Vann's death in detail.

10. Sheehan, *A Bright Shining Lie,* 790.

11. Ibid., 32; B. G. Burkett and Glenna Whitley, *Stolen Valor: How the Vietnam Generation Was Robbed of Its Heroes and Its History* (Dallas: Verity Press, 1998), 607.

12. 17th Aviation Group (Combat) Pleiku, Operations Report, Lessons Learned (ORLL), for the period 1 May–31 Oct. 1972, Inclosure [*sic*] 10, pp. 46–48, NND927622, RG 472, National Archives.

13. John C. Burns, *XM-26 TOW: Birth of the Helicopter as a Tank Buster* (Quantico, VA: Marine Corps Command and Staff College, 1994), 15.

14. Quoted in Gene Famiglietti, "TOWs on Target, An Ace Dealing Weapon," *Redstone Rocket,* 26 July 1972, reprinted from *Army Times,* 26 July 1972.

15. Philip D. Chinnery, *Vietnam: The Helicopter War* (Annapolis, MD: Naval Institute Press, 1991), 163; S. L. Christine, "1st Combat Aerial TOW Team: Helicopter vs Armor," *U.S. Army Aviation Digest* 20, no. 2 (Feb. 1974), 5.

16. Jack G. Heslin (Lieutenant Colonel, Ret.), email to the author, 1 Mar. 2005.

17. Burns, *XM-26 TOW,* 55, 68, 70.

18. Message from Vann to Abrams, "Daily Commanders Evaluation for 24 Hours from 1000H 26 May," RG 472, National Archives.

19. Ian Ward, "Why Giap Did It: Report from Saigon," in *North Vietnam's Blitzkrieg: An Interim Assessment,* edited by Brian Crozier (London: Institute for Study of Conflict, Oct. 1972), 4.

20. *The Nguyen Hue Offensive,* Military Assistance Command Directorate of Intelligence Study 73-01 (Saigon: Intelligence Support Liaison Branch, Intelligence Production Division, Directorate of Intelligence, USMACV, 12 Jan. 1973), 5.

21. James G. Lowenstein and Richard M. Moose, *Vietnam: May 1972*, a staff report for the Committee on Foreign Relations, US Senate (Washington, DC: US Government Printing Office, 1972), 11.

22. Giap Phuc Hai, MD, interviewed by the author, 18 Apr. 2008, Denver.

23. Lewis Sorley, ed., *Vietnam Chronicles: The Abrams Tapes, 1968-1972* (Lubbock: Texas Tech University Press, 2004), 874.

24. Ibid.; Peter A. W. Liebchen, *Kontum: Battle for the Central Highlands, 30 March-10 June 1972*, USAF Southeast Asia Monograph Series, vol. 2, monograph 3, USAF Project Contemporary Historical Examination of Current Operations Report (Washington, DC: USAF, Oct. 1972), 67–68.

25. Lowenstein and Moose, *Vietnam*, 10.

26. Lieutenant Colonel (Ret.) Stanislaus J. Fuesel, former artillery adviser to ARVN II Corps, telephone interview by the author, 27 June 2005.

27. Liebchen, *Kontum*, 67–68.

28. Lewis B. Sorley, *A Better War: The Unexamined Victories and Final Tragedies of America's Last Years in Vietnam* (New York: Harcourt Brace, 1999), 337.

29. "South Viet Nam: Pulling Itself Together," *Time*, 22 May 1972.

30. Harry G. Summers Jr., "Snatching Victory from Defeat," *Vietnam* (Apr. 1999), 38. George D. Moss, *Vietnam: An American Ordeal* (Upper Saddle River, NJ: Prentice Hall, 1998), 386; Lewis Sorley, *Reassessing ARVN* (pamphlet produced from lecture) (Lubbock: Texas Tech University, 17 Mar. 2006), 26.

31. Douglas Kinnard, *The War Managers: American Generals Reflect on Vietnam* (Burlington: University of Vermont, 1999), 148–49.

32. Michael Clodfelter, *Vietnam in Military Statistics: A History of the Indochina Wars, 1772-1991* (Jefferson, NC: McFarland, 1995), 199.

33. Lowenstein and Moose, *Vietnam*, 4–5.

34. Dale Andradé, *Trial by Fire: The 1972 Easter Offensive, America's Last Vietnam Battle* (New York: Hippocrene Books, 1995), 521.

35. John D. Howard, "They Were Good Ol' Boys! An Infantryman Remembers An Loc and the Air Force," *Air University Review* 26, no. 2 (Jan.–Feb. 1975), 35.

36. Sorley, ed., *Vietnam Chronicles*, 867–68, emphasis in original.

37. Dave R. Palmer, *Summons of the Trumpet: U.S.-Vietnam in Perspective* (San Rafael, CA: Presidio Press, 1978), 255.

38. Quoted in Lowenstein and Moose, *Vietnam*, 2.

39. Harry G. Summers Jr., *On Strategy: A Critical Analysis of the Vietnam War* (Novato, CA: Presidio Press, 1982), 1.

Selected Bibliography

Although not perfect, the most accurate, official, blow-by-blow account of the battle is *United States Military Assistance Command Vietnam (MACV), Command History, January 1972-March 1973,* 2 vols., especially the annex to volume 2, *Annex K, Kontum: The NVA Buildup,* prepared by the Military History Branch, Office of the Secretary, Joint Staff, MACV. Lieutenant Gary R. Swingle interviewed participants soon after the battle while memories were still fresh, maps were still on hand, and many of the defensive positions, destroyed aircraft, and dead tanks were still in place. There are only minor differences between Swingle's final draft and the published history, but he received no credit as the author.

Contemporary accounts recorded in the hectic confusion of battle were sometimes less accurate than later accounts based on additional information. The Daily Staff Journal or Duty Officer's Log was a standard form used by all US Army headquarters from the adviser teams in the field to MACV headquarters in Saigon. These logs are useful in confirming the date and time of some actions, but most entries were extremely brief, and some were inaccurate or incomplete initial reports. Nevertheless, they were often the basis for later narrative accounts produced by various headquarters or historians. Another useful source for what happened and when it happened is the Daily Commanders Evaluation that the II Corps senior adviser, Mr. John Paul Vann, sent to the MACV commander, General Creighton W. Abrams, in Saigon. Although these messages ostensibly cover a 24-hour period starting with 1000Z each morning, Vann sometimes discussed actions that took place earlier than the period his evaluation was supposed to cover, which can be confusing to a researcher.

The most useful repositories were the Modern Military Records of the National Archives at Archives II in College Park, Maryland; the US Army Center of Military History at Fort Leslie J. McNair in Washington, DC; the US Army Heritage and Education Center at Carlisle Barracks, Pennsylvania; and the Library of Congress in Washington, DC. The Library of the US Army Command and General Staff College at Fort Leavenworth, Kansas; the US Marine Corps Historical Center in the Washington Navy Yard; the Vietnam Archive at Texas Tech University in Lubbock; and the USAF Historical Research Agency at Maxwell AFB, Alabama, also have relevant documents. Some items at the Library of Congress and in the Modern Military Records at Archives II were still classified almost 30 years after the Vietnam War ended. Having them declassified was usually a lengthy process and sometimes took several years. The staffs at all these facilities were knowledgeable and helpful.

Except for personal papers, personal electronic records, and specific items from archives, the sources cited in the endnotes are included in this bibliography. The former items are cited only in the notes. The bibliography also includes some sources not cited in the notes.

Interviews

Most interviews were conducted by the author in person or by telephone, letter, or email. Journalist and author Neil Sheehan donated his sound recordings, typed transcripts, and handwritten notes on his interviews to the Library of Congress. When material from them is used, this information is included in the endnote. The three men interviewed by Neil Sheehan only are indicated by (S) in the list given here. Ranks and assignments during the battle are as of June 1972. The date, place, and type of each interview are given in the note citations.

Barker, James N. Sergeant, US Army Vietnamese language specialist.

Bricker, James W. "Bill." Lieutenant colonel, G-3 adviser, 23rd ARVN Division.

Cao Van Vien. ARVN general and chief of Joint General Staff. (S)

Cloninger, James M. Lieutenant, 3rd ARVN Armored Cavalry Regiment adviser.

Duck, William A. Major, B-52 navigator who flew Arc Light missions.

Engram, Bart J. Lieutenant, G-2 Targeting Branch, ARVN II Corps.

Finch, John R. Lieutenant colonel (ret.), G-3 air adviser, 23rd ARVN Division.

Fuesel, Stanislaus J. Lieutenant colonel, artillery adviser, ARVN II Corps.

Giap Phuc Hai. Captain (doctor), commander 230th ARVN Medical Company.

Gudat, Richard C. Major, G-4 adviser, 23rd ARVN Division.

Hall, Raymond W. Captain, signal adviser, 23rd ARVN Division.

Heslin, John G. Captain, pilot, and operations officer, 17th Combat Aviation Group.

Hill, John G., Jr. Brigadier general, deputy senior adviser, ARVN II Corps. (S)

Ivars, Richard. Sergeant, C-130 loadmaster, 21st Tactical Air Squadron.

James, Stephen. Captain, Huey helicopter pilot, "Pallbearer 32," B Troop, 7th Squadron, 17th Air Cavalry Regiment.

Kaplan, Phillip. Colonel, senior adviser to 22nd ARVN Division.

Kleiner, Martin S. Captain, operations officer and forward detachment commander, C Troop, 7th Squadron, 17th Air Cavalry Regiment.

Lovings, Wade B. Major, deputy senior adviser, 44th ARVN Infantry Regiment.

Ly Tong Ba. Brigadier general, commanding general 23rd ARVN Infantry Division.

McClellan, James R. Lieutenant, forward air controller, Covey 507.

McInnish, Hugh J., Jr. Civilian engineer, TOW Project officer.

Millard, David M. Sergeant, crew chief, 57th Assault Helicopter Company.

Mulkey, Reed C. Lieutenant colonel, USAF C-130 pilot.

Page, William B. Specialist/4, Company D, 1st Battalion, 12th Cavalry.

Peters, John E. "Jed." Captain, adviser, 72nd Border Ranger Battalion, FSB 5.

Plaster, John L. Staff sergeant, MACV SOG soldier and Covey FAC rider.

Rhotenberry, R. M. Colonel, senior adviser, 23rd ARVN Infantry Division. (S)

Scudder, Christopher E. Captain, air operations adviser, ARVN II Corps.

Stein, James E. Captain, scout helicopter pilot, B & H Troops, 7th Squadron, 17th Air Cavalry Regiment.

Stevens, Lowell W. Master sergeant, MACV SOG soldier, and Covey FAC rider.

Sweeney, Brian. Captain, C-130 pilot, 21st Tactical Air Squadron.

Truby, John O. Colonel, senior adviser, 23rd ARVN Infantry Division.

Truhan, Stephen M. Captain, adviser, ARVN 95th Border Ranger Battalion.

Vaughan, James T. Captain, II Corps TOC duty officer.

Wear, George E. Brigadier general, deputy senior adviser, ARVN II Corps.

Secondary Sources

The 1972 Quang Tri Offensive Campaign (Secret). Hanoi: Military Art Faculty of the Military Science Institute, 1976.

"1972 Vietnam Counteroffensive." Chap. 7 of *RB-100-2*, vol. 1 of *Reference Book: Selected Readings in Tactics*. Fort Leavenworth, KS: US Army Command and General Staff College, April 1974.

"350,000 Refugees on Move." *Pacific Stars and Stripes*, 3 May 1972.

374th Tactical Airlift Wing History, 1 Jan.-30 June 1972. Vol. 2. Maxwell Air Force Base, AL: Department of the Air Force, Air Force Historical Research Agency, 1972.

"5 Safe after 2 Weeks in Jungle: A Most Dangerous Game of Hide-and-Seek." *Pacific Stars and Stripes*, 9 May 1972.

"Adviser Reports B52 Helped Cripple 2 NVA Divisions." *Pacific Stars and Stripes*, 18 May 1972.

"The Air War Grows." *Newsweek*, 24 Apr. 1972.

Andradé, Dale. *America's Last Vietnam Battle: Halting Hanoi's 1972 Easter Offensive*. Lawrence: University Press of Kansas, 2001. (Newer edition of *Trial by Fire*.)

——. "Tigers, Blue Dragons, and White Horses." *Vietnam* (Dec. 1989): 47–53.

——. *Trial by Fire: The 1972 Easter Offensive, America's Last Vietnam Battle*. New York: Hippocrene Books, 1995.

——. "Why Westmoreland Was Right." *Vietnam* (Apr. 2009): 26–32.

Annex K, Kontum: The NVA Buildup. Annex to *United States Military Assistance Command Vietnam (MACV), Command History, January 1972-March*

1973, vol. 2. Saigon: Military History Branch, Office of the Secretary, Joint Staff, MACV, 1973.

"Army Tank Ace KOs 8." *Armed Forces Journal* (Aug. 1972): 24.

"Army Tank Aces." *Armed Forces Journal* (July 1972): 15-16.

Baker, Bob. "Battle of the Bulge vs. Eastertide Offensive, Lessons Learned." *Vietnam* (Apr. 1999): 34-40.

Ballard, Jack S. *Development and Employment of Fixed-Wing Gunships, 1962-1972*. Washington, DC: Office of Air Force History, 1982.

"Battle for City Looms / They 'Have to Get Out' of Imperiled Kontum." *Pacific Stars and Stripes*, 13 May 1972.

BDM Corporation. *A Study of Strategic Lessons Learned in Vietnam*. Vol. 6: *Conduct of the War*. Report submitted to Department of the Army, 9 May 1980.

Berger, Carl, ed. *The U.S. Air Force in Southeast Asia, 1961-1963*. Washington, DC: Office of Air Force History, 1982.

Berman, Larry. *No Peace, No Honor: Nixon, Kissinger, and Betrayal in Vietnam*. New York: Free Press, 2001.

———. *Planning a Tragedy: The Americanization of the War in Vietnam*. New York: W. W. Norton, 1982.

Booth, Waller B. "The Montagnards of Vietnam, Tragic Warriors of the Highlands." *Army* (May 1975): 47-50.

"Both Sides of Debate over Vietnam Bombing." *U.S. News & World Report*, 1 May 1972.

Bowers, Ray L. *Tactical Airlift: The U.S. Air Force in Southeast Asia*. Washington, DC: Office of Air Force History, USAF, 1983.

Boyne, Walter J. "The Easter Halt." *Air Force* 81, no. 9 (Sept. 1998): 60-65.

Brigham, Robert K. *ARVN: Life and Death in the South Vietnamese Army*. Lawrence: University Press of Kansas, 2006.

Browne, Malcolm W. "Thousands Flee Kontum in Panic as Enemy Nears." *New York Times*, 1 May 1972.

Buckley, Thomas. "The ARVN Is Bigger and Better, but—." *New York Times Magazine*, 12 Oct. 1969.

Burkett, B. G., and Glenna Whitley. *Stolen Valor: How the Vietnam Generation Was Robbed of Its Heroes and Its History*. Dallas: Verity Press, 1998.

Burns, John C. *XM-26 TOW: Birth of the Helicopter as a Tank Buster*. Quantico, VA: Marine Corps Command and Staff College, 1994.

Candlin, A. H. S. "The Spring Offensive in Vietnam." *Army Quarterly and Defense Journal* (July 1972): 411-18.

Cao Van Vien and Đong Van Khuyen. *Reflections on the Vietnam War*. Indochina Monograph Series. Washington, DC: U.S. Army Center of Military History, 1980.

Cao Van Vien, Ngo Quang Truong, Dong Van Khuyen, Nguyen Duy Hinh, Tran Dinh Tho, Hoang Ngoc, and Chu Xuan Vien. *The U.S. Adviser*. Indochina Monographs. Washington, DC: U.S. Army Center of Military History, 1980.

Carhart, Tom. *Battles and Campaigns in Vietnam, 1954-1984*. New York: Crescent, 1984.

Chinnery, Philip D. *Vietnam: The Helicopter War.* Annapolis, MD: Naval Institute Press, 1991.

Christine, S. L. "1st Combat Aerial TOW Team: Helicopter vs Armor." *U.S. Army Aviation Digest* 20, no. 2 (Feb. 1974): 3–5.

Clarke, Jeffrey J. *The U.S. Army in Vietnam, Advice and Support: The Final Years, 1965-1971.* Washington, DC: US Army Center of Military History, 1988.

Clodfelter, Michael. *Vietnam in Military Statistics: A History of the Indochina Wars, 1772-1991.* Jefferson, NC: McFarland, 1995.

Colvin, John. *Giap, Volcano under the Snow.* New York: Soho Press, 1996.

Det One Report: Yearbook Supplement for the People Who Fly and Support the C-130E Hercules Aircraft of the 374th Tactical Airlift Wing. Tan Son Nhut Air Base, Vietnam: 374th Tactical Airlift Wing, 4 July, 1972.

Doglione, John A. *Airpower and the 1972 Spring Invasion.* Washington, DC: Office of Air Force History, 1985.

Doleman, Edgar C., Jr. *The Vietnam Experience: Tools of War.* Boston: Boston Publishing, 1985.

Dougan, Clark, and Stephen Weiss. *The American Experience in Vietnam: The Complete History with Eye-witness Accounts.* New York: W. W. Norton, 1988.

Dunstan, Simon. *Vietnam Tracks: Armor in Battle, 1945-1975.* Novato, CA: Presidio Press, 1982.

Famiglietti, Gene. "TOWs on Target, an Ace Dealing Weapon." *Redstone Rocket,* 26 July 1972. Reprinted from *Army Times,* 26 July 1972.

"The Flow of Red Arms U.S. Is Trying to Halt." *U.S. News & World Report,* 22 May 1972.

"Foe's Thrust into Kontum Is Repulsed." *Washington Post,* 26 May 1972.

Franjola, Matt. "Smart Bombs Wreck Key N. Viet Bridge." *Pacific Stars and Stripes,* 29 May 1972.

———. "Viets Take Most of Kontum as Reds Appear in Retreat." *Pacific Stars and Stripes,* 31 May 1972.

Greenberg, Lawrence M. "'Spooky': Dragon in the Sky." *Vietnam* (Apr. 1990): 22–28.

Halloran, Bernard F. "Soviet Armor Comes to Vietnam." *Army* (Aug. 1972): 18–23.

"Hanoi's High-Risk Drive for Victory." *Time,* 15 May 1972.

"The Harrowing War in the Air." *Time,* 1 May 1972.

Herring, George C. *America's Longest War: The United States and Vietnam, 1950-1975.* New York: Wiley, 1979.

Heslin, John G. *Combat Power: An Ontological Approach.* Newport, RI: US Naval War College, 1978.

Higbee, Arthur. "N. Viet Tanks Sweep Down on Kontum; 7 Knocked Out." *Pacific Stars and Stripes,* 28 May 1972.

"Highlands Fighting Flares over Vital Highway Link." *Pacific Stars and Stripes,* 7 May 1972 and 8 May 1972.

Hill, John G., William J. Maddox Jr., and James H. Patterson. "Discussions of Combat Use of Helicopters." *U.S. Army Aviation Digest* 22, no. 3 (Mar. 1976): 1–5, 28–29.

History of the Central Highlands People's Armed Forces in the Anti-U.S. War of Resistance for National Salvation. Translated by US Government Foreign Broadcast Information Service. Hanoi: People's Army Publishing House, 1980.

Howard, John D. "An Loc: A Study of U.S. Power." *Army* (Sept. 1975): 18–24.

———. "They Were Good Ol' Boys! An Infantryman Remembers An Loc and the Air Force." *Air University Review* 26, no. 2 (Jan.–Feb. 1975): 26–39.

———. "The War We Came to Fight: A Study of the Battle of An Loc, April–June 1972." Student paper, US Army Command and General Staff College, Fort Leavenworth, KS, 1974.

Hubbard, Bob. "Testing TOW under Fire." *Army Logistician* (Mar.–Apr. 1973): 10–14.

Isaacs, Arnold R. *Without Honor: Defeat in Vietnam and Cambodia.* Baltimore: Johns Hopkins University Press, 1983.

Jenkins, Brian M. *Giap and the Seventh Son.* Santa Monica, CA: Rand Corporation, 1972.

Karnow, Stanley. *Vietnam: A History.* New York: Viking, 1983.

Kasper, Paul. "Arsenal: The M-132 Mounted Flamethrower Produced Devastating Battlefield and Psychological Effects." *Vietnam* (Oct. 2004): 14, 62.

Kieu My Duyen. *Chinh Chien Dieu Linh.* N.p.: n.p., 1994. Downloaded 25 Mar. 2007 from http://www.bietdongquan.com/article1/rgr62.htm.

King, Bart. "John Paul Vann's Reluctant Tiger." *Vietnam* (Oct. 2001): 20–21.

Kinnard, Douglas. *The War Managers: American Generals Reflect on Vietnam.* Burlington: University of Vermont, 1999.

Kissinger, Henry. *The White House Years.* Boston: Little, Brown, 1979.

Knappman, Edward W., ed. *South Vietnam.* Vol. 7: *U.S.-Communist Confrontation in Southeast Asia, 1972-73.* New York: Facts on File, 1973.

"Knock Out 26 Tanks, Army's New TOW Choppers Bat .802." *Pacific Stars and Stripes,* 29 June 1972.

"Kontum Hit from 3 Sides." *Washington Post,* 13 and 27 May 1972.

"Kontum Readies for Fight, Families Flown to Safety." *Pacific Stars and Stripes,* 17 May 1972.

Kutler, Stanley I. *Encyclopedia of the Vietnam War.* New York: MacMillan, 1997.

Larson, Stanley R., and James L. Collins Jr. *Vietnam Studies: Allied Participation in Vietnam.* Washington, DC: Department of the Army, 1975.

Lea, Charles, as told to Phil Powell. "Downed in the Jungle." *Vietnam* (Oct. 2002): 26–32.

Le Gro, William E. *Vietnam from Cease-Fire to Capitulation.* Washington, DC: US Army Center of Military History, 1981.

LePore, Herbert P. "The Role of the Helicopter in the Vietnam War." *U.S. Army Aviation Digest* (July–Aug. 1994): 33–39.

Leslie, Jacques. "S. Vietnam Troops Turn Back Red Attack at Kontum." *Los Angeles Times,* 15 May 1972.

Lester, Robert, ed. *Records of the Military Assistance Command Vietnam.* Part 1: *The War in Vietnam, 1954-1973.* MACV Historical Office Documentary Collection, microfilm ed. Bethesda, MD: University Publications of America, 1988.

——, ed. *U.S. Army Build-up and Activities in South Vietnam, 1965-1972.* Vietnam War Research Collections. Microfilm ed. Bethesda, MD: University Publications of America, 1989.

Liebchen, Peter A. W. *Kontum: Battle for the Central Highlands, 30 March-10 June 1972.* USAF Southeast Asia Monograph Series, vol. 2, monograph 3. USAF Project Contemporary Historical Examination of Current Operations Report. Washington, DC: USAF, Oct. 1972.

Lowenstein, James G., and Richard M. Moose. *Vietnam: May 1972.* A staff report for the Committee on Foreign Relations, US Senate. Washington, DC: US Government Printing Office, 1972.

"Many Will Flee, Others Vow to Fight / Red Tanks, Troops near Kontum." *Pacific Stars and Stripes,* 30 Apr. 1972.

McInnish, Hugh J., Jr. "Germany Tests Airborne TOW." *U.S. Army Aviation Digest* (Mar. 1972): 10–13.

"Message to Nixon: U.S. Moves Are Blunting Hanoi's Drive." *U.S. News & World Report,* 29 May 1972.

Metcalf, Donald J. "Why Did the Defense of Quang Tri Province, SVN Collapse?" Student essay, US Army War College, Carlisle Barracks, PA, 1972.

"*Midway,* on the Job Early, Aids Defenders of An Loc." *Pacific Stars and Stripes,* 7 May 1972.

Military History Institute of Vietnam. *Victory in Vietnam: The Official History of the People's Army of Vietnam, 1954-1975.* Translated by Merle L. Pribbenow. Foreword by William J. Duiker. Lawrence: University Press of Kansas, 2002. English translation of 1994 edition of the People's Army of Vietnam official history.

Moore, James K. "Giap's Giant Mistake." *Vietnam* (Feb. 1992): 27–32.

Moss, George Donaldson. *Vietnam: An American Ordeal.* Upper Saddle River, NJ: Prentice Hall, 1998. Reprint, Lawrence: University Press of Kansas, 2002.

Mrozek, Donald J. *Air Power and the Ground War in Vietnam: Ideas and Actions.* Maxwell Air Force Base, AL: Air University Press, 1988.

"New Missiles Hit Hard in Vietnam." *Pacific Stars and Stripes,* 3 June 1972.

Ngo Quang Truong. *The Easter Offensive of 1972.* Indochina Monograph Series. Washington, DC: US Army Center of Military History, 1980.

——. "The Tactical Adviser." In *The U.S. Adviser,* by Cao Van Vien, Ngo Quang Truong, Dong Van Khuyen, Nguyen Duy Hinh, Tran Dinh Tho, Hoang Ngoc, and Chu Xuan Vien, 40–43. Indochina Monographs. Washington, DC: US Army Center of Military History, 1980.

The Nguyen Hue Offensive. Military Assistance Command Directorate of Intelligence Study 73-01. Saigon: Intelligence Support Liaison Branch, Intelligence Production Division, Directorate of Intelligence, USMACV, 12 Jan. 1973.

Novak, C. James. "Linebacker II." *The Retired Officer Magazine* (Nov. 1992): 40–43.

Novak, Paul. "Fondly Called the BUFF (Big Ugly Fat Fellow) in Vietnam, the B-52 Stratofortress Still Plays a Vital Role in Today's Air Force." *Vietnam* (Aug. 2005): 10–12, 48.

"N. Viet Tanks, Troops Open Attack on Kontum." *Washington Post,* 14 May 1972.

Ott, David E. "1972 Enemy Offensive." *Field Artillery Journal* 45, no. 1 (Jan.–Feb. 1977): 42–47.

"Over Half Million under Red Control as Drive Continues." *Pacific Stars and Stripes,* 31 May 1972.

Paine, David J. "Kontum Is Next—and It Knows It." *Pacific Stars and Stripes,* 26 May 1972.

Palmer, Bruce, Jr. *The 25-Year War: America's Military Role in Vietnam.* Lexington: University Press of Kentucky, 1984.

———. "How Bright, How Shining? Sheehan's Portrait of Vann and Vietnam." *Parameters* (U.S. Army War College) 19, no. 2 (June 1989): 18–23.

———. *U.S. Intelligence and Vietnam.* Special issue of *Studies in Intelligence* 28 (1984).

Palmer, Dave R. *Summons of the Trumpet: U.S.-Vietnam in Perspective.* San Rafael, CA: Presidio Press, 1978.

Parks, Michael. "Trapped Refugees at Kontum Pack and Await Attack." *Baltimore Sun,* 30 Apr. 1972.

Phan Vu. "The Vietnam War: A Free Vietnamese's Viewpoint." Unpublished manuscript, copy in author's files.

"Pilots Fear Reds' New Portable Rocket." *Cleveland Plain Dealer,* 28 May 1972.

Plaster, John L. *Secret Commandos: Behind Enemy Lines with the Elite Warriors of SOG.* New York: Simon and Schuster, 2004.

"The President's Report to Nation on Vietnam." *U.S. News & World Report,* 8 May 1972.

Randolph, Stephen P. *Powerful and Brutal Weapons: Nixon, Kissinger, and the Easter Offensive.* Cambridge, MA: Havard University Press, 2007.

"Red Barrage Turned the Tide." *Pacific Stars and Stripes,* 4 May 1972.

"Red Drive Slowed in Viet Highlands." *Pacific Stars and Stripes,* 28 Apr. 1972.

"Reds Batter An Loc Relief Column." *Pacific Stars and Stripes,* 31 May 1972.

"Reds Squeezed Out of Ben Het; 11 Tanks Blasted." *Pacific Stars and Stripes,* 11 May 1972.

"Refugees Moved to Pleiku." *Pacific Stars and Stripes,* 4 May 1972.

"ROK Casualties Higher." *Pacific Stars and Stripes,* 29 Apr. 1972.

Ross, John F. "Landing Party." *Smithsonian* (Nov. 2004): 39–40.

Rottman, Gordon L. *North Vietnamese Army Soldier 1958-75.* London: Osprey, 2009.

"Saigon Forces Recover Some Parts of Kontum." *Washington Post,* 1 June 1972.

"Scared S. Viets Refused to Fight at Hoai An—Adviser." *Pacific Stars and Stripes,* 22 Apr. 1972.

Schuster, Carl Otis. "North Vietnam's Light Anti-Aircraft Artillery." *Vietnam* (Oct. 2007): 21–22.

———. "The SA-7 Grail: Man-Portable Missile Packs a Punch." *Vietnam* (Feb. 2010): 15.

Serong, A. P. *The 1972 Easter Offensive*. Special issue of *Southeast Asian Perspectives*, no. 10 (Summer 1974).

"Sharp-Eyed Pilot Leads Cobras to NVA Tank." *The Observer* (MACV), 16 June 1972.

Sheehan, Neil. *After The War Was Over: Hanoi and Saigon*. New York: Vintage, 1993.

———. *A Bright Shining Lie: John Paul Vann and America in Vietnam*. New York: Random House, 1988.

"Showdown over Vietnam." *U.S. News & World Report*, 22 May 1972.

Sigler, David Burns. *Vietnam Battle Chronology: U.S. Army and Marine Corps Combat Operations, 1965-1973*. Jefferson, NC: McFarland, 1992.

Sloniker, Mike. "The Easter Offensive of 1972 to the War's End." In *Vietnam Helicopter Pilots Association Membership Directory*, 16:248–72. Grapevine, TX: Vietnam Helicopter Pilots Association, Oct. 1999.

Sobel, Lester A., ed. *South Vietnam, U.S.-Communist Confrontation in Southeast Asia*. Vol. 6: *1971*. New York: Facts on File, 1973.

Sorley, Lewis B. *A Better War: The Unexamined Victories and Final Tragedies of America's Last Years in Vietnam*. New York: Harcourt Brace, 1999.

———. "Courage and Blood: South Vietnam's Repulse of the 1972 Easter Invasion." *Parameters* (U.S. Army War College) 29, no. 2 (1999): 38–56.

———. *Reassessing ARVN* (pamphlet produced from lecture). Lubbock: Texas Tech University, 17 Mar. 2006.

———. *Remembering Vietnam* (pamphlet produced from lecture). Washington, DC: National Archives, Apr. 2002.

———, ed. *Vietnam Chronicles: The Abrams Tapes, 1968-1972*. Lubbock: Texas Tech University Press, 2004.

"South Vietnam in the Balance." *U.S. News & World Report*, 15 May 1972.

"South Viet Nam: Pulling Itself Together." *Time*, 22 May 1972.

Stanton, Shelby L. *Vietnam Order of Battle*. New York: Galahad Books, 1986.

Starry, Donn A. *Armored Combat in Vietnam*. Vietnam Studies. Washington, DC: Department of the Army, 1978.

Stern, Laurence. "Vann Calls the Shots in the Skies over Kontum." *Hong Kong Standard*, 14 June 1972.

Summers, Harry G., Jr. *On Strategy: A Critical Analysis of the Vietnam War*. Novato, CA: Presidio Press, 1982.

———. "Snatching Victory from Defeat." *Vietnam* (Apr. 1999): 38.

———. *The Vietnam War Almanac*. New York: Ballantine, 1985.

"S. Viets Battle for Kontum; Report Reds Lose 12 Tanks." *Chicago Tribune*, 27 May 1972.

"Tells How Reds Died: Chained Inside of Tanks." *Pacific Stars and Stripes*, 18 Apr. 1972.

Theodoracopulos, Taki. "What Makes Charlie Run?" *National Review*, 7 July 1972, 743.

Thompson, W. Scott, and Donaldson D. Frizzell, eds. *The Lessons of Vietnam.* New York: Crane, Russak, 1977.

Tran Van Hien. "The Communist Assault on Quang Tri." In *Vietnamese Marine Corps History,* part III: *1972.* Formerly available online. Copy in author's files.

Truhan, Mark. "The Battle of Ben Het—May 1972." Available on the Battle of Kontum Web site at http://www.thebattleofkontum.com/memories/27.html.

Turley, G. H. *The Easter Offensive: The Last American Advisors* [sic], *Vietnam, 1972.* Novato, CA: Presidio Press, 1985.

Turley, William S. *The Second Indochina War: A Short Political and Military History, 1954-1975.* Boulder, CO: Westview Press, 1986.

Ulsamer, Edgar. "Airpower Halts an Invasion." *Air Force Magazine* (Sept. 1972): 60–71.

United States Military Assistance Command Vietnam (MACV), Command History, January 1972-March 1973. 2 vols. Saigon: Military History Branch, Office of the Secretary, Joint Staff, MACV, 1973.

"U.S. Adviser: Red Offensive 'Major Blunder' by N. Viets." *Pacific Stars and Stripes,* 26 May 1972.

"U.S. Advisers Saved in Daring Rescue." *Louisville Courier-Journal,* 25 Apr. 1972.

"The U.S. Army in Vietnam: From Tet to the Final Withdrawal, 1968–1973." In *American Military History,* rev., edited by Richard W. Stewart, 333–43. Army Historical Series. Washington, DC: US Army Center of Military History, 2005. Available at http://www.history.army.mil/books/AMH-42/AMH%20V2/chapter 11.htm.

"U.S. May Up Air War to Hit North." *Stars and Stripes,* 7 Apr. 1972.

"Vietnamization: A Policy Put to the Test." *Newsweek,* 17 Apr. 1972.

"Vietnamization: A Policy under the Gun." *Time,* 17 Apr. 1972.

"Vietnam—Why the Standoff." *U.S. News & World Report,* 19 June 1972.

"Viets Push Close to An Loc." *Pacific Stars and Stripes,* 20 May 1972.

"Viets Push Open Highlands Link." *Pacific Stars and Stripes,* 19 May 1972.

"Waiting for Another Tet." *Time,* 31 Jan. 1972.

Walsh, Alden C. "Soviet Artillery Weapons." *Field Artillery* (July 1962): 33–41.

Ward, Ian. "Why Giap Did It: Report from Saigon." In *North Vietnam's Blitzkrieg: An Interim Assessment,* edited by Brian Crozier, 1–10. London: Institute for Study of Conflict, Oct. 1972.

"The War That Won't Go Away." *Newsweek,* 17 Apr. 1972.

Whitney, Craig B. "Government to Remove 30,000 Civilians Still in Kontum." *New York Times,* 7 May 1973.

Willbanks, James H. *Abandoning Vietnam: How America Left and South Vietnam Lost Its War.* Lawrence: University Press of Kansas, 2004.

———. *The Battle of An Loc.* Bloomington: Indiana University Press, 2005.

Index

Names of military units are alphabetized as spelled rather than by numerical order. For example, the 44th Infantry Regiment will appear before the 42nd Infantry Regiment. *Italics* within personal names indicate pseudonyms.

A-1 fighter-bombers (Skyraiders), 11, 34
A-37 fighter-bombers, 11, 232
Abrams, Creighton W., 201
  on advisers, 163
  on air power, 148–49, 185
  antitank weaponry approved by, 177
  Arc Light airstrikes ordered by, 47
  on ARVN performance, 153–54, 185, 190–91, 266
  challenges facing, 72–73
  Easter Offensive and, 63
  Hill and, 125
  on Kontum defense prospects, 144, 145–46
  as MACV commander, 8
  military messages sent to, xiii
  NVA troop movements and, 52–53
  retaliative authority requested by, 42
  Tan Canh/Dak To deployments and, 80–81
  upgrading program of, 9–10
  Vann reports to, 94, 161, 222, 224, 239, 251–52
  Vietnam withdrawal and, 19, 30
AC-47 gunships, 11, 34, 200
  See also Spooky gunships

AC-119 gunships, 33–34
  See also Stinger gunships
AC-130 gunships, 33, 122, 196, 260
  See also Spectre gunships
advisers, 42–43
  ARVN retrained by, 10–11
  E&Es of, 108–10, 155–56, 170, 192–93
  number of, during Easter Offensive, 262
  NVA capture of, 198
  significance of, xii–xiii, 163, 191, 245, 266
  wounding/evacuation of, 251–53
Aerial Port Team, 214
Agnew, Spiro, 190–91
AH-1G gunships, 21
  See also Cobras
Airborne Division (ARVN), 9, 84, 85, 116, 121
Air Force (magazine), 71–72
airlifts, 64–65
air support, 33–39, 266–67
alcoholism, 89
All Weather Airdrop System, 227
America's Last Vietnam Battle (Andradé), xiii
Anderson Air Force Base (Guam), 39
Andradé, Dale, xiii
An Khe
  author stationed at, 51–52, 140
  NVA sapper attack in, 50
  US 1st Cavalry Division stationed at, 51
  US 7th Squadron stationed at, 89
An Khe Pass
  ARVN retaking of, 76–79